Microsoft®
Power BI

A Wiley Brand

Microsoft® Power BI

2nd Edition

by Jack Hyman

Microsoft® Power BI For Dummies®, 2nd Edition

Published by: **John Wiley & Sons, Inc.,** 111 River Street, Hoboken, NJ 07030-5774, www.wiley.com

Contents at a Glance

Table of Contents

Introduction

Data isn't just everywhere — it is everything. In today's connected world, every click, swipe, purchase, and interaction generates data. The challenge? Organizations drown in their data because they struggle to transform raw information into the actionable intelligence required to drive positive business outcomes.

Enter the era of democratized analytics, where *business intelligence* isn't just a buzzword in your IT department or unique to the data science expert. Today, every employee handles data, from frontline workers to C-suite executives. The expectation is that employees — folks like you and me — explore, understand, and act on that data.

Transforming raw data to produce valuable insights requires that you do more than use "just another tool" that sits on the proverbial shelf, waiting to be used ad hoc. Sure, spreadsheets served their purpose last decade (and still do today), but modern businesses require a platform that can handle massive datasets, provide real-time analysis, integrate artificial intelligence, and enable collaboration across teams and departments. The question is not whether your organization will need sophisticated business intelligence tools; it's how quickly you will acquire and begin to use them.

Microsoft Power BI has evolved far beyond its humble beginnings as a SQL Server reporting extension tool. What started in 2010 as a bunch of Excel add-ins has matured into a comprehensive analytics ecosystem that sits at the heart of Microsoft Power Platform alongside Power Apps, Power Automate, and Power Pages. As you see in this book, Power BI uses the newest available AI capabilities and can connect to hundreds of other data platforms, not just those owned by Microsoft. Power BI also provides enterprise-grade security and governance features for all users, from individual users to global organizations.

Whether this is the first time you are noodling around building a dashboard or architecting an enterprise solution that requires real-time analytics, you can be assured that Power BI will transform how you think and act with data. It bridges the gap between the raw information and strategic decision-making. Users throughout an organization can use Power BI to create stunning visualizations, discover hidden patterns, and share insights that propel business outcomes.

About This Book

I wrote this book for anyone interested in business analytics who wants to find out how they can apply the general capabilities of the Power BI platform to their work. It doesn't matter whether you're a novice or a power user — you'll benefit from reading this book.

The second edition of *Microsoft Power BI For Dummies* reflects the dramatic evolution of both the Power BI user experience and the broader analytics landscape. This edition incorporates and expands on the fundamental concepts introduced in the first edition. You get more information about intelligent automation, artificial intelligence, data warehousing tools, and methods for managing scalable datasets. You also discover the expanded collaboration possibilities that didn't exist just a few years back.

This book is intended for the following business roles:

>> **Business analyst:** As a business analyst, you're tasked with many responsibilities. Maybe you're the requirements-gathering expert, the configuration guru, the designer, or even the quasi-developer. This book can serve as a valuable resource for many of the critical tasks you may encounter in the field. The reality is that your role will expand with the use of Power BI. You'll be expected to be part detective, part designer, and part strategist. For you, this book serves as a practical framework to tackle real-world analytics challenges, from gathering requirements to delivering solutions.

>> **Data professional:** Data is complex — make no mistake about it. This book doesn't help you tackle the formulas behind the scenes or tell you how to construct and programmatically code many sophisticated reports, dashboards, visuals, and KPIs. It does, however, help you understand the foundational activities across the Power BI platform if this is your first foray into using Microsoft's business intelligence (BI) platform. You'll be able to ingest data quickly, conduct data analysis, and build relatively sophisticated reports after reading this book. You now operate in an ecosystem where technical skills must blend with business acumen. This book won't make you a world-renowned DAX expert or a Power BI master ninja overnight, but it provides you with the foundational knowledge needed to architect your scalable solutions, implement best practices, and communicate effectively to business stakeholders, not just technical wizards.

>> **Developer:** This book isn't specifically for you, but you can find plenty of tips, tricks, and techniques you can learn throughout the book. Power BI is a collection of products that require users to understand several fundamental programming languages, including DAX and SQL. This book scratches the surface of these topics ever so slightly. Take a look at the chapters on DAX in

Part 4 if you want an introduction or a refresher. As you learn more about the integration between Microsoft Fabric, pipelines, and the various data lake options, you can dabble with Power BI's expanded API capabilities, custom visualizations, and embedded analytics to support application integration. Remember, this book is not meant to be a technical deep-dive; it highlights the integration patterns and opportunities to help build your solution.

>> **IT professional:** If you're a cloud expert, systems engineer, or database professional, or you fill another IT role, this book doesn't provide you with all the technical answers you're looking for. Instead, the book serves as a starting point if you want to leap into the world of Microsoft enterprise business intelligence. Today, you must strike a balance between user empowerment and governance, security, and scalability requirements. This book addresses operational aspects of Power BI deployment such as tenant management, data source connectivity, and the security considerations — the basics that allow you to sleep at night, knowing your organization's data is safe and sound.

>> **Manager or executive:** Often, the deliverables created in Power BI are built for managers and executives. Power BI now offers hundreds of data connectors for data extraction, report development, visualization support, and dashboard creation. Under your guidance, these deliverables are created by analysts, developers, and data professionals. Reading *Microsoft Power BI For Dummies,* 2nd Edition, can help you better understand the art of the possible. In your role, you act on data as both a strategic asset and a practical tool to help move the organization forward. With Power BI, you can accelerate data analysis, integrate with countless data sources to get a 360-degree picture of your data universe, and guide meaningful conversations with teams and customers.

Foolish Assumptions

I've written this book for users who want to learn about the critical features across the three Power BI platforms: Desktop, Service, and Mobile. This book isn't intended to be a crash course for certification or a deep dive into administration or coding for Power BI. You can find other books for these purposes.

Power BI is a pretty big application, as you can probably already tell. Microsoft assumes that its interfaces are relatively simple to figure out, and that most users can create reports and dashboards without too much trouble. Here's the truth: The interfaces can be overwhelming, depending on which product you're using. Just to keep users on their toes, a great deal of bells and whistles appear across each Power BI platform.

Now I need to forewarn you here about what you should expect from time to time in this book. You'll be able to utilize the free features provided by Microsoft to learn Power BI for most exercises. That said, Power BI Service, Microsoft Fabric, and Copilot do require premium licenses; therefore, you'll need to spend money or have your system administrator provide you access. If you begin to scratch your head and wonder why you can't access the feature, you've probably run into a premium roadblock.

Since the last edition, the Power BI user experience has become more intuitive, and the platform has incorporated hundreds of new features, meaning that there is a bit more to learn. This new edition helps you know about the key features and updates, as well as how to use such features as a business professional rather than a data scientist.

Throughout this book, I point you directly to the Microsoft Power BI website, when appropriate, where you can find resources to dig a bit deeper from time to time, on technical capabilities you may need to know about.

Because Power BI is made up of many components, I've made some assumptions about your configuration for this book as you follow along on the journey:

>> **You have downloaded a copy of Power BI Desktop.** Some things in life are free, and this is one of them. Microsoft provides its users with the Desktop client for free. The Desktop client is designed to enable users to build data models, reports, and dashboards for personal use. That's where it ends, though. You do need an online account to share and collaborate. About half of the steps listed in this book can be completed using the Desktop client. Power BI serves as your primary development environment, as the Desktop is where individual productivity begins. Power BI Service, on the other hand, is meant for online collaboration and sharing.

>> **You have at least signed up for a Power BI and Fabric Trial account, but preferably, you have a Power BI Pro account (at a minimum).** A free account allows basic functionality so that you can test the exercises in this book, but if you intend to collaborate or share work, you need to get a Power BI Pro license (at a minimum). With the online companion, you can distribute your outputs in read-only format. If you want others to edit and manipulate the data, you have to pay for the Pro or Premium per-user version. The larger your dataset, the more likely you will want the upgrade, anyway.

>> **You have access to the Internet.** Even with the Desktop client, you need an Internet connection to access datasets from the Internet. Power BI Desktop also heavily relies on Internet connectivity for the advanced features covered in this book's second edition.

>> **You have a meaningful dataset.** *Meaningful* generally means at a minimum hundreds, if not thousands of records with at least 10 – 20 columns. In the example used throughout the book, you are provided a dataset with 3000+ rows and 275 columns. I point you to open-source datasets on sites such as Kaggle.com so that you can truly appreciate the power available in Power BI.

What's New in This Edition

Beyond advancements Microsoft introduced to the Power BI user experience, which means that many features were moved to other locations within the platform, Power BI now incorporates artificial intelligence capabilities, new data preparation tools, extensible visualization options, and hundreds of new integration possibilities. In *Microsoft Power BI For Dummies*, 2nd Edition, you see how to deploy Power BI based on real-world experiences and become more familiar with the latest best practices.

Icons Used in This Book

Throughout *Microsoft Power BI For Dummies*, you see some icons along the way. Here's what they mean:

TIP

Tips highlight shortcuts or essential suggestions for doing things quicker, faster, and more efficiently in Power BI.

REMEMBER

If you see the Remember icon, pay particular attention because these gotchas can make Power BI a bit difficult to understand. Don't worry, though — I'll help you find a workaround.

TECHNICAL STUFF

Technical Stuff is a way for you to consider exploring the inner workings of Power BI and perhaps how it integrates with other applications in a bit more detail. That means there may be a configuration to a data source that has a nuance or an advanced reporting feature that may help shape your data a smidgen. These items are here to help you on a case-by-case basis.

ON THE WEB

This icon points to useful content available to you out there on the World Wide Web.

WARNING

Do not take warnings as a sign of panic. They appear once in a while, though, to make you aware of a common issue or product challenge many users face. Again, do not fret!

Beyond the Book

In addition to the content you're reading in this book, you have access to a free Power BI Cheat Sheet that can give you a hand when it comes to creating compelling dashboards, valuable reports, and structured DAX code. To find the Cheat Sheet, go to www.dummies.com and enter **Microsoft Power BI For Dummies** in the Search box.

You can find the dataset used in this book on Kaggle.com, located at https://www.kaggle.com/jackhymanpowerbi/datasets.

Where to Go From Here

This book is designed as both a road map and a reference. For beginners, the chapters build step by step, from foundational concepts (Part 1) to data modeling (Part 2), visualization (Part 3), programming (Part 4), and advanced features like Microsoft Fabric and Copilot (Part 5). But each part also stands on its own, so you can jump directly to the topics that matter most to your work without losing context.

As you continue your Power BI journey, remember that the platform is constantly evolving. Fabric adds scalability and governance, and Copilot accelerates analysis with AI-driven insights. The key is to continue experimenting, applying these concepts to your own data, and leveraging the Power BI community. Whether you follow the book in order or chart your own path, you now have the tools to move from beginner to confident practitioner and beyond.

1

Put Your BI Thinking Caps On

Understand the three types of data.

Learn key Power BI terminology.

Explore the Power BI licensing model.

Master the fundamentals needed to transform your organization's data into meaningful insights.

IN THIS CHAPTER

» Figuring out the different types of data Power BI can handle

» Understanding your options for business intelligence tooling

» Familiarizing yourself with Power BI terminology

Chapter 1

A Crash Course in Data Analytics Terms: Power BI Style

Data is everywhere — literally. From the moment you awaken until the time you sleep, some system somewhere collects data on your behalf. Even as you sleep, data is being generated that correlates to some aspect of your life. What is done with this data is often the proverbial million-dollar question. Does the data make sense? Does it have any structure? Is the dataset so voluminous that finding what you're looking for is like finding a needle in a haystack? Or is it more like you can't even find what you need unless you have a special tool to help you navigate?

I answer that last question with an emphatic yes, and that's where data analytics and business intelligence join the party. And let's be honest: The party can be overwhelming if data is consistently generating something on your behalf.

REMEMBER

Dealing with data isn't always a chore — data can be fun to explore as well. Sometimes it's easy to figure out precisely what is needed to solve a problem, but at other times you need to put on your Sherlock Holmes deerstalker cap. Why? Because the data you're working with may lack structure and meaning. Of course, you're bound to take up tools to help you play the role of detective, evaluator, designer, and curator.

In this chapter, I discuss the different types of data you may encounter along your journey. I review the key terminology that you should become familiar with upfront. Don't worry: It's not like you need to memorize a dictionary. You learn a few key concepts to give you a head start in Power BI and business intelligence. Are you ready to go?

What Is Data, Really?

Ask a hundred people in a room what the definition of data is and you may receive one hundred different answers. Why is that? Because, in the world of business, data means a lot of different things to a lot of different people. So, here's try to get a streamlined response. Data contains facts. Sometimes, the facts make sense; sometimes, they're meaningless unless you add a bit of context.

The facts can sometimes be quantities, characters, symbols, or a combination of sorts that come together when collecting information. The information allows people — and more importantly, businesses — to make sense of the facts that, unless brought together, make absolutely no sense whatsoever.

When you have an information system full of business data, you also must have a set of unique data identifiers you can use so that, when searched, it's easy to make sense of the data in the form of a transaction. Examples of transactions may include the number of jobs completed, inquiries processed, income received, and expenses incurred.

The list can go on and on. To gain insight into business interactions and conduct analyses, your information system must have relevant and timely data that is of the highest quality.

REMEMBER

Data isn't the same as information. *Data* is the raw facts. That means you should think of data in terms of the individual fields or columns of data you may find in a relational database or perhaps the loose document (tagged with some descriptors called *metadata*) stored in a document repository. On their own, these items are unlikely to make much sense to you or to a business. And that's perfectly okay — sometimes. *Information* is the collective body of all those data parts, that results in the factoids making logical sense.

Working with structured data

Have you ever opened a database or spreadsheet and noticed that data is bound to specific columns or rows? For example, would you ever find a United States zip code containing letters of the alphabet? Or, perhaps when you think of a first name, middle initial, and last name, you notice that you always find letters in those specific fields. Another example is when you're limited to the number of characters you can input into a field. Think of Y as Yes; N is for No. Anything else is irrelevant.

What I'm describing here is called *structured data.* When you evaluate structured data, you notice that it conforms to a tabular format, meaning that each column and row must maintain an interrelationship. Because each column has a representative name that adheres to a predefined data model, your ability to analyze the data should be straightforward. This embodies your classic relational data system.

If you're using Power BI, you notice that structured data conform to a formal specification of tables with rows and columns, commonly referred to as a *data schema.* In Figure 1-1, you find an example of structured data as it appears in a Microsoft Excel spreadsheet.

FIGURE 1-1:
An example of
structured data.

	A	B	C	D	E	F	G	H
1	Employee ID	First Name	Last Name	Birth Date	Email Address	Mobile Number	Department	Office Location
2	123-45-453	Joe	Smith	1/3/2000	joe.smith@dataco.com	555.421.9051	Data Management	Seattle
3	123-45-459	Bob	Jones	2/14/1974	bob.jones@dataco.com	555.429.9082	Data Management	Seattle
4	123-49-907	Jane	Richards	3/15/1978	jane.richards@dataco.com	555.904.2852	Data Management	Seattle
5	190-90-223	Sally	Frank	2/28/1967	sally.frank@dataco.com	555.229.1804	Accounting	Atlanta
6	229-29-004	Emma	Donaldson	10/21/2002	emma.donaldson@dataco.com	555.867.5309	Marketing	San Francisco

REMEMBER

Whether you're using Power BI for personal analysis, educational purposes, or business support, the most accessible data sources for BI tools are structured. Platforms that offer robust structured data options include Microsoft SQL Server, Microsoft Azure SQL Server, Microsoft Access, Azure Table Storage, Oracle, IBM DB2, MySQL, PostgreSQL, Microsoft Excel, and Google Sheets.

Looking at unstructured data

Unstructured data is ambiguous, having no rhyme, reason, or consistency whatsoever. Pretend that you're looking at a batch of photos or videos. Are there explicit data points that one can associate with a video or photo? Perhaps, because the file itself may consist of a structure and be made of some metadata. However, the byproduct itself — the represented depiction — is unique. The data isn't replicable; therefore, it's unstructured. That's why video, audio, photos, text files, and social media posts are considered unstructured data.

Adding semi-structured data to the mix

Semi-structured data does have some formality, but it isn't stored in a relational system, and it has no set format. Fields containing the data are by no means neatly organized into strategically placed tables, rows, or columns. Instead, semi-structured data contains tags that make the data easier to organize and manage in some form of hierarchy. Nonrelational data systems or NoSQL databases are best associated with semi-structured data, in which the programmatic code, often serialized, is driven by the technical requirements. There is no hard-and-fast coding practice.

Common examples of semi-structured data include JSON files from web APIs, XML documents, and data from cloud applications. Power BI can work with these formats, making it possible to analyze data from modern web services and applications alongside your traditional databases and spreadsheets. This flexibility makes Power BI particularly valuable in today's business environment, where data comes from many different sources and formats.

Looking Under the Power BI Hood

The Power BI platform combines cloud-based apps and services to help you organize, collect, manage, and analyze your data. Whether you're working with a few hundred rows or millions of records, Power BI can handle datasets of various sizes and reveal patterns and trends that may not be obvious from the raw data. Unlike a tool such as Microsoft Excel, Power BI can simultaneously connect to and evaluate multiple data sources. The sources don't need to be structured like a spreadsheet, either. They can include unstructured and semi-structured data. After connecting to these data sources and processing them, Power BI helps you create visually compelling outputs such as charts, graphics, reports, dashboards, and KPIs (key performance indicators).

As you see throughout this book, Power BI isn't just a single application. It has desktop, online, and mobile components.

REMEMBER

Across the Power BI platform, you are certain at some point to encounter one (or more) of the following products:

>> **Power Query:** A data connection tool you can use to transform, combine, and enhance data across several data sources

>> **Power Pivot:** A data modeling tool

>> **Power BI Visualizations:** Built-in tools for creating interactive charts, graphs, maps, and other visuals

- **Power Q&A:** An AI-powered engine that allows you to ask questions about your data and receive responses using plain language.

- **Copilot in Power BI:** An AI assistant that helps create reports, write DAX formulas, and answer questions about your data

- **Power BI Desktop:** A free application that brings together data connection, modeling, and visualization capabilities in a single interface

- **Power BI Service:** A cloud-based platform for collaboration, sharing, and distributing reports and dashboards with others

In the following sections, I explore each product's core functionality.

Posing questions with Power Query

Power Query is the capability that allows Power BI to create data connections and transform data among many different data sources, from databases like SQL Server and Oracle to cloud services, spreadsheets, and web APIs. Power Query also serves as your trusty helper to clean and shape (or *transform*) your raw data before analysis, handling tasks like removing empty rows, changing data types, and combining information from multiple sources. The transformed data can then be used in your Power BI reports and dashboards, enabling you to work more easily with information that may otherwise be messy or difficult to analyze. For the data analyst and engineer, these tools are invaluable.

Power Pivot is the Power BI data modeling tool that helps you create relationships between data sources, craft models of varying complexities, and build calculations for your analysis. With Power Pivot, you can connect tables from various sources and define how they relate, which enables you to analyze data across multiple datasets. For example, a sales manager can link customer records from a CRM system with revenue data from an ERP system to quickly see which customer segments are driving the most profit. Power Pivot uses a formula language called DAX (Data Analysis Expressions) to create custom calculations, but don't worry — Power BI includes many built-in calculations, so you can get started without writing formulas. I cover DAX in Chapters 15 and 16.

Mastering Power BI Visualizations

Power BI visualizations help you see your data in a way that makes sense. For example, instead of scanning a long list of numbers, a bar chart can quickly show which department spends the most on travel. A map can display where most service requests come from so that you can spot regional patterns right away.

The key is that these visuals are interactive. You can click, filter, and drill into the details to answer specific questions. Later in this book, I walk you through the complete set of chart types available in Power BI and talk about when each one works best.

Interpreting data with Power Q&A

One of the biggest challenges for many users is data interpretation. Say, for example, that you've built this incredible data model using Power Pivot. Your data sample is significant in size, meaning that you need some way to make sense of all the data you've deployed in the model. But is the model useful? Possibly not, unless you have a way to interpret the data. That's why Microsoft created Power Q&A, an AI-powered feature that allows you to ask questions about your data using plain English and get instant visual answers.

Power Q&A comes with AI assistance to help you ask better questions by suggesting queries based on your data. For example, you may type, "How many customers purchased red shirts in our Chicago store last month?" From there, Power Q&A can suggest follow-up questions such as "Which day of the week had the most sales?" or "How does this compare to last year?" Of course, this only works if your dataset includes those details. Power Q&A can't generate insights from data you don't have. When your data model is well-designed, these AI-driven prompts can guide you toward insights you may not think to ask on your own.

Guiding the way with Copilot

At first glance, Q&A and Copilot may seem to be the same thing, seeing as though both are AI assistants. Here's how they differ: Copilot in Power BI is an AI assistant that helps you learn and use Power BI itself, whereas Power Q&A allows you to explore and analyze your data. Although Power Q&A helps you discover what's in your data by asking questions like "How many red shirts sold last month," Copilot enables you to figure out how to work with Power BI as a tool. For example, if you need to create a calculation, Copilot can write DAX formulas when you describe what you want to calculate. It can also suggest the best visualization types for your data and even help create entire reports based on your requirements. Whether you're wondering "How do I calculate year-over-year growth" or "What's the best chart to show regional sales trends," Copilot provides step-by-step guidance to help you accomplish your goals. This makes it particularly valuable for beginners who know what they want to achieve but aren't sure how to use Power BI's features to get there.

Power BI Desktop

Power BI Desktop is a free application that combines Power Query, Power Pivot, Power BI Visualizations, and Power Q&A. Using Power BI Desktop, you can complete all your business intelligence activities under one umbrella — from connecting to data sources and building models to creating reports and dashboards. Power BI Desktop is where you do all your development work on your local computer. Microsoft updates Power BI Desktop monthly with new features and improvements, so you can always access the latest capabilities.

Power BI Service

Accessible at `https://app.powerbi.com` from any device with an Internet connection, Power BI Service allows you to publish the work you create in Power BI Desktop and share it with colleagues across your company.

Power BI Service is the cloud platform where your reports and dashboards come to life for your organization. You can access it at `https://app.powerbi.com` from any device with an Internet connection, but you'll also need an organizational or educational email account to sign in. This means personal email addresses (like Gmail, Yahoo, or `Outlook.com`) won't work for publishing and sharing reports in Power BI Service.

Once you're set up, you can publish the reports you've built in Power BI Desktop, share them securely with colleagues, and even schedule automatic refreshes so your data stays up to date. Administrators can manage permissions to ensure that the right people see the right information, keeping your data protected.

REMEMBER

Your Power BI license determines which sharing, refresh, and collaboration features you can access.

Knowing Your Power BI Terminology

Whether Microsoft or another vendor creates it, every product you come across has its own terminology. It may seem like a foreign language, but if you visit a vendor's website and do a simple search, you're sure to find a glossary that spells out what all their mysterious terms mean.

Microsoft, unsurprisingly, has its own glossary for Power BI as well. In Microsoft Power BI-speak, some concepts resonate across vendors no matter who you are. For example, all vendors have reports and dashboards as critical concepts. Of course, not all vendors adopt Microsoft's practice and call dataflows a type of workflow. But even though they have their own names for these features, the features generally work the same way.

Microsoft has done a pretty good job of trying to stick with mainstream names for critical concepts. Nevertheless, some of the more advanced product features specific to AI or machine learning and security adopt the specialized terminology of Microsoft products such as Microsoft Entra ID or Azure Machine Learning.

Capacities

The first concept you must be familiar with is *capacities,* which are central to Power BI. Capacities are the sum total of system resources needed for you to complete a project you create in Power BI. Resources include the storage, processor, and memory required to host and deliver Power BI projects. Both the type and quantity of your data can affect the capacity required to deliver your projects.

When you use Power BI, you must consider two types of capacity: shared and dedicated. A *shared* capacity allows you to share resources with other Microsoft end users. *Dedicated* capacities fully commit resources to you alone. Shared capacity is available for both free and paying Power BI users, and dedicated capacity requires a Power BI Premium subscription.

Workspaces

Workspaces are a means of collaborating and sharing content with colleagues. Whether it's personal or intended for collaboration, any workspace you create is created on capacities. Think of a workspace as a container that allows you to manage the entire lifecycle of dashboards, reports, workbooks, datasets, and dataflows in the Power BI Service environment. (Figure 1-2 shows the My Workspace, which is a personal Power BI workspace.)

My Workspace isn't the only type of workspace available. You also have the option to collaborate. If you want to collaborate, you have no choice but to upgrade to a Power BI Pro, Premium Per User, or Premium Per Capacity plan. Features that come with collaboration include the ability to create and publish Power BI-based dashboards, reports, workbooks, datasets, and apps with a team.

To upload the work you've created using Power BI Desktop, or to manipulate the work online without collaborating with anyone, you can use My Workspace — this is all that is necessary. You only *require* the use of Power BI Free. As soon as you want to collaborate with others, you need to upgrade to a Power BI Pro, Premium Per User, or Premium Per Capacity subscription.

So now you know that your work is stored in a workspace. Next question: What happens with the data in that workspace? When you work with Power BI data, you primarily deal with two key concepts: datasets and reports. A dataset contains your data and any relationships or calculations you've defined. Think of it as the

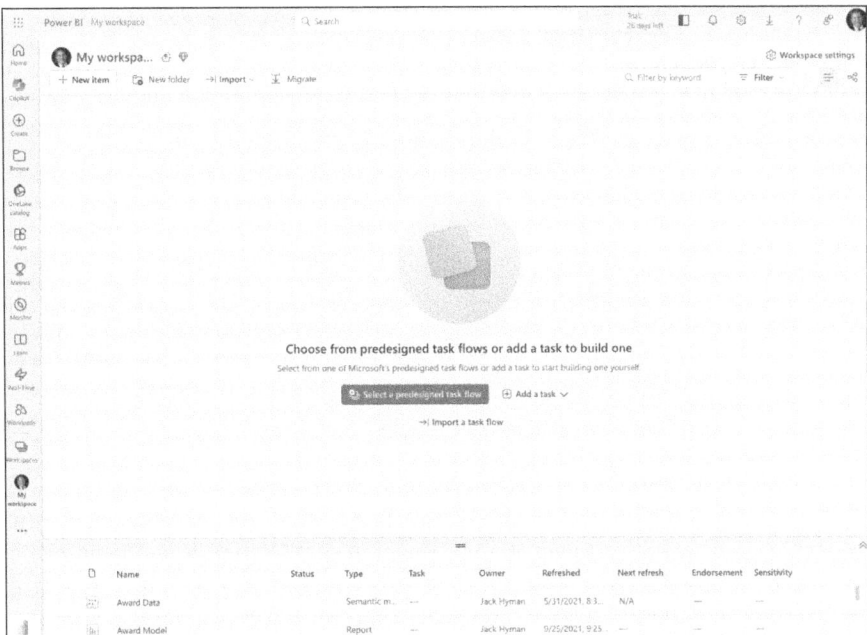

FIGURE 1-2:
My Workspace in
Power BI Service.

foundation that holds all your information. Reports are then built on top of datasets to create the visualizations you see. The Power BI Service Workspace is where both assets are managed behind the scenes, so you can focus on analyzing and presenting your information.

Dataflows and datasets

Power BI works with two main types of data containers: datasets and dataflows. A *dataset* is like a digital filing cabinet that holds your data, relationships, and calculations — it's what you'll work with most often when creating reports. A *dataflow* is a more advanced feature that helps prepare and clean large amounts of data before it becomes a dataset. Think of dataflows as a preprocessing step for complex data scenarios.

TIP

Most users starting with Power BI primarily work with datasets. Dataflows are helpful when dealing with large, complex data sources that need significant cleaning and transformation before analysis, as you see when you dig into Part 3 of this book.

REMEMBER

After you manipulate the data on your own, you must publish the data you created in Power BI to Power Bi Service. Otherwise, it remains on your desktop and only you can access the file. Microsoft assumes that you intend to share the data among users. If you want to share a dataset, you must have a Power BI Pro, Premium Per User, or Premium Per Capacity license.

Reports

Data can be stored in a system indefinitely and remain idle, but what good is it if no one ever looks at it to understand what it means? That's where Power BI reports come in. A report transforms your raw data into visual stories that make sense at a glance.

For example, imagine you're a sales manager who needs to understand your team's performance. You can create a Power BI report that shows monthly sales trends in a line chart, top-performing products in a bar chart, and regional performance on a map — all on different pages of the same report. Whether you're working with hundreds of sales records or thousands, Power BI helps you see patterns and insights that would be impossible to spot in spreadsheet rows.

Power BI reports translate your data into one or more pages of visualizations — line charts, bar charts, pie charts, treemaps, and dozens of other options. You can view your data at a high level to spot big trends, or drill down into specific details when something catches your attention. Creating a report is straightforward: connect to your data source (like an Excel file, database, or cloud service), choose the information you want to display, and select the best visualization to tell that part of your data's story. The result is a report (see Figure 1-3) that transforms rows and columns of data into meaningful insights you can use.

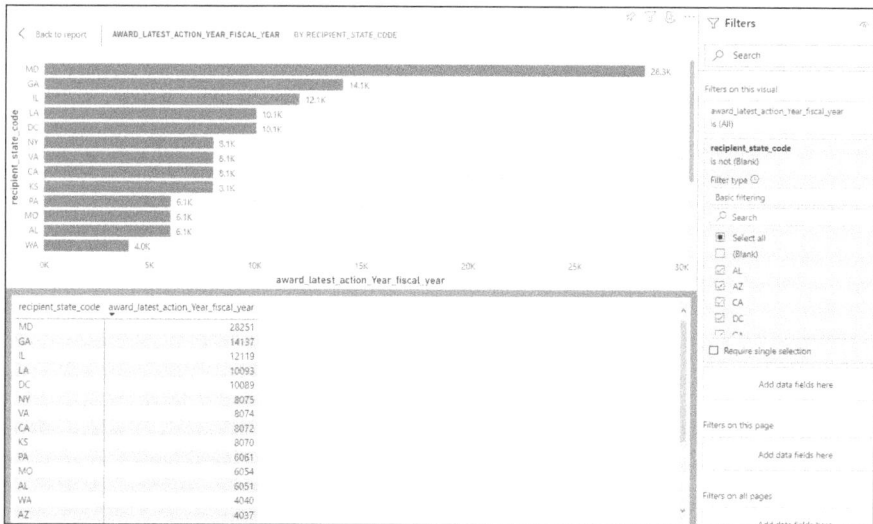

FIGURE 1-3:
A sample
Power BI report.

TIP

Power BI offers two Report view modes: Reading view and Editing view. When you open a report, it opens in Reading view. You can switch to Editing view to modify a report if granted Edit permissions. Your ability to edit depends on your role in the workspace and your Power BI license.

TECHNICAL STUFF

Users with administrative, member, or contributor roles in a workspace can create and edit reports. Other users can view and interact with these reports but cannot make changes to them. Reports in a workspace can be found under the Reports tab, as shown in Figure 1-4. Reports can contain multiple pages and are built using data from one or more datasets.

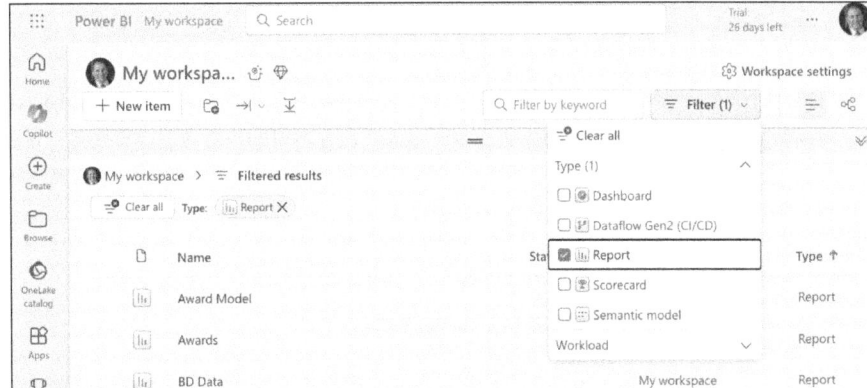

FIGURE 1-4: The Reports tab in Power BI Desktop.

Dashboards

If you've had any experience with Power BI, you already know that it's a highly visual tool. In line with its visual nature, the Power BI dashboard brings your data story to life. If you want to take all the pieces of your data puzzle and capture a moment, you use the dashboard. Think of it as a blank canvas. As you build your reports, widgets, tiles, and KPIs over time, you pin the ones you like to the dashboard to create a single visualization. The dashboard represents the large dataset that you feel covers your topic. As such, it can help you make decisions, support you in monitoring data, or allow you to drill down in your dataset by applying different visualization options.

To access a particular dashboard, you must first open a workspace. Then all you need to do is click the Dashboards tab. Remember that every dashboard represents a customized view of an underlying dataset. To locate your dashboards, go to your My Workspace (see Figure 1-5) and then choose Dashboards to see what's available.

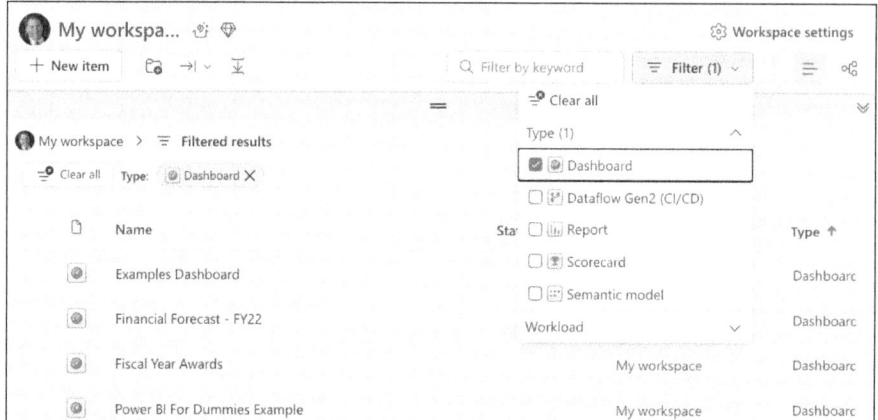

FIGURE 1-5:
Locating your
dashboards.

REMEMBER

If you own a dashboard, you have permission to edit it. Otherwise, you only have read-only access. You can share a dashboard with others, but they may not be able to save any changes. Keep in mind, however, that if you want to share a dashboard with a colleague, you need, at minimum, a Power BI Pro license. (For more on the ins and outs of licensing, see Chapter 3.)

Navigation pane

In this chapter, I talk about many of the must-know concepts in Power BI, but I want to cover one more important element — the Navigation pane. The Navigation pane is your road map to everything in Power BI Service. All the capabilities I discuss in this chapter — workspaces, dashboards, reports, datasets — are accessed through the Navigation pane (see Figure 1-6). You'll use the Navigation pane to move between workspaces and find the Power BI content you want to work with.

Your Navigation pane options are endless. For example, a user such as yourself can

>> Expand and collapse the Navigation pane

>> Open and manage your favorite content with the help of the Favorites option

>> View and open the most recently visited section of content

FIGURE 1-6:
The Navigation
pane.

Although Power BI Desktop has its own interface for building reports locally, the Navigation pane explicitly refers to the online Power BI Service experience, where you'll collaborate, share, and manage your published content.

Chapter **2**

The Who, How, and What of Power BI

Modern organizations rely on teams of people who work across multiple job roles to achieve the results they want from Power BI. Whether you're building your first report or managing an enterprise deployment, understanding who does what — and when — is key to knowing how to run a successful Power BI project. In most organizations, you'll find a mix of business and technically focused individuals working together whose goal is to transform raw data into meaningful insights. To understand how each person's role complements the others, and where each person fits into the Power BI workflow, you need to understand how the analytics lifecycle works in business.

In this chapter, I describe the who, how, and what of the data analytics lifecycle, which should set you up for success when you build your next business project.

Highlighting the Who of Power BI

There once was a time when you could point to a single person in a company and say, "Tag — you're *it!*" You knew that this one person was responsible for running the reports and accounting for the companywide data on the hard drive, so you knew who to turn to if you had a problem. Those days are long gone.

Power BI projects typically involve six key roles, though the exact structure varies by organization size and complexity. In a smaller company, one person may wear multiple hats, handling everything from data evaluation and data cleansing to report design. Larger enterprises often have dedicated people on a team responsible for a specific function, with clear handoffs between roles. Understanding these roles helps you identify who should get involved in your Power BI projects and ensures that nothing falls through the cracks.

Business analyst

The business analyst is the equivalent of the conductor to most organizations, bridging between business stakeholders and the technical team. Business analysts focus on understanding the business problem with the data, rather than how to build the solution (although most analysts also tinker with solution building). A business analyst typically begins a Power BI project by conducting interviews with stakeholders to understand the data landscape. This involves talking with both functional and technical stakeholders to learn about decision-making processes, key performance indicators, and reporting requirements.

Business analysts often spend their time creating requirement documents that specify exactly what to do with the data and how a report or dashboard should appear. They may develop mockups using tools like PowerPoint or Visio to help stakeholders visualize the possibilities before the data engineer or developer takes control. Once reports are built, the business analysts test the final deliverables with actual business users to ensure that the solutions meet real-world criteria. The business analyst also plays a crucial role in user adoption by conducting training sessions and creating user guides to help individuals effectively use the new Power BI content.

Data analyst

Unlike business analysts, data analysts are less focused on requirements and more focused on being the hands-on builders who translate the requirements into working Power BI products. Once data enters the enterprise information systems, these assets become the analyst's most valuable tool. The data analyst seeks to understand value through the use of visualization and reporting tools, such as Power BI. As the builder, the data analyst spends most of their time immersed in Power BI Desktop, connecting data sources, building data models, and creating visualizations that business users will ultimately use.

REMEMBER

Data analysts typically begin their work by understanding the available data sources and determining the best way to structure the data for reporting purposes. The data analyst is more tool-focused, using Power Query Editor extensively to clean and transform data, ensuring that information from different systems can work together effectively. Much of their day involves writing DAX (Data Analysis Expressions) formulas to address complex calculations in columns or measures that support business logic. They also select the most appropriate visualization type and configure the formatting within those visualizations to make information easy to understand. Once reports are complete, data analysts publish them to Power BI workspaces and work with business stakeholders to refine the solution based on feedback.

Data engineer

Because data isn't a one-size-fits-all kind of concept, you can imagine that the individuals who implement the data need to know a thing or two about the different flavors of data delivery available to them. For example, the people implementing BI solutions must be able to address both on-premises data and data in the cloud. Moreover, the data you're managing and securing often requires that you evaluate the flow of both structured and unstructured data sources. Sometimes, it may be just the one source, but more often than not it involves many different sources. The platforms themselves run the gamut, ranging from typical relational databases to non-relational databases, and even from data streams to file stores. One thing is for sure, though: Data must always be secure and seamlessly integrated, regardless of the data service.

Just like the data analysts, data engineers are forced to wear many hats — it's just that, while wearing those many hats, they're implementing data tools rather than analyzing processes. That means that the engineer must know how to use both on-premises service tools and cloud data service tools to ingest and transform data across various sources. Finally, keep in mind that you can't plan on sources being bound solely to the organization itself because data sources often reside outside your organization's four walls.

TECHNICAL STUFF

There are many similarities between the data engineer and the database administrator. You may wonder why a data engineer isn't also called a database administrator. The thing is, a data engineer doesn't just supply advisory services, manage the hosted infrastructure, or support operational data needs. The data engineer is the main person responsible for crafting the agenda for business intelligence and data science initiatives. The role requires the engineer to have a thorough understanding of data in all shapes and formats. As such, the data engineer must master *data wrangling,* in which they use the latest technology to transform and map data from its raw form to a more streamlined one — a form that is easier for BI or analytics to exploit, in other words.

Data scientist

Data scientists are seldom responsible for managing infrastructure. Most data scientists typically don't install much software. The data scientist is laser-focused on creating and executing advanced analytical capabilities for Power BI projects, with a focus on statistical analysis, machine learning, and predictive modeling. As I explain later in this chapter, the data scientists perform analytics routines on descriptive, diagnostic, prescriptive, predictive, and cognitive data. Although other roles primarily focus on historical reporting, data scientists help organizations understand what might happen in the future and identify the factors that drive business outcomes.

REMEMBER

In Power BI, data scientists will often find themselves working with R and Python integration using tools such as Jupyter Notebook or Anaconda to create sophisticated analytical models that go beyond standard reporting capabilities. The data scientist may also apply forecasting models that help organizations plan for future scenarios, and then create what-if analysis tools that allow business users to explore different assumptions. With the integration of Copilot in Power BI, the data scientists may also leverage Power BI's AI capabilities, such as the Key Influencers visual and decomposition trees, to help users understand the patterns that align with key metrics. Much of their work involves experimenting with various analytical approaches to identify models that best meet the needs of a business and its data consumers. You can learn about these advanced visuals in Chapters 11 and 12

Database administrator

Your database administrator handles the implementation and management of the database infrastructure. In some organizations, the database is entirely cloud-enabled. Legacy organizations, on the other hand, have often kept their database on-premises or in a state of flux, resulting in a hybrid data platform deployment. When using Power BI, you'll likely have your database administrator build solutions on top of Microsoft Azure-based data services, including Microsoft Azure SQL. Although the database administrator may not create reports directly, their work is crucial for maintaining the smooth operation of Power BI solutions in production environments.

Whereas the data engineer or analyst may handle the availability and performance of the database solution, ensuring that stakeholders can identify and implement the necessary policies and procedures to support the data environment properly, the data administrator has a quite different set of responsibilities. The database administrator is like a doctor: This person ensures the health and wellness of the database as well as the infrastructure that the organization's data runs on. In organizations using Power BI Premium, database administrators often monitor capacity utilization and work with Power BI administrators to optimize resource allocation.

REMEMBER

When you try to sum up who does what in the Power BI data lifecycle, keep these two points in mind:

>> **Your business analyst, data analyst, and data engineer are involved in the creation of data and its manageability.** The keywords here are *ingestion, transformation, validation, cleansing,* and *creation.*

>> **Your database administrator, on the other hand, handles the systems that ensure that the data remains healthy.** The responsibility isn't just limited to data reliability, but also to security.

Power BI administrator

Think of the Power BI administrator as the air traffic controller for your organization's entire Power BI operation. While other team members focus on building reports and analyzing data, the Power BI administrator makes sure that everything runs smoothly behind the scenes. This role has become increasingly critical as companies transition from having a handful of Power BI users to supporting hundreds or thousands of users across the organization.

The Power BI administrator spends most of their time managing tenant-level settings — essentially the master system that determines how Power BI works throughout your company. The Power BI administrator also decides which features are available, who can use them, and how data flows between different parts of the organization. When your company purchases Premium capacity (extra computing power for Power BI), the administrator allocates these resources to ensure that the most critical reports and dashboards receive priority treatment.

Security and the governance behind it consume a significant portion of the Power BI administrators' activity. Power BI administrators set up and maintain policies that ensure users only see the data they're authorized to view. This includes configuring row-level security, which may sound technical but simply means that a sales manager in California can't accidentally access payroll data for employees in New York. They also manage workspaces — think of these as folders where teams collaborate, controlling who can create them, publish content, and invite others to join.

Beyond security, Power BI administrators monitor the system's performance and troubleshoot issues when problems arise. They're often the first people called when reports load slowly or when someone can't access a dashboard they need for the meeting. Part troubleshooter, part strategist, they also help establish best practices, including data and application governance, for how teams should organize their data and build their reports. If you're wondering who to ask about Power BI capabilities, licensing questions, or why something isn't working the way you expect, the Power BI administrator is your one-stop shop. They're the ones who truly understand how all the pieces fit together.

Understanding How Data Comes to Life

Data takes time to nurture. Treat the process as though you're starting at the center of a bull's-eye, where the focus is on preparation. As you learn more about the organization's people, processes, and technologies, your data requirements evolve, and these evolving requirements ultimately inform your data model. As models mature and the data volume increases, the visualizations available to you become more detailed, varied, and comprehensive. You're in a position to complete far more analyses, which may run the gamut from qualitative to quantitative and occur either sporadically or in real time. Ultimately, data management is all-encompassing because it overlays every phase of the data lifecycle. Figure 2-1 illustrates what a typical organization's leaders should expect when they nurture data using an enterprise BI solution such as Power BI.

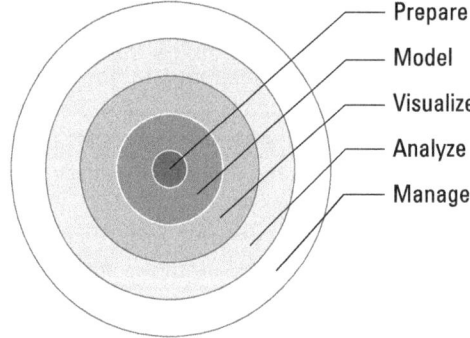

Prepare

Model

Visualize

Analyze

Manage

FIGURE 2-1:
A prototype data lifecycle for an organization using Power BI.

Prepare

Though the preparation stage is the most focused and tedious, the entire data lifecycle is influenced by preparation. Why, you ask? Well, what do you end up with if you start out with insufficient data? Poor reporting or poorly constructed visualizations can lead to flawed analyses, which in turn can have a devastating impact on an organization.

The primary tool for data preparation is the Power Query Editor, which provides a user a visual interface for connecting to various data sources and transforming the data as needed. During this phase, you connect a data source, whether it is a database, one or more files, web services, or other sources, to Power BI to initiate the report creation process. Power Query Editor enables you to preview your data and identify potential issues, such as missing values, inconsistent formatting, or data type errors.

TIP

Most people want to jump right into creating their Picaso on the Power BI canvas. Don't rush things. Instead, you want to invest significant time in data preparation. Making the upfront investment yields dividends later on when you need to manipulate your data. Clean, well-structured data makes every subsequent step easier and leads to more reliable insights. Use Power Query's error-handling capabilities to manage missing or invalid data.

Model

Okay, you say your data preparation is complete. Data scrutiny is at a high level, with many eyes confirming that the data is in tip-top shape. Now what? Organizations often take this opportunity to model the data. In this context, data modeling can be seen as a process in which all raw pieces of data are formalized and structured. The goal is to determine how the organized datasets can be related to each other. After you define the relationships, you can then build on the models by creating metrics, calculations, and rule sets. To accomplish these objectives, you use Power BI Desktop's Model view and Relationship view, where you define how different tables relate to each other.

During the modeling phase, your data analyst or data engineer may also write DAX formulas to create calculated columns and measures to support your reporting requirements. Two areas where folks spend a considerable time before visualization are crafting calculated columns and measures to support specific mathematical behaviors. Calculated columns add new data to your tables, and measures create dynamic calculations that respond to user interactions like filtering and slicing.

The model is a critical component in the data lifecycle. Without a model, the end user cannot produce reports or conduct analyses for an organization. A properly designed model is the key to delivering accurate and trusted results, especially as more organizations begin to work with large datasets. If at all possible, your goal is to create a star schema, in which fact tables containing measures are connected to dimension tables containing descriptive attributes.

Anytime you experience performance issues using Power BI, start by evaluating your model. Examples that may indicate performance issues include report refresh rates taking a bit longer than expected, data loading and preparation lagging, or data rendering from an often-accessed dataset that takes a tad too long to query.

Visualize

Visualizing data helps organizations better understand business problems in ways that plain text can't convey. Imagine the thickness of this book as a single dataset for a report. Is it easy for a person to summarize the contents of this book after reading it for two minutes? How much effort would it take to come up with five or six key data points discreetly? I sense that it would take a superhuman effort unless you use Copilot to synthesize this for you. The old saying "A picture is worth a thousand words" surely applies here. That's why visualization can bring data to life. Visualizations tell compelling stories, enabling business decision-makers to gain needed insights reasonably quickly. Picking the correct visualization is the key to mastering analysis.

A good BI tool such as Power BI incorporates many visualization options that make report outputs easier for decision-makers to understand. The visualizations generally aggregate the data to guide the professional through the dataset quickly. Different chart types serve other purposes, and understanding when to use each type helps ensure that your reports communicate effectively. Bar and column charts are well-suited for comparing categories, and line charts excel at illustrating trends over time. Pie charts can effectively show parts of a whole, but should be used sparingly as they can be difficult to read accurately. Tables and matrices are excellent for displaying detailed data that users may need to export or reference precisely. As you can see, each visualization type has its advantages and disadvantages, so thinking through the process is essential. In Part 3 of this book, you see how to best determine the optimal visualization.

Power BI has built-in AI capabilities that guide the best-fit visualization for reporting, eliminating the need for code. You may also use the Questions and Answers feature to explore the various visualization options or utilize Quick Insights to map your data model with the best-fit solution in Power BI.

Analyze

No two individuals analyze data in the same way. The analysis task is another step in the process when crafting your data model and interpreting your visualizations. Consider analysis as an overarching activity that often coincides across roles. It would be best if you continually analyzed your data, the model you derived, and your visualization output to ensure that accuracy is maintained. You should ensure accuracy in finding patterns, noticing trends, communicating with others, and even predicting outcomes based on data, even if you find anomalous tendencies. Platforms such as Power BI make data analysis more accessible because the process is simplified for business stakeholders when it comes to completing each one of those tasks.

REMEMBER

Power BI is both a desktop solution and a cloud-based one. You can do most of your business analysis, data analysis, data modeling, and visualization activities using Power BI Desktop. You can also analyze the data on your own using Power BI Desktop, provided you've connected your data model to the correct data source. However, if you want to share your data or analyze it with others, you must use Power BI Service.

Manage

When you have a chance to look more closely at Power BI, you soon see that, as a platform, it consists of a ton of different apps. The outputs produced are plentiful: reports, dashboards, workspaces, datasets, KPIs, and even other apps. On a well-organized team, every member typically manages one or more byproducts that support the management of Power BI assets, enabling the sharing and distribution of data. Whether you're the data analyst who oversees the validation of the data or the database administrator who must ensure the health and well-being of the hardware infrastructure, everyone has a role in managing the platform.

When you complete activities using Power BI Desktop, the ultimate goal is to share the deliverable with a broader audience. As soon as the deliverable is made available, the content you created using the Power BI Desktop fosters collaboration between teams and individuals. Sharing of content means ensuring that the right stakeholders gain access to the product you created.

REMEMBER

Security can be challenging in large organizations. Your business analyst, data analyst, and data engineer each play a role in ensuring that the right people have access to only what they need. The data scientist makes sure that the data assets being created are of high value. And of course, the database administrator ensures that the data house is always open for business by managing the infrastructure that all stakeholders support as part of the data lifecycle for business intelligence using Power BI. Therefore, ensure that each data asset, whether it is a model, report, or dashboard, is accessible only to those who need access. You'll learn more about access in Part 5 of this book.

Identifying Your Who and What

Previous sections in this chapter explain the who and how of Power BI. Now it's time to bring it all together and identify what type of developer you are. Power BI is designed to support two distinct user types: citizen developers and professional developers.

Citizen developers are business users who create reports and dashboards using Power BI's intuitive, self-service tools. These individuals are subject matter experts in their business domains but typically lack deep technical skills for implementing comprehensive business intelligence and data strategies. Business analysts often fall into this category, as they understand the functional requirements but focus on analysis rather than technical implementation.

Citizen developers don't need extensive technical expertise to get started. They typically build straightforward reports using trusted data sources that IT has already prepared and made accessible — think Excel files or approved databases. Although citizen developers can create basic reports and understand fundamental concepts, they generally don't delve into advanced features like complex DAX formulas or intricate data modeling.

The key responsibilities for citizen developers include handling data correctly, designing clean and effective reports, and — crucially — knowing when to escalate to IT support when requirements exceed their technical scope.

Professional developers bring deep technical knowledge to Power BI implementations. This group includes BI developers, data analysts, and data engineers who specialize in developing enterprise-scale solutions. These professionals have formal training in data modeling and coding, and they typically work on projects serving dozens, hundreds, or even thousands of users. Professional developers excel at combining data from multiple sources, writing complex business logic, and creating reusable data models with robust security controls. They also handle performance optimization, manage system resources, and build deployment pipelines to ensure smooth rollouts of updates and new features. In essence, professional developers are technical generalists who can wear multiple hats, depending on the project's needs.

So, the critical question remains: Which developer type are you — citizen or professional? Understanding your role will help you focus your learning efforts and set appropriate expectations for your Power BI journey.

Examining the Various Types of Data Analytics

Earlier in this chapter, I describe those stakeholders in an organization who would typically use Power BI. I try to show, at a very high level, how each of these stakeholders takes data that has been created and transforms it into something useful by using Power BI Desktop or Power BI Service. The only thing left for you to do before I let you loose in the Power BI forest involves knowing the type of analytics produced by Power BI. If you have ever read a generalist book on business intelligence, this section may not hold new information for you. If this is your first foray into BI or learning what makes Power BI different among the analytic product outputs, this section is your one-stop shop to summarize the details.

You can produce five types of analytics using Power BI: descriptive, diagnostic, predictive, prescriptive, and cognitive. Depending on the business goal and application within Power BI, the analytic products differ slightly. Table 2-1 describes the five types of analytics, including each one's purpose and where you're most likely to experience success using each analytics type.

TABLE 2-1   **Types of Analytics Produced in Power BI**

Analytic Type	What It Does
Descriptive	Helps answer questions based on historical data. Descriptive analytics also summarize large datasets and describe outcomes.
Diagnostic	Explains why events happen. Typically, diagnostic analytics support descriptive analytics as a secondary form of analytics that allows you to discover the cause of events. Analysts look for anomalies in datasets, reports, and KPIs. The use of statistical techniques available within Power BI helps users discover relationships in the data and trends.
Predictive	Helps answer questions about what might potentially happen in the future. Taking historical trends and finding patterns, the resultant output is an observation of what is likely to occur. Techniques used to derive results involve combinations of statistical methodologies and machine learning capabilities available in Power BI.

(continued)

TABLE 2-1 *(continued)*

Analytic Type	What It Does
Prescriptive	Answers the question about which actions one must take to meet a goal. Taking the data gathered, organizations can address issues based on unknown conditions. Such analytics also rely heavily on big data analytics and existing datasets being evaluated by Power BI's machine learning engine to find patterns, which helps deliver on different outcomes.
Cognitive analytics	Referred to at times as inferential analytics; lets the analyst pull together data from across the datasets to detect patterns, develop conclusions, and set up a knowledge bank for future learning. The keyword here is *future* because what is learned and seen is used to self-guide for the future. If conditions change, the knowledge bank adjusts accordingly. Because inferences are unstructured thoughts and hypotheses, it's up to machine learning solutions within Power BI to process the data change, make sense of the existing data sources, and create data correlations.

Taking a Look at the Big Picture

Understanding these roles and the business process behind building a business intelligence solution is foundational to building a Power BI project. Whether you're a citizen developer creating your first report or a professional building enterprise solutions, several key principles should be considered as you embark on your Power BI journey:

» **Start with clear requirements:** You should be able to specify exactly what questions your Power BI solution needs to answer. Too many projects struggle because they begin with lots of available data rather than business questions. Most people forget to ask what the data should do, how it should be used, and why things need to be organized in a specific way. The results are solutions that may be technically impressive but fail to help anyone make better decisions.

» **Invest in data preparation:** Unless you're stuck with an absolute deadline to deliver a project, don't skimp on the data preparation stage. Clean data that is well-structured makes every subsequent step easier and more reliable. The impact on product delivery later on will make all the difference. Why? Whether you are purposefully using the data for Power BI only or as the basis for a model-driven app using Power Apps, clean data sets the stage for improved performance and less rework later on. Rushing through data preparation to get to the "interesting" visualization work almost always leads to problems later in the project.

>> **Keep your models simple:** You may want to add many relationships among tables, but are they necessary? If you are building a solution using Dataverse, a secure, scalable data platform that enables users to store, manage, and share data used by business applications across Microsoft Power Platform including Power BI (which I cover in Chapter 5), is it better to use a lookup table, adding complexity to a data model, or make it a choice if there are just a few options? These are the considerations that a data analyst, data engineer, and data scientist should work through as they establish basic relationships. It is perfectly okay to add complexity gradually as you better understand your requirements and user needs. But to start, keep it simple. Over-engineering data models early in a project often creates unnecessary complexity that becomes difficult to maintain.

>> **Design with your users in mind:** Don't create for yourself, develop solutions that are purposeful for the business and the end user. You need to create visualizations and interactions, whether in reports or dashboards, that match how people work, rather than what is technically possible or visually impressive in your mind. The best Power BI solutions often look simple because they hide complexity behind intuitive interfaces.

>> **Implement proper governance from the outset:** Data is only as good as the people who control and manage it. You must ensure that the right people have access to the data only as needed. This involves consistently applying the right security policies, as well as ensuring that processes are in place to manage changes and updates to production solutions.

Now that you know how to tackle project team formulation and the process, Chapter 3 helps you determine the version of Power BI that best suits your business needs.

.

IN THIS CHAPTER

» Comparing Excel and Power BI

» Understanding the Power BI product ecosystem within Microsoft Fabric

» Selecting between Desktop and cloud-based services

» Navigating current licensing options and pricing

» Exploring new AI-powered features and capabilities

Chapter **3**

Oh, the Choices: Power BI Versions

hoosing the correct license type of Power BI is like trying to pick the best sweet treat from the world's biggest candy store: You can choose from a plethora of alternatives, and each alternative differs only subtly from the others.

Since the first edition of this book, Microsoft has fundamentally transformed its business intelligence strategy by integrating Power BI into Microsoft Fabric. This unified analytics platform combines data engineering, data warehousing, and AI capabilities with traditional business intelligence tools. Power BI continues to excel at data modeling, visualization, and reporting. Still, it now benefits from enhanced AI capabilities, real-time analytics, and simplified data management through the broader Fabric platform. This chapter helps you factor in this shift as you determine which license type best serves your organization's needs, whether you're a solo analyst or managing enterprise-wide analytics initiatives.

Why Power BI Rather Than Excel?

Microsoft markets Power BI as a way to connect and visualize data using a unified, scalable platform that offers self-service and enterprise business intelligence (BI), helping you gain deep insights into your data. Sounds like a lot of hyperbole, right? Within the Microsoft Fabric ecosystem, Power BI also offers AI-powered analytics, real-time data processing, and seamless integration with advanced data engineering tools.

You may wonder whether Microsoft Excel already has these capabilities, and what makes Power BI different. Ask yourself these questions:

>> **What level of analytics does your organization need?**

Power BI is a tool for data visualization and analysis that allows for collaboration with enterprise-grade security and governance. Power BI offers an array of advanced analytics capabilities that Excel doesn't include, such as the ability to create dashboards, key performance indicators (KPIs), advanced visualizations, and alerts. Excel works best for individual or small team analysis, and Power BI scales to enterprise-wide deployments with thousands of users.

>> **Is collaboration an issue?**

Power BI has significant collaboration capabilities. Excel has limited data collaboration options, as only one person can interact with or edit a document at a time.

>> **What is the size of your dataset?**

Power BI can extract and format data from hundreds of different data sources simultaneously. Because Power BI handles extensive data ingestion — specifically automating data import and transformation — the process is, by nature, much faster. Furthermore, because Power BI can connect to various data sources, the range of outputs — including dashboards and reports — is more interactive, whereas Excel is limited in scope.

>> **Is there a pricing issue?**

There is no single free version of Excel. On the other hand, you can start with Power BI for free. Power BI Desktop remains completely free for report creation, and Fabric (Free), a lightweight version of Power BI Service, provides basic cloud capabilities for personal use to manage large datasets. You can also purchase premium alternatives if you need advanced features, ranging from a few dollars per month to several thousand dollars, to handle either large data volumes or data that require speed.

>> **How meaningful are visualizations to you or your team?**

Power BI integrates business intelligence (BI) and data visualization, enabling users to create custom and interactive dashboards, KPIs, and reports. As part of Microsoft Fabric, it also provides unified data management, AI-powered analytics, and real-time processing capabilities. Microsoft Excel excels at spreadsheet-based calculations, financial modeling, and detailed data manipulation, but lacks the enterprise BI capabilities for large-scale datasets, given its limit of 1,048,576 rows.

>> **Do you need AI-powered insights and natural language querying?**

Power BI includes Copilot for natural language queries, automated insights, and machine learning integration (at an extra cost, of course). Excel incorporates AI to a limited extent. Though Excel can help when it comes to creating advanced reports, if you want to build data models that include predictive and machine learning assets, you need a specific version of Power BI, specifically Premium Per User or Fabric capacity licenses.

>> **Is real-time data monitoring important for your business?**

Power BI enables real-time collaboration with role-based security, workspace management, and enterprise governance features. Excel does not offer comparable features.

REMEMBER

Both Excel and Power BI can handle many requirements, but Power BI is a significant upgrade for several reasons. Data volume, breadth of visualization options, cost, AI capabilities, and collaboration are differentiators with Power BI.

Power BI Products in a Nutshell

Microsoft has restructured its business intelligence offerings around Microsoft Fabric. This transformation, which began in early 2023 and continues to evolve, creates a unified analytics platform that integrates Power BI with data engineering, data warehousing, and AI capabilities. The Power BI ecosystem now includes several key components that work together within the broader Fabric platform — think of it as Microsoft putting all their data tools under one roof.

Power BI licensing options have evolved as part of Microsoft's broader move to integrate Fabric into its business intelligence and analytics ecosystem. Because Fabric connects Power BI with other Microsoft data tools behind the scenes, you'll notice the benefits directly within Power BI through improved storage, faster performance, and expanded data connection options.

The following sections outline each Power BI license option, explaining what's included and how different versions of Power BI and their relationship with Microsoft Fabric affect features such as sharing, data refreshes, and capacity.

Introducing the Power BI license options

You can choose from three product license options for end users like you and me: Power BI Desktop, Power BI Pro, or Power BI Premium. You may be scratching your head because Microsoft also lists a few other Power BI products on its website, including two versions of Power BI Premium, as well as Power BI Mobile, Power BI Embedded, and Power BI Report Server. If you're confused, you're not alone. The good news is that some of these products are included with all three product licensing options, whereas others are specific to either the Pro or Premium version.

Here's a basic description of each Power BI product license:

>> **Power BI Desktop:** The free, downloadable authoring tool for creating reports and data models. Power BI Desktop remains your primary development environment for building visualizations and preparing data, accessible from your Desktop.

>> **Power BI Service:** The cloud-based platform accessible via app.powerbi.com that enables sharing, collaboration, and consumption of reports. Your Desktop creations become available for organizational use when you click the Publish button from within Power BI Desktop.

>> **Power BI Report Server:** An on-premises reporting solution that enables organizations to host Power BI reports within their own data center or cloud infrastructure. This solution is ideal for regulated industries and other scenarios that require data residency or offline access.

>> **Power BI Mobile:** The native application is available for iOS and Android mobile devices so that users can access reports and dashboards with offline capabilities.

>> **Power BI Embedded:** An embedded solution that enables you to integrate Power BI reports and dashboards into custom applications or websites.

>> **Microsoft Fabric:** The unified platform extending Power BI with advanced data engineering (Azure Data Factory), real-time analytics (Azure Synapse), and AI capabilities (Copilot).

As you can see, Power BI isn't a one-trick pony but part of a broader business intelligence platform designed to handle everything from personal analysis to enterprise-scale analytics.

Understanding license options and pricing

Microsoft offers several licensing paths, each designed for different use cases and organizational needs. If you are a one-person organization and don't intend to share your data, you can find affordable options for that. Suppose that you need to collaborate with others and store large data models. In that case, you'll likely require a more robust version, such as Power BI Pro (at a minimum) or, preferably, Power BI Premium Capacity. The key is matching your requirements to the right combination of tools and licenses, as shown in Table 3-1. Pricing listed is as of October 2025.

TABLE 3-1 Power BI License Types

License Type	Monthly Cost (Est.)	Best For	Limitations
Power BI Desktop	Free	Individuals who require data cleansing and visualization without sharing	No sharing online. Everything is done from your desktop. Limited ability to export into report formats.
Fabric (Free) (formerly Power BI Online Free)	Free	Personal use, learning online	No sharing whatsoever. Available online for personal use only.
Power BI Pro	Starting at $14 per user	Great for team collaboration	1GB data set limitation. 8 data refreshes daily.
Premium Per User	Starting at $24 per user	Power users needing AI features and large datasets	100GB datasets; 48 daily refreshes; PPU users only.
Fabric Capacity (formerly Power BI Premium Capacity)	Starting at $260+ per month (Fabric SKU, minimum F2 capacity for usage-based pricing)	Enterprise deployments with 50+ users	Consumption-based pricing varies with usage.

Assessing the licensing options

The old saying that nothing in life is free rings true when it comes to Power BI. If you want to share, you have to pay up. The amount you have to pay depends entirely on the features your organization requires.

Fabric (Free) replaced the old Power BI Free. Like Power BI Free, Fabric Free provides a small amount of cloud storage for personal reports. You'll get a "My Workspace," which I talk about more in Chapter 4 and Chapter 19 of this book, for individual use. Basic data refresh capabilities are also extended to free users. The downside is that you cannot share content with others or participate in organizational workspaces. You'll need to spend a little bit of money to get these new features. If you fall into one of these categories, Fabric Free may be sufficient for your needs to get started: Individual contributors, students, consultants conducting personal analysis, or anyone exploring Power BI capabilities before organizational adoption.

Once you realize, "Hey, I need to share," you'll need to choose how much you'll share and how often your data must be freshened by those collaborating with you. A Power BI Pro license, priced at $14 per month per user, enables the fundamental collaboration features that most organizations need. Pro users can create workspaces, share reports and dashboards, and collaborate with other Pro users. There is a 10GB storage per user allocation and a 1GB dataset limit, which can generally handle most departmental scenarios effectively. However, if your data model exceeds 1GB, you will need to perform data refreshes more frequently (think real-time analytics) or utilize artificial intelligence functionality with Copilot in Power BI. In this case, your only option is to purchase a Premium Per User license at $24 per month per user. The general rule of thumb is that if you are an organization with 2–50 users and small data models, or have data that doesn't need to be refreshed often, consider Power BI Pro. Otherwise, making the extra investment for Premium Per User licenses is a safe bet. Why? Because you get 100x the capacity for your data model (100GB vs. 1GB), have access to AI-powered insights with Copilot, and get more frequent data refreshes (48 versus 8). Power BI Pro is typically sufficient for most end users who require collaboration features. If you are a data analyst, power user with extensive data demands, or need AI capabilities, Power BI Premium is your only option.

What happens to organizations that have millions or billions of records flowing through their organization yearly? In this case, you should purchase not only Power BI Pro or Premium licenses (as these are tied to individual usage), but also Fabric Capacity. Fabric represents Microsoft's future direction, as it allows enterprises to share computational resources that many users can consume, not just for one-off requirements. You'll find that the bigger the organization, the more cost-effective the Fabric becomes because with scale comes discounts and greater access to storage and speed, which Power BI individual premium licenses don't allow.

Fabric Capacity is based on memory and storage allocation as well as refresh capabilities. For most enterprises starting with Fabric, F2 is good enough. However, when you have many users with a standard set of data requirements, the most efficient way to procure is to check out F64 and above. The reason is that this capacity allows users with Fabric Free licenses to consume Power BI content, as well as dramatically reducing the per-user cost for large-scale enterprises. With a Fabric Capacity plan, the more you consume, the higher the price. That is why you want to ensure that you monitor your consumption and optimize your solutions as effectively as possible.

For an overview of the various licensing options, check out Table 3-2.

TABLE 3-2 **Comparison of Power BI Licensing Options**

Features	Desktop	Fabric Free	Pro	Premium Per User	Fabric (Capacity)
Delivery method	Offline	Cloud	Cloud	Cloud	Cloud
Cost	Free	Free	$14 per month per user	$24 per month per user	Starting at $260+ per month (F2)
Model size limit	N/A	1GB	1GB	100GB	Up to 400GB (varies by F-SKU)
Refresh rate	N/A	8/day	8/day	48/day	48/day
Maximum storage capacity	N/A	10GB/per user	10GB/per user	100TB	100TB
Works with Power BI Mobile	No	Yes	Yes	Yes	Yes
Connect to more than 100 data sources	Yes	Yes	Yes	Yes	Yes
Connect to Power BI Desktop for report creation and visualization	N/A	Yes	Yes	Yes	View only
Integrate with Power BI Embedded	N/A	Limited	Yes	Yes	Yes
Sharing and collaboration	Requires publishing	No	Only with Pro users	Only with Premium users	Free users can Consume (F64+), Pro users can publish
AI visualization	No	No	No	Yes	Yes
Unstructured data (text analytics, image detection, machine learning)	No	No	No	Yes	Yes
XMLA connectivity	No	No	No	Yes	Yes
Data flow integration	No	No	No	Yes	Yes
Data warehousing storage options	No	No	No	Yes	Yes

(continued)

TABLE 3-2 *(continued)*

Features	Desktop	Fabric Free	Pro	Premium Per User	Fabric (Capacity)
Security and encryption	Limited	Yes	Yes	Yes	Yes
Application lifecycle management	No	Yes	Yes	Yes	Yes
Distributed geographic deployment	No	NO	Yes	Yes	Yes
Bring your own key (BYOK)	No	No	No	Yes	Yes
Autoscaling	No	No	No	Limited	Yes
Can Be Used with Power BI Report Server for offline access	Yes (with Desktop Version)	No	No	No	Yes

TECHNICAL
STUFF

Note that I didn't discuss Power BI Embedded, as it's an Azure-based service. Power BI Embedded enables organizations to integrate reports and dashboards directly into custom applications, websites, or portals. Operating Power BI Embedded through Azure, combined with the Fabric capacity model, allows end users to access analytics without requiring individual Power BI Pro licenses, making it cost-effective for customer-facing applications.

Unlike Power BI Pro or Premium, Power BI Embedded does not provide the traditional Power BI report viewer experience. Instead, the embedded experience supports customization to match organizational branding and provides enterprise-grade security through Microsoft Entra ID integration and row-level security features.

What's nice about Power BI Embedded is that whether you're building internal business applications or external customer portals, Power BI Embedded scales from departmental solutions to enterprise-wide analytics platforms. The only downside is that it comes with a premium price tag, starting at several hundred dollars per month.

Building a Decision Framework

When you're the point person in your organization who must select the right mix of licenses, you need to build a framework for deciding which Power BI product each person on your team requires. Everyone should have a copy of Power BI

Desktop, regardless of the use case. Deciding who gets which online capability is where the rubber meets the road.

Here is how you should pick and choose the right version for you and your team:

>> **Fabric (Free):** You're learning Power BI, doing personal analysis, or building proof-of-concepts without sharing requirements. In other words, your online workspace is limited to just a single user.

>> **Power BI Pro:** You have 2–50 users who need to collaborate on reports and dashboards with standard datasets under 1GB. The key here is smaller datasets and basic collaboration or sharing.

>> **Premium Per User:** You work with large datasets (up to 100GB), need AI-powered features like Copilot, or require near real-time data refreshes (48 times per day versus 8 times for Pro).

>> **Fabric Capacity:** You have 50+ report consumers, need embedded analytics, or want access to the whole Microsoft Fabric platform beyond Power BI, including the use of Azure Synapse or Azure Data Factory.

TECHNICAL STUFF

When you visit `app.powerbi.com`, Microsoft now refers to this as the *Power BI Service* rather than the previous *Power BI Free*. The previous free tier has been replaced by Fabric (Free), which supports only My Workspaces. Pro and Premium Per User licenses are now the only options for organizational sharing and collaboration.

Planning Your Power BI Governance and Licensing Strategy

Every user's journey with Power BI starts at the Desktop. Fortunately, Power BI Desktop is free and provides full authoring capabilities. You can connect to hundreds of data sources, create sophisticated data models, and build rich visualizations without paying for a license.

To make your work available for collaboration beyond your personal Desktop, you have to publish it from Power BI Desktop to a cloud service. If you want even one other person to explore your work, you need to have a clear strategy for online collaboration. This step is where most organizations choose to formulate a *governance strategy*, which begins with selecting the correct license type, such as Power BI Pro or Premium (Service) or Fabric Capacity.

WARNING

Without proper planning, your organization can end up with sprawling, ungoverned Power BI deployments that become security and compliance nightmares. Be sure to formulate a governance strategy that matches your needs with the correct license type.

Cloud services enable each Desktop asset to be shared with others within your organization or with external partners. Here's the rub: Not one but several license types are available, and each license comes with bells and whistles that will explicitly shape your organization's needs.

When determining your data governance strategy, consider these questions:

>> Who am I sharing my data with? (determines license type)

>> How secure does my data security need to be? (shapes architecture)

>> How often will data need refreshing? (affects license features)

>> Is mobile device access required? (affects user experience)

>> Should I expect to integrate with other applications? (affects platform choice and license type)

By answering these questions, your team can establish governance rules on how users should create, deploy, and consume data. As an example, here is a common delivery practice in Power BI:

1. Create in the Desktop.

2. Publish to Power BI Service.

3. Share with others.

4. Consume via device.

Chapter **4**

Power BI: The Highlights

P ower BI belongs to two Microsoft product families — Microsoft Power Platform (alongside Power Automate and Power Apps) and the Microsoft Fabric unified analytics platform. As a business intelligence platform that bridges product families, Power BI serves everyone from business users seeking to create simple reports to enterprise data teams that build complex analytics solutions.

This chapter helps you determine when and why to use Power BI Desktop versus Power BI Service during your workflow. Most new users of Power BI start off working with the Desktop version. Power BI Desktop is ideal for practicing data manipulation, including data ingestion and modeling, as the software is designed to be used while working independently from your personal computer. Whether you're manipulating data to make the model just right, tackling data transformation through wrangling, or trying to create beautiful visualizations, you do the heavy lifting from Power BI Desktop.

Modern Power BI also comes with AI-powered features, including Copilot and Visual Calculations, that allow you to ask questions about your data in plain language and receive instant visual answers. This chapter highlights some basic tasks for which you may find these AI-powered features most helpful. These features are also covered throughout the book.

After you create and refine your dataset, you're ready to share your work with others. To share your work, you must use Power BI Service. In this chapter, I explain where Power BI Service fits into the typical workflow. I also describe the collaboration and advanced visual tools available in Power BI Service.

Power BI Desktop: Connecting, Transforming, and Visualizing Data

Think of Power BI Desktop as a hub where users perform all their self-directed activities. Users install the application on their computer, and then they can get right to work connecting to, transforming, and visualizing data.

Here is a breakdown of the activities users typically perform with Power BI Desktop. The sections that follow discuss each of these activities in detail:

>> Ingest data across one or more data sources.

>> Model data to create reports and dashboards.

>> Refine, cleanse, and visualize the data through analysis.

>> Create reports for sharing and consumption.

REMEMBER

Power BI Desktop is designed specifically for the work individual users typically perform — it isn't intended for groups. You can complete the same activities online with Power BI Service, but Power BI Desktop provides AI features, such as Copilot (available with Premium or Fabric capacity) and Visual Calculations, that can assist during development. If you use the Desktop platform, you also don't need to share your work before you're ready. You choose when you make your work available on Power BI Service or Fabric workspace.

Finding the best view for the job

Before you can do anything in Power BI Desktop, you need to make sure you're in the right view. Power BI Desktop provides three views: Report, Data, and Model. You access these views from the left-side navigation of Power BI Desktop, as shown in Figure 4-1. Although these features are also available in Power BI Service, Power BI Desktop offers more options for individual analysis.

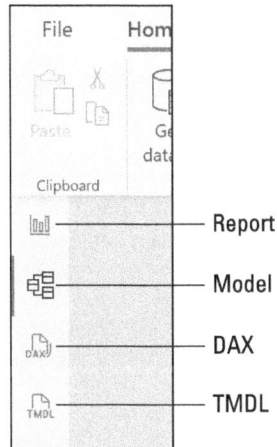

FIGURE 4-1:
Power BI Desktop
navigation.

Each Power BI Desktop view pertains to specific tasks:

>> **Report:** You can create reports and visualizations after ingesting and model-ing the data. Features available in Power BI, such as Visual Calculations and Copilot, can assist with chart creation and analysis. That said, users spend most of their time here on post-data ingestion, transformation, and modeling.

>> **Model:** Like creating a relational data model in Microsoft SQL Server, Azure SQL Server, or even Microsoft Access, you can fully manage the relationships among the structured tables you've created after you've ingested the neces-sary data using Power BI. This creates what's called your semantic model.

>> **DAX view:** This view lets you create and edit DAX (Data Analysis Expressions) formulas, which are used to build calculated columns, measures, and tables. DAX view is where you define the logic behind your analytics, similar to writing formulas in Excel but on a model-wide scale in Power BI.

>> **TMDL view:** The Tabular Model Definition Language (TMDL) view provides a structured, text-based way to see and edit the semantic model behind your data. A replacement for JSON-based scripting, TMDL is useful for advanced users who want to review or fine-tune model definitions, relationships, and metadata in a human-readable format.

Ingesting data

Without data, you can't do all that much with Power BI. Whether you're trying to create a chart or a dashboard or you're posing questions with Questions and Answers (Q&A), you must have data that comes from an underlying dataset.

Each semantic model comes from a particular data source, either found on your local desktop (if you're using Power BI Desktop) or acquired from other online data sources. These sources may be Microsoft-based applications, a third-party database, or even other application data feeds.

In Power BI Desktop, you either use the Power BI Ribbon (shown in Figure 4-2) or click the Power BI Data Navigation icon to access a data source (see Figure 4-3).

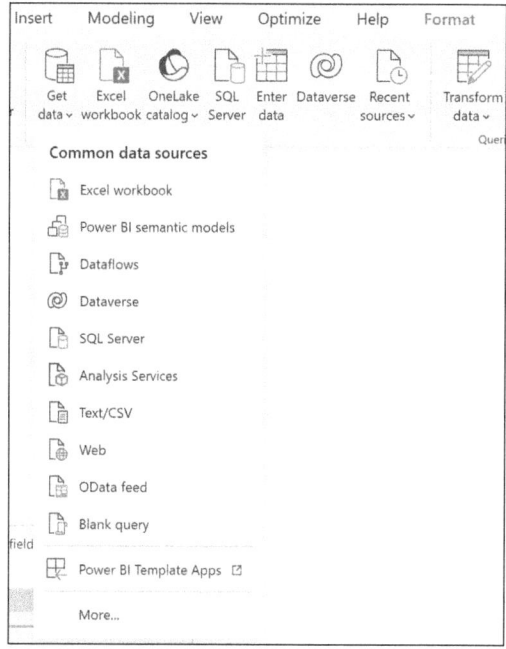

FIGURE 4-2:
Getting data from the Power BI Ribbon.

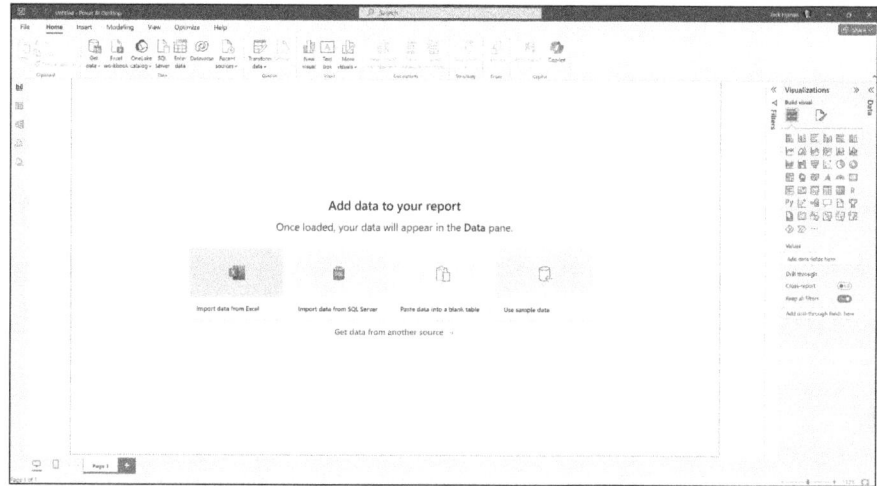

FIGURE 4-3:
Accessing a data source.

Files or databases?

In Power BI, you can create or import content yourself. When it comes to the type of content users can create or import, it boils down to either files or data stored in a database. A word to the wise: Files can be a bit more complicated than databases. With files, you typically need a three-step process: obtain, transform, and import the data into a usable format.

For example, when importing an Excel or .csv file with multiple data types, you click the Get Data button to first load the data into Power BI. Then you use Power Query's transformation tools to format the data and prepare it for your semantic model. Power Query streamlines this entire process, making data preparation much easier.

If you don't want to store your data directly in Power BI Desktop, you have options. You can store data files in cloud locations like OneDrive for Business, which may be easier for sharing and getting automatic updates, or you can keep files on your local drive for complete control. Each approach has trade-offs between convenience and control.

REMEMBER

Where you store your data makes a difference when dealing with data refresh. Consider the frequency of your data updates when you select a data storage location. When the data is stored on your local drive, you'll generally find better performance, even with large datasets. With shared data accessible over the Internet, performance relies on network connectivity and other users accessing the data source. One person manages data stored on your local drive — you.

TIP

You don't always have to store the data directly in Power BI Desktop. You can use Desktop to query and load data from external sources. When you're ready to share your work with others or collaborate on your data model, you can publish your Power BI Desktop file to the Power BI Service or Fabric workspace.

Databases differ from files in that they can connect to a live data source, which requires an Internet connection. Databases are also often made available for consumption to either a small subset of users or to many users. This is especially true when the database is available "as a service," such as Azure SQL Database, Azure Cosmos DB, Azure Synapse Analytics, or Azure HDInsight. With live database connections, you can either import a snapshot of the data or query the database directly each time someone views your report. Once you connect to and appropriately model the data, you can explore the data, manipulate it, and create data visualizations.

REMEMBER

The term *data* gets thrown around a lot — you're probably already confused about data, datasets, dataflows, semantic models, and even databases. And believe me, I throw lots of data words at you in this book. When it comes to data ingestion, *dataset* and *data source* are treated the same, even though they're actually just distant relatives that support the same mission.

You create a *semantic model* in Power BI whenever you use the Get Data feature. A semantic model is also referred to as a data model; these terms are interchangeable. It's what lets you connect to and import data, including from live data sources. A semantic model stores all the details about the data source and its security credentials. A *data source,* on the other hand, is where all the data stored in the semantic model is derived, which can be a proprietary application data source, a relational database, or a stand-alone file storage alternative, such as a hard drive or network file share.

Building data models

The *data model*, also known as a *semantic model*, enables users to create visual representations of their data. Some BI tools aren't data-model-dependent; Power BI isn't in that camp. Power BI is a data-model-based reporting tool. First, let me help you understand what makes a data model unique.

These are the key characteristics of data models:

>> Tables hold meaningful data.

>> Relationships exist between the loaded tables with data.

>> Formulas, also known as *measures,* apply business rules and calculations to your data to create meaningful business insights and key performance indicators.

>> Visual calculations allow you to add calculations, like running totals, moving averages, and percentages, directly to charts without writing complex DAX formulas.

REMEMBER

Power BI isn't alone in including these attributes that create a data model. Other Microsoft products, including Power Pivot for Excel and Microsoft Fabric's data engineering tools, offer this feature set.

You may wonder why you even need a data model. Think of it like a cake recipe. If you follow the recipe, it's easy to make the same cake repeatedly. When the cake ingredients vary, the inconsistencies can make your cake a flop, possibly an epic one. As with a cake recipe, following a data model helps prevent inconsistencies that lead to data irregularity and continual rebuild efforts. Data requires handling and refinement. With BI solutions like Power BI, users can streamline business issues using a data model. Modern Power BI includes AI features that can help you understand and optimize your data model as you build it.

To summarize, models are helpful for these reasons:

» **Reusability:** Users can solve a reporting requirement or business challenge using a formulaic approach without having to reinvent queries or rebuild datasets.

» **Management:** Business users are in a position to manage the data on their own after models are built. Modern features like Copilot and Visual Calculations make this even easier for nontechnical users. Seldom is a database expert or technical professional needed to handle infrastructure requirements.

» **Adaptive models:** You can build a logical model with minimum code. Changes can accommodate technical and business requirements, including the use of measures (formulas) and rule sets.

You can choose from among many tools, including Microsoft Excel and BI-based reporting tools, but not all tools offer the ability to build data models. A BI tool that does not incorporate data models requires the analyst or data engineer to generate a query to fetch the data manually. Though many of these tools have graphical user interfaces to support query generation, you need to reinvent the process each time you use it, with little extensibility available. In Power BI, the relationships you need to keep track of are mapped out in the Model Viewer with the help of a data model (see Figure 4-4).

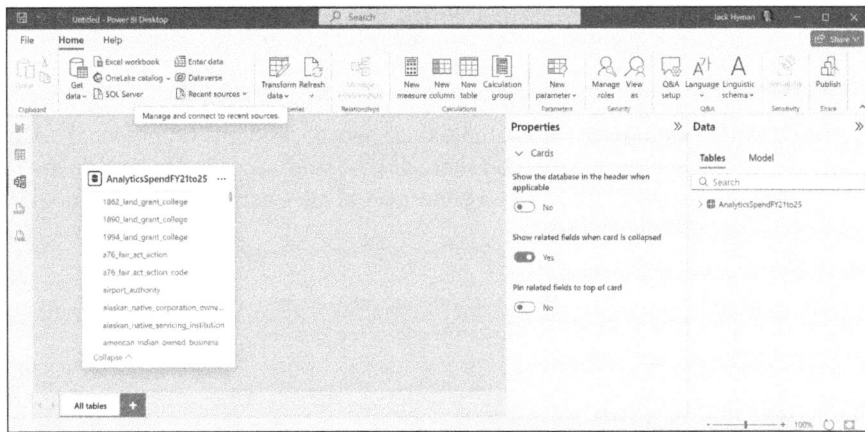

FIGURE 4-4:
A data model in the Model Viewer.

REMEMBER

You know the old saying "Reuse, reduce, recycle"? It applies perfectly to data models. A data model is a reusable asset that, when tailored to different business needs, can significantly reduce development efforts and lower costs. You can often build new solutions on top of existing models or enhance them for new requirements.

Analyzing data

Before you share data with a team, you must carry out your own personal data analysis using Power BI Desktop. You can conduct several forms of analysis. At the most basic level, when the data enters the system, you must review it to ensure that it appears correctly and accurately. If it doesn't, you manipulate the data by cleansing it — a task often carried out by an analyst or engineer. The process usually takes a while because it's quite laborious, kind of like preparing a big holiday dinner. Yet when the results are available, they're easy to read in a matter of seconds. As much as this strategy sounds like a hassle, the results are what you want to aim for in business intelligence.

Once the data source has been cleaned up and you've mapped the data into refined datasets, it's time to create the necessary visualizations. Here I'm referring to pictures that can serve as examples of your data sources, such as charts, maps, indicators, and gauges. You'll find these visuals in deliverables such as reports and dashboards. Even the Q&A feature in Power BI produces visuals after you ask focused questions.

ON THE WEB

Power BI has an extensive catalog of visuals available, but you may want more options for complex visuals. Industry-specific options that aren't part of Power BI Desktop or Service may also be available. To view additional options, visit Microsoft AppSource at https://appsource.microsoft.com.

You eventually want to reach a point where you can use Power BI to rapidly generate reports and access data through dashboards. A Power BI designer builds out dashboard visualizations, referred to as *tiles,* using data in reports and semantic models. Users can build their own dashboards for personal use or share them with others. (*Note:* If you share dashboards, security credentials are tied to each visual.) Figure 4-5 shows a collection of tiles across a dashboard organized by role and responsibility.

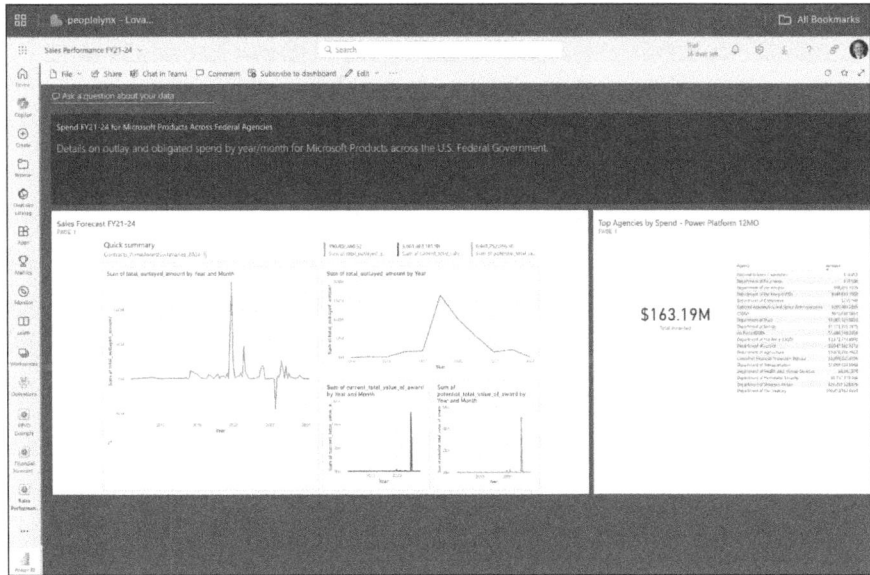

FIGURE 4-5:
A sample dashboard that aggregates many visual sources.

Creating and publishing items

You may want to learn more about Power BI by trying out the free Desktop client to tackle more complex data projects. And, at some point, you may want to post that data project on the web in a read-only format to a limited audience. And you certainly can for free. Suppose, however, that you want others to edit and collaborate with you beyond read-only support. In that case, you must pay for such features.

When you publish items from Power BI Desktop to Power BI Service, the files are workspace-bound. Similarly, if you've produced any reports, they appear in Report view. Datasets migrate from the desktop with the same name, as do any reports to the workspace. The relationship is typically one-to-one, with rare exceptions.

In Power BI Desktop, you can publish your files by choosing Publish ⇨ Publish to Power BI from the main menu (see Figure 4-6) or by selecting Publish on the Ribbon (see Figure 4-7).

REMEMBER

When you publish an item from the Power BI Desktop to Power BI Service, you're performing the same action as pressing Get Data, essentially. You're connecting to a data source, uploading a file from Power BI Desktop, and then sending it to Power BI Service.

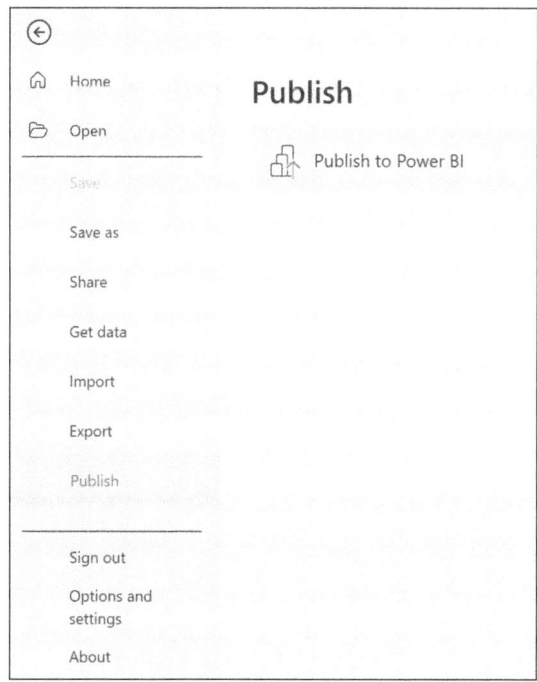

FIGURE 4-6:
Publishing items
using the Power
BI Desktop
File menu.

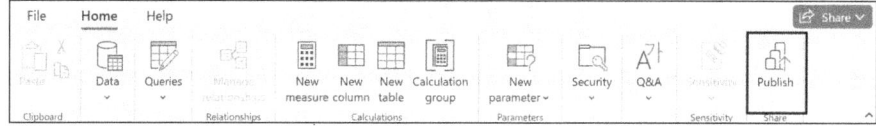

FIGURE 4-7:
Publishing items
using the Power
BI Desktop
Ribbon.

WARNING

Saving in Power BI Service doesn't make changes to the original Power BI Desktop files. Therefore, don't expect any updates when you or your colleagues add, delete, or change a dataset, visualization, or report.

Power BI Service: Sharing Your Work Far and Wide

Power BI Service (sometimes called *the Service*) isn't meant for you to do your work alone; that's what Power BI Desktop is for. Instead, Power BI Service is built for collaboration. It's where you take your Power BI Desktop creations and publish them online so that you and your teammates can explore, share, and manage your data together. Accessible at https://app.powerbi.com, Power BI Service acts as a hub for teamwork. Here, you can organize reports, create dashboards, manage permissions, and connect your data with others. As your analytics needs grow, you may find that a Power BI Pro, Premium Per User, or Premium capacity license unlocks advanced sharing, refresh, and performance options.

Differences between Power BI Desktop and Service

Power BI Desktop users can update and republish datasets, data models, and reports as often as needed. Power BI Service doesn't update data stored locally on your computer, so it's up to you (or your scheduled refreshes) to keep things in sync. Power BI Service focuses on sharing, collaboration, and visualization since it's where you publish and explore your reports and dashboards. Taking it one step further, for large-scale analytics (think gigabytes and terabytes of data), Microsoft Fabric serves as the unified data platform that underpins Power BI. Fabric handles the heavy lifting by storing, integrating, and preparing data across your organization. At the same time, Power BI Service delivers the polished, interactive insights that everyone can see and use. In short, Fabric manages the data foundation, and Power BI Service brings that data to life.

Power BI Service offers multiuser access and features designed for teamwork, things like viewing and editing reports online, managing dashboards, refreshing data on a schedule, and integrating with other Microsoft 365 apps. Because Power BI Service is cloud-based, which means your data, reports, and dashboards are available anywhere you log in, whether you're on your laptop, tablet, or phone, you'll always be looking at the exact source of truth.

Viewing and editing reports

Reports typically begin in Power BI Desktop, where a user builds the semantic model, models the relationships, and designs visuals. Once complete, you can then publish the report to the Power BI Service to make it available for others. Publishing to Power BI Service gives you and your organization access to the report through one of two workspace types, a personal workspace, called my workspace or one or more shared workspaces. Reports can then be refined collaboratively. If you are given the appropriate credentials, you can make edits directly online or continue making changes in Desktop and republish updates incrementally.

Many organizations use online services and SaaS applications (like CRM or ERP systems) to manage business data. Power BI Service connects to applications via prebuilt connectors and REST APIs that directly link to platforms such as Dynamics 365, Salesforce CRM, Azure DevOps, and Google Analytics. Once connected, Power BI creates a live or scheduled refresh connection to the dataset in the connected applications, so your reports in Power BI Service always reflect the latest information without manual uploads. You learn more about connecting to data sources in Chapters 5 and 6.

Sharing insights within Power BI Service

What you develop using Power BI Desktop is for one person: you. That's why you need to share your insights by publishing to Power BI Service. Publishing your reports isn't just about putting data in the cloud; it's about collaboration and sharing with others. Power BI Service makes it easy to share three key items: dashboards, reports, and apps across your team, department, or organization, so everyone works from the same up-to-date information.

How you share determines how others can interact with your content. Some users may only be able to view dashboards and reports, depending on how your organization manages data permissions, and others may be able to edit, comment, or collaborate directly. All of this is controlled by workspace permissions, which act like a shared folder for your Power BI projects.

You can open and explore all your Power BI content saved online, such as reports, dashboards, semantic models (datasets), and apps, right inside Power BI Service. Here are the main ways to find what you need:

>> **Home:** Your personal starting point that shows your recent, favorite, and recommended items so you can quickly jump back into your work.

>> **Browse:** Explore everything you have permission to access, organized by type — reports, dashboards, apps, and semantic models.

>> **My Workspace:** Your personal workspace where you can build and store your own reports and dashboards before sharing them with others. It's private to you.

>> **Workspaces:** Shared areas where teams collaborate to create, edit, and manage reports, dashboards, and datasets together.

>> **Apps:** Ready-to-use collections of dashboards and reports that your organization has published for wider distribution.

>> **Dashboards:** One-page summaries that highlight key visuals; click any tile to open the related report or explore the data behind it.

>> **Data hub:** A central place to find and connect to shared datasets (semantic models) you can use when building your own reports.

Many organizations find it helpful to collaborate in small teams while a semantic model is still being developed. Once the semantic model and reports are stable, the team will then bundle them into an app for broader use. This approach ensures that both data consistency and security are maintained.

Collaborating inside Power BI Service

Most users transition from Power BI Desktop to Power BI Service for the collaboration tools, which are not included in Desktop. You may want to share with a small subset of users, or perhaps the group of users you're looking to share information with is distributed. Depending on the Power BI Service option you're working with, you have these options:

>> **Using the workspace:** The most common way to share reports and dashboards is by using the workspace. Suppose that another user is given access to a report or dashboard. In that case, the user either views or edits the workspace area in Power BI Service.

>> **Using Microsoft Teams:** Microsoft Teams integration allows for enhanced collaboration on reports and dashboards with Power BI.

>> **Distributing your reports and dashboards via an app:** If your results are focused, the user can build a single app and create a working executable for sharing among other users.

>> **Embedding reports and dashboards on websites:** Sometimes, the reports and dashboards you create may be helpful for targeted public consumption on an external or internal-facing website. You can create an iteration of a Power BI report or dashboard that's viewable. Any user who visits that website may view the data if they're assigned permission to do so.

>> **Printing reports:** When in doubt, you can always print your reports and distribute paper copies. Of course, each time the data is refreshed, you need to print a new copy of the report. For dashboards, each output is printed separately.

>> **Creating a template app:** If your deliverables are repetitious, distribute them so that Power BI users can access them using Microsoft AppSource. You must assume that these items are publicly consumable for other businesses to use.

Collaboration requirements depend on your organization's Power BI setup and the features you want to use. Although some basic sharing can be done with free accounts, advanced collaboration features typically require Power BI Pro, Premium Per User licenses, or access to Premium/Fabric capacity. Licensing requirements vary depending on whether users are viewing, editing, or managing content. Check with your administrator to determine your organization's needs.

Refreshing data

Every time you access a report or a dashboard on Power BI Service, you must query the data source. If there are new data points, the results are updated in the dataset as part of the visualization. Depending on the refresh requirements, one or more processes may be needed. The refresh process consists of several phases, depending on the storage operation required for the dataset. You have two concepts to consider: storage mode as well as data refresh type.

Storage modes and dataset types

Power BI offers several modes for allowing access to data in a dataset:

» **Import mode:** Datasets are imported from the original data source into the dataset. Power BI can query the reports and dashboards submitted to the dataset and return results from the imported tables and columns. You may find this to be a snapshot copy — a dataset representing a moment in time, in other words. Each time Power BI copies the data, you can query the data to fetch the changes.

» **DirectQuery/LiveConnect:** Two connection types that don't rely on importing data directly are DirectQuery and LiveConnect. Data results come in from the data source whenever the report or dashboard queries the dataset. Power BI will then transform the raw data into usable datasets. Only DirectQuery mode, though, requires that Power BI not use queries using the Power Query Editor Extract Transform Load (ETL) engine. The reason for this is that the queries are processed directly using Analysis Services, without having to consume resources. Data refreshes aren't required because no imports occur in the Power BI Desktop environment. Features that are still updated include tiles and reports, in which the data updates about every hour. The schedule can be changed to accommodate business needs.

» **Push mode:** In Push mode, there's no formal definition for a data source, so there's no requirement for a data refresh. Instead, you push the data into the dataset through an external service, which is quite common for real-time analytics processes in Power BI.

Data refresh types

For a Power BI user, *data refreshes* are defined as importing data from the original data sources into one or more datasets. The refresh is based on a schedule or can be in real time. Depending on your Power BI license, the refresh rate varies from 8 updates to as many as 48 per day. You're limited to eight daily dataset refreshes for shared capacity, which are executed by the schedule using a plan. The updates reset daily at 12:01 a.m.

Licensed users are limited to eight refreshes per day for Power BI (free) and Power BI Pro. If you buy Power BI Premium capacity or Power BI Premium Per User, your refresh allotment increases to 48 refreshes per day.

A Power BI refresh operation can have multiple refresh types, including a standard data refresh, OneDrive refresh, query cache refresh, tile refresh, dashboard refresh, and of course visualization refresh. Power BI decides the individual refresh steps with each of these examples. A precedence must be applied based on operational complexity, as shown in Table 4-1.

TABLE 4-1   ## Comparison of Power BI Refresh Types

Storage Mode	Data Refresh	OneDrive Refresh	Query Caches	Tile Refresh	Report Visuals
Import	Scheduled and add-on	Yes, for connected data	If enabled on Premium Capacity	Automatic and on-demand	No
DirectQuery	Not applicable	Yes, for connected data	If enabled on Premium Capacity	Automatic and on-demand	No
LiveConnect	Not applicable	Yes, for connected data	If enabled on Premium Capacity	Automatic and on-demand	Yes
Push	Not applicable	Not applicable	Not practical	Automatic and on-demand	No

Regardless of the refresh approach, you must ensure that reports and dashboards use current data for a business to be successful. If you find that your data is stale, address the problem with the data owner or the gateway administrator.

When refreshing data, keep the following points in mind:

>> For optimal performance, schedule refresh cycles for off-peak business hours, especially if you use Power BI Premium capacity or Premium Per User.

>> Consider the number of refreshes your organization is allowed under its license and the volatility of the data. Refresh only when you know it makes sense.

>> Make sure the dataset refresh doesn't exceed the refresh duration, or else the data won't refresh properly, causing business issues.

>> Optimize your data by including only the necessary data for your reports and dashboards. Any extra overhead can be costly, especially when it comes to the consumption of memory and processing resources.

» Apply the appropriate security settings for both Power BI Desktop and the Power BI Service. The settings don't carry over from one environment to another.

» Be mindful of the visuals used, as more outputs result in performance degradation and potential data refresh issues down the line.

» Use only reliable data gateways to connect data sources, whether on-premise or cloud-based. If data refresh failures happen, you may need to deploy additional infrastructure to handle needed capacity.

» If data refresh failures happen, put a notification method in place so that you can quickly deal with any technical concerns.

2

It's Time to Have a Data Party

IN THIS PART . . .

Understand how to prepare, connect, and manage data sources, including Power BI dataflows.

Examine and integrate data from diverse data sources.

Address data transformation and cleansing techniques to create reliable foundations for analysis.

Optimize query performance and implement proper storage modes for efficient data handling.

Troubleshoot common data challenges using tools available in Power BI.

Chapter **5**

Preparing Data Sources

odern organizations generate more data than ever — from spreadsheets and cloud applications to real-time streams and enterprise systems. Thankfully, Microsoft Power BI allows users to connect to that data using hundreds of built-in connectors across Power BI Desktop, Power BI Service, and Microsoft Fabric. The connection is often the easy part; transforming and preparing data for analysis still takes some thought. In this chapter, you explore the different ways to connect, prepare, and load data — whether it's from Excel files, cloud folders, databases, or Fabric-native sources like OneLake and Dataverse in order to build reports and dashboards quickly.

Getting Data from the Source

You literally cannot do anything in Power BI without data. Microsoft has made it easy to establish a connection to almost any data source you can imagine. Whether you're working with local files, cloud storage, databases, APIs, or real-time streams, Power BI offers hundreds of connectors across Desktop, Service, and

Microsoft Fabric. However, before you dive into a maze of connectors, it's worth taking a moment to establish the business requirements behind the data. Ask yourself this question: Are you analyzing a static file updated monthly, or tapping into a continuously refreshed enterprise data source? Your answer to this question determines your data management tactic, and these tactics can vary radically.

REMEMBER

Microsoft continually adds data connectors to its Desktop and Service platforms. In fact, don't be surprised to find at least one or two new connectors released monthly as part of the regular Power BI update. As a result, Power BI offers well over 300 data connectors. The most popular options include files, databases, and web services.

ON THE WEB

You can find a list of all available data sources at

https://learn.microsoft.com/en-us/power-bi/connect-data/
desktop-data-sources

To correctly map your data in Power BI, you must determine the exact nature of the data. For example, would you use the Excel Connector if the document type were meant for an Azure SQL database? That wouldn't produce the results you're looking for as a Power BI user.

ON THE WEB

Throughout *Microsoft Power BI For Dummies,* 2nd Edition, I refer to a dataset with publicly accessible federal procurement data on the topic of acquiring data analytics services, particularly those related to Microsoft Power BI. To access this dataset, you'll need to complete a one-time registration and set up an account. To access the data, go to https://www.kaggle.com/jackhymanpowerbi/datasets.

When you download the dataset, it comes in a CSV file format. Don't worry—Power BI makes it easy to open. Just follow these steps:

1. **Open Power BI Desktop.**

   On the Ribbon at the top of the window, click Home ⇨ Get Data. If you don't see CSV listed right away, click More to see the complete list of options (see Figure 5-1).

2. **Pick the correct file type.**

   In the Get Data window, choose File ⇨ Text/CSV. Then click Connect. A file browser will pop up (see Figure 5-2).

3. **Find your file.**

Navigate to where you saved the CSV file on your computer. Double-click the filename (or select it and press Open). Power BI shows you a preview of the data.

4. **Choose what to do with the data.**

You see two buttons, Load and Transform Data:

- *Load:* If you click this button, Power BI drops the data straight in, but you have to fix any issues later by hand.

- *Transform Data:* Clicking this button gives you a chance to clean and shape your data before importing it into Power BI.

5. **Access Power Query Editor (see Figure 5-3).**

After you click the Transform Data button, you enter the Power Query Editor. From this interface, you can tidy up your data — remove extra columns, rename things, and make sure that everything looks right before loading it into Power BI.

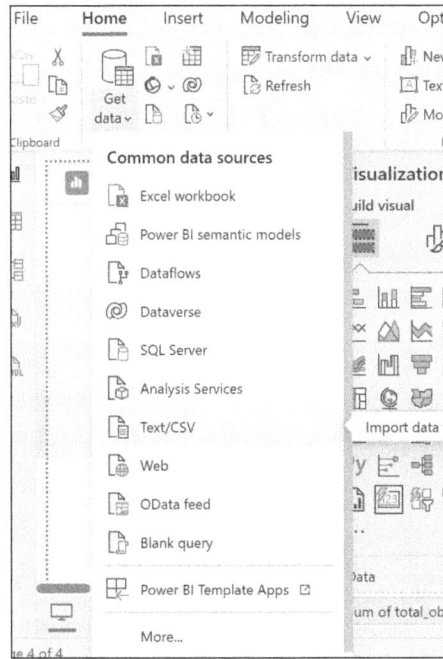

FIGURE 5-1: Finding the CSV File Connector in Power BI Desktop.

REMEMBER

When you load data into Power BI Desktop, it's stored as a snapshot — a frozen copy of the data at a specific point in time. To view the most current data, click the Refresh button on the Home Ribbon periodically to re-import the latest values from your data source if you are updating the file and want to see the updates.

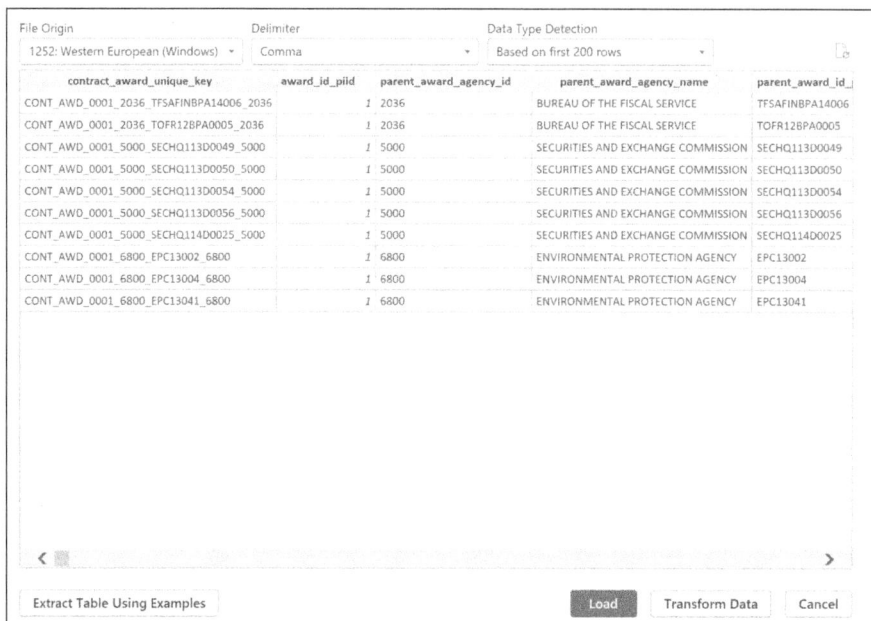

FIGURE 5-2:
Selecting data in
the Navigator.

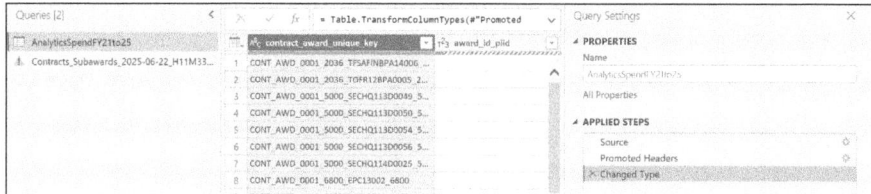

FIGURE 5-3:
Your data, loaded
into the Power
Query Editor.

When you need to work with more than one file, folders can make your life much easier. Imagine having a set of reports or spreadsheets that you receive every month. Instead of connecting to each file one at a time, Power BI allows you to connect to an entire folder. Power Query then combines those files into a single dataset for you.

There's one catch: The files in that folder must appear identical. That means they should have the same columns, with the same names and data types. For example, if one file refers to a column as *PeopleID* and another refers to it as *People_ID*, Power BI won't recognize that they belong together. Consistency is the secret that makes the process work. You must have both column names be PeopleID or People_ID.

This folder connection is convenient when you're dealing with recurring files such as Excel, CSV, or Google Sheets. By maintaining a consistent file structure, Power BI can automatically detect new files, merge them into the dataset, and refresh your reports without additional work on your part.

To connect the folder, follow these steps:

1. **Open the Home tab on the Ribbon and click the Get Data button.**

2. **Choose All ⇨ Folder from the menu, as shown in Figure 5-4.**

   Want to try another way? Go to the Home tab on the Ribbon, click New Source, choose More from the menu that appears, and then choose Folder.

3. **Whichever way you select Folder, your next step is to click the Connect button.**

   Clicking the Connect button enables access to a single data source.

4. **Locate the folder path specific to where you've stored files and browse to the location where you've placed the file, like** `C:\Downloads\` `<name_of_file>`.

   The files from the folder you just selected load into a new screen, shown in Figure 5-5, which indicates that your file is now part of the Power BI local data store.

5. **Select one or more tables that have loaded.**

6. **Click the Transform Data button.**

   Clicking the Transform Data button combines and transforms your data files into a single table. If you click Load, your files load as is.

   When you connect to a folder, Power BI consolidates all the files into a single Power Query Editor window. From there, you can view the datasets from each file and combine them into a single, unified table.

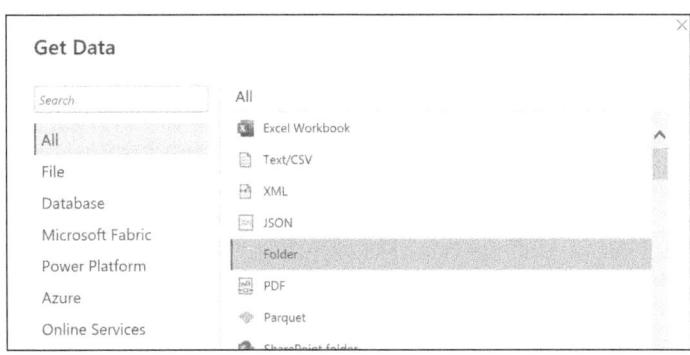

FIGURE 5-4:
Selecting Folder
from Get Data.

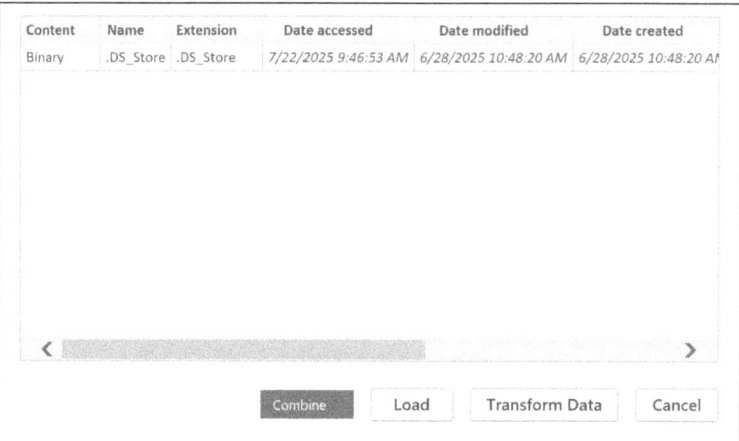

Content	Name	Extension	Date accessed	Date modified	Date created
Binary	.DS_Store	.DS_Store	7/22/2025 9:46:53 AM	6/28/2025 10:48:20 AM	6/28/2025 10:48:20 AM

Combine · Load · Transform Data · Cancel

FIGURE 5-5:
Files from a
folder load
into Power BI.

TIP

When you connect to data in Power BI, you see three options: Load, Transform Data, and, in the case of folders, Combine and Transform Data. Choosing Load brings the data directly into your report without requiring you to open Power Query. This option works well if your file or dataset is already clean and consistent and doesn't need any shaping. However, it also means that you don't get a chance to adjust anything, such as renaming columns, filtering rows, or changing data types, before the data is loaded.

If you need more control, the Transform Data option opens the Power Query Editor, where you can clean and shape the data before bringing it into your model. This option is available for all sources, including single files, databases, web connections, and folders, giving you the flexibility to prepare the data exactly as you want it.

When you work with a folder of files, you also see the Combine and Transform Data option. This choice is designed for situations in which all the files in the folder share the same structure. When you choose this option, Power BI selects a sample file, generates query steps, and then automatically applies them to every file in the folder, merging them into a single unified dataset. If your files are consistent, this is usually the fastest way to consolidate them.

Managing Data Source Settings

Commonly, your dataset requirements change over time. That means if the data source changes, so will some of the settings that were initially loaded when you configured Power BI. Suppose that you move the csv files folder from C:\Desktop to C:\Documents. Such a change in folder location would require you to modify the data source settings.

If you move your CSV file or need to point Power BI to a new location, you can easily fix it in Power Query by following these steps:

1. **Pick your query.**

   In the left pane, under Queries Pane, click the query you want to update.

2. **Look at Query Settings.**

   On the right side of the screen, find the Query Settings pane.

3. **Find the Source step.**

   Under Applied Steps, click Source (see Figure 5-6).

   This opens a small window showing the file path and type of file Power BI is using.

4. **Update the file location.**

   Change the path (for example, if you moved the file to a new folder) or switch the file type if needed.

   Repeat these steps for each query that needs updating.

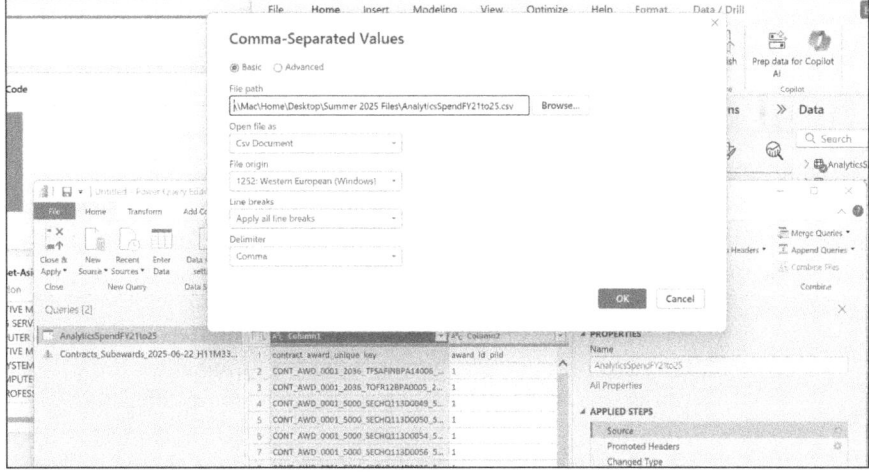

FIGURE 5-6:
Using the Applied Steps area to update the data source settings.

Though the steps outlined here may seem easy at first blush, they may become laborious because you need to make a change to each file listed for each query. That process can be time-consuming, and if you have a lot of queries, you're bound to make errors, given the tedious nature of the work. That's why you want to consider an alternative option — one where you can change the source location in one fell swoop rather than tackle each query independently with this option. Follow these steps for the other method:

1. **In the Power Query Editor, open the Home tab and click the Data Source Settings button. (The Data Source Settings button is the one sporting a cog — see Figure 5-7.)**

   A new window opens showing all the data sources for your current report. This is where you can view and manage the source locations.

2. **Make the changes you want to make to the source location.**

3. **(Optional) Change and clear associated security credentials by selecting Edit Permissions or Clear Permissions and then re-enter them the next time you connect or refresh the data.**

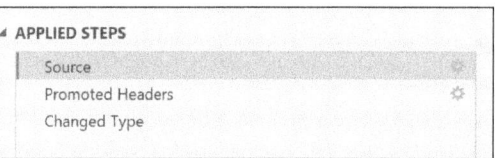

FIGURE 5-7:
The Data Source
Settings button.

Working with Shared versus Local Datasets

So far, the focus in this chapter has been on local datasets that you handle by creating and managing them using Power BI Desktop. After you publish and share a dataset with others — either through your own workspace or a shared one — that dataset is referred to as a *shared dataset*. Unlike with Power BI Desktop, in which you have to continually update the dataset on the local hard drive, a shared dataset is stored on the cloud, which means that, whether the dataset is stored in your workspace or with others, updates can be more consistent.

You can find many other benefits to using a shared dataset over a local dataset, including

» Consistency across reports and dashboards

» Reduction in dataset copying due to centralization of a data source

» The ability to create new data sources from existing sources with little effort

REMEMBER

Although you may have your own needs with a dataset, once you share it with a team, the desired outputs may differ. In that case, you may want to create a single dataset and allow the other users to develop reports and dashboards from the single dataset.

TIP

Connecting to a published dataset in Power BI Service requires a user to have Build permission. You can also be a contributing member of a shared workspace where a dataset exists. Make sure that the owner of the dataset provisions your access according to your business needs.

You can connect to a shared dataset using either Power BI Desktop or Power BI Service. To do so, follow these steps:

1. **Using Power BI Desktop, click the Home tab's Get Data button and then choose Power BI semantic models from the menu that appears (see Figure 5-8).**

   The data is transferred from Power BI Desktop to Power BI Service for you to consume.

2. **With Power BI Service, go to the workspace where you published your data, and then choose New ⇨ Report, as shown in Figure 5-9.**

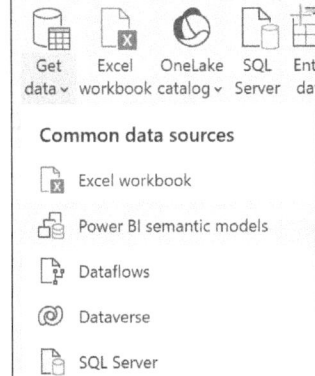

FIGURE 5-8:
Accessing a Power BI semantic model.

Whether you're using Power BI Desktop or Power BI Service, your ability to connect to a semantic model without having to worry about data refresh issues or version control becomes a bit easier. You also have the choice to select Save a Copy in the Power BI Service next to any report in My Workspace or a shared workspace without having to re-create a semantic model. This action is similar to connecting to data using Power BI Desktop; it involves creating a report without the base data model.

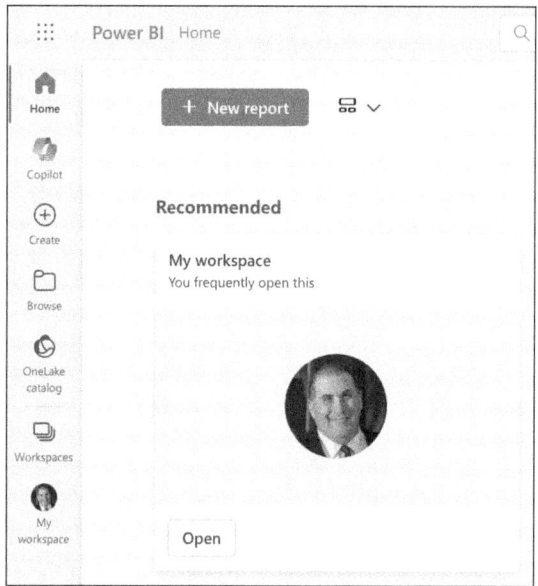

FIGURE 5-9:
Connecting to a
shared dataset in
Power BI Service.

WARNING

Don't be surprised if certain buttons in Power BI Desktop become unavailable when working with a semantic model from the Power BI Service. When you connect to a published model — often through the Datahub — you're limited to report-building only. You won't be able to open the Power Query Editor or view the Data pane, because the underlying model is managed in the cloud.

To confirm whether you're working with a connected semantic model versus one on your desktop, look in the lower-right corner of Power BI Desktop. You'll see the semantic model name and your user ID, which indicate that you're connected to a cloud-based model. If, for some reason, you are not the owner of the semantic model, ask for a downloadable copy (PBIX or PBIP) or work in a development workspace where you have full permissions. Follow these steps:

1. **Open a new Power BI Desktop file.**

   Click File ⇨ New to start a fresh report.

2. **Connect to your data source.**

   Click Home ⇨ Get Data and choose your source (Excel, SQL Server, SharePoint folder, or whatever). If you're pulling from a Fabric resource, such as OneLake or Dataverse, those are also considered valid connections.

3. **Click Transform Data.**

   This opens Power Query, where you can shape and clean your data before loading it.

4. **When you are ready, go to the top of the Home Ribbon and click Close and Apply.**

   Your data is loaded into the report's semantic model.

You're now working with a local dataset in the context of a semantic model, which gives you full control over transformations, relationships, calculations, and DAX without any restrictions from shared or managed datasets.

Accessing Data via Storage Modes and Modalities

Power BI gives you several options to bring data into your reports and dashboards, depending on the structure, size, and freshness of your data. The most common method is Import mode, in which Power BI makes a snapshot copy of your data and stores it inside the report file or workspace. However, as data volumes and real-time needs increase, so do your options for ingesting real-time data. Options such as DirectQuery, Direct Lake, and composite models offer additional flexibility — particularly when working with enterprise-grade or Fabric-based data sources.

Here are the five Power BI modalities you can choose from:

>> **Import:** This is the most common modality, in which data is copied into the report's semantic model. It's fast and supports full Power Query and DAX features. Import allows you to work offline, but it must be refreshed manually or on a schedule.

>> **DirectQuery:** Power BI doesn't store the data locally. Instead, it queries the source live every time you interact with a visual. DirectQuery allows for real-time data refreshes, which is great for meeting data needs that require up-to-the-minute updates. That said, performance depends on the source system. A slow system or a lot of data yields slow querying.

>> **Direct Lake:** With the introduction of Microsoft Fabric for premium capacity users, Direct Lake allows Power BI to read data directly from OneLake Delta tables. Direct Lake enables semantic models to read data directly from Delta tables stored in OneLake. This setup allows for Power BI to maintain the high-speed performance of in-memory import models while ensuring that the same data is accessible to other tools and users across various data-intensive platforms, not just Power BI.

>> **Composite model:** The Composite model lets you combine multiple storage modes in one. You may have a need for a local dataset and live feed. With composite, you can combine the best of both worlds in Power BI.

>> **Dual mode:** Taking Composite mode one step further, dual mode enables a table to act as both imported (for fast performance on the desktop) and DirectQuery (for real-time updates), depending on how it's queried — offering the best of both worlds dynamically.

REMEMBER

The Power BI modalities enable you to access your data at the desktop or online using services. They are useful whether you want to focus on data performance, ensure your data can scale, or aim for data freshness.

Considering the Query

In my Power BI discussions, I always emphasize that you can choose from various methods to prepare and load data into Power BI. When you're in doubt, the method that ensures you and your organization the most accuracy is Import mode — hands down. In some cases, however, the user experience with direct import isn't ideal. Consider the circumstances described in this list:

>> DirectQuery may be the better choice when dealing with a very large dataset. However, the performance of the import correlates directly to the system that the import is coming from.

>> Data frequency and freshness are two reasons to use DirectQuery. This is the case because data sources must always show the return of results in a reasonable length of time.

>> Suppose that the data must reside in its original data source and that the location of the source cannot change. In that case, DirectQuery is better suited for data movement.

WARNING

DirectQuery isn't the best lifeboat if you think that direct importing doesn't solve your problems. You may face an uphill battle using DirectQuery under the following conditions:

>> **The state of your infrastructure dictates the results for DirectQuery.** That means slow or old hardware won't work the way you think it will when dealing with large datasets.

>> **Not all query types are usable with DirectQuery.** This is especially true for native queries that have table expressions or stored procedures.

>> **Data transformation is limited, unlike direct import.** You must interact with the interface each time a change is required.

>> **Data modeling limitations exist, especially when you're addressing calculated tables and columns.** As you see in Chapter 15, DAX functionality is limited when you use DirectQuery to import data.

Data querying varies, depending on the data connectivity mode used in Power BI. Table 5-1 explores the differences between Import, DirectQuery, and Live Connection.

TABLE 5-1 **Comparing Data Connectivity Modes**

Feature	Import	DirectQuery	Direct Lake	Composite Model
Storage mode	Based on license type	Limited by the data source	Optimized by Microsoft Fabric	Varies based on the data source
# of Sources	Unlimited	Unlimited	Only OneLake Delta tables	Multiple source types; can be unlimited with performance issues
Security	Row Level security (RLS) via Power BI roles	RLS enforced at source or in Power BI Desktop	Integrated RLS with Fabric	RLS is delegated on a per table basis
Refresh cycle	Scheduled refresh for Pro is up to 8/day. Premium is unlimited.	Live query every visual interaction	Instant access based on OneLake status	Mixed depending on data source
Performance	Optimize because of in-memory engine.	Depends on source query speed and performance.	Near-import level performance via Direct Parquet/Delta Reads	Varies
Data transformation	Power Query & DAX	Limited to query folding and source transformation support	PowerQuery supported via Lakehouse pipelines	Varies
Modeling features	Full: calculated columns, tables, measures, relationships	Limited modeling (no calc tables; DAX limited)	Full modeling with semantic models on top of Delta data	Supports full semantic model across multiple modes with caveats

Addressing and correcting performance

At some point, you connect to a data source and stare at the screen and wonder, "Why are things so slow?" You may experience slow performance in Power BI for several reasons, many of which can be diagnosed and corrected in no time.

Power Query transforms your data sources using a native query language pre-configured by Microsoft within the product. A translation language called M is used in Power BI to convert the data source. The language conversion process is referred to as *query folding*. Though query folding is usually quite efficient, hiccups do occur. An example where query folding may result in issues is when a dataset is only partially retrieved from the data source. As a result, rather than loading all columns, the dataset loads a subset of the data, making it more difficult for you to pick and choose what you want to keep and what you want to remove.

TIP

To inspect how Power Query is interacting with your source, you can view the native query being sent via the Power Query Editor. To view the query, right-click a step under Applied Steps, and choose View Native Query.

REMEMBER

Native Query isn't always available. For example, some data sources don't support query folding. In addition, the query step may not be translated depending on the native language used, in which case the option is grayed out.

Diagnosing queries

Power BI includes a built-in query diagnostics toolset that helps you identify and resolve performance issues that may arise during data loading or transformation. These tools are particularly useful for evaluating queries generated during dataset refresh cycles, especially when diagnosing query folding anomalies.

To use the Query Diagnostics feature, you must have a data source already loaded into Power Query — ideally with some transformations applied. Once that's in place, follow these steps:

1. **In Power BI Desktop, click Home ⇨ Transform Data to open the Power Query Editor.**

2. **In the Power Query Editor, open the Tools tab from the Ribbon.**

3. **Click Start Diagnostics to begin capturing performance events, and then click Stop Diagnostics when finished (see Figure 5-10).**

4. **(Optional) To diagnose a specific transformation step, click Diagnose Step on the Tools Ribbon or right-click a step and choose Diagnose. This isolates the performance of an individual step and opens a comparison view.**

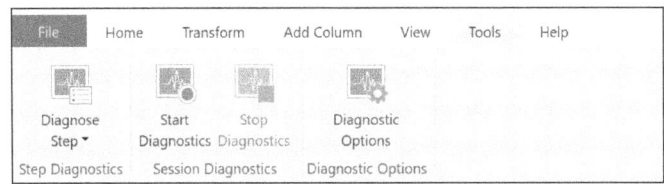

FIGURE 5-10:
Start and Stop
query diagnostics.

This step-level diagnostic capability marks a significant improvement over earlier Power BI versions, in which all performance tuning had to be done in-code. Now, Power BI supports a more low-code, user-friendly approach to performance analysis.

TIP

Query Diagnostics is most effective when working with imported or partially imported data, in which Power Query transformations can be inspected in detail. However, if your dataset is large or expected to update frequently, and you're using Import or Hybrid tables (such as those backed by OneLake or Fabric Lakehouses), consider enabling an incremental refresh policy. This approach preserves historical data while only processing new or updated records during each refresh cycle, helping to improve performance, reduce refresh times, and optimize resource usage.

**TECHNICAL
STUFF**

EXPLORING THE MICROSOFT DATAVERSE

Power BI is a component of the Microsoft Power Platform, a suite that includes Power Apps, Power Automate, Power Pages, and Copilot Studio. At the heart of this ecosystem is Microsoft Dataverse (formerly known as the Common Data Service). Microsoft Dataverse is a cloud-based data platform designed for low-code app development, automation, and analytics. Dataverse isn't a strict relational database management platform, though. Microsoft touts the product as a managed, cloud-native data platform built on a combination of Azure SQL, Azure Blob Storage, metadata services, and integrated security, combining relational storage, business logic, and low-code extensibility in a single product.

So how do Dataverse and Power BI work together? Dataverse serves as a central repository, not just for Power Apps and Automate but also for Power BI dataflows, including Fabric-integrated pipelines. As long as users have appropriate environment-level permissions and security roles, access is seamless — no manual connection strings needed.

If you want to read more about Dataverse and Power Platform, check out my other book, *Microsoft Power Platform For Dummies* (Wiley).

Chapter **6**

Getting Data from Dynamic Sources

R emember when getting data meant begging your IT department for access to a file store, just for an Excel spreadsheet? Those days are over! Power BI can connect to practically everything these days — your company's sales system, that cloud app your marketing team loves, even real-time data that updates as you watch. The best part? You don't need to be a tech wizard to make it happen. Whether your data lives in a simple Excel file or a fancy enterprise system, Power BI speaks its language. In this chapter, you discover how to tap into all sorts of data sources without breaking a sweat (or calling IT every five minutes).

Getting Data from Microsoft-Based File Systems

In Chapter 5, I discuss loading data directly from Power BI Desktop and even from folders stored locally on your desktop computer. In this chapter, I focus on integrating with Microsoft-based applications, such as OneDrive for Business and SharePoint Online, both of which are Microsoft 365 applications.

REMEMBER

To use OneDrive, you need to be logged in to Microsoft 365. If you're logged in, you can access files and folders as though you're accessing your local hard drive. The only difference is that your hard drive is Microsoft OneDrive. In Figure 6-1, you can see that the path to a OneDrive folder is no different from the path for a standard file or folder on your hard drive.

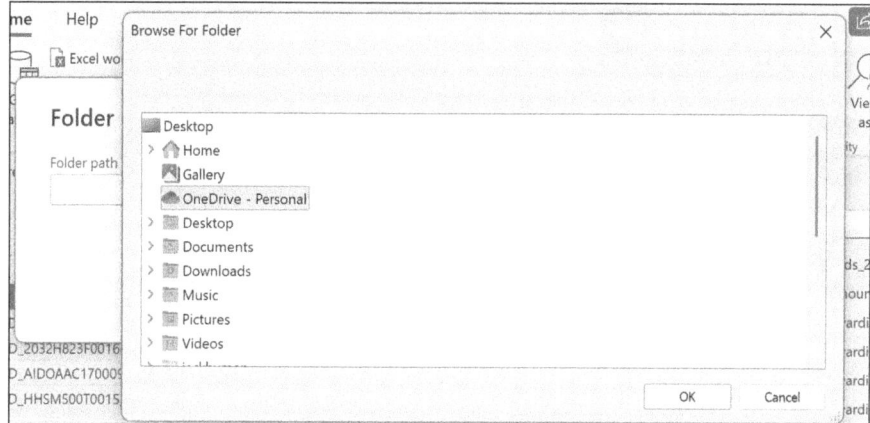

FIGURE 6-1:
OneDrive
file path.

On the other hand, SharePoint Online offers a variety of options for document management and collaboration. The first option is to search a site collection, site, or subsite (referred to in Power BI as a SharePoint Folder). In this case, you must enter the complete SharePoint site URL. For example, if your company has an intranet, the site may be something like `https://asitecollection.sharepoint.com`. An example of what you'd see after you enter a complete URL and log in with your Azure Entra ID credentials is shown in Figure 6-2.

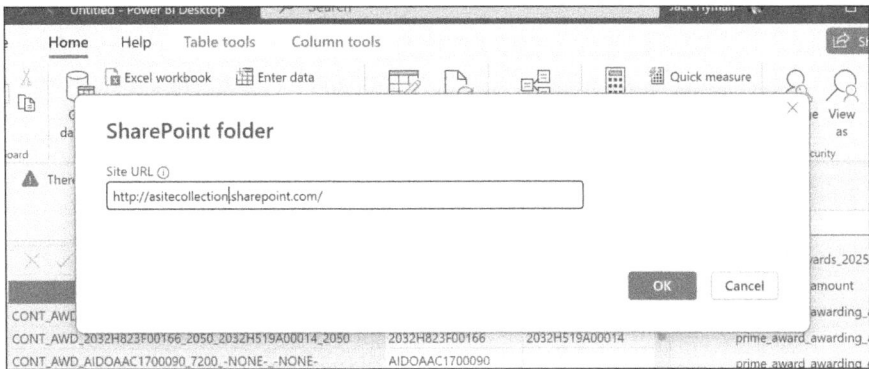

You can also collect, load, and transform one or more SharePoint lists in Power BI. (In SharePoint, a *list* looks like a simple container.) Lists are a great tool to use with Power BI when combined with metadata columns, versioning, and workflow automation using Power Automate. With a list, data is gathered in rows, with each row represented as a row item similar to a database or spreadsheet item. To load a SharePoint list, you must know the URL path of the SharePoint site collection, site, or subsite. Once a user is authenticated, all available lists are loaded for that person.

TIP

When you're first starting out with Power BI, you may be tempted to keep all your files on the computer's hard drive as a way to manage your data. After a while, though, dealing with numerous versions of the same dataset becomes unmanageable. That's why you should use a cloud option, such as OneDrive or a SharePoint site, to manage your files, datasets, reports, dashboards, and connection files. It helps keep everything streamlined.

Working with Relational and Non-Relational Data Sources

Many organizations use relational databases to record transactional activity. Examples of systems that typically run relational databases are enterprise resource planning (ERP), customer relationship management (CRM), and supply chain management (SCM)-based systems. Another type of system may be an e-commerce platform. Each of these systems has one thing in common: They can all benefit from having a business intelligence tool, such as Power BI, evaluate data by connecting with a relational database instead of extracting individual data files.

Businesses rely on solutions like Power BI to help them monitor the state of their operations by identifying trends and forecasting metrics, indicators, and targets. Suppose a relational database isn't enough for your business demands. In that case, you may also consider the use of non-relational data solutions coupled with relational data sources to jump-start your data journey with Power BI. This may include cloud-native warehouses such as Snowflake, BigQuery, or Microsoft Azure Lakehouse. Power BI supports all of these, allowing you to query, model, and visualize data regardless of where it lives.

In the example shown in Figure 6-3, I have Power BI connect to an Azure SQL Database, Microsoft's web-based enterprise database. Depending on your relational database solution, you have a few choices. One would be to choose Get Data⇨ More from the Ribbon Home tab and then look for Database. Here you will find Microsoft-specific databases. If you are looking for another type of data source, choose Get Data⇨ More and look for Other. Then click the appropriate choice. Whether you're working with your traditional Microsoft SQL Server, Azure SQL Database, PostgreSQL, Oracle, or even a data lake using Parquet files, Power BI has you covered with native connectors and built-in query optimization features.

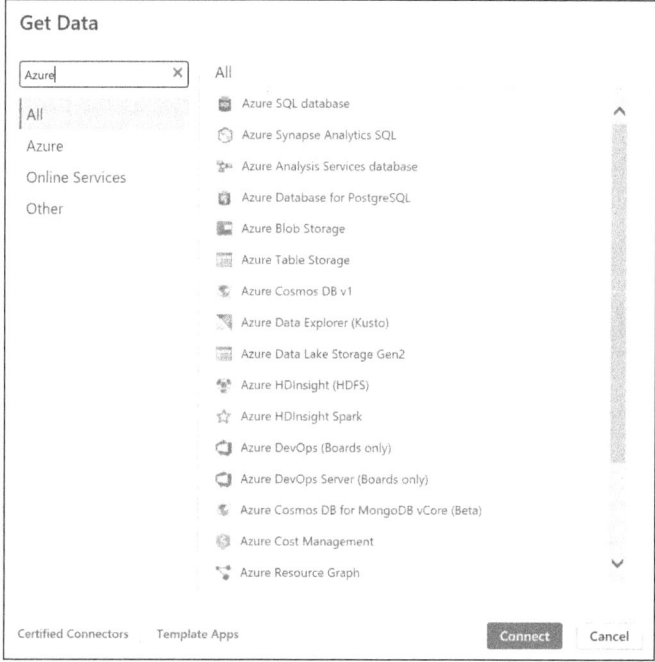

FIGURE 6-3: Azure SQL database location.

A Microsoft Azure SQL database is shown in the previous example. You can either search for the product in the Search box or click the Azure option after selecting More.

After you select the database source type under Get Data, you must enter the credentials for the relational database. In this case, you enter the following info:

» Server name

» Database name

» Connection mode — Import or DirectQuery

Figure 6-4 provides you with an example of the fields that must be filled out. (You don't need to add unique command lines or SQL query statements unless you're looking for a more granular data view.)

FIGURE 6-4:
Entering credentials for a SQL-based relational database.

REMEMBER

In most cases, you should select Import. The circumstances in which you choose DirectQuery are for large datasets. The data updates are intended for near real-time updates.

After you've entered your credentials, you're prompted to log in with your username and password using your Windows, database, or Microsoft account authentication, as shown in Figure 6-5.

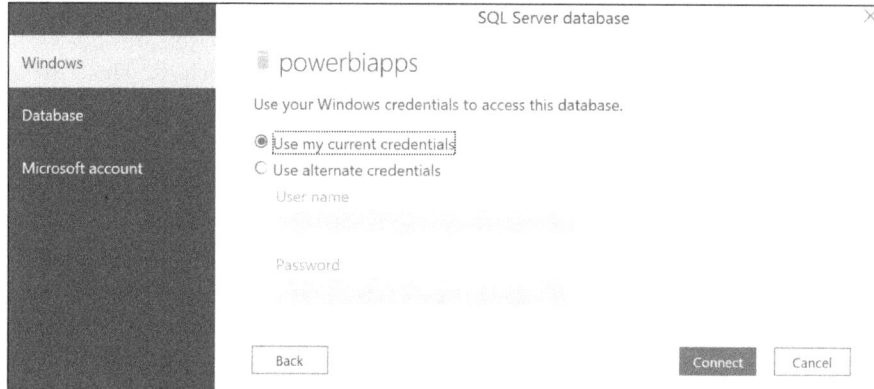

FIGURE 6-5:
Selecting the authentication method to connect.

Importing data from a relational and nonrelational data source

Connecting to the data source can be tricky because you need to ensure that your database source and naming conventions are set up correctly. However, once you get past these two facts, you often have smooth sailing — well, at least until you need to pick the data to import. You may become overwhelmed if the database contains a large number of tables.

After you've connected the database to Power BI Desktop, the Navigator displays the data available from the data source, as shown in Figure 6-6. In this case, all data from a Dataverse instance is shown. You can select a table or one of the entities to preview the content.

REMEMBER

The data loaded into the model *must* be accurate before proceeding to the next dataset. To import data from the relational data source that you want to ingest into Power BI Desktop, and then either load or transform and load the data, follow these steps:

1. **Select one or more tables in the Navigator.**

   The data selected will be imported into Power Query Editor.

2. **Click the Load button if you're looking to automate data loading into a Power BI model based on its current state with no changes.**

3. **Click the Transform Data button if you want Power BI to execute the Power Query engine.**

   The engine performs actions such as cleaning up excessive columns, grouping data, removing errors, and promoting data quality.

FIGURE 6-6:
Selecting the
tables from the
Navigator
for import.

Importing Data from a Nonrelational Data Source

Not all data lives in neatly organized tables. Many organizations rely on nonrelational (NoSQL) databases — such as Microsoft Azure Cosmos DB, MongoDB, or Apache Hadoop-based systems — to handle massive volumes of semistructured or unstructured data. What separates a relational database from a nonrelational database is how data is organized and stored. These systems don't use traditional tables. Instead, they store data in formats such as documents, key-value pairs, wide-column stores, or graphs — making them highly flexible and scalable for large data workloads (think terabytes and petabytes).

Power BI can connect to many NoSQL sources, but each database typically requires access to an API or at least one native connector. The authentication and connection process differs from traditional databases, as you usually need to provide an endpoint URL, access keys, or API tokens — not just your server or database name, along with the username and password.

For example, to connect Power BI to Microsoft Azure Cosmos DB, a globally distributed NoSQL database platform, you need to follow these steps:

1. **Choose Get Data ⇨ More from the Home Tab in Power BI.**

2. **In the submenu that appears, locate the Azure submenu.**

3. **Search for Cosmos.**

4. **Click to select the Azure Cosmos DB v2 option (as shown in Figure 6-7).**

   You are now able to create a nonrelational database connection.

5. **Enter the URL of the Cosmos DB in the URL field and then click OK. (See Figure 6-8.)**

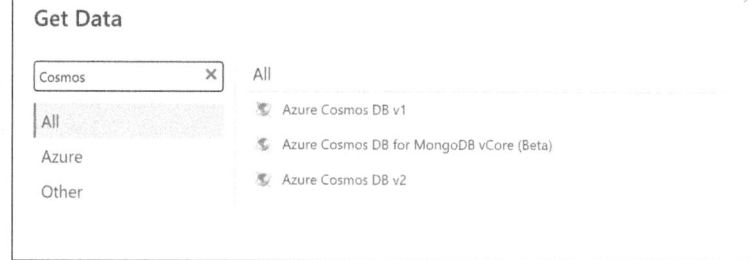

FIGURE 6-7:
Selecting the
Cosmos DB
data source.

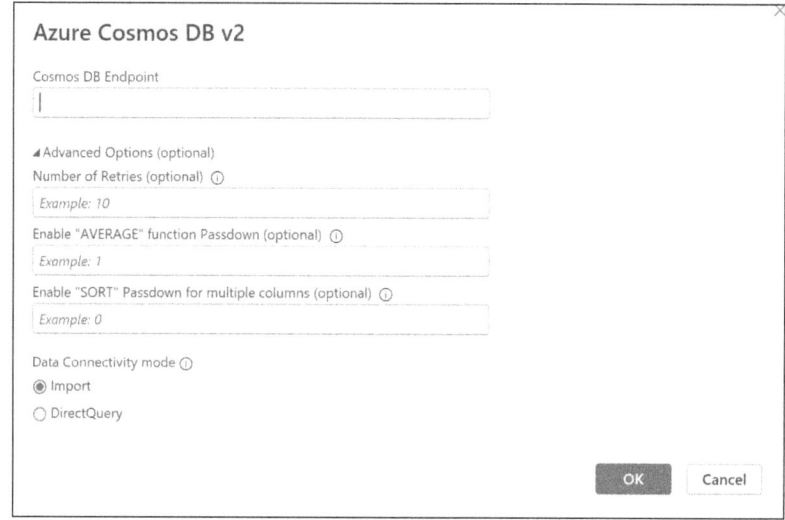

FIGURE 6-8:
Connecting to
the Cosmos DB,
a Microsoft
NoSQL database.

WARNING

When you're using a NoSQL database, you need to know the keys to authenticate. For Cosmos DB, you can find those keys in the Azure portal under the Cosmos DB Instance Settings, Key Link. Be sure to copy down the primary and secondary read-write keys and the primary and secondary read-only keys.

Importing JSON File Data into Power BI

JSON (JavaScript Object Notation) is one of the most common formats for exchanging data today, within both Power BI and Fabric. Whether you're pulling data from an API or a Power Automate flow, or exporting records from cloud services like Dataverse or Cosmos DB, chances are you'll encounter a .json file at some point in time. Unlike CSV or Excel, JSON is a semi-structured data file; its data is stored as nested key-value pairs, often with inconsistent shapes across records. That makes it flexible for developers, but it also means that you need to transform it before you can use it in Power BI. The following sections cover bringing JSON file data into Power BI Desktop, and cleaning and loading your JSON data.

Bringing JSON file data into Power BI Desktop

To bring JSON into Power BI Desktop:

1. **Click Home ➪ Get Data ➪ JSON and select your file.**

   Power BI opens the Power Query Editor and displays a hierarchical list of the JSON data elements, with expandable nodes that show the file's nested structure, including objects, arrays, and fields.

2. **Click To Table from the Transform tab to convert the list into a tabular format.**

3. **Use the expand icons to flatten nested records or lists into rows and columns.**

There will be times when your data doesn't load accurately. When this happens, you'll want to tweak the file by clicking the Gear icon next to the Source Step in the Query Settings Pane. From there, you can reconfigure steps such as the file origin, encoding type, and delimiter settings.

Clean up and load your JSON

You've transformed your JSON data into a table using Power Query – now what? It's time to get it ready for reporting. Before loading, you should take the time to clean up your JSON data by conducting a data hygiene exercise with the file created. You'll want to

>> Remove unnecessary columns, especially ones filled with null values or repeated metadata.

>> Use Replace Values to fill in missing data or standardize entries.

>> Rename columns for clarity and consistency.

You do this for two reasons — first, unnecessary and excess data results in slower performance. Second, bad data creeping into your dataset will affect your ability to create reports later on.

Once you have completed your cleanup, click Close & Apply to load the data into Power BI's model. This locks in your transformations and lets you start building visuals immediately. If you ever need to make changes later, just go back to Transform Data — Power BI keeps track of every step. This process is as easy as rinse, repeat, and recycle.

Importing Data from Online Sources

Enterprise applications and third-party data feeds are widely available in Power BI. Microsoft has over 300 connectors to applications developed and managed by other vendors, including those from Adobe, Denodo, Oracle, and Salesforce, among others. Of course, Microsoft also supports its own enterprise application solutions, including those in the Dynamics 365, SharePoint 365, and Power Platform families. Online sources can be found across several categories using the Get Data feature in Power BI Desktop. Still, your best bets are under the Online Services heading or the Other heading, as this is where most of your traditional enterprise applications are found.

In the example, shown in Figure 6-9, I've set up a connection to Dynamics 365 Business Central.

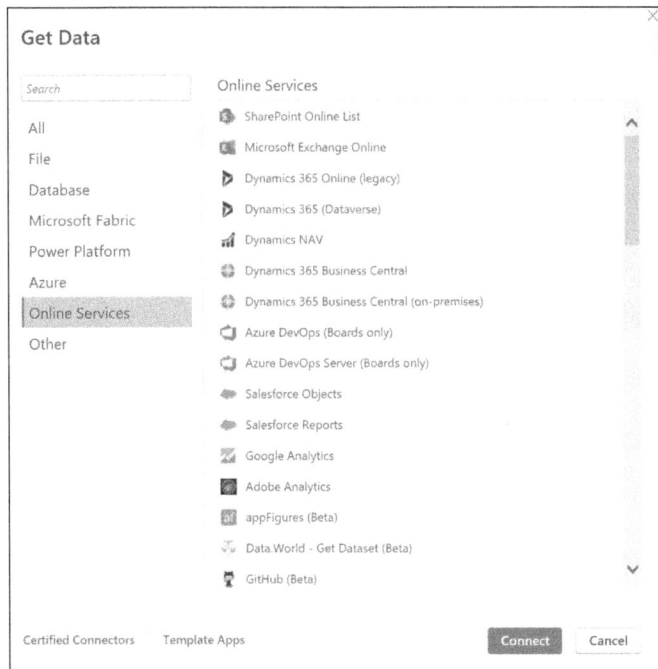

FIGURE 6-9:
Connecting to an online service in Power BI Desktop.

To connect to an online service, follow these steps:

1. **Click Home ⇨ Get Data from Power BI Desktop.**

2. **At the bottom of the Go Data menu, click More.**

   Selecting More displays more data source options.

3. **Choose Online Services from the More submenu.**

   Online Services include enterprise applications, where you can access large datasets (assuming you have access to user credentials).

4. **On the right side, click Dynamics 365 Business Central.**

   Doing so allows for a connection to Microsoft's Small Business ERP Solution (see Figure 6-10).

5. **At the bottom of the screen, click Connect.**

   You have now established a connection to Microsoft Dynamics 365 Business Central.

You're then asked to enter your online organizational credentials. Generally, this part is already prepopulated because it's your Single Sign-On login associated with Azure Entra ID. (See Figure 6-10.)

FIGURE 6-10:
Common
interface to
enter login
credentials for
online services.

After you authenticate a session, all data available from the database for the specific source is loaded in the Navigator pane within the Power Query Editor. Power Query transforms the data before loading it in Navigator.

TIP

Some connectors (such as Dynamics 365, Salesforce, or ServiceNow) offer multiple APIs; ensure that you select the one labeled v2.0 or OData for full schema support and optimal query performance.

Discovering Modern Semantic Modeling in Power BI and Microsoft Fabric

When your data comes from multiple sources — such as SQL, APIs, Excel, and Dataverse — you may become overwhelmed when ensuring that your reports are accurate, fast, and easy to understand, yet built properly. Power BI uses the DAX language to define relationships, calculations, and business rules. As things scale, however, managing all of this in a single report file becomes increasingly difficult. This is where enterprise semantic modeling comes in.

Power BI enables you to publish a centralized data model, which can comprise multiple data sources, as a dataset to either the Power BI Service or a Microsoft Fabric workspace. This dataset can become the single source of truth for your team. Once published, multiple report creators can reuse consistent calculations and KPIs, avoid duplicating data loads, and apply security measures such as row-level security (RLS) to protect sensitive information. These datasets can also be accessed through other tools, such as Excel or additional Power BI reports, enabling broader collaboration and consistency across your organization. Think of it as a "define once, reuse everywhere" approach to enterprise reporting.

As you explore in Chapter 19, Microsoft Fabric takes enterprise data modeling to the next level — especially when you're working with large, shared datasets across multiple teams. Although Power BI offers robust modeling features on its own, there are times when building your semantic model in Fabric is the practical choice. Fabric enables you to create high-performance models using Direct Lake, eliminating the need to import data and allowing Power BI to query delta tables directly from OneLake (which I cover in Chapter 18). You gain faster performance and lower memory usage — especially with large or constantly updated datasets.

Other reasons to use Fabric for your semantic models include support for datasets over 400 GB, built-in version control and CI/CD workflows, and the ability to use Live Connections without duplicating data. These features make it ideal when you're building a centralized, governed data model that multiple reports and teams will connect to — helping you scale Power BI across your organization without complexity.

Dealing with Modes for Dynamic Data

The tried-and-true method of importing data reliably with no restrictions is to use the Import method. *Importing* data means that the data is housed in a Power BI file and published with reports to Power BI Service from Power BI Desktop by a user. Thus, you can rest assured that if it's possible to interact directly with the dataset, the data is transformed and cleansed the way you want it to be converted. Sometimes, of course, this approach may not be suitable for you or your organization.

Don't use Direct Import in either of these two instances:

>> An environment with complex security requirements

>> Large, unmanageable datasets where the potential for bottlenecks is high

TIP

In such cases, go with DirectQuery for dynamic data because you can query the data sources directly without worrying about importing a copy of the dataset into Power BI. This dataset can potentially be excessively large. Using DirectQuery also helps you avoid another issue that Direct Import often poses as a challenge: data recency and relevancy. You always know that your data is fresh with DirectQuery. In contrast, with Direct Import, you must update the dataset yourself.

If you need to switch storage modes, you can do so by navigating to Model view in Power BI. First, select the data table that requires modification in the Properties pane. Then change the mode by selecting an option from the Storage Mode drop-down menu, located at the bottom of the list (see Figure 6-11). There are three options: Import, DirectQuery, and Dual.

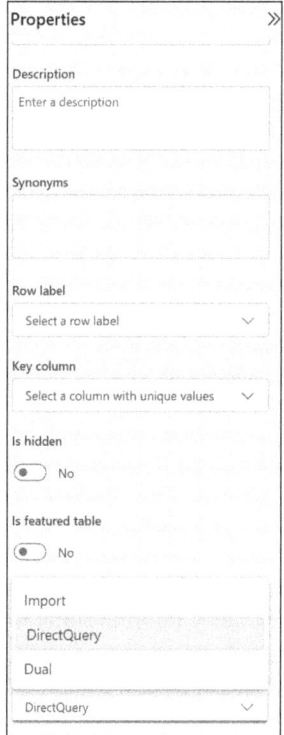

FIGURE 6-11:
Changing
modes in
Properties pane.

Fixing Data Import Errors

Along the way, don't be surprised if you find yourself coming across an import error or two. Most of the time, the issue is caused by query timeouts, data mapping errors, or data type issues. These problems are easy to fix after you understand the error message. Table 6-2 addresses how to accommodate these most common issues.

REMEMBER

Always specify the correct data type at the data source from the get-go. Completing an import versus a DirectQuery also eliminates many of the standard data source errors.

TABLE 6-2 ## Common Data Errors and Fixes

Error Message	Why It Happens	How to Fix It
`Time-out expired`	Power BI limits how long queries can run before timing out. This error means the data source took too long to respond, typically due to large data volumes, source performance issues, or query complexity.	You need to optimize the query. You do this by reducing the number of columns or required conditions for the query. Another option is to switch to a faster connection method, such as Import, instead of DirectQuery.
`The data format is not valid`	If you don't properly label the headers if your file, Power BI will not be able to properly map the data.	Databases usually don't have this issue. The issue is often seen with file imports. You need to make sure that the first row in your file contains column headers (not blank rows or merged cells). Once you get that taken care of, reload the data into Power Query.
`Missing data files`	If file dependencies exist within your uploaded file or access is limited to the file as a user, you may encounter this type of error message.	Here is a simple test: Open Power Query. Locate the query with the error and edit the source step. Then update the file path or permissions to reflect the correct configuration.
`Transformation is error prone`	A column may contain errors or unexpected data types due to import or conversion issues. Another issue may be data misinterpretation. A string field may be converted to a number, all because the first character in the text is a number.	In Power Query, check each column to make sure that the correct column data types are enforced. If they aren't, you should swap the column type to reflect the data. You may need to remove invalid column and then rebuild it using just the Load option instead of using Transform and Load because Microsoft may make the same mistake twice.

Chapter **7**

Cleansing, Transforming, and Loading Your Data

E ffective data cleansing and transformation requires everyone in an organization to think like detectives — but detectives equipped with both traditional investigative skills and modern AI tools such as Copilot. The core challenge remains the same as it has always been: You must rigorously analyze data before it enters your system or after it is stored in its intended data store. Superficial reviews won't uncover the subtle inconsistencies, hidden patterns, and data quality issues that can undermine your analysis. Only a human being can be the data conductor.

What has changed is how you can approach this detective work. Although the step-by-step analysis process remains essential for understanding the true nature of your data, you now have intelligent assistants built into Power BI, thanks to Copilot, that can automatically flag anomalies and suggest transformations, as well as predict potential issues before they occur. The goal is to ensure data consistency across all columns, values, and keys.

This chapter guides you through the complete modern data preparation lifecycle. First I discuss foundational techniques, and then I show how AI-enhanced approaches can accelerate the process of data preparation and cleansing. You see when to rely on traditional analysis methods, when to leverage automation, and how to combine human expertise with artificial intelligence to engineer optimized queries and transformations. By the end of this chapter, you will be able to make any data source shine for analysis, consumption, and visualization, regardless of its initial condition or complexity.

Engaging Your Detective Skills to Hunt Down Anomalies and Inconsistencies

Anomalous data comes in many forms, and Power BI provides both traditional investigative tools and AI-powered detection capabilities to uncover it. Using Power Query, you can find unusual data trends and subtle ambiguities that may otherwise slip through manual review. Whether it's an out-of-context dollar amount, unexpected format variations, or missing values that skew results, these real-life data quality scenarios can now be addressed through a combination of human analysis and intelligent automation.

The foundational approach to spotting errors remains looking directly at your data in the Power Query Editor. You can evaluate the quality of each column using the Data Preview features, which provide immediate visual feedback about potential issues. To begin your manual investigation, choose View ⇨ Data Preview ⇨ Column Quality from the main menu in Power Query. This traditional approach provides you with direct control over the analysis process, allowing you to understand precisely what you're examining. In Figure 7-1, you can see that the Contract Details column has just a small amount of data missing, shown by the <1% number reported as empty, whereas 38% of the Award Number data is empty. You should be more concerned about data quality issues in the Award Numbers column than in the Contract Details.

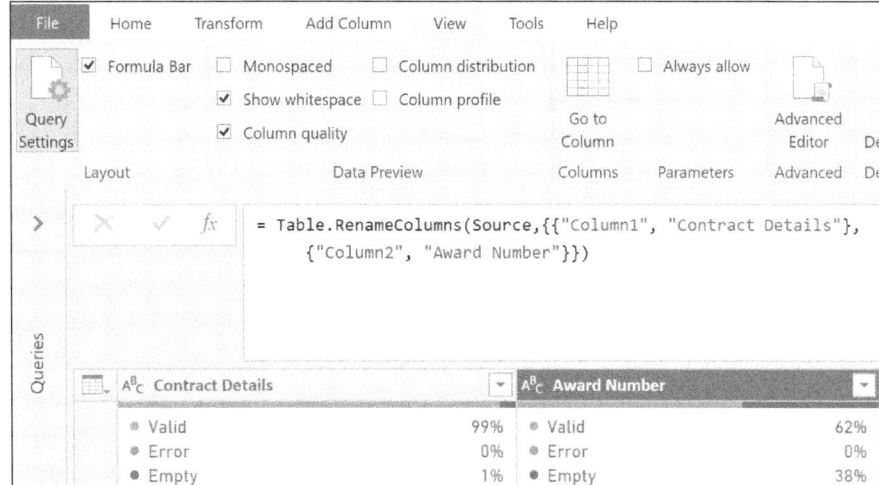

FIGURE 7-1:
Address-
ing column
quality issues.

Checking those data structures and column properties

Beyond basic column completeness, understanding column value distribution provides deeper insights into data structure issues and helps identify patterns that can impact your analysis. Column value distribution measures all distinct values in a selected column, showing the percentage of rows that each value represents and offering a comprehensive view of how your data is structured.

To enable this analysis, choose View ⇨ Data Preview ⇨ Column Distribution in the Power Query Editor. In Figure 7-2, the `prime_award_awarding_office_name` column displays a high number of distinct and unique values, revealing important details about the data's granularity.

The distinction between these metrics is crucial:

>> **Distinct:** Represents the count of different values when duplicates are removed

>> **Unique:** Counts values that appear exactly once

A column with many distinct values but few unique values suggests repetitive data, and high numbers in both categories indicate highly granular data.

The distribution graph tells an even more compelling story. Although there are many distinct data points in the dataset, only 40 percent of the fields contain actual values — 60 percent are empty. This 40/60 split immediately flags a significant data quality concern that warrants investigation and potentially indicates incomplete data collection processes or system integration issues.

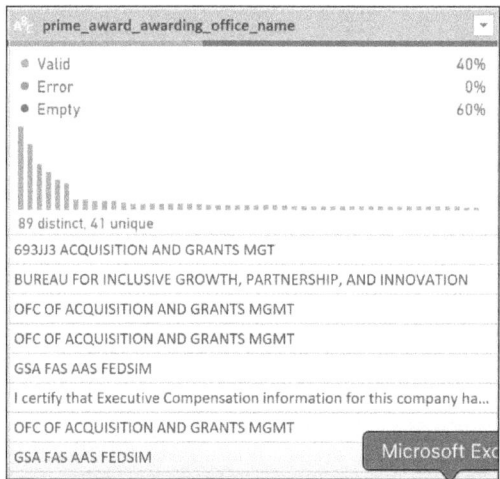

REMEMBER

Use column distribution analysis to make informed decisions about your data model. Columns with excessive missing values (such as the 60 percent empty example) may require improvements in data sourcing. In contrast, columns with very few distinct values may be candidates for removal if they don't add business value. Eliminating problematic or low-value columns creates more efficient queries and cleaner visualizations.

Finding a little help from data statistics

Statistics can sometimes be your best friend, which is why you want to consider using them for profiling and understanding the nature of your data. To enable data preview for statistics, open the Power Query Editor, choose View ⇨ Data Preview from its main menu, and then select the Column Quality and Column Profile check boxes, as shown in Figure 7-3.

FIGURE 7-3:
Data preview options in the Power Query Editor.

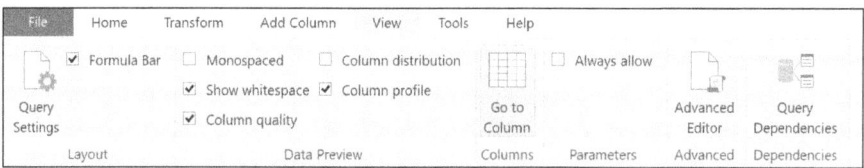

After enabling the features, select a column header requiring further statistical analysis. In Figure 7-4, you find the profile of the `prime_award_funding_sub_agency_name` column. Notice the general-statistics panel on the bottom and then the individual column statistics. Your options aren't limited to column profile and column quality, either. You can also review data for whitespace, monospacing, and column distribution.

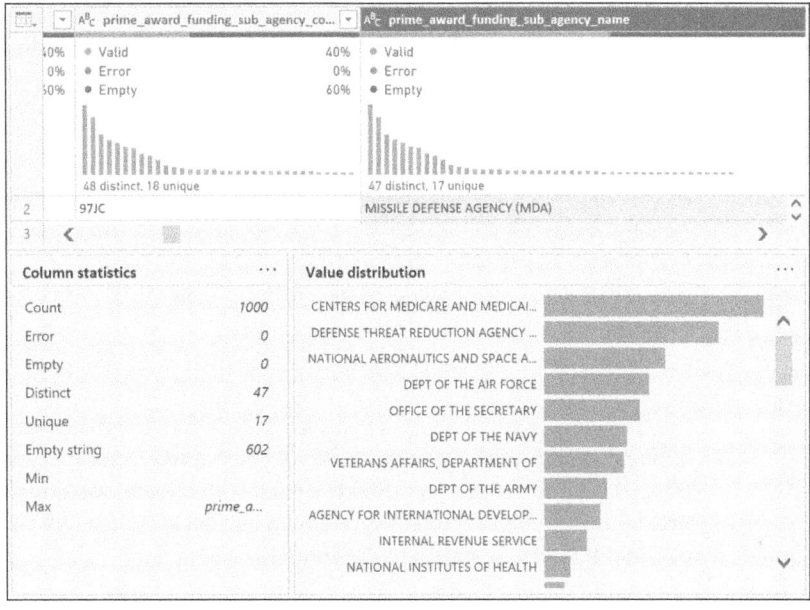

FIGURE 7-4:
Data preview of the column profile and column quality.

These are the key column statistics you can evaluate:

>> **Count:** Total number of rows (records) evaluated in a column

>> **Error:** Number of cells with errors (for example, type conversion failures or invalid values)

>> **Empty:** Number of null (missing) values in a column

>> **Distinct:** Number of different (unique) values, regardless of repetition

>> **Unique:** Number of values that appear only once in the column

>> **Empty string:** Number of cells containing blank text, not null

>> **Min:** The smallest value (for numeric or date columns)

>> **Max:** The largest value (for numeric or date columns)

REMEMBER

If the column has text, the statistics vary in comparison to numerical columns. With text columns, the number of empty strings and values is highlighted. In contrast, in numeric columns you're limited to empty values alone.

Stepping through the Data Lifecycle

Rarely is raw data ready for analysis. Most of the time, especially when connecting to dynamic or unstructured sources, you'll need to clean, reshape, and enrich the data before using it in Power BI. Power Query is the tool that handles such activities in Power BI. It allows you to extract, transform, and load (ETL) your data using the Get Data and Transform Data options. With Power Query, you can filter, merge, split, pivot, and shape your data into a usable format without writing traditional code.

REMEMBER

Power Query is not exclusive to Power BI. It's also a part of Excel and is integrated into tools like Dataflows, Microsoft Fabric, and Azure Data Factory, offering a consistent low-code experience across the Microsoft ecosystem.

Power Query uses a case-sensitive, functional language called M (short for *mashup*). M drives the transformations you apply in the Query Editor. In contrast, DAX (Data Analysis Expressions) is used for calculations after the data is loaded into your Power BI model. M prepares your data; DAX helps you analyze it. Head over to Chapters 15 and 16 to dig more into DAX.

The more data you have, the more you have to be on the lookout for inconsistencies, unexpected values, null values, and other data quality issues. Power BI, with the help of Power Query, supports users with several ways to deal with inconsistencies. These include replacing values, removing rows, and completing root cause analysis.

Resolving inconsistencies by replacing values

You can replace undesired or missing values directly in the Power Query Editor using the Replace Values option. This is useful for handling nulls, correcting data entry errors, or standardizing inconsistent entries (for example, replacing nulls or N/A with "blanks"). To apply a replacement, right-click the column and choose Replace Values (see Figure 7-5), or use the command in the Transform tab on the Ribbon.

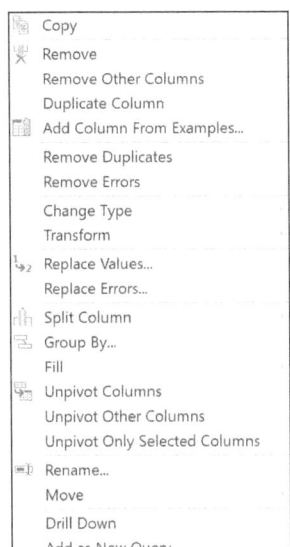

FIGURE 7-5:
Replace Values
menu option.

To replace values that are causing errors, follow these steps:

1. **Right-click a column header and choose Replace Errors from the menu that appears in the Power Query Editor.**

2. **Enter the values you want to replace in the Value box.**

3. **Click OK.**

Replacing values in a column follows a similar process, as shown in Figure 7-6. Follow these steps:

1. **Right-click a column header and choose Replace Value from the menu that appears in the Power Query Editor.**

2. **On the new screen that appears, fill in the Value To Find and the Replace With fields.**

3. **When you finish, click the OK button.**

WARNING

The file or data system where your data resides does not change when you use the Replace Value feature. This feature applies transformations only during the data load process. If your source updates, your replacements are reapplied each time the data is refreshed. You need to ensure that your replacement logic still makes sense when source values change.

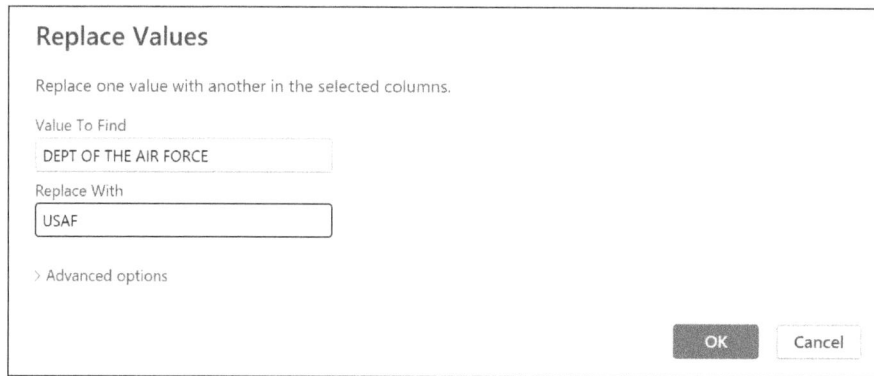

Replace Values

Replace one value with another in the selected columns.

Value To Find

DEPT OF THE AIR FORCE

Replace With

USAF

> Advanced options

OK   Cancel

FIGURE 7-6:
Replacing values.

TECHNICAL STUFF

In Power Query, you can select multiple columns by pressing and holding Ctrl (for non-adjacent selections) or Shift (for adjacent ones) to handle bulk actions like removing, renaming, or changing data types. However, the Replace Values transformation only works on one column at a time. To apply a replacement to multiple columns, you need to do it individually for each column.

Removing rows using Power Query

From time to time, you find that you must remove entire rows of data because something in the rows is creating an abundance of errors. To remove a row, you may assume that correcting the error should be as simple as right-clicking the column and choosing Remove Errors from the contextual menu. Using this method removes only rows where known errors are present. Suppose that you prefer to remove all rows in a table that meet a particular condition that can lead to errors. In that case, you click the Table icon to the left of the column header, select the affected rows, and then choose Remove Errors from the menu that appears.

Digging down to the root cause

When an error occurs in a column, you can inspect its cause by selecting the affected cell and viewing the errors message that appears in the Preview pane at the bottom of Power Query. This information helps you troubleshoot issues related to records, tables, lists, or embedded errors.

As shown in Figure 7-7, this error occurs in a custom column expression because the + operator is being used to combine two text fields. In Power Query, the + operator can only be applied to numeric values, not text. To concatenate text values, you must use the & operator instead. Expression and type conversion errors like this are among the most common issues you encounter in Power Query.

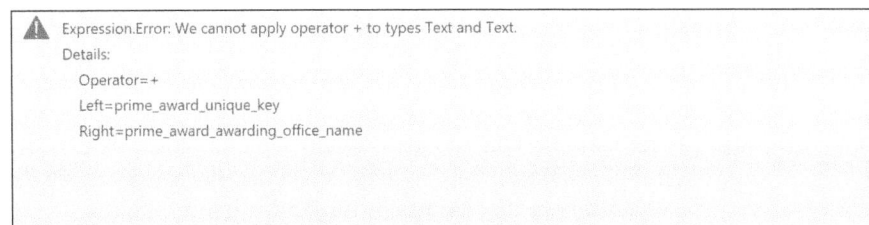

⚠ Expression.Error: We cannot apply operator + to types Text and Text.
Details:
    Operator=+
    Left=prime_award_unique_key
    Right=prime_award_awarding_office_name

**TECHNICAL
STUFF**

From time to time, you may need to convert a column from one type to another (from Text to Number, for example). In Power BI, this is referred to as a *type conversion*. Most times, you make type conversion changes immediately after data is transformed using Power Query.

Evaluating and Transforming Column Data Types

Most raw data sources aren't ready for reporting out of the box. You typically need to clean, reshape, and standardize the data using Power Query before it can be deemed usable by Power BI. This is especially true for flat files, such as CSVs and Excel sheets, although even structured databases often require transformation if they don't fit report-specific requirements.

As you work through a dataset, you add query steps to manage rows, columns, and data types. Even basic tasks, such as transposing columns or merging tables, require careful attention to data structure. In this section, I show you the steps you can take that help shape data into a reliable, analytics-ready format.

Finding and creating appropriate keys for joins

Power BI supports users by combining data from tables in several ways — but no matter which way you choose, you have to use a join in your query. (A *join* is a way to combine data from multiple tables; it brings together these tables using a common key from two or more tables.) Using Power Query Editor, you can complete this action using the Merge functionality. If you want to create relationships using the Power BI data model instead of Power Query, you're not technically performing a *join*; you're establishing a relationship. This is sometimes referred to informally as an *implicit join*, but in Power BI terminology, it's simply called a relationship. The use of a join depends on the business requirements.

Of all the many join types out there, the two you most often hear about are implicit and explicit joins. An *implicit* join performs a left outer join with a table field, pulling from another table. *Explicit* joins specify the integration of two tables. There are many benefits to using implicit joins. A key benefit is syntax because it's a useful substitute for explicit join syntax. In fact, an implicit join can appear in the same query that maintains an explicit join syntax.

Joining tables requires that a criterion be set up. One clear criterion is to identify the key in each table. If you were to look at the Primary and Sub Awards in the sample `FiscalYearAwards.xlsx` file, you'd see that one obvious choice to play this role is the Agency Key column for each table. (Though data often appears cleaner if your keys are named the same way, it's not a requirement.)

Tables can be represented by one or many join statements. If a table is represented on the One side of the join, the key in the table is unique in every row. If the table is represented by the Many side of the join, not all keys are unique, which yields some duplication. As you may have guessed, the One side is represented as a primary key, and the Many side can be a foreign key. One-to-one (1:1) and many-to-many (M:M) relationships do exist at times; however, the results produced in Power Query may not be suitable; a one-to-one relationship may produce a narrow result set, whereas a many-to-many often produces too many results.

Here are two key terms to remember when data modeling:

>> **Relationship:** A *relationship* is the connection between entities in a data model, which in turn reflect business rules. Relationships between entities can be either one-to-one, one-to-many, or many-to-many.

>> **Join:** A *join* is a bit different, in that you're setting up a relationship between two or more tables to pull data. The data is commonly mapped together using a primary key, a foreign key, or a combination, which is referred to as a *composite key.*

Consider the following information as it relates to joins and relationships:

>> **Keys for joins:** You can perform joins based on one or more columns at a time. Creating composite keys isn't a requirement to merge tables using Power Query. When you create joins in Power Query, pay particular attention to the column type. You must match the data types with one another or else a join won't work.

>> **Keys for relationships:** Power BI will try its best to resolve different data types, including converting data types, if possible. Ideally, however, you should ensure that the data type in the relationship is the same to ensure accuracy and prevent model performance issues.

REMEMBER

Power BI allows only for physical relationships between two tables on a single column pair. This statement means that if you have a composite key in a table, you must combine the key columns into a single column to create the necessary physical relationship. You can carry out this task by either using Power Query or setting up a calculated column with the help of DAX.

You can combine columns in two different ways using Power Query: by creating a new column or by merging values and then optionally removing the original columns. To add a new merged column, first select the columns you want to combine using the Ctrl key, then choose Add Column ⇨ Merge Columns from the Power Query Editor Ribbon. If you want to overwrite the original columns, you can select Transform ⇨ Merge Columns, which replaces them with a single merged result.

Regardless of which method you choose, the outcome is the same: a new column containing the merged values. Figure 7-8 shows the Merge Columns interface in Power Query. For example, you may combine two fields — such as agency code and program code — within the same table (like Prime Awards or Sub Awards) to create a single composite key. These merged values can then be used to support relationships between tables in the Power BI data model.

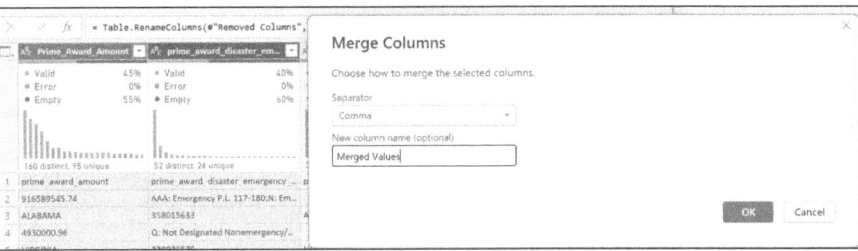

FIGURE 7-8:
The Merge
Columns option.

A final step in the process is to define separators from the Separator drop-down menu, located on the Merge interface. You can either select a predefined separator or create your own by choosing Custom from the menu. If you choose the latter method, you're given a choice to enter a new column name. Once you complete it, click OK.

In the example, a comma is being used as a separator. Finally, the new column is titled Merged Field, as shown in Figure 7-9.

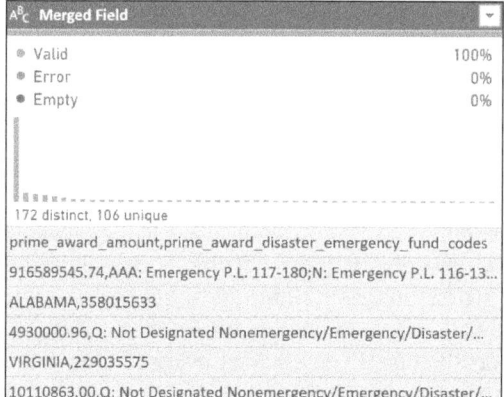

FIGURE 7-9: Columns that have been merged.

Shaping your column data to meet Power Query requirements

Not every data source you ingest may have the correct data type. Power Query does its best to detect the appropriate data type based on characteristics found in the dataset. For example, you may be using a U.S.-based zip code as part of your dataset. Power Query may (incorrectly) interpret zip codes that start with zeros as whole numbers. As a result, those leading zeros are removed. Why? Because when stored as a number, the leading zero has no value and is discarded. In this case, the zip code should be assigned a Text data type, not a whole number.

As you begin evaluating your data in columns, keep in mind that Power Query tries to convert any data it receives as one of the data types shown in Figure 7-10. You can keep Power Query on the right track by making sure you're using the correct data type in the first place.

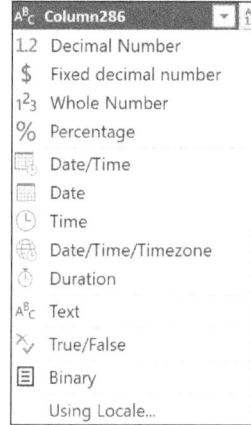

FIGURE 7-10: The available data types.

REMEMBER

You encounter complex data types, such as functions, lists, records, and tables every so often. Keep in mind that not all data types may be available after loading the data.

If you want to change the data type, you can do so by right-clicking a column header and selecting Change Type from the menu. Then choose the type you want, as shown in Figure 7-11. After changing a data type once in a column, you see a prompt asking whether you agree to change the column type and insert a step. Figure 7-12 shows an example of inserting a step.

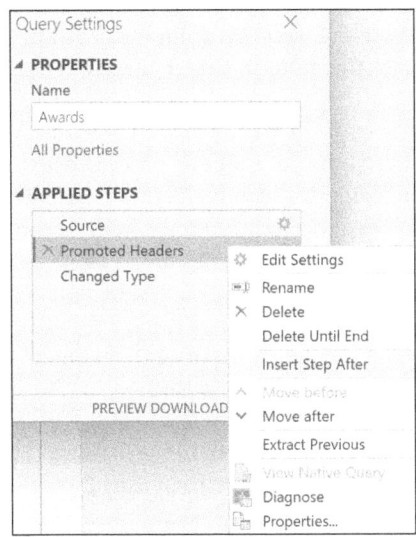

FIGURE 7-11:
Changing the data type.

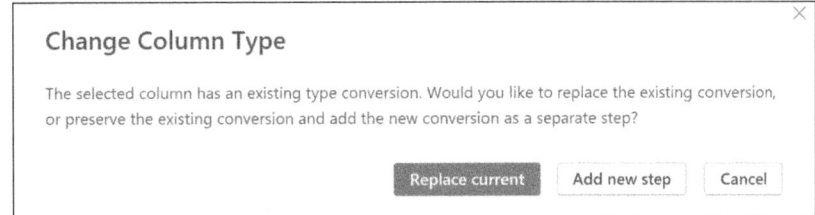

FIGURE 7-12:
Inserting a step.

Combining queries

In Power BI, you can combine queries using Power Query in one of two ways. First, you can append queries. That means you add other queries to an existing set of queries as though you're stacking the data. When you create appended queries, you often use patterns such as SQL's UNION ALL operator. On the other hand, combining queries using the merge structure is based on the supplied primary and foreign keys. You need to set up JOIN statements with Merge queries. In Power Query, merging requires selecting matching columns between the two tables and defining the join type. There is no explicit JOIN statement, but the operation behaves like SQL joins.

Appending queries

You can always make tables taller or wider. When you append, the table is taller. The reason is that your queries include the same number of columns. If columns are missing from one of the queries, Power Query will include them anyway and fill those cells with null values. In some cases, the resulting tables contain columns from all queries; in other instances, columns that were not present in the original query may populate the dataset. Under these circumstances, each of the rows keeps null values.

A Power BI user can either append a query or create a new query with the appended results. To append queries, you make this choice when there are one or more queries to select. No new queries need to be built — simply reuse whatever exists. Appending queries without creating new ones is the default choice in Power BI.

When you take many new rows of data and string them together using the original query, you should choose Append Queries As New.

To access Append Queries as New, go to the Power Query Editor Home Ribbon. Then select Append Queries as New. You're then asked to concatenate rows from two or more tables. Once you select the tables and rows, click OK.

Merging queries

When you merge queries, you combine them, which yields a wider table. Because you inherit more columns, it's only natural for horizontal growth to occur. The critical consideration is which set of keys you use. The columns must have matching values in both tables to ensure that one table can be combined with the rows in the second table.

Much like when appending queries, you have two merge options — create a new query or merge two queries directly into an existing one using Merge Queries. Merging queries involves selecting matching columns and choosing one of several join types using Power Query, as shown in Table 7-1.

TABLE 7-1   **Join Types**

Join Type	Description
Inner	Only matching rows are visible.
Left Outer	All rows from the first table appear. Matching rows from the second table are included; if no match exists, null values are shown.
Right Outer	All rows from the second table appear. Matching rows from the first table are included; if no match exists, null values are shown.
Full Outer	All rows appear.
Left Anti	Returns all rows from the first table where a match in the second table does not exist.
Right Anti	Returns all rows from the second table where a match in the first table does not exist.

When you try to use one of these queries, you may realize that your data isn't perfect. To alleviate some of the quality concerns, Power Query supports fuzzy matching when performing merges. *Fuzzy matching* occurs when you can compare items from separate lists. A join is formed if there's a close match. You have the ability to set the matching tolerance and similarity threshold when establishing a fuzzy match. Your fuzzy matching options include those in Table 7-2.

TABLE 7-2   **Fuzzy Matching Options**

Fuzzy Matching Option	Description
Similarity threshold	Values range from 0 to 1. A threshold of 0 allows very loose matching, even if values are quite different. A threshold of 1 returns only exact matches.
Ignore case	Treats upper- and lowercase the same.
Maximum number of matches	Limits the number of rows from the second table that matches the first, which is helpful when the result set produces multiple matches.
Match by combining text parts	Attempts to combine separate words into a single entity, looking to find matches between keys.
Transformation table	Acts as a mapping table, where one column defines the original value and the other defines the replacement value. Requires at least two columns.

To merge a query, follow these steps:

1. **On the Home tab of the Power Query Editor, locate Merge Query.**

2. **Select Merge Queries (or Merge Queries As New if you want to create a new query).**

3. **Select the tables and columns you want to combine in the Merge Queries interface.**

4. **Select the key that is common to both tables.**

   Notice that the appropriate key column is highlighted.

5. **Choose the desired Join from the drop-down list.**

6. **Click OK.**

When you merge the two tables, one or more new columns appear, depending on which JOIN statement you select. Figure 7-13 shows the interfaces for completing the merge. After you select one or more matching columns from each table and click OK, the Power Query Editor displays new columns with the results from the JOIN statement.

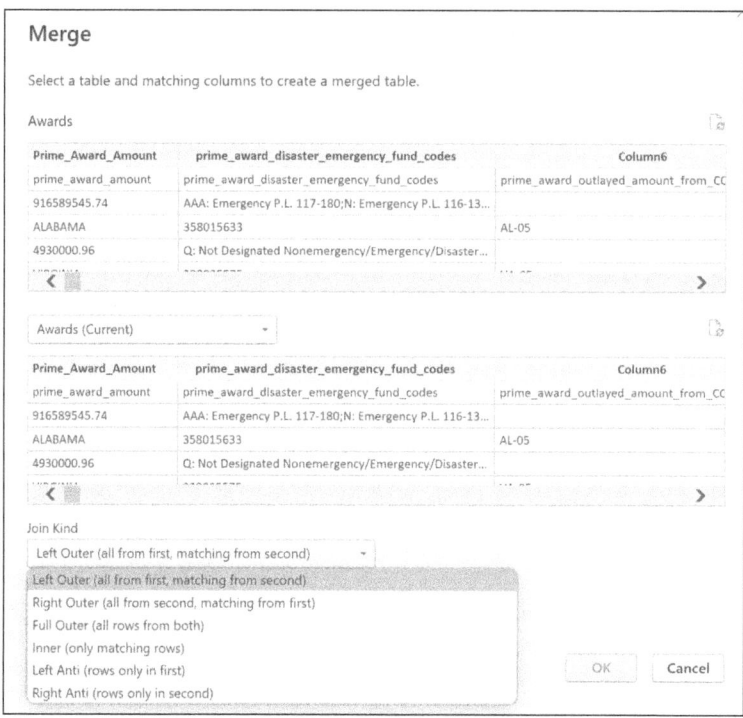

FIGURE 7-13:
Merging
datasets using
Merge Query.

When you select any cell in the new column, a preview of the content contained in the merged table appears.

When expanding a table, you can either *expand* or *aggregate:*

>> **Expand:** Select a column from the merged table that you want to add to the current table. If the merged table has multiple matches for a row in the current table, Power BI duplicates the current row once for each match.

>> **Aggregate:** If you want to combine rows without duplication in the current table, this is your best choice. Aggregates enable you to summarize matched data using functions like Sum, Count, or Average directly in the Power Query interface.

Configuring Queries for Data Loading

When developing a Power BI semantic model, you can use Help queries. These helper tools are available by processing your model using the Get Data option and the Transform Data option. Also, when you're trying to combine files or even merge datasets, Power Query supports helper queries.

REMEMBER

Helper queries are embedded in Power BI Power Query to assist users in creating query strings. Rather than making the coding process complex, you can use the built-in API to simplify the most difficult parts of query development. Helper queries support standard terms, phrases, ranges, and geospatial functions.

Of course, you may have queries that you don't need or want to load, because not all data is helpful. In this case, right-click the Queries pane and then clear the Enable Load section. When queries are already packed, you may get errors. Otherwise, select which queries you want to omit from the load process.

One common scenario occurs when you don't want to load queries that are appended or merged with other queries. To segregate queries that should not be included, follow these steps:

1. **Right-click the first query you want to omit.**

2. **Choose Enable Load from the menu that appears in the Queries pane.**

3. **Uncheck Enable Load to exclude the table from the model.**

4. **Make sure that each table you want to omit from the query is deselected.**

5. **Repeat this process for each query you don't want to load.**

The result is removing unwanted entities from the data model for future querying and loading. In Figure 7-14, you can see an example of the drop-down menu for selecting or deselecting Enable Load. Any query that's deselected isn't loaded, and it's noted by text that's italicized.

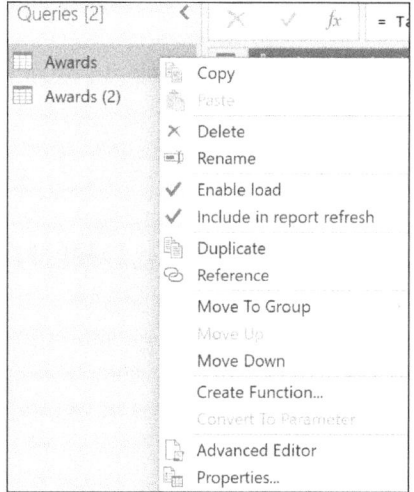

FIGURE 7-14:
Removing
queries.

After you've modified the entities to be included in the queries, save your changes by pressing the Close & Apply button on the Ribbon's Home tab.

Resolving Errors During Data Import

Sometimes, when you load data, you may encounter query errors in Power BI. Don't panic!

Errors come in many forms. Values alone don't cause a query to fail blatantly. Power BI displays the total number of errors for each query. *Error values,* or values ignored during querying, are considered blank values. Simply put, they have no text in the field — not even a zero.

To get to the bottom of what's causing errors in Power Query, make use of the View Error hyperlink, which can be found in the Power Query Editor column. When you click the hyperlink, you can see the specific details related to the query. Common reasons why errors are thrown in Power Query are often linked to data conversion. For example, a value originally N/A, which is considered text, would not work in a column intended for numbers.

To correct an error such as this one, you need to change the column type. To make such a modification, follow these steps:

1. **In the Power Query Editor, select the query in question.**

2. **Right-click the column presenting an error.**

3. **Choose Change Type from the menu that appears and then change the selection from Number to Text.**

4. **Select Replace Current when the pop-up appears to validate that you want to change the column data type.**

   You have now changed the column data type from Numerical to Text. Now, alphanumeric values, not just numeric values, can be added to the column for the specific dataset. After you click the Close & Apply button for a dataset that's been corrected, the error messages disappear.

Curating Data Using Microsoft Copilot for Power BI

Throughout this chapter, I've described traditional Power Query methods you can use to prepare data better. Even using these methods, you may miss a thing or two. Although artificial intelligence (AI) isn't perfect, it can speed up your efforts to find errors and perform data cleansing.

Suppose you are licensed to use Microsoft Copilot for Power BI. In that case, you can sift through your data quickly by accomplishing tasks such as data cleansing, addressing errors, and subsequently debugging them, as well as automating routine data transformations. Taking the traditional approach can take hours, but using Copilot can accelerate your work to minutes.

REMEMBER

AI doesn't replace your analytical skills; it amplifies them by allowing you to focus on the business while this extra tool set helps you identify issues that may not be so obvious.

For the examples in the following sections, I use the downloadable dataset provided on Kaggle for this book. You can find instructions for downloading the dataset from Kaggle in this book's Introduction and in Chapter 5.

Enhancing anomaly detection and quality assessment

Copilot transforms the traditional detective work of data quality assessment by automatically scanning your entire dataset for anomalies, inconsistencies, and quality issues. Assume that you have a semantic model with forty columns and one million rows. Rather than manually enabling Column Quality and Column Distribution views, as discussed earlier in this chapter, you can ask Copilot to provide analysis by entering a prompt such as:

> **Prompt:** Analyze this dataset for quality issues and provide recommendations to address them.

For the example shown in Figure 7-15, that's exactly what I did using the downloadable dataset provided on Kaggle for this book. The results of this query yielded the results shown in the figure.

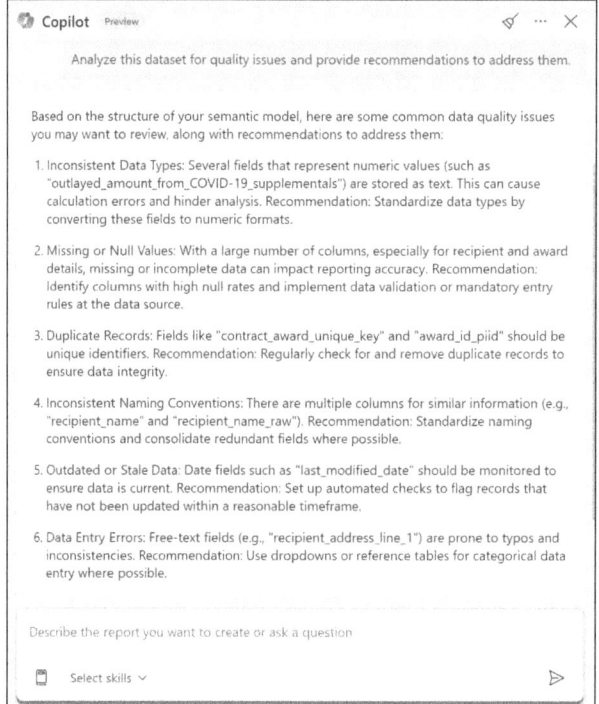

FIGURE 7-15: Using Copilot to identify quality issues and recommendations.

Focusing on intelligent data transformation and error resolution

Copilot can assist with many of the repetitive or error-prone steps of data transformation. Instead of writing individual transformation steps by hand or clicking through multiple Ribbon options, you can now issue simple natural language prompts to drive your data prep tasks. For example, imagine working with a column containing mixed date formats or text-based numeric values. Instead of manually applying split columns, replace value, or change type transformations, you can prompt Copilot with something like:

> **Prompt:** Standardize the award_base_action_date column into a consistent YYYY-MM-DD format and remove any rows where the column is blank or contains invalid entries.

Copilot figures out what you mean, applies the necessary steps, and gives you instructions on how to accomplish this task. In Figure 7-16, you can see how a prompt-based transformation created multiple steps automatically, including data type conversion, null removal, and date formatting.

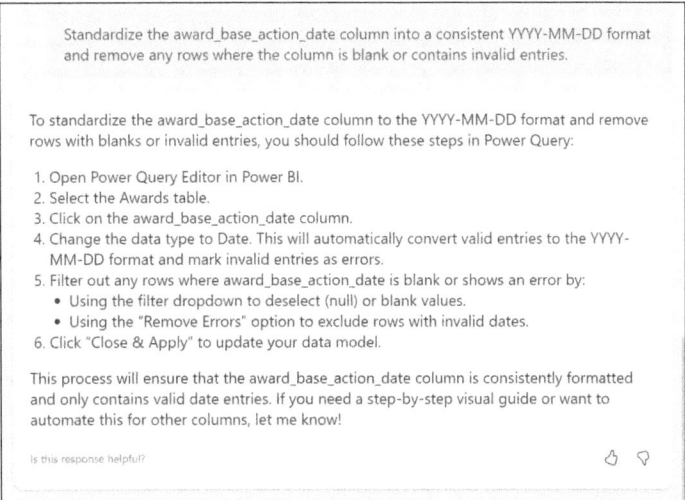

FIGURE 7-16: Using Copilot to identify quality issues and recommendations.

What used to take five or six clicks (and a good deal of M code under the hood) now takes just a sentence. The reason is simple: Copilot guides you on your journey, but it is up to you to make the decision and take action on what should or should not be completed. If you tell Copilot to make the changes, which was not the case in this exercise, it will still validate that you want to take action.

TIP

You can always toggle the Advanced Editor in Power Query to review the M code Copilot generates. This is a great way to learn what's happening behind the scenes and deepen your skills.

Getting smart about query operations and relationship discovery

One of the lesser known yet key features of Copilot in Power BI is its capability to assist with relationship discovery, particularly when working with unfamiliar or complex datasets. In large semantic models, figuring out how tables connect can be time-consuming and error prone. Copilot can help by analyzing column names, data types, and patterns to suggest potential relationships across tables. If you are trying to connect two tables together, you may prompt Copilot with:

> **Prompt:** Identify potential foreign key relationships between these tables and suggest a merge strategy based on the best match.

For this example, I use Prime Award Data and Sub Award Data from the Kaggle dataset to create the example.

This doesn't just save time; it surfaces relationships you may overlook or not even think of, especially when naming conventions vary between source systems. Copilot can provide a ranked list of candidate keys and propose a join type (such as left outer or inner) based on the data overlap. In addition to key matching, Copilot can assist with query optimization. If your current queries are inefficient or contain redundant steps, you can ask to conduct an analysis similar to:

> **Prompt:** Optimize this query for performance and remove unnecessary steps.

In response, Copilot rewrites the query to minimize data movement, streamline filters, and combine redundant transformations. In Figure 7-17, the optimized query shows fewer steps and improved refresh performance compared to the original.

REMEMBER

Copilot for Power BI serves as a practical assistant to streamline tasks that would otherwise require multiple manual steps. It helps surface potential issues more quickly, suggests repeatable fixes, and proposes ways to improve model structure without replacing the need for human judgment. Although Copilot can accelerate many aspects of the data preparation process, its suggestions should constantly be reviewed for accuracy and relevance because AI isn't perfect (like us humans). Whether resolving column errors, applying joins, or transforming mixed data types, it's still up to you to ensure that the logic aligns with your business data.

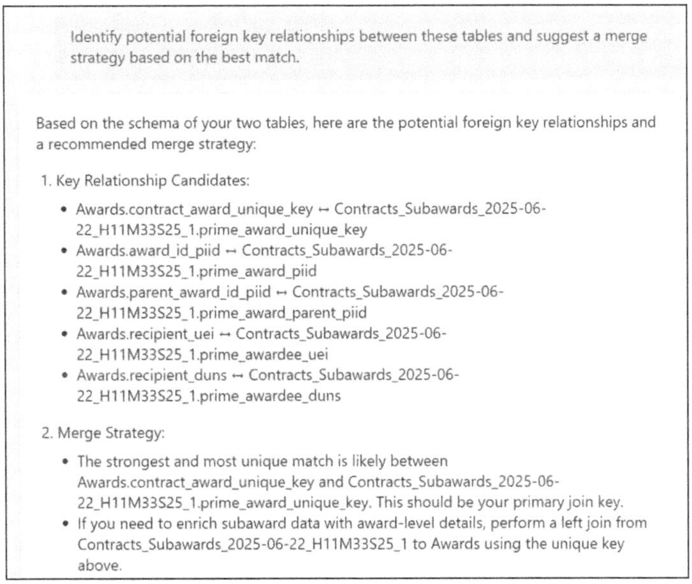

Identify potential foreign key relationships between these tables and suggest a merge strategy based on the best match.

Based on the schema of your two tables, here are the potential foreign key relationships and a recommended merge strategy:

1. Key Relationship Candidates:

- Awards.contract_award_unique_key ↔ Contracts_Subawards_2025-06-22_H11M33S25_1.prime_award_unique_key
- Awards.award_id_piid ↔ Contracts_Subawards_2025-06-22_H11M33S25_1.prime_award_piid
- Awards.parent_award_id_piid ↔ Contracts_Subawards_2025-06-22_H11M33S25_1.prime_award_parent_piid
- Awards.recipient_uei ↔ Contracts_Subawards_2025-06-22_H11M33S25_1.prime_awardee_uei
- Awards.recipient_duns ↔ Contracts_Subawards_2025-06-22_H11M33S25_1.prime_awardee_duns

2. Merge Strategy:

- The strongest and most unique match is likely between Awards.contract_award_unique_key and Contracts_Subawards_2025-06-22_H11M33S25_1.prime_award_unique_key. This should be your primary join key.
- If you need to enrich subaward data with award-level details, perform a left join from Contracts_Subawards_2025-06-22_H11M33S25_1 to Awards using the unique key above.

FIGURE 7-17: Optimizing queries with Microsoft Copilot.

3

The Art and Science of Power BI

IN THIS CHAPTER

» Describing different semantic
  modeling techniques

» Configuring properties to meet
  semantic model requirements

» Designing a model to meet
  performance requirements

Chapter **8**

Crafting the Semantic Model

You probably thought that after the data is transformed by Power BI you'll have smooth sailing. In some instances, this is correct. Of course, when you have created a detailed model with numerous tables, some work is required to refine the dataset. Data modeling is both an art and a science because you're constantly trying to shape data so that the insights gained are as precise as possible. Once your data is loaded and transformed, the next phase, refining the model, begins.

In this chapter, you learn about schema designs and modeling techniques, including modern approaches like composite models and Direct Lake, which provide you with the information you need to design and develop scalable data models that support visualization and reporting across Power BI and Microsoft Fabric.

An Introduction to Semantic Models

Semantic models (sometimes called *data models)* are the building blocks of visualization and reporting. A semantic model consists of one or more tables and several relationships, assuming that more than just one or two tables exist. Well-designed semantic models enable users to articulate their data effectively and build upon existing insights. As such, semantic modeling requires considerable effort; it cannot be accomplished in a single step. You first need to load your data and then define the relationships between tables within the Power BI modeling environment or Microsoft Fabric.

REMEMBER

The best time to build a semantic model is during the initial phase of Power BI or Fabric report development. To create efficient measures, enable AI-generated insights, or ensure that Copilot provides accurate suggestions, you must hone the model early to emphasize relationship definitions, table roles, cardinality, and metadata configuration.

Working with data schemas

You've imported all this data that was transformed into one or many tables — now what? Your first business aim is to address how to overcome the challenge of creating complicated semantic models. In Power BI, semantic modeling can be streamlined.

Your first goal is to start with the data schema. If you start there, you likely soon recognize that your data is coming from one or more transactional systems. Under these circumstances, having many tables will likely overwhelm you. You don't want data clutter — you want to organize and simplify your understanding of the data. That's where schemas come in.

In Power BI and Fabric, you have several approaches to data schema design and simplification, including flat, star, snowflake, denormalized, and hybrid schema designs. Understanding when to use each model type can help support data performance and granularity across visualization and reporting. The following sections are designed to help you gain that understanding. In case you're in a hurry, Table 8-1 provides a quick overview of the schema types and when to use them.

TABLE 8-1 **Comparison of Schema Types**

Schema	Best For	Description
Flat	Simple spreadsheets	Single-table models
Star	Reporting and slicing/dicing	Fact + dimension layout
Snowflake	Enterprise data warehouses	Normalized dimension relationships
Denormalized	Large data volumes (Direct Lake/Import)	Wide tables for performance
Hybrid	Real-time + historical analytics	Mixed import, DirectQuery, Direct Lake

Flat schemas

Consider a listing of sales transactions, customer identities, or awards. What do all these things have in common? Suppose that you were to lay out the data in an Excel spreadsheet. In that case, you'd likely need only a single table to present the essential data. When that's the case, you'd want to use a *flat schema* — the one that uses just a single table, similar to the one you see in Figure 8-1.

CustomerID	CustomerName	POCName	DateCreated
U123X456	The Art School Inc.	Michael Angelo	1/3/2021 05:00 PM
U123X567	Music Academy LLC	Fred Chopin	2/4/2021 04:00 PM
U123X789	Sports Stadium Inc.	Babe Ruthie	3/7/2021 03:00 PM
U123X678	Bookbinder Corp.	Bill Bookman	4/9/2021 02:00 PM
U123X987	Jingle Cleaning LLC	Jana Jingle	5/8/2021 01:00 PM
U123X756	Gentle George Air Inc.	George Gentle	6/7/2021 12:00 PM
U123X911	Milkman Foods Corp.	Deborah Milkman	5/7/2021 11:00 PM

FIGURE 8-1: A flat schema.

Note the four columns in Figure 8-1. Each of these data columns may have a unique identifier, including a specific time/date stamp indicating when the customer data was entered, the company name, the customer ID, and the company's point of contact. Each of these data points can be used as a lookup to assess detailed customer information more independently. When you examine the model, however, it can stand on its own. You would consider a flat schema when reporting requirements are linear and unsophisticated, requiring no more than a single table.

TIP

Flat schemas tend to have a limited value. When you're looking to bring information from a spreadsheet into Power BI for fundamental analysis — a task that may involve adding a column of values or filtering of data — this approach is perfectly adequate. As soon as you introduce multiple tables, you must adopt an alternative approach.

If you deploy just one table, it can be used for reporting, but the scope is limited. Perhaps you can filter the data or extract one or two key data points to create simplified visuals or basic calculated outputs. That's where the usefulness of a flat schema ends.

TECHNICAL STUFF

In Microsoft Fabric, flat schemas are commonly used in Direct Lake scenarios, in which high-performance queries are executed over a single large denormalized table. This enables faster performance at scale — but at the cost of flexibility in relationship modeling.

Star schemas

Most organizations have a model that represents the star schema approach. You often find models with one or two large tables known as fact tables, and then a few dimension tables. When a data modeler plans a model, it's a common practice to model tables as either dimensions or facts. Here's how they differ:

>> **Fact tables** are representative of observations or events. Consider patterns such as sales transactions, account balances, and personnel records. The fact table connects to one or more dimension key column that relates to a given dimension. For example, a transaction table with a sales transaction (fact table) may map to a manufacturer (dimension table). The dimension key column decides an item's *dimensionality* — the details within a fact table. Dimension key-values offer product granularity.

>> **Dimension tables** describe the business entity in granular detail. These are attributes of the product, people, places, and concepts that are part of the fact table. Think of a dimension as a quality attribute that can provide a greater level of granularity.

REMEMBER

Dimension tables often have a finite number of rows because these are widely used descriptors. Fact tables can hold many rows and grow over time because they contain transaction records. Consider that the dimension table is an excellent utility for filtering and grouping, whereas the fact table is an example of summarization.

Whenever a Power BI report visualization is generated, you notice that a query is generated against the semantic model. The query is designed to filter, group, and summarize the model data. Your primary goal is to develop a model that can effectively meet each of these specific business objectives. Figure 8-2 shows the fact-versus-dimension-tables concept; Figure 8-3 shows a prototype star schema.

REMEMBER

With a star schema, no properties exist to classify a table as a fact or a dimension. The relationship itself decides the model's behavior. A model relationship is established between two entities, and the attributes maintained within each entity are defined.

Cardinality — the property of the relationship, in other words — determines the table types. Common relationships are one-to-one, one-to-many, or many-to-many. One side is always the dimension table, whereas the Many side is always a fact table. However, seldom do you ever find a one-to-one relationship within a star schema, because the fact table tends to repeat dimensions more than once.

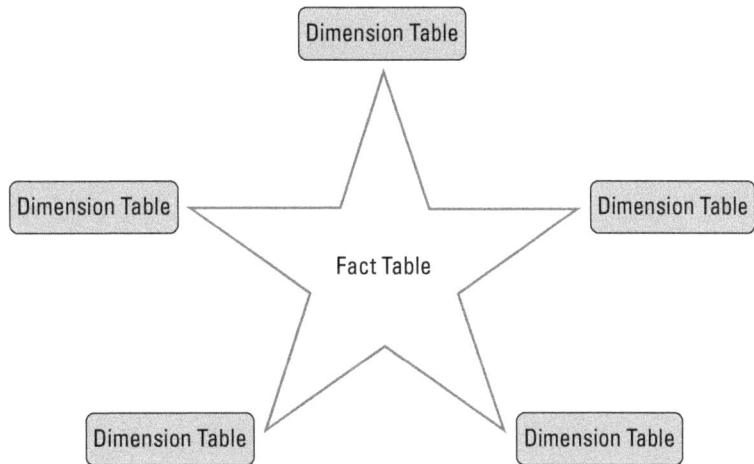

FIGURE 8-2:
Facts versus
dimensions.

FIGURE 8-3:
A star schema
prototype.

TIP

With semantic modeling, a well-structured model design includes distinct tables that are either dimension tables or fact tables. Don't mix table types to create a single table. If you make a single table, you quickly realize that the data in place is poorly formed. That's why you should evaluate your data to ensure that you have the right number of tables with the correct relationships in place.

Snowflake schemas

The *snowflake schema,* an extension of the star schema, is a schema in which you have a set of normalized tables that drill down against a single business entity. Normalized data helps you reduce data redundancy and promote data integrity. Suppose that each of your products falls into a category or subcategory.

The branching outward from the single business entity, products, to its associated category and subcategory reminds some people of a snowflake. (Okay, you do have to squint at it sideways for a few minutes before its snowflakeyness becomes evident — try it with Figure 8-4.)

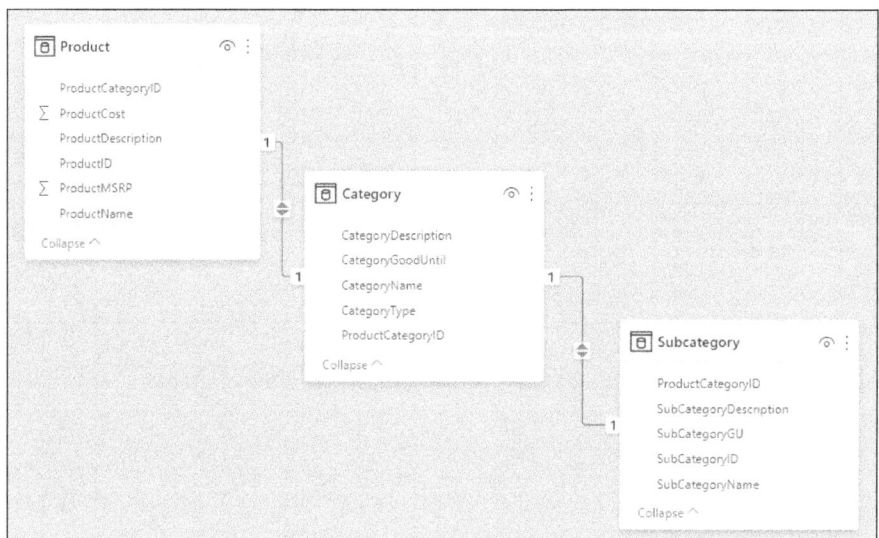

FIGURE 8-4:
A snowflake
schema.

TIP

Snowflake schemas are the ideal modeling tool for enterprise data warehouses, but they can degrade performance in DirectQuery or Direct Lake scenarios. When Power BI is combined with Fabric, avoid snowflake schemas when latency or high query concurrency is a concern.

Denormalized and hybrid schemas

Traditional schemas, such as the star and snowflake schemas, are considered legacy modeling approaches because they were designed for centralized systems with structured relational data. As Power BI has evolved, users often work across cloud-based, distributed environments; some are optimized for speed, and others are optimized for scale or real-time access. When schematic models are rich in data, albeit with massive data volumes or complex table relationships (some of which may not be relational) consider the denormalized and hybrid schemas.

Which of these models is better suited for big data analytics and nonrelational schemas? *Denormalized schemas* reduce complexity and improve performance, especially in Direct Lake scenarios where queries must return results quickly over large datasets. Meanwhile, *hybrid schemas* give you the flexibility to connect real-time, historical, and warehouse data in a single semantic model. This wasn't possible with the flat, star, or snowflake models. You can even pair the decentralized model with a legacy model to create a hybrid model, given that Power BI allows for a more adaptive design when used with Microsoft Power BI and Fabric together.

A *denormalized schema* flattens related tables into a single wide table. You avoid the complexity of managing joins by storing all relevant fields in a single semantic-based table. This approach is common in Direct Lake or Import mode scenarios, where query speed is prioritized over relational flexibility. Keep in mind that if you use the denormalized pattern, the goal is for performance across large datasets. Reporting logic should not be overly complicated either. If you increase the file size and expect to change business logic frequently, but have massive data volumes, denormalization is your best bet. Figure 8-5 illustrates a denormalized table.

FIGURE 8-5:
A denormalized schema.

Let's assume you need to combine various schemas across multiple applications. Some may require the data to be imported into Power BI, and others you can only connect to using DirectQuery or Direct Lake. If creating a tightly coupled semantic model so that your data can talk across sources (and applications, even) is your goal, you'll choose the hybrid schema. A hybrid schema combines Import, DirectQuery, and Direct Lake tables within the same semantic model. It enables you to integrate real-time data sources with high-performance Fabric data (which requires Premium Capacity) or historical imports stored in the application together. This scenario is ideal for enterprise analytics, in which not all data is stored uniformly. Figure 8-6 shows the hybrid schema.

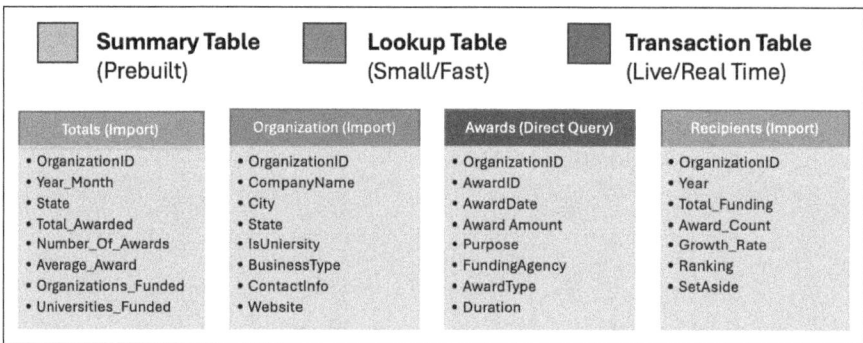

FIGURE 8-6:
A hybrid schema.

The hybrid schema shown in Figure 8-6 displays four tables that work together through `OrganizationID` as the primary key. The Organization table serves as the central lookup, connecting to all other tables via this shared identifier. The Awards table contains live transactional data using DirectQuery for memory efficiency. In contrast, the two summary tables pre-calculate common aggregations and store them using Import mode for lightning-fast dashboard performance. This design offers the best of all worlds: instant answers from pre-built summaries when possible, along with the ability to drill down into detailed, real-time data when needed, all connected through proper relationships that maintain data integrity.

Storing values with measures

Measures are dynamic calculations written in DAX that return a single value based on filters applied in a report. Unlike columns in a table, measures aren't physically stored in the data model; they're computed at query time. Therefore, as the data in a column changes, so does the value in a measure.

Power BI provides two main types of aggregations: *implicit* and *explicit* measures. Implicit measures are created automatically when you drag a numeric column into a visual. Then, Power BI applies a default aggregation, such as SUM or AVERAGE, without requiring any DAX coding. Power BI uses the values in those columns to compute the aggregate directly within the visual. Implicit values are quick and easy for simple reports but lack reusability since they are built for a singular purpose. On the other hand, *explicit measures* are defined manually by the report author using DAX formulas. These measures offer greater control, consistency, and portability because they're formula-based and independent of visual-specific aggregations.

To create an explicit measure, you can use the New Measure button on the Modeling tab of the Power BI Ribbon, which opens a Formula bar where you can write your DAX expression.

Power BI also offers a helpful feature called *quick measure*, which provides a menu of common calculation templates that generate DAX for you. To use the Quick Measure feature, follow these steps:

1. **Head to the Ribbon and open the Modeling tab.**

2. **Locate the Calculations area of the Modeling tab and click Quick Measure (see Figure 8-7).**

   Power BI prompts you to choose from categories such as Aggregate per category, Filters, Mathematical operations, Text, Time intelligence, and Totals (see Figure 8-8).

3. **Enter the parameters specific to the column or columns you are looking to create a measure for in the pane.**

   Once configured, Power BI creates the DAX formula for you, which you can then edit or use as a learning tool (see Figure 8-9).

TIP

You can also use Copilot to guide you in the creation of your measures.

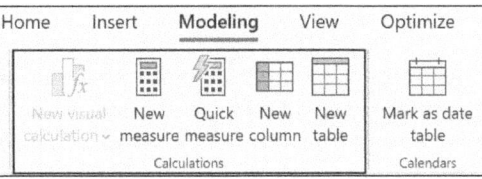

FIGURE 8-7: Calculation capabilities on the Modeling tab.

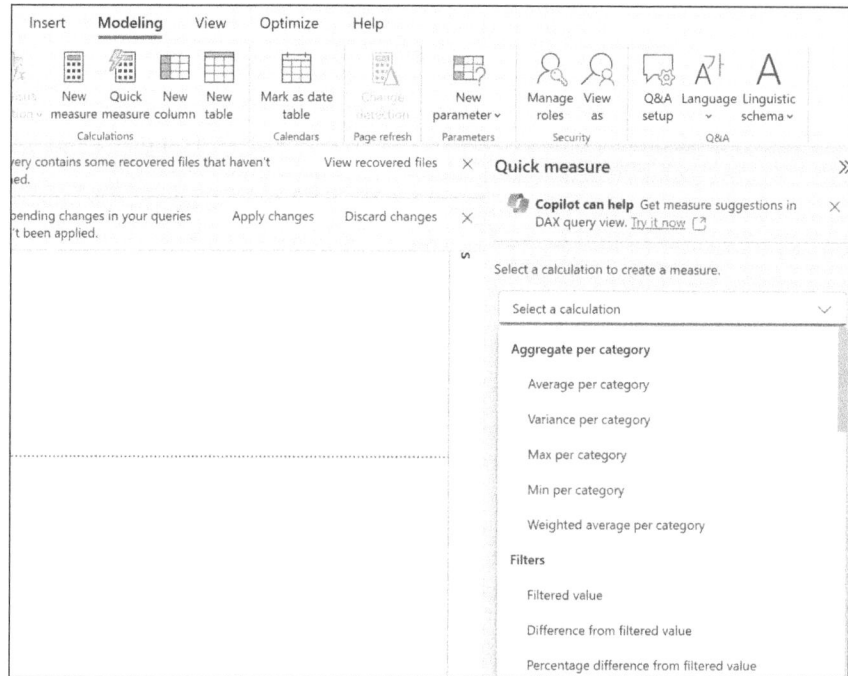

FIGURE 8-8:
Some Quick
Measure options.

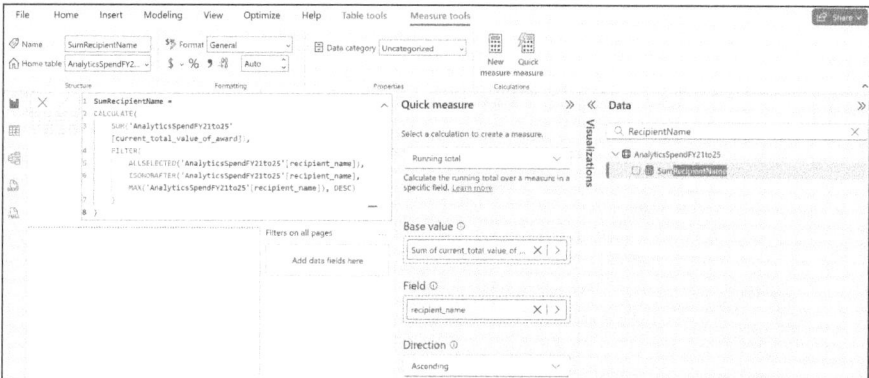

FIGURE 8-9:
The completed
quick measure
for the sum of
running totals
calculation.

Although implicit measures work well for quick analysis, developing a strong foundation in explicit measures will give you more power and flexibility in your data modeling and reporting. As your models grow more complex, relying on well-crafted measures becomes essential for accurate and consistent analysis. To create complex measures, focus your attention on using the New Measure button versus Quick Measure.

To create a formula using New Measure, follow these steps:

1. **Head to the Ribbon. Open the Modeling tab and click New Measure.**

   You also can access New Measure by right-clicking a column or clicking the ellipses in the Data pane and choosing New Measure from the menu that appears.

   Choosing New Measure enables you to start a new measure with a predefined formula. (By default, a new measure begins as Measure =.) Some data may be prepopulated on the Formula bar, as shown in Figure 8-10.

2. **Replace Measure = with the name of a new column and an equal sign and then add a pre-built DAX formula.**

   I cover DAX formulas in Chapters 15 and 16. An example measure could be TotalBid = Sum(Awards[Bids]).

FIGURE 8-10:
Populating New
Measure on the
Formula bar.

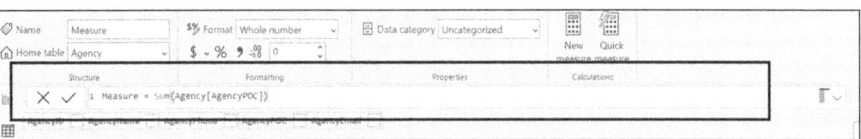

The resulting product is a DAX–based formula if you're using New Measure. Otherwise, the Formula bar displays the generated code for the formula. You'll likely use IntelliSense, which helps you populate the formula as you type. You can find more information about DAX in Chapters 15 and 16.

Working with dimensions and fact tables (yet again)

With Power BI, you'll quickly notice a typical pattern when building data models: You often work with two types of tables, dimension tables and fact tables. *Dimension tables* store descriptive information, like details about a product, customer, or manufacturer. *Fact tables,* on the other hand, store measurable events or transactions, things like sales, orders, or inventory movements.

Think of it this way: dimensions describe and facts calculate. Dimensions hold the "who," "what," or "where," and fact tables capture the "how much" or "how many."

In the example shown earlier in Figure 8-2, you see one fact table surrounded by several dimension tables. That's a standard layout known as a star schema. Typically, dimension tables have many columns but fewer rows, as they describe entities such as product names, categories, and regions. Fact tables are the opposite — they tend to have fewer columns but many rows, as each row represents a transaction or event that occurred.

When you design a semantic model, you can structure your dimension tables in several ways. Table 8-2 outlines the most common approaches and their respective applications.

TABLE 8-2　**Dimensional Data Approaches**

Approach	What It Means
Slowly changing	Manages change of dimensions over time.
Role-playing	Filters facts against many criteria.
Junk	Combines low-cardinality attributes with few values into a single dimension to reduce clutter in the model.
Degenerate	Requires an attribute to a fact table that is needed for filtering. In this case, a primary key is an example.
Factless fact	Contains no measures, only dimension keys.

Flattening hierarchies

A *hierarchy* is a set of fields organized in levels, in which each level is a parent of the one below it. The value at a parent level can be drilled down to reveal more detailed data in a lower-level category. A parent-child hierarchy may show data for accounts, customers, or salespeople in a retail environment. These hierarchies can vary in depth. For example, you may illustrate data based on Country → State → City → Street when describing a business territory. An organization may also be tied to a region. In this case, you're working with a four-level hierarchy.

A common practice in Power BI is to flatten a hierarchy, which means breaking the structure into separate columns for each level. Instead of nesting parent-child relationships in a single column, a flattened hierarchy uses one column per level. This approach simplifies filtering, slicing, and visualizing the data.

In Figure 8-11, you see an example of a two-level hierarchy, in which the Product Category ID is linked to both Product Name and Product ID. Each entry is tied to a standard parent value — the Product Category ID — and each level is stored in its distinct column. Because every item is mutually exclusive under the same category, this structure represents a clean, two-level hierarchy.

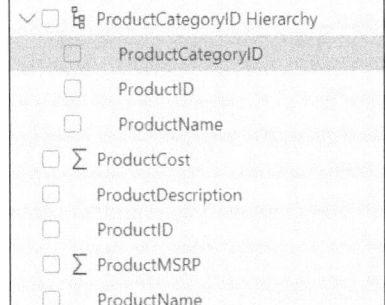

FIGURE 8-11:
Flattening a
hierarchy.

You have a couple of options when creating a hierarchy. The following set of instructions is the most efficient way to create a parent-child hierarchy — you need to be in Report view to complete this series of actions:

1. **In the Data pane, right-click a field you want to use as the top level of your hierarchy and choose Create Hierarchy from the menu that appears.**

   Power BI creates a new hierarchy and places that field as its first item.

2. **Right-click another field you want to include in the hierarchy and choose Add to Hierarchy.**

3. **In the submenu that appears, click the arrow next to the column from which the hierarchy you just created is derived.**

   For example, you may add "County Name" and "City Code" to the "City Name" as part of the hierarchy.

To change the order of columns within a hierarchy:

1. **In the Data pane, expand the hierarchy to see its levels.**

2. **Right-click the field you want to move and choose Move Up or Move Down from the menu that appears.**

TIP

You can also drag the field to the required position if no existing relationship is in place yet.

An alternative method for creating a hierarchy is to use the Table view in connection with the Formula bar. In this example, I use a hypothetical Subcategory table (not included in your downloaded dataset from Kaggle) to demonstrate how to create a more complex hierarchy.

To build a custom hierarchy using the PATH and PATHITEM functions in Power BI Desktop, follow these steps:

1. **In Power BI Desktop, click the Table View button in the Navigation pane on the left side of the screen.**

2. **In the Data pane, select the table where you want to create the hierarchy column.**

   For this example, I use the Subcategory table.

3. **On the Modeling tab of the Ribbon, click New Column.**

   This action enables you to create a calculated column based on existing fields in the table.

4. **In the Formula bar, enter the following DAX expression and then press Enter.**

   ```
   Path = PATH(Subcategory[SubcategoryID], Subcategory[Product
       CategoryID])
   ```

   This expression creates a parent-child path that defines the hierarchy relationship between subcategories and product categories using their IDs.

5. **Click New Column from the Modeling tab to create a second column.**

6. **In the Formula bar, enter the following and then press Enter:**

   ```
   Level 1 = PATHITEM(Subcategory[Path], 1)
   ```

   You can repeat this step using PATHITEM as many times as you want with different index numbers (2, 3, and so on) to extract deeper levels of the hierarchy.

   Figure 8-12 shows the output of using the PATH and PATHITEM functions on the Formula bar.

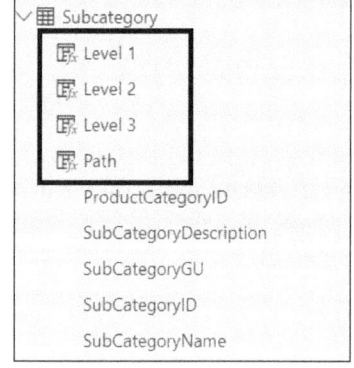

FIGURE 8-12: Example of a multi-level hierarchy.

Dealing with Table and Column Properties

Earlier in this chapter, I show how to design tables and columns in your data model. One thing these elements have in common is that both include a wide range of configurable properties that determine how your data appears and behaves in reports. All these properties can be viewed and modified in Model view, which provides a unified workspace for managing your model's structure and metadata.

To view or edit the properties of a table, column, or measure, you first need to select an object. Once an object is selected, the Properties pane on the right displays the available options for that item. To try this out, choose Model view from the navigation pane on the left side of the Power BI Desktop interface. After entering Model view, click on a table to view its table-level properties. If you want to view or edit the properties of a specific column, click on that column within the table. The Properties pane automatically updates to display the relevant fields.

You can see examples of table and column properties in Figures 8-13 and 8-14.

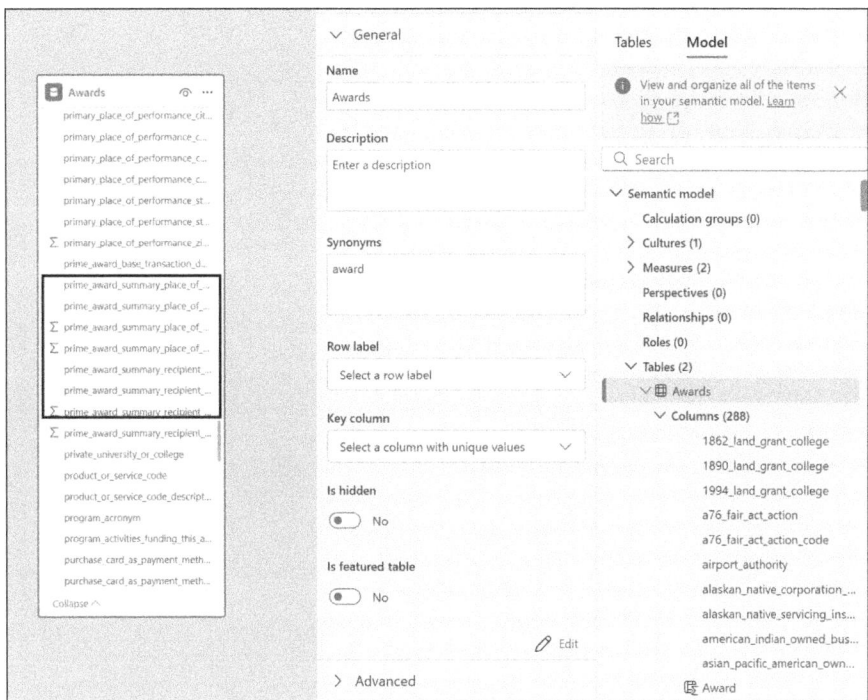

FIGURE 8-13: Table property selection.

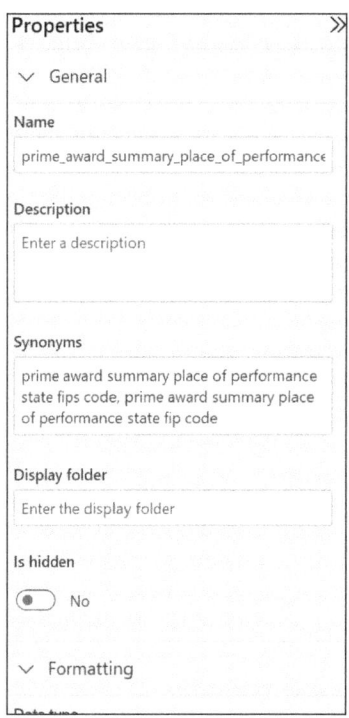

FIGURE 8-14:
Column
properties.

Here are some of the key table property options:

>> Name

>> Description

>> Synonyms

>> Row label

>> Key column

>> Is hidden

>> Is featured table

And here are the column properties:

>> Name

>> Description

>> Synonyms

>> Display folder

- ❯❯ Is hidden
- ❯❯ Data type
- ❯❯ Format
- ❯❯ Sort by column
- ❯❯ Data category
- ❯❯ Summarize by
- ❯❯ Is nullable

TIP

Although most measure properties overlap with column properties, a few column-specific properties — including Sort by column, Summarize by, and Is nullable — aren't available for measures.

Managing Cardinality and Direction

In the earlier section "Dealing with Table and Column Properties," I briefly discuss the relationships between fields and tables. The critical thing to remember is whether you're trying to set up a one-to-one, one-to-many, many-to-one, or many-to-many relationship; these are all referred to as relationships *between* tables — its cardinality, in other words. To edit the relationship between tables, click on the relationship link in a semantic model. Doing so brings up a window that you can use to set up the cardinality more effectively, as shown in the Model view. (Figure 8-15 provides an example of such an editable relationship.) You can change the relationship cardinality on this page. You can view a preview of each dataset to select a column that will be part of the relationship.

To ensure that a relationship is active, select the Make This Relationship Active check box (see Figure 8-15). There can be only one active relationship between two tables. If you choose to use DirectQuery, be sure to check the Assume Referential Integrity check box. (Referential integrity helps improve query performance.)

Cardinality

The relationship (cardinality) between two tables comes in four flavors: one-to-one, one-to-many, many-to-one, or many-to-many. Most of the time with Power BI, you use many-to-one relationships to implement parts of a data model. Table 8-3 describes the differences between the four relationship types.

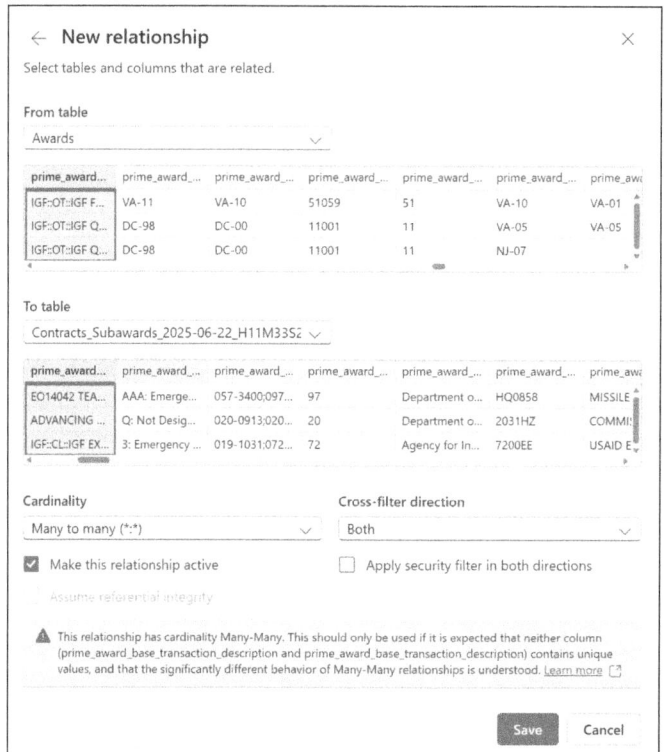

FIGURE 8-15:
Editing
relationships.

TABLE 8-3   **Table Relationship Types**

Relationship Type	What It Means
One-to-one (1:1)	Key data appears in both tables only once.
One-to-many (1:M)	*Many* refers to the fact that a key may appear more than once in a select column. *One* means that a key-value appears only once in the selected table. When you have a 1:M relationship, one key on the left side of the relationship acts as a unique identifier, whereas many items on the right side can match.
Many-to-one (M:1)	Similar to a one-to-many (1:M) relationship, many items can often be tied to a single key. The only difference is the direction and order of the key data.
Many-to-many (M:M)	A relationship exists between two tables; however, there is potentially no unique value between both tables.

Cross-filter direction

Just because you have set up a relationship type between two tables doesn't mean that the data will flow the way you want. In fact, Figure 8-15, shows a Cross Filter Direction drop-down menu in the lower right corner of the screen. When setting up a relationship, you can also show the direction in which filters flow. For one-to-many or many-to-one, you have the choice of selecting Single or Both:

>> **Single:** Filters data from the table on the One side to the table data on the Many side. A single arrow points to the relationship line in Model view.

>> **Both:** Filters from both tables in both directions. These relationships are bidirectional. Two arrows appear in the relationship line in Model view.

TECHNICAL STUFF

When you select Both for Apply Cross-Filter Direction, you can also choose Apply Security Filter. Adding these features introduces row-level security, a method for implementing restrictions on data based on individual row access.

In Figure 8-16, note the bidirectional relationship between the NAICS Code table and the Award List table. On the other hand, there is a many-to-one relationship — hence, a single cross-filter direction — between the Agency Contacts table and the Award List table. This means that many agency contacts can be associated with a single Award List entry. The number of records between the two tables varies depending on whether the relationship is 1:M or M:1, and whether the relationship is bidirectional.

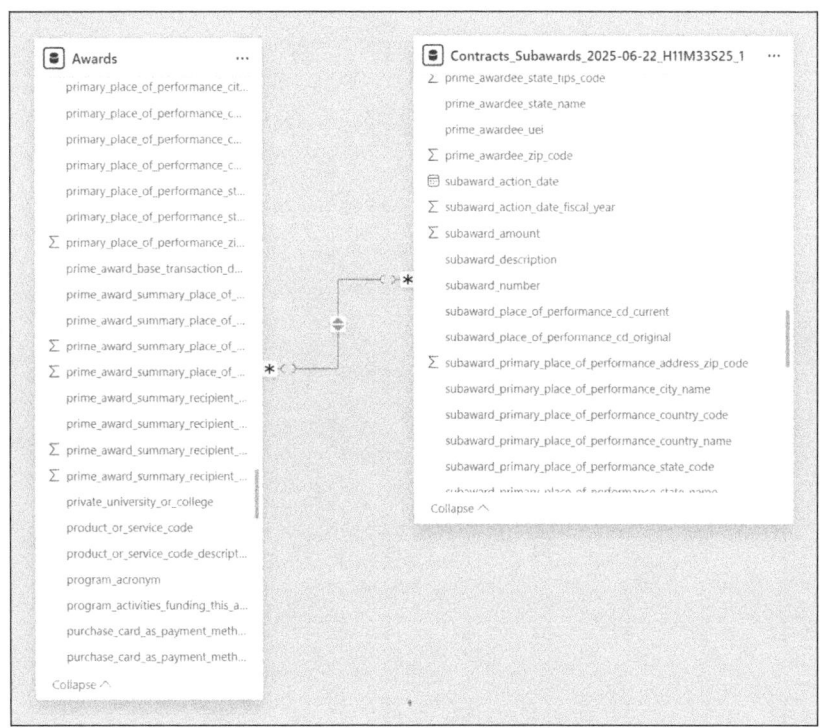

FIGURE 8-16: A cross-filter direction example.

REMEMBER

Granularity, which refers to the level of detail in your data, directly affects how relationships behave in your model. In a one-to-many (1:M) relationship, the *One side* typically represents data at a higher level (lower granularity), like product categories or customer IDs. In contrast, the *Many side* holds detailed transactions (higher granularity). A mismatch in granularity, such as trying to link two high-detail tables using many-to-many (M:M), can cause ambiguous results when producing reports, especially in filters and visuals. When you create relationships, always verify that your columns match in granularity, and exercise caution with M:M joins, which may require composite models or DAX workarounds to behave predictably.

Chapter **9**

Designing and Deploying Semantic Models

Before you can build stunning dashboards in Power BI, you need a good foundation for your data. That foundation is called the *semantic model.* Think of the semantic model, or *data model,* as the blueprint that tells Power BI how your data tables connect, what kind of information each column represents, and how numbers should be calculated. A well-defined semantic model enables you to analyze the data effectively and gain both prescriptive and descriptive insights.

In this chapter, I show you how to shape and organize your data in Power BI Desktop to be ready for analysis. You work with Table view (formerly known as Data view) and Model view to understand both the details and the broader context of your data. You see how to create relationships, fix data types, hide clutter, and add descriptions. Along the way, you also see how Microsoft Service, Fabric, and Copilot can help make this process easier.

Creating a Semantic Model Masterpiece

Creating visualizations requires a semantic model — it's just one of those things. Your data source also needs to be correct, specific, and well-crafted. Fortunately, the Power BI ETL (extract, transform, and load) framework provides support for these and other development and design activities. You use this framework to transform data, often across multiple datasets, as described throughout Part 2 of this book. After the data is safely stored in Power BI Desktop, you need to prepare it so that the model can be crafted and can function as a well-oiled semantic model for visualization and reporting.

When in doubt, Power BI also supports AI-assisted modeling through Copilot, allowing for advanced scenarios such as Direct Lake and reusable semantic models across Microsoft Fabric.

REMEMBER

The Table View tab presents the full contents of your semantic model. The Model view naming remains the same. (Table view was formerly called Data view.)

Working with the Table view and Model view

After importing data into the Power BI Desktop environment, your goal now is to manipulate the data so that it works the way you need it to work for your models. The first stop on this journey is to explore the Table View and Model View tabs. The Table View tab presents all data imported into the semantic model, and the Model View tab displays the model's visualization based on what Power BI has inferred, including tables, fields, and relationships at a given point in time.

You are responsible for updating the model, because it's part of your responsibility after importing the data. You can do this on either the Table View tab (by viewing all data instances) or the Model View tab (by reviewing the model itself). Modern versions of Power BI also allow you to define and manage semantic model-level metadata directly in Model view, including descriptions, formatting, and role-level security. Figure 9-1 shows an example of the output on the Table View tab; Figure 9-2 shows the output from the Model View tab.

FIGURE 9-1:
The Table View tab.

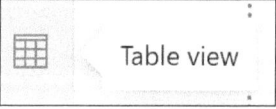

FIGURE 9-2:
The Model
View tab.

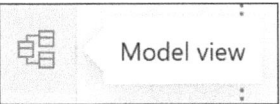

The Home Ribbon for Model view is considered the cockpit for managing many of your data actions, regardless of which view you're in within Power BI Desktop. As shown in Figure 9-3, the Home Ribbon for Model view is divided into sections: Data, Queries, Relationships, Calculations, Security, and Share. Each section has its own set of features, as described in Table 9-1.

FIGURE 9-3:
The Home Ribbon
in Model view.

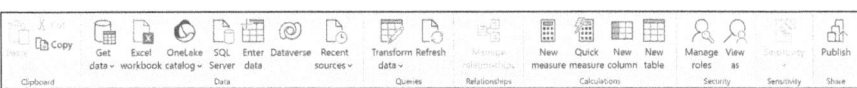

TABLE 9-1 **Sections of the Power BI Model View Home Ribbon**

Section	What It Does
Data	Brings in data from various sources.
Queries	Manages and transforms how to retrieve data from sources.
Relationships	Handles how tables relate to one another.
Calculations	Creates DAX-based modeling objects.
Security	Controls user access.
Sensitivity	Supports data labeling and metadata tied to governance. Requires Microsoft Purview.
Share	Pushes your semantic model and related reports to Power BI Service or Microsoft Fabric workspace.

The Power Query Editor shares many of the same features shown in Table 9-1, although it also has (unsurprisingly) a broader set of tools focused on data transformation and cleansing, including column shaping, row filtering, and AI-assisted insights, as shown in Figure 9-4. You'll also find access to tools for combining queries, applying parameters, managing data types, and leveraging Azure AI for text, vision, or sentiment analysis.

FIGURE 9-4:
The Power Query
Editor Ribbon.

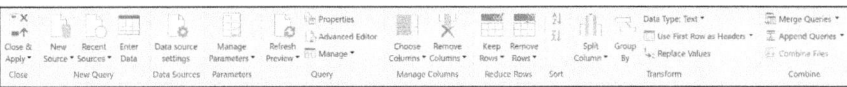

Importing queries

You can import queries into Power BI Desktop by using one of several import options. Start by using the Navigation pane on the left side of the screen to switch to Table view, where all existing tables are available.

From Table view, you can choose to start fresh by opening a new file, or you can import a file or data source into Power BI. To start fresh with a new file, choose File ⇨ New from the menu bar. To import, follow these steps:

1. **Click the Get Data button to open the Get Data pane and select the type of file or source you want to import.**

   Once you select your data source, the Navigator window opens, as shown in Figure 9-5.

2. **To load data, pick one or more datasets, and then click the Load button.**

3. **To transform data, pick one or more datasets, and then click the Transform Data button.**

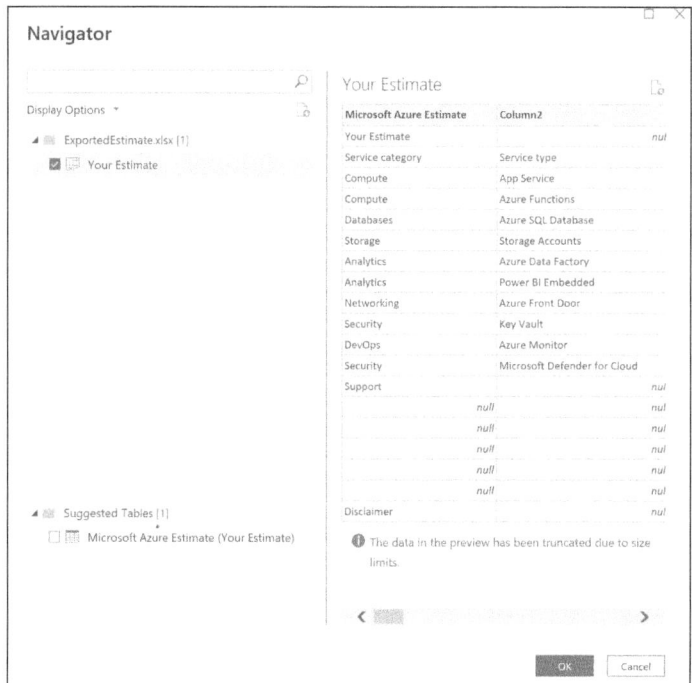

FIGURE 9-5:
The Navigator window in Table view.

REMEMBER

If you choose to load data, the data isn't mapped to a specific data type. When you transform data, Power BI does its best to map against the proper data type based on ETL properties. See Chapter 7 to find out more about data types and their corresponding ETL properties.

TECHNICAL STUFF

Although Table view is similar to the Power Query Editor, keep in mind that only a sample of your data is shown in the Power Query Editor. In contrast, all data is available in Table view after it's imported into the data model. In Table view, you work with your entire dataset, and modifications are made live according to the dashboard's requirements and specifications. Both Table view and the Power Query Editor can handle the creation of calculated columns in real time, though. Also, if you are importing text or CSV files, you won't find the Navigator window. Virtually all other data source types present the Navigator window, though.

After the data is loaded, you can manipulate it, add queries, add or delete columns, or manage the existing relationships. The following sections provide detailed instructions on how to complete each of these activities.

Defining data types

When Power BI imports a dataset, it automatically assigns a data type to each column based on the detected values. For example, in Figure 9-6, the `parent_award_agency_id` field is initially recognized as a whole number in the Kaggle dataset. However, this column may sometimes include letters or leading zeros, which would be lost if treated as a numeric type. In such cases, it's best to change the field type to Text.

FIGURE 9-6:
Using the Column Tools tab to change the data type.

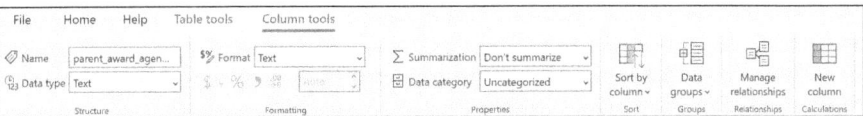

Similarly, numeric columns representing monetary values may default to Whole Number or Decimal Number. To ensure accurate financial calculations, you should use the Fixed Decimal Number type, which maintains higher precision. You can also apply a Currency format to these fields to make the monetary context clear and visually consistent across your report.

To review the data types for a given column, follow these steps:

1. **Open Table view.**
2. **Select the column you want to review and highlight it.**

3. **Make sure you're on the Column Tools tab (refer to Figure 9-6).**

4. **On the Column Tools tab, check the Name property to make sure it reflects your desired column name.**

5. **Verify that the Data Type drop-down menu is set to the correct data type (see Figure 9-7).**

   In this case, it's set to Whole Number.

6. **Switch the option to Text.**

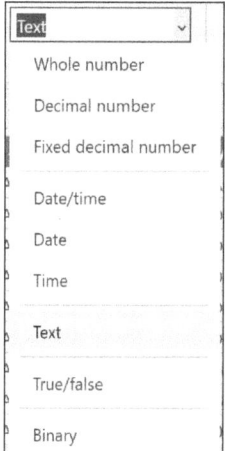

FIGURE 9-7: A list of data type options.

This process is consistent throughout Power BI for modifying data types, whether you're trying to change numerical data to text or text to numeric.

Handling formatting and data type properties

The Format drop-down menu on the Column Tools tab lets you assign properties that determine how each column's data is displayed and interpreted. This ensures that the column's behavior matches the type of information it contains. For instance, as I mention earlier, if a column represents monetary or decimal values, you should apply the Decimal Number or Fixed Decimal Number format to maintain accuracy. On the other hand, if a column contains only whole numbers, such as counts or identifiers, you should select the Whole Number format. Setting the correct format not only improves data accuracy but also helps Power BI display values in a way that clearly reflects their meaning.

Keep in mind that column data can be text or numeric, and the data type you choose determines which formats appear in the Format drop-down menu. If you select Text for the data type, for example, only the text option appears. If you choose a data type with numerical values, only numeric-based formatting choices appear, as shown in Figure 9-8.

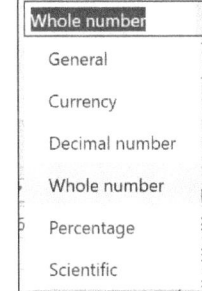

FIGURE 9-8:
Numeric formatting options.

Suppose you're looking to apply properties such as Measures, Geographic markers, or Mathematical Behaviors against a column. In that case, you can use a *summarization* (a way to evaluate data further mathematically) or a data category (a way to classify geographically-based data). Figure 9-9 shows the summarization options for the Column Tools tab, and Figure 9-10 shows the Data Category options.

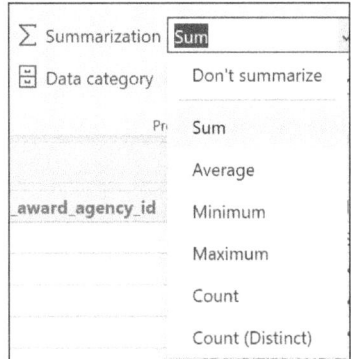

FIGURE 9-9:
The Summarization options on the Column Tools tab.

FIGURE 9-10:
The Data Categories options.

REMEMBER

Summarization options enable the summarization of any column of numeric data in a table as a single value. Data Category options are applicable for Power BI mapping — specifically, latitude and longitude or degrees.

Managing tables

Sometimes, the name of a table you've imported is not exactly what you want. Or maybe you want to delete a table. Data experts commonly perform these actions in Power BI Desktop as they work their way through the design, development, and deployment of their semantic model.

Adding tables

You may need to add one or more tables to your semantic model after the initial data load. Perhaps you want to create an additional fact table for transactional data or a dimension table to support a new lookup. Both scenarios are pretty standard — and fortunately, adding a table is straightforward. (If you enter data manually, you still need to configure relationships and enrich metadata as necessary.)

Here is how you add a table:

1. **From Model view, open the Home tab of the Model view Ribbon, and click the Enter Data button (see Figure 9-11).**

The Create Table Interface appears.

2. **Enter the column names and data you want into the appropriate table cells.**

3. **Enter a table name in the Name field.**

The table should resemble the one shown in Figure 9-12.

4. **Click the Load button when you finish creating your table.**

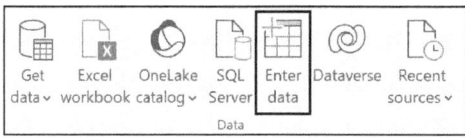

FIGURE 9-11:
The Enter
Data button.

The result is a brand-new table that appears as part of the Semantic model, accessible in both Table view and Model view.

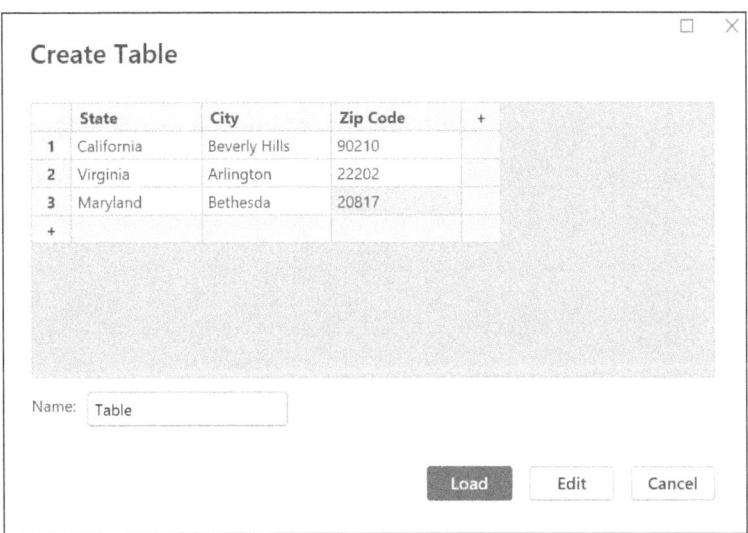

FIGURE 9-12:
Creating a table.

Renaming tables

Renaming a table is a straightforward activity, provided that no other table already has the same name. With Power BI, every table in a data model must have a unique name. For example, two tables cannot have the name Product. (You can have a table named Product and another named Products, but that would be pretty confusing.) Best practices suggest being as descriptive as possible.

To rename a table in Power BI Desktop, follow these steps:

1. **In either Table view or Model view, go to the Data pane.**

2. **Right-click the table name you want to change.**

3. **Choose Rename from the menu that appears, as shown in Figure 9-13.**

4. **Enter a new name for your table in the highlighted field and then press Enter.**

   The table name refreshes within 30 seconds.

Deleting tables

If you want to delete a table from a model, you face a few risks. If relationships are associated with the table, those relationships will break. If calculated fields are embedded within a report, they will also disappear. That said, removing a table, like moving a column, is a relatively simple process.

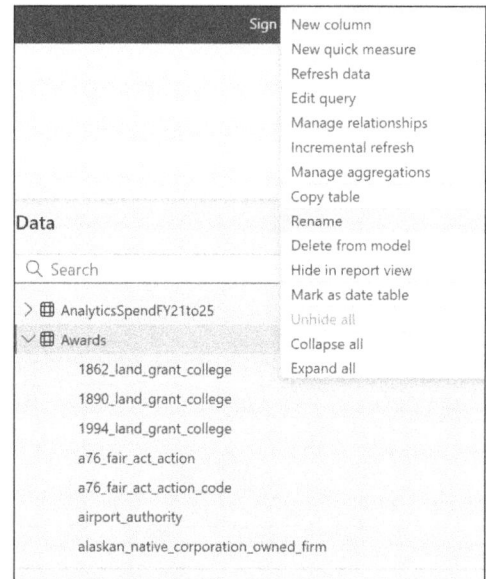

FIGURE 9-13:
Updating the
table name in
Model view.

To remove a table, follow these steps:

1. **In either Table view or Model view, go to the Data pane.**

2. **Right-click a table to remove and then choose Delete From Model from the menu that appears, as shown in Figure 9-14.**

   A prompt appears, asking whether you're sure you want to delete the table, as shown in Figure 9-15.

3. **Click Delete.**

   The table is deleted from the model.

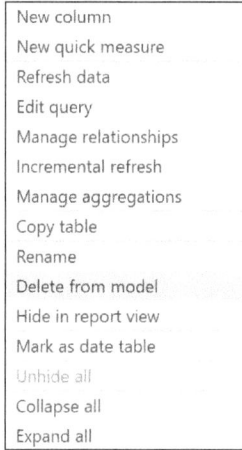

FIGURE 9-14:
Deleting a table
from the model.

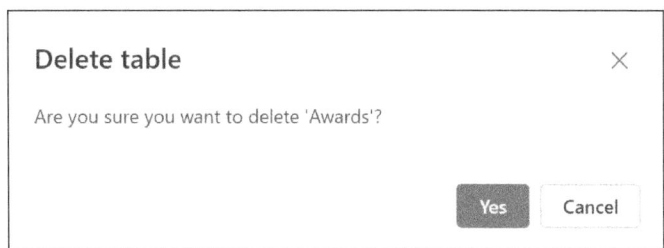

FIGURE 9-15:
Asking whether
you're sure.

Renaming and deleting columns

Renaming or deleting a column follows the same practice as renaming or deleting a table. The only caveat is that when dependencies, such as key enforcements, occur, deleting a column can result in potentially broken relationships.

To rename a column, follow these steps:

1. **In either Table view or Model view, go to the Data pane.**

2. **Right-click the column name you want to rename.**

3. **Rename the column.**

    The column name refreshes automatically.

    If relationship updates require revision, they are updated accordingly.

To delete a column, follow these steps:

1. **In either Table view or Model view, go to the Data pane.**

2. **Right-click the column name and choose Delete From Model from the menu that appears.**

    You're alerted that the column is about to be deleted.

3. **Click Delete.**

    The column is deleted, and the model updates automatically.

    If relationships are broken, the links between the tables are updated accordingly.

Adding and modifying data in tables

To add or modify data in an existing table, you use the Power Query Editor. The process is simpler for data that you created yourself within Power BI than for datasets that were imported using a file or ingested using DataQuery, which I cover in the next section.

To add rows or modify cells to rows of tables you created yourself, follow these steps:

1. **In Model view, open the Home tab of the Ribbon, and from the Queries section, click the Transform Data button.**

    The Power Query Editor appears.

2. **Select the model you created.**

3. **Click Source under Applied Steps.**

4. **Click the Gear button (see Figure 9-16).**

    A window opens that allows you to add or update additional rows or fields.

FIGURE 9-16:
Clicking the
Gear to open the
Source under
Applied Steps.

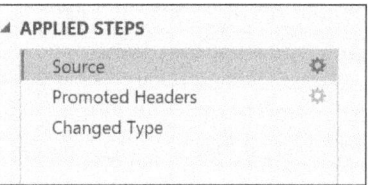

Adding and modifying data to imported, DirectQuery, and composite models

When you import or use DirectQuery and then transform the data in Power BI, your ability to add or change the data is limited to the native data source, with one exception: If you create custom columns or calculated columns, those are editable and managed within Power BI.

Assume that you want to modify the Location table, as shown in Figure 9-17. The data exists in the file you added. You can add, change, or delete data in the table, which is precisely what was done. As soon as you update the file, click the Refresh button in the Queries section of the Model view Home Ribbon. The results are instantly updated, as shown in Figure 9-18.

FIGURE 9-17:
Before
modifications
were made to the
source file and
then refreshed.

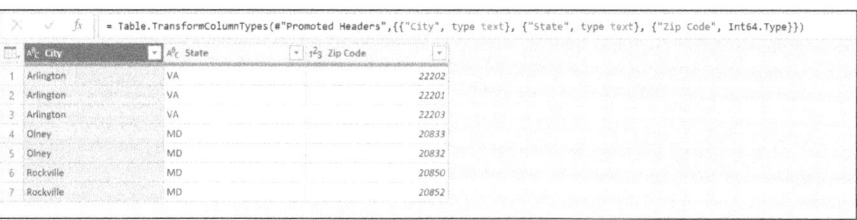

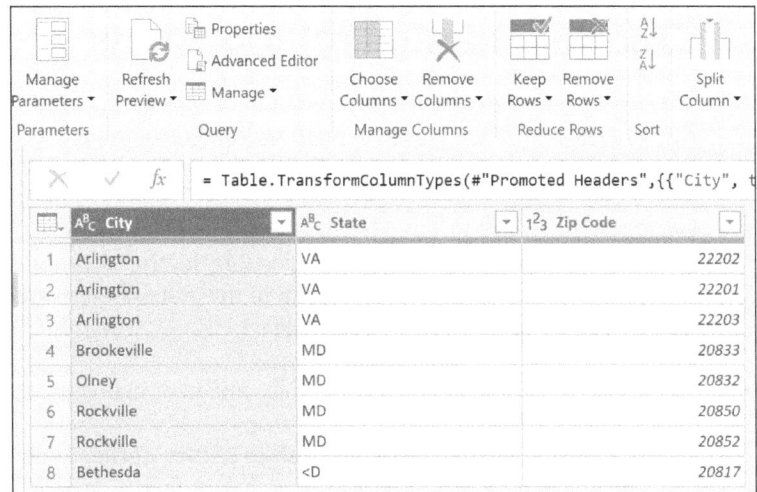

FIGURE 9-18:
Refreshed
dataset based on
changes made in
the source file.

Managing Relationships

When a common bond connects two tables, it often signifies that a relationship exists through a key. It can be a primary-primary key or a primary-foreign key relationship. In certain circumstances, a table may even be joined together in a single field. That single field can be mapped to another table with a corresponding field, creating a lookup. In this section, I cover the value of relationships in designing and developing the data model.

Creating automatic relationships

Power BI recognizes that when data is transformed, a relationship between the original data and the transformed data exists. For example, if you have two tables with a numeric data type and they're named similarly, they're considered to be in a relationship. Power BI detects these relationships as part of the ETL process. The automatic detection helps reduce the manual work required to identify relationships yourself. Also, you can reduce the risk of errors from occurring between tables.

To see how Power BI views relationships between datasets, follow these steps:

1. **In Model view, from the Relationships section of the Home Ribbon, click the Manage Relationships button.**

   Relationships that exist when the datasets are imported are automatically matched.

2. **(Optional) If you want the systems to autodetect the relationships, click the Autodetect button.**

Creating manual relationships

Sometimes the names of primary and foreign keys don't match, but you know that the data between them creates a relationship. For example, LocationID and CityID may be the same, as may StateID and StateAbbreviation. These are examples where data analysts need to manually map the relationship between two tables, even though Power BI should have been able to identify the pattern. In the example shown in Figure 9-19, the relationship in the Location table (which was created within an Excel file) is mapped to the State Column and the Awards table (*primary_place_of_performance_state_code*).

To establish relationships between tables and keys manually, follow these steps:

1. **In Model view, from the Relationships section of the Home Ribbon, click the Manage Relationships icon.**

2. **Click the New button.**

3. **The New Relationship interface appears, as shown in Figure 9-19.**

4. **Select the two tables that are in a relationship.**

5. **Using the Cardinality and Cross-Filter Direction drop-down menus, choose the settings you want.**

6. **Click OK when you finish.**

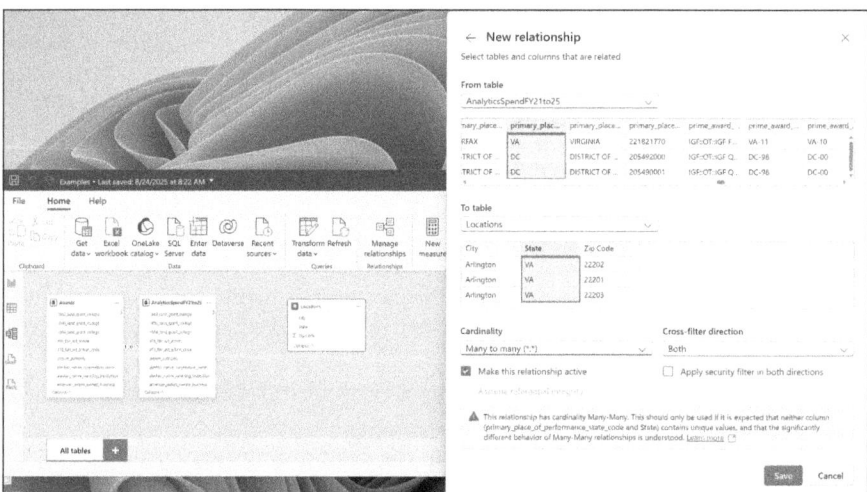

FIGURE 9-19:
The New Relationship interface.

Deleting relationships

Deleting relationships occurs in one of three ways. You either remove the field in one of the two tables that sets up the join between the two tables, or you use the Manage Relationships interface to disconnect the relationship the same way you created the interface. You uncheck the Active box. Then you click Delete. A warning appears, showing a break in the relationship. You acknowledge the relationship to be broken, and then click OK.

The easiest way to break a relationship is to open Model view and right-click the link. Choose Delete. You're prompted to acknowledge that the relationship will be broken.

Classifying and codifying data in tables

As you build your data collection in Power BI over time, it is essential to add context so that any user accessing those datasets you've created can put the puzzle pieces together. Whether your descriptive data is tied to a single dataset or to many, it's an ongoing activity for the person responsible for managing the data. A way to help any user who comes across your data better understand precisely what they are reviewing is to add *metadata* — data that provides a more detailed description of your data, in other words, within each table or column property.

To add metadata to each table or column, follow these steps, depending on whether it's a table or a column:

1. **Open Model view.**

2. **Click to select the table (to describe an entire table) or a column inside the table. (You need to select the specific column among the tables.)**

3. **In the Properties pane, enter a description in the Description box.**

   You can enter an extended sentence regarding the specific item.

4. **Enter synonyms that can also describe the table or column name.**

WARNING

Be careful not to confuse data categories with data types. Data *categories* are a way to group data in a model; data *types* are specific to determining whether the data is text, numeric, or mixed. Think of Cities as a data category and the data type as Text.

Arranging Data

Arranging data in a dataset differs from what you experience when data is transformed for visualization. Arranging data in Power BI can be classified into three categories: Sort By, Group By, and Hide Data. The following sections provide a detailed examination of each type.

Sorting by and grouping by

You can easily be confused by the Sort By and Group By options. Sort By sorts data in ascending order (A–Z) and descending order (Z–A) on a column basis. To ascend or descend the data in a dataset, you need to use the Power Query Editor to complete any form of sort-by action. You can sort by only one column at a time.

Group By allows a field to be grouped against a mathematical operation (count, sum, and mean) and another field, as shown in Figure 9-20. Selecting advanced options enables you to group by one or more fields.

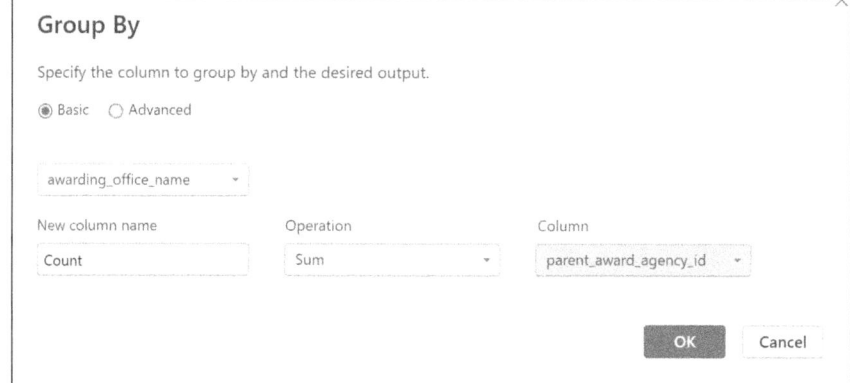

FIGURE 9-20: Grouping by capabilities.

Hiding data

At times, you may want to suppress column data from a table. The column may offer little value in the dataset when presenting results, or the data may add too much complexity to the visualization. It may be that the column, when included in the dataset, provides inaccurate data. The reasons for hiding data can be many. However, rather than deleting a column when you may still need the data later, you can hide it temporarily.

To hide a column, as shown in Figure 9-21, follow these steps:

1. **In Model view, go to the table containing the column in question.**

2. **Click to select the field.**

3. **Go to the Properties pane (see Figure 9-21).**

4. **Locate the Is Hidden slider.**

5. **Slide the option from No to Yes.**

   You see an eye with a line through it appear in the field, indicating that it has been hidden.

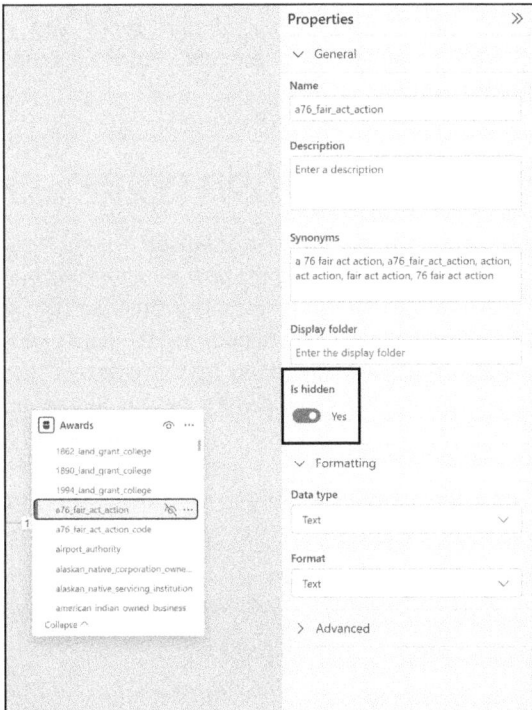

FIGURE 9-21:
Hiding data.

If you want to unhide the column at any point, repeat these steps, but this time slide the Is Hidden slider to No.

Working with Extended Semantic Models

Regardless of which import method you use for Power BI Desktop, you face limitations. Not all semantic models require calculations, but the underlying requirement is that mathematical calculations are needed to help analyze qualitative data at some point. Calculations of percentages and comparing figures are all too familiar.

DAX (short for Data Analysis Expression) is the language written for calculation in Power BI Desktop. This formula-based language comprises over 300 formulas used either alone or in combination to create mathematically oriented metrics. Many of the formulas found in DAX are identical to those you find in Excel.

The following sections cover the calculation types you may need to use when working with extended data models. To read more about DAX, see Chapters 15 and 16.

Knowing the calculation types

Every time you import data or connect to a data source via DirectQuery to create a visualization, you discover all over again how much easier Power BI makes your life when you see how little you must do to transform the datasets. There's a catch, though: Suppose that you need to quantify the data you're visualizing. Your goal may be to develop calculations from tables to extend your datasets. Power BI Desktop allows for all metric types to be calculated and imported from the source.

These techniques are essential not only to visualization efforts but also to DAX calculations:

>> Components that are used to filter the visualization

>> Components that are used in the classification of data

>> Order and rank for datasets

>> Weighting and values to datasets

>> Adding new columns to datasets

Regardless of why you need to extend a dataset, you'll quickly find that these techniques become necessary because imported or live datasets in Power BI aren't designed to handle advanced calculations right away. They're not what you'd call quantitative-ready or formula-rich out of the box. Bear in mind that the preceding list isn't exhaustive; plenty of other ways exist to approach data calculation. The key idea is that you can't always predict the patterns, trends, or needs of a dataset when you first start working with it.

Working with column contents and joins

I tend to talk in this chapter about importing data from a single source, but enterprise organizations often import data across multiple sources into a single source. Under these circumstances, organizations must merge the columns from these data sources and connect them into tables and columns.

Suppose that you want to create a column with the data on NAICS codes associated with the Awards Data. The data sources are housed in two different sources. What you need to do is create a new column that combines the data from both columns, creating a single entry in one of the tables after the data is imported and transformed.

If you want to join the two tables on `naics_code`, follow these steps:

1. **In Power BI Desktop, open Table view and then choose Home ➪ Transform Data.**

2. **In Power Query, select the `Awards` table in the Query pane.**

3. **Choose Home ➪ Merge Queries.**

4. **Pick the `AnalyticsSpendFY21to25` table.**

5. **Select `naics_code` in both tables as the key.**

6. **Choose the join type (usually Left Outer if you want all Awards rows, or Inner for only matches).**

7. **Click OK and expand the merged column to keep only the fields you need.**

8. **Click Close & Apply.**

If all you want to do is create a relationship, you apply this logic:

1. **Load both tables into Power BI.**

2. **Open Model view.**

3. **Drag `Awards[naics_code]` to `AnalyticsSpendFY21to25[naics_code]`.**

   Power BI creates a relationship.

4. **Use** `RELATED( )` **in DAX to pull columns over.**

   Here's an example of how that may look written in DAX:

   ```
   SpendFY21to25 = RELATED(AnalyticsSpendFY21to25[Spend])
   ```

If your goal is to create a union on NAICS codes from both tables (one list of codes without joining), consider the following:

1. **In Power Query, select Append Queries instead of Merge Queries.**

2. **Append the two tables, keeping only** `naics_code`**.**

3. **Click OK.**

Publishing Data Models

When a data model is ready to be published to Power BI Service, the process is as easy as clicking a button — assuming that you've set up your online account with Microsoft's Power BI Service at `https://powerbi.microsoft.com`. You're asked to supply your username and the email address that logs you in to all Power Platform and Microsoft 365 applications. Depending on the type of license you have, the data volume and refresh rate of your model vary.

To publish your model, open the Home tab in Power BI Desktop, and click Publish, as shown in Figure 9-22.

FIGURE 9-22: The Publish button for deploying the data model and reports to Power BI Service.

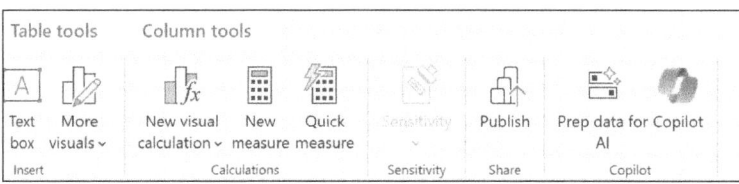

Chapter **10**

Perfecting the Semantic Model

H ere's a common problem: Your reports look great in a test environment. They run fast, smoothly, and experience no hiccups in Power BI Desktop. But the moment you publish them with Power BI Service, everything slows down. Pages take forever to load, visuals refresh too slowly, and users get frustrated.

Most of the time, the semantic model is the culprit when performance slows down. The model may have unnecessary columns, poorly written DAX formulas, or messy relationships between tables. Add more data into the mix, and the problems only get worse.

The good news? You can fix most of these issues early, before they snowball. In this chapter, I show you practical ways to optimize your semantic model. You see how you can trim excess data, write better measures, and use tools like Copilot and Fabric to keep your reports running smoothly in real-world conditions.

Matching Queries with Capacity

Every version of Power BI has its limits. Power BI Desktop, Pro, Premium, and now Fabric all manage queries a little differently. Think of it like lanes on the interstate: the more lanes you have, the more cars (queries) can get through without causing a traffic jam. If too many queries hit your data model simultaneously, performance suffers. Reports load slowly, refreshes drag on, and users start wondering whether Power BI is broken. That's why it's smart to keep your data models lean and load only what you really need. In Fabric, capacity works differently from older versions. With Direct Lake and OneLake, models can scale more effectively and perform nearly as well as imported data. Still, the same golden rule applies: The less clutter you send through your model, the faster things run.

TIP

Before publishing, prune unnecessary tables, columns, and rows. This optimized model improves performance, reducing strain on system capacity and allowing more queries to flow smoothly.

Deleting Unnecessary Columns and Rows

You've probably heard the saying that too much of a good thing can be bad. That's definitely true in Power BI. Just because you can load every column and row into your data model doesn't mean you should. In fact, one of the fastest ways to slow down your reports is to carry around a bloated dataset that's full of information no one is ever going to use.

The trick is to load only what you need. If a column isn't being used in a visualization or calculation, it's just dead weight; you should drop it. The same goes for rows. If your report is only concerned with the past two years of data, why burden your model with ten years' worth unless there is a mandatory requirement to retain historical data? Power BI makes this easy: You can filter data at the query level so only the rows you care about are loaded, or you can disable query loading for tables you don't need right now. With Copilot, you can actually point out unused fields and even suggest ways to slim down your dataset before it becomes a performance problem.

Ditching columns

Columns in your model should provide value. Each column should either support a visualization, feed into a calculation, or give some real value to your users. If a column isn't doing any of those things, it's just clutter, and clutter slows everything down. One common culprit is high-cardinality columns, which are those with a large number of unique values. Think of something like an invoice number or a transaction ID. Those fields are helpful in auditing in a database, but in a Power BI report, they usually don't add much value except for filling up space on a piece of paper or screen.

Primary keys are another example. They're great for maintaining relationships in a database. Still, when you try to import them into a fact table in Power BI, they often bloat your model without providing much reporting benefit. Unless you really need them, do not incorporate them into a model. When a column doesn't serve a purpose for your reports, whether that's building visuals, enabling relationships, or feeding calculations, don't load it. Your model and the refresh times behind the models will thank you.

Limiting the number of rows from the get-go

Including a filtering criterion is a must-have for a dataset from the onset when building a data model in Power BI. The requirements can be anything from an attribute set to a series of dates. But it's essential to limit the number of rows you have. Suppose that you're concerned only with analyzing a finite dataset. Why not just reduce the number of rows from the onset? It's senseless to include data with little value or parameters that can be added later if they create extraneous performance concerns with reporting.

TIP

This advice holds even with new technologies such as Direct Lake, which comes with Fabric, and mirrored sources. Although these features can handle much larger datasets, your reports will still perform faster and refresh more smoothly if you start with a lean approach.

TIP

Power BI Copilot can now suggest filters or highlight unused data, making it easier to keep your dataset focused on what matters most.

Swapping Numeric Columns with Measures and Variables

Too many Power BI users despair when it comes to managing columns, yet there's no good reason to get so frustrated. Creating measures and authoring variables in your DAX formulas can provide you with far less complex code and calculation options. Newcomers to Power BI Desktop often underuse variables when creating data models.

When you put your data modeler hat on, you are often tasked with a tall order of being the code guru, debugging detective, and budding artist for those killer visualizations you produce. But to successfully deliver for each of these roles requires you to come up with some nifty code (and a pull a few tricks from your sleeve now and then), especially when you are crafting DAX calculations. You've already seen a few examples of DAX and know that it takes a dash of compound and complex expressions to create a formula. That's why you'd bring your handy-dandy friend, the variable, into the mix (which I cover in depth in Chapters 15 and 16). A variable is a way to store a DAX calculation efficiently, with the goal of reuse. Variables can help you write more complex calculations with efficiency and style. Better yet, a variable enables you to strengthen your code's performance and reliability, readability, and, of course, to reduce complexity.

TIP

You don't have to rely only on your own DAX skills. Power BI Copilot can generate draft measures, suggest variables, and even explain existing formulas in plain English. You can focus on the logic of your analysis while Copilot handles some of the grunt work of writing and optimizing DAX.

REMEMBER

You're often forced to use nested functions and reuse logic — the processes that are associated with calculating data, in other words — to come up with effective expressions. To be successful, the most effective shortcut is to leverage variables. Without variables, expressions can get long, slow to process, and challenging to debug. Using measures and DAX variables helps reduce processing time.

Variables in a data model offer the following benefits:

>> **Improves performance:** Reduces the need to evaluate expressions multiple times. In many cases, queries return results in half the time.

>> **Enhances readability:** Variables are ideal when you're looking to replace extended expressions. If you need a way to read and understand formulas more readily, variables can help you.

>> **Assists with debugging:** Variables are also a debugging tool. If you need to test formulas or test expressions, variables are the go-to utility for troubleshooting.

The following example shows how a traditional DAX expression can be transformed into one that includes variables to improve performance, enhance readability, and make it easier to debug.

Without variables:

```
SalesGrowth % =
DIVIDE(([ProductSales] - CALCULATE([ProductSales],
```

```
PARALLELPERIOD('Date'[Date], -12, MONTH))),
CALCULATE([ProductSales], PARALLELPERIOD('Date'[Date], -12,
MONTH))
)
```

With variables:

```
SalesGrowth % =
VAR SalesLastYear = CALCULATE([ProductSales],
PARALLELPERIOD('Date'[Date], -12, MONTH))
RETURN
DIVIDE(([Sales] - SalesLastYear), SalesLastYear)
```

TIP

Power BI Copilot can suggest how to rewrite formulas such as the one presented above automatically. You can paste a complex DAX formula into Copilot, and it will recommend ways to simplify it with variables. This means less trial and error and more time focusing on insights.

Reducing Cardinality

You may not realize it, but I talk about cardinality in earlier chapters, just in disguise. When you examine the number of elements in a set of data, you are evaluating its *cardinality.* Consider this example: I have lived in many cities, but in each of those cities, I could have lived in one or more houses. Cities are represented as many (M), and the places I've lived in each town could be one or many (1 or M). The cardinality or relationship described in a data model would likely be notated as a many-to-many (M:M) relationship.

As you aim to refine your model, part of the process involves reducing cardinality to create the most reliable dataset possible. When you try to improve model performance, you may not immediately consider that cardinality plays a role, but it often does. One clear sign is in the Power Query Editor, where the column distribution shows the number of distinct and unique values in each column.

Distinct values represent all the different values in a column (for example, the list of all cities you've lived in). Unique values are those that appear only once (for example, a street address that occurs only once in the data). Columns with too many unique values are considered high cardinality, and that can slow down your model. Reducing cardinality, in other words, trimming down columns to only those values that matter for reporting, makes your model smaller, faster, and easier to manage. Table 10-1 illustrates the four types of relationships in Power BI and their connection to cardinality.

TABLE 10-1   Cardinality and Direction

Cardinality	What It Means
One-to-one (1:1)	Both tables have only a single instance of a particular value.
Many-to-one (M:1)	The most common cardinality and thus the default type. The column in one table can have many instances of a value. The other related table is often a lookup table with only one instance.
One-to-many (1:M)	A column in one table has a single instance of a particular value. The related table has one or more values.
Many-to-many (M:M)	Appropriate for composite models and can be used as many-to-many between tables. There is no specific requirement for unique values. There is also no need to establish new tables for relationships.

TIP

During data model development, creating and editing relationships is a standard practice. No matter the relationship type (or cardinality) in your model, Power BI enforces consistent data types. Remember, though, that relationships will fail if two columns don't share the same data type.

Power BI now offers several ways to reduce the amount of data being loaded into models. Summarization and aggregation can help keep your model lean. The smaller your model, the easier it is to maintain healthy relationships, especially if you know it will grow over time. With Fabric and Direct Lake, you can query massive datasets more easily, but keeping models small and tidy is still one of the best ways to ensure speed and reliability.

Reducing Queries

Under Power BI Desktop's Options and Settings (found on the File menu), you can access the Query Reduction page (see Figure 10-1). This page gives you a few options to control how many queries are sent, grouped into three areas:

» **Reduce number of queries sent by:** You can use this option to disable cross-highlighting in reports. This reduces backend queries and can make navigation feel smoother. Unless you have a specific need, it's best to leave cross-highlighting enabled.

» **Slicers:** You can choose whether slicer changes apply instantly or only after clicking an Apply button. Instant apply is best for most cases, but if your queries take longer or require multiple steps, using the Apply button can improve performance.

>> **Filters:** As with slicers, you can choose whether filter changes apply instantly or require an Apply button. For most reports, instant apply works best, but an Apply button can be useful when filters interact with more complex queries.

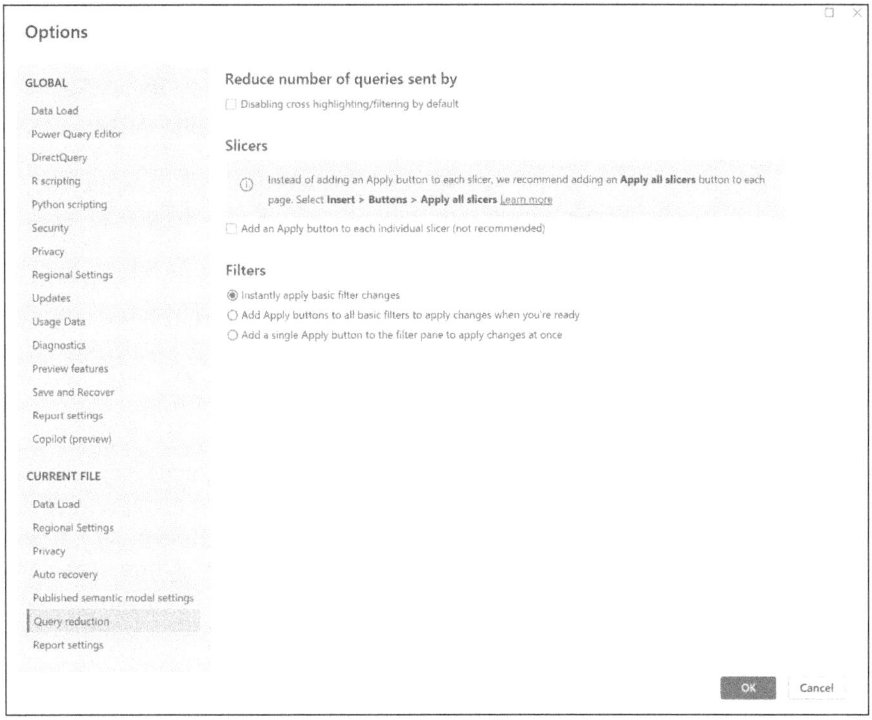

FIGURE 10-1:
Query
reduction
options.

If you notice that report interactions (like slicers or filters) are slowing things down, Power BI gives you the ability to reduce the number of queries being sent in the background. This doesn't change your data, it simply limits how often queries run, which can make your report feel more responsive. Follow these steps:

1. **Choose File ⇨ Options and Settings from the main menu and then choose Options from the menu that appears.**

2. **Under the Current File heading in the listing that runs down the left side of the screen, select Query Reduction.**

3. **The main window refreshes to show your query reduction options (refer to Figure 10-1).**

4. **Select the radio button to add the Instantly Apply basic filter changes to apply changes when you are ready.**

This changes the filtering from instant to one where you control the filtering. As you can see, there are alternative options to make changes to all configurations at once.

Converting to a Composite Model

Sometimes, direct import and DirectQuery results need to be combined into a single model to balance storage and performance better. Power BI supports this through composite models, which enable you to combine different storage modes within a single dataset. A table can even be set to dual mode, meaning it can act as both DirectQuery and Import depending on the query.

As a refresher, a composite model enables you to connect to multiple data sources and use them together as if they were a single entity. You may have one or more DirectQuery connections alongside imported tables, or even several DirectQuery sources combined. This flexibility provides you with more options for building a model that meets your reporting needs.

The main advantages to using a composite model concern performance and flexibility. By integrating multiple sources into a single model, you can reduce the query load, support aggregations, and optimize data access. With Direct Lake available on Fabric, you now have a third option that behaves almost like an import but can scale to massive datasets, making composite models even more powerful.

WARNING

Your first choice is to create a direct import model whenever possible. Import provides the best design flexibility, control, and performance. However, there are times when composite models (or Direct Lake) are more appropriate, such as when

>> You need to consolidate multiple sources into a single source of truth.

>> You want to combine DirectQuery models with additional imported datasets.

>> You need to combine two or more DirectQuery sources into one model.

>> You're working in Fabric and want to combine Direct Lake data with imported or DirectQuery data.

REMEMBER

The DirectQuery method connects directly to data in its source repository from within Power BI Desktop. It's an alternative to importing data, but the user experience depends heavily on the performance of the underlying system. Slow source performance, timeouts, or an excessive number of concurrent users can all lead to delays in your reports.

External factors, such as network latency and server load, also impact the performance of DirectQuery. Because of this, DirectQuery can pose a risk if performance optimization is your top priority. If you have limited control over the source files or database, you may have limited success with DirectQuery. If you are looking for a mitigation strategy, consider using Direct Lake in Fabric, which delivers near-instant query speeds while allowing you to work with data in place. When performance matters most, Import or Direct Lake are often better options than relying on DirectQuery alone.

Creating and Managing Aggregations

A central theme of this chapter is that excessive data can lead to performance issues. One of the best ways to improve speed is to summarize your data at a higher level. For example, instead of storing every individual sales transaction, you may aggregate sales by product, vendor, or region. By doing so, you reduce table size and make queries faster, while still keeping the insights you need. Your organization may decide to use aggregations in its data models for the following reasons:

» **Handling big data:** Aggregation makes it possible to analyze very large datasets quickly, especially when the results are cached. Fewer resources are required, and queries can be completed in a fraction of the time.

» **Optimizing data refreshes:** Because the dataset is smaller, refresh times are faster. Users gain access to fresh data sooner, and your cache doesn't get bogged down by massive volumes of records.

» **Managing model size:** Large models can get out of control. Aggregating tables helps keep your model lean and prevents unnecessary growth.

» **Keeping the model relevant:** By aggregating proactively, you avoid future performance hiccups caused by data volume concerns. It's easier to keep the model responsive and user-friendly as your data grows.

The creation part

Aggregation isn't an activity to take lightly. You first need to decide the right level — or grain — at which to aggregate. For example, in the Awards dataset (`https://www.kaggle.com/jackhymanpowerbi/datasets`), should you summarize data at the Agency level, the NAICS Code level, or somewhere else? Aggregating at the Agency level often provides the best insight, since it captures the broadest relationships and allows you to roll up information tied to NAICS codes and awards beneath it.

After you decide on the grain, you must choose how to build the aggregation. There are several methods, but the result is the same: a smaller, faster dataset. Consider these two approaches:

>> **At the database level:** If you have access to the source system, you can create a new table with your aggregated fields and import it directly.

>> **In Power BI Desktop:** You can use the Power Query Editor to build aggregations on the fly. For instance, you may reduce an Awards List table down to three fields (AgencyID, VendorID, NAICSID) and then use the Group By function to summarize by AgencyID.

The effect on performance is dramatic. Instead of carrying multiple detailed columns, you now have a single aggregated column that combines those details into one. The model refreshes faster, the tables are smaller, and performance improves.

If you haven't already done so, download the dataset included with this book (go to Kaggle at https://www.kaggle.com/jackhymanpowerbi/datasets) and import it into Power BI Desktop as I describe in Chapter 5. Then follow these steps:

1. **Open the Power Query Editor (Home ⇨ Transform Data).**

2. **In the Queries pane, select the Awards List table.**

3. **Click the Choose Columns button in the Manage Columns area of the Ribbon's Home tab (see Figure 10-2).**

FIGURE 10-2:
The Choose Columns icon on the Ribbon Home tab.

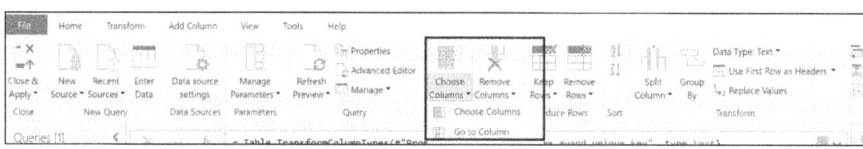

4. **Choose Columns (see Figure 10-3).**

   By selecting the Awards List table, all the fields available from that table will appear in the Choose Columns screen.

5. **Select** prime_award_funding_agency_name, prime_awardee_name, **and** prime_awards_naics_code **in the Choose Columns screen.**

   Selecting these three columns will be the first step in creating an aggregation entry.

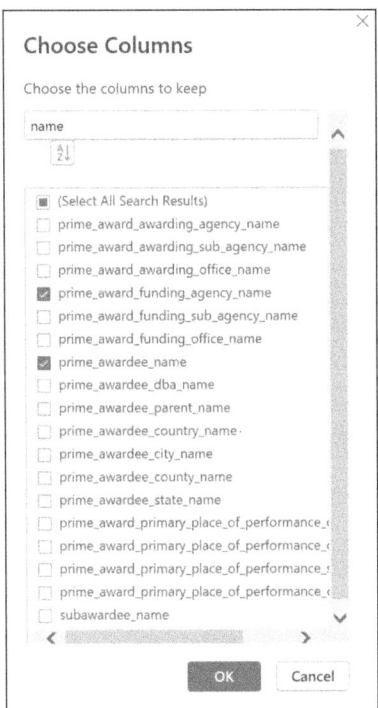

6. **Click OK.**

   You've now removed all but three columns. As noted in the Query Settings pane, you can see that the Power Query Editor acknowledges the columns being removed (Remove Other Columns). You now see just those three columns within the Power Query Editor, as shown in Figure 10-4.

7. **After the three columns are displayed in the Power Query Editor, click the Group By icon in the Transform area of the Ribbon's Home tab.**

8. **In the Group By window that appears, choose the item you want to group by (see Figure 10-5).**

   In this case, I chose prime_award_funding_agency_name.

   You should create a name for the new column. The name I have made is AgencyCount. In this case, I've created a new column name, selected Count Rows as the aggregation action, and chosen prime_award_funding_agency_ name to be the item aggregated when grouping by prime_award_funding_ agency_name, as shown in Figure 10-6.

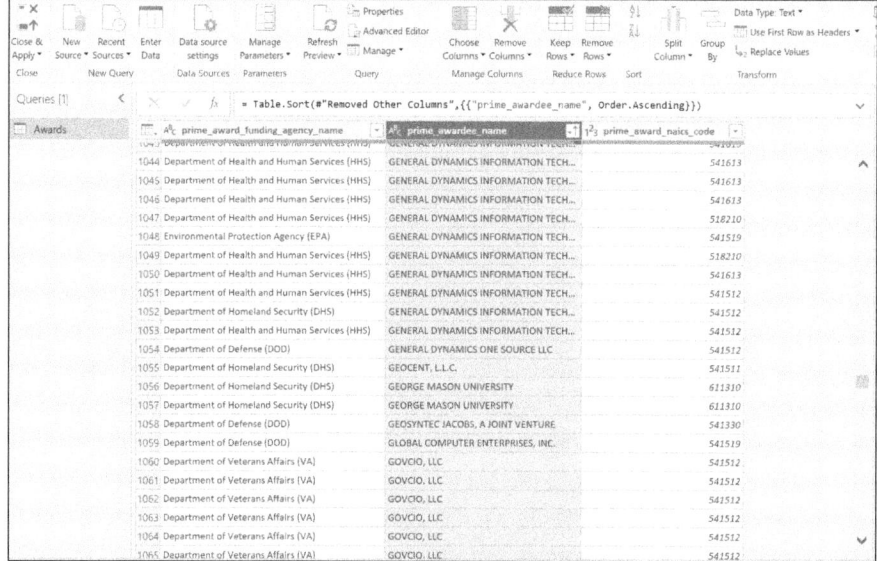

FIGURE 10-4:
Aggregated
columns in the
Power Query
Editor.

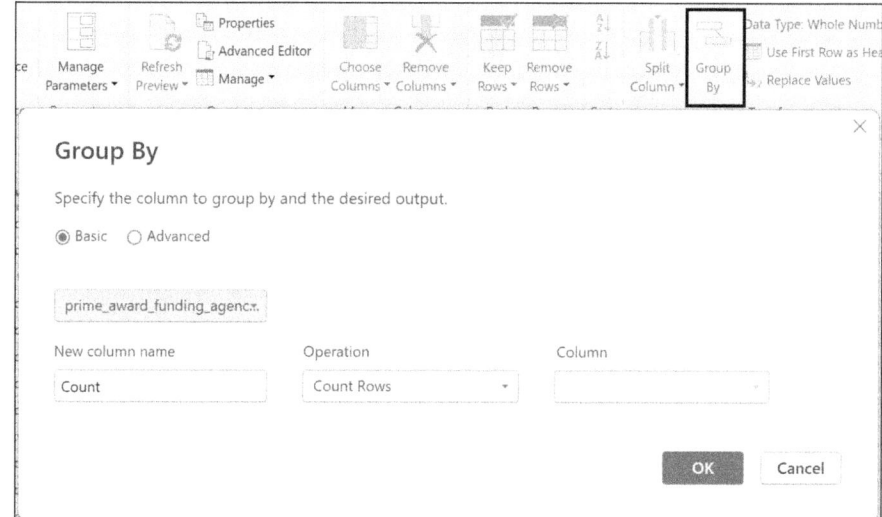

FIGURE 10-5:
The Group By
dialog box and its
interface in
Power Query.

The result is the aggregate count of rows grouped by prime_award_funding_ agency_name, so that instead of having multiple columns, you now only have one aggregate column with each prime_award_funding_agency_name. You've combined several columns into one, which supports better performance. You can see the aggregated result in Figure 10-7.

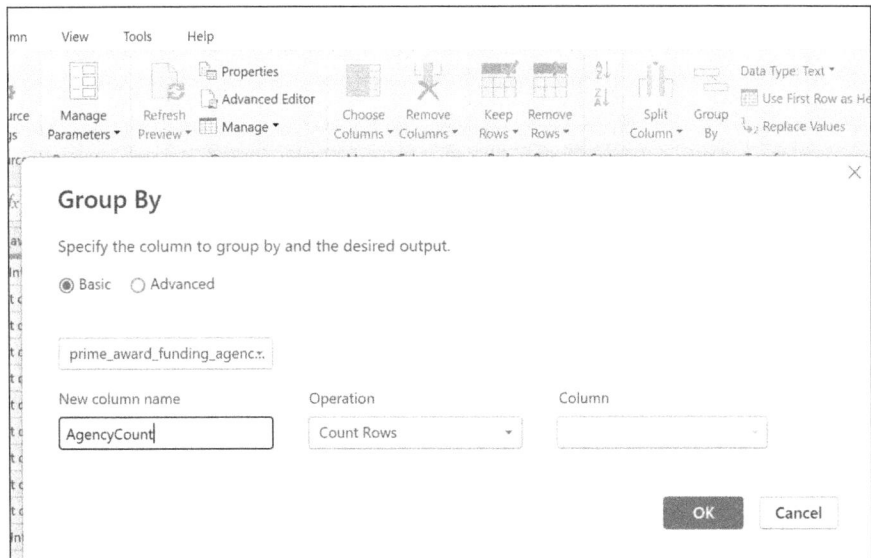

FIGURE 10-6:
Setting up the Group By feature to count rows for each funding agency.

	A^BC prime_award_funding_agency_name	1²3 AgencyCount
1	Department of Defense (DOD)	834
2	Department of the Treasury (TREAS)	70
3	Agency for International Development (USAID)	59
4	Department of Transportation (DOT)	71
5	Department of Health and Human Services (HHS)	360
6	Department of Homeland Security (DHS)	204
7	Department of Veterans Affairs (VA)	101
8	Department of Justice (DOJ)	10
9	Social Security Administration (SSA)	11
10	Department of Energy (DOE)	19
11	Department of Education (ED)	18
12	Environmental Protection Agency (EPA)	30
13	Department of Commerce (DOC)	7
14	Commodity Futures Trading Commission (CFTC)	10
15	National Aeronautics and Space Administration (N...	176
16	National Science Foundation (NSF)	6
17	Department of Housing and Urban Development (...	53
18	Department of the Interior (DOI)	8
19	Department of State (DOS)	7
20	Executive Office of the President (EOP)	2
21	Department of Agriculture (USDA)	3
22	Securities and Exchange Commission (SEC)	2

FIGURE 10-7:
The aggregated column.

9. **Click the Close & Apply button on the Ribbon Home tab to close the Power Query Editor.**

   You are now closing the Power Query Editor and going back to the Data Model View tab. This action saves all changes to the data model. The data model automatically refreshes, resulting in a significantly smaller data model because you've just pared down the criteria using the aggregation conditions. As shown in Figure 10-8, your new model has two columns instead of the 275+ columns from the original dataset you imported with the Awards Dataset.

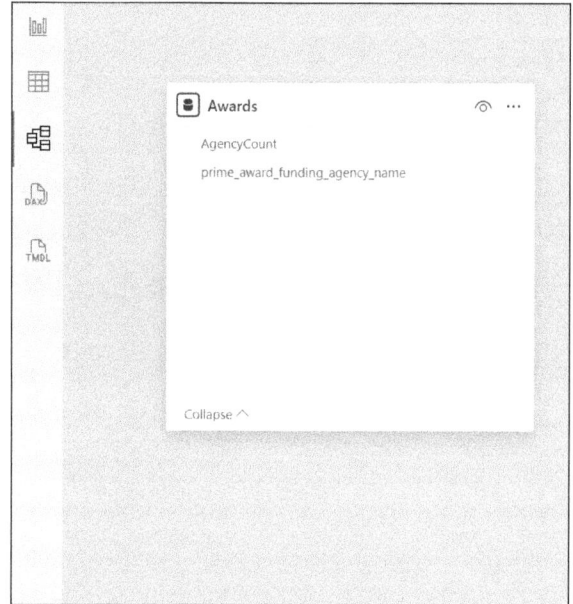

FIGURE 10-8:
The updated Data
Model view.

The managing part

It should come as no surprise that you need to manage the model, which may include relationships and aggregations in the Power BI Desktop environment after creating them, including managing their behavior.

Assuming that you want to add a third-party data source, such as an XLS, CSV, or TXT file, to your existing tables and there are some commonalities among the columns, you can make modifications to the model. To manage relationships from any Power BI Desktop environment, follow these steps:

1. **In the Data Model view, navigate to the Data pane on the right side of the model.**

2. **In the Data pane, right-click a table whose relationships you want to manage.**

   In this case, I selected the Awards List table to manage the aggregation created in the last section.

3. **Select Manage Relationships from the menu that appears (see Figure 10-9).**

   The Manage Relationships window appears in the list of options. You'll click it to create a new relationship between two tables.

4. **Click New Relationship.**

5. **In the Relationships Window, select the first table you want to establish a relationship.**

6. **Choose the column in the first table, and then select the related column in the second table.**

   Ideally, these columns should share the same name and data type.

7. **Pick the appropriate cardinality and cross-direction filtering based on your particular use case.**

8. **Click the Save button (see Figure 10-10).**

   You've now changed the original model aggregation based on the updated conditions you specified.

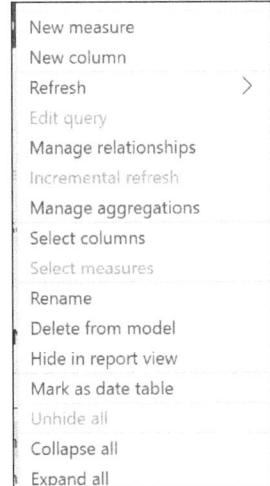

New measure
New column
Refresh   >
Edit query
Manage relationships
Incremental refresh
Manage aggregations
Select columns
Select measures
Rename
Delete from model
Hide in report view
FIGURE 10-9:   Mark as date table
Manage   Unhide all
aggregations   Collapse all
from the
Data pane.   Expand all

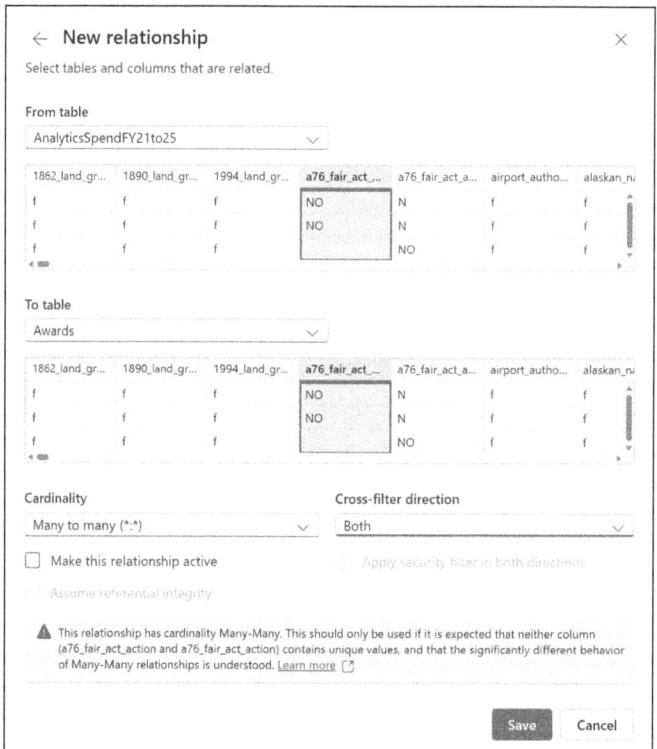

FIGURE 10-10:
Managing
aggregations.

Chapter **11**

Visualizing Data

ongratulations! You've got your data imported — maybe thousands, maybe millions of records — and now you're staring at it thinking, okay, what's this telling me? A visualization makes it easier to see patterns and trends, or perhaps even find that needle in the haystack. If you had to go row by row, column by column, it would be a bear. Depending on the type of data you want to explore, choosing the right visualization helps make your analysis more straightforward and gets you exactly where you need to be in a jiffy. In this chapter, I show you how to turn those boring rows and columns into charts and graphs that make sense.

Looking at Report Fundamentals and Visualizations

REMEMBER

Power BI has two main parts:

» **Power BI Desktop:** The app on your computer where you build your reports

» **Power BI Service:** An online interface that enables you to share your reports with others

You'll probably start most projects in Power BI Desktop, but here's the thing — Power BI Service has gotten much more powerful. You can edit charts, create new reports, and work with your team right in your web browser. These days, you can do most of what you used to need Power BI Desktop for right online. The upshot? You have flexibility. Do you need to make a quick edit while you're out of the office or on your tablet? Use Power BI Service. Want the complete set of tools? Power BI Desktop has you covered.

Creating visualizations

Assume that you have a semantic model stored in Power BI Desktop and want to create visualizations from it. Navigate to the Report view by clicking the Report button on the left-side navigation bar (see Figure 11-1).

FIGURE 11-1: The Report view button.

After you click the Report button, you enter the visualization interface. To create a chart or graph, select a visualization type from the Visualizations pane on the right side, and it will appear on the report canvas. Figure 11-2 shows the Report view in Power BI Desktop, where you build your visualizations.

In Report view, you can do the following:

➤➤ Select a visual type from the Visualizations pane

➤➤ Choose which data fields to include in a visual

➤➤ Add fields by dragging them from the Fields pane to a visual

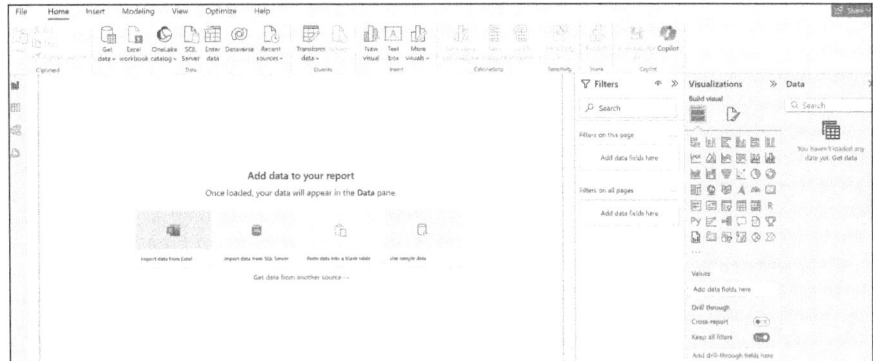

FIGURE 11-2:
Overview of
Report view
in Power BI.

>> Use the Ribbon tools to format and customize visuals

>> Ask questions about your data using natural language Q&A

You can add text boxes, shapes, and images to make your reports clearer and visually appealing. For multipage reports, you can include buttons and bookmarks to help users navigate between different pages and sections.

Choosing a visualization

The Visualizations pane of the Power BI Desktop Report view hosts a buffet's worth of visualization options that you can drag to the Report canvas. Out of the box, you get about twenty, but you can add more by downloading them from other app sources. Each visualization requires a user to select one or more fields from the Fields pane after dragging the visual to the canvas. A user must select the check box to include the field from the Data pane for a visual. Figure 11-3 shows an example of the Visualizations pane, and Figure 11-4 illustrates the associated Data pane.

TIP

Don't go check box crazy! It's tempting to throw every field you have into a chart, but that's a recipe for data glut. Stick to the fields that matter for what you're trying to show. Sometimes less really is more — a clean chart with three key data points beats a cluttered nightmare with fifteen any day of the week. Plus, your report will load faster!

Visualizations
Build visual
R
Py
Values
Add data fields here
Drill through
Cross-report
Off
Keep all filters
On
Add drill-through fields here

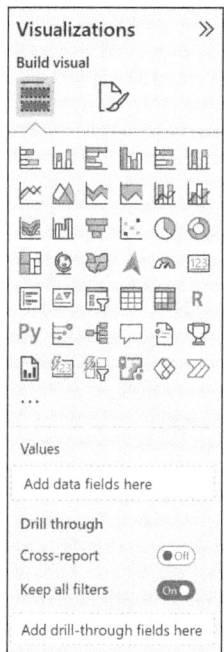

FIGURE 11-3: The Visualizations pane.

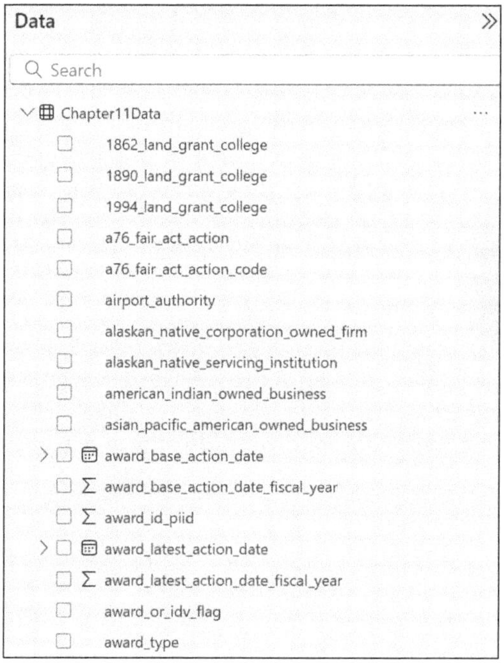

Data
Search
Chapter11Data
1862_land_grant_college
1890_land_grant_college
1994_land_grant_college
a76_fair_act_action
a76_fair_act_action_code
airport_authority
alaskan_native_corporation_owned_firm
alaskan_native_servicing_institution
american_indian_owned_business
asian_pacific_american_owned_business
award_base_action_date
award_base_action_date_fiscal_year
award_id_piid
award_latest_action_date
award_latest_action_date_fiscal_year
award_or_idv_flag
award_type

FIGURE 11-4: The Data pane.

Filtering data

You'll often need to filter your data while building a visualization. When you add fields to your chart, each one becomes something you can filter. If you're working with a large dataset, you'll probably want to narrow things down to what matters. Suppose that you have a field called *Award* with five different categories, plus a *Select All* option. You can pick which categories to show and hide the rest — maybe you only care about three of them (see Figure 11-5). Other times, you may want to filter by numbers. For example, if you're analyzing awards and only want to see the big ones that are worth more than $100,000, you can set up that filter condition (see Figure 11-6). Now you're looking at only the data that's relevant to your analysis.

ON THE WEB

To download the data used to build the visualizations, visit `https://www.kaggle.com/jackhymanpowerbi/datasets`. Once downloaded, you can import the dataset into Power BI Desktop (see Chapter 5) and start building the visuals step by step. Given the scope of the chapter, consider creating a separate file and calling it "Chapter 11 Dataset" for this data. This way, you can use the original dataset as intended for the chapter, not the one that you've modified in previous chapters.

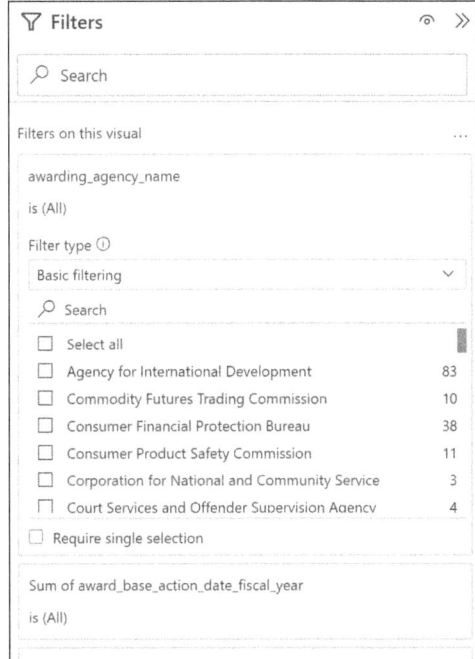

FIGURE 11-5:
Filtering data based on a category.

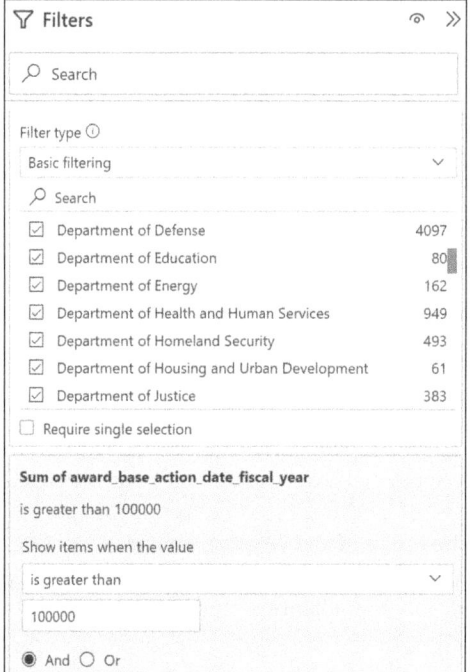

FIGURE 11-6:
Setting
up filtering
conditions with
quantitative data.

Working with bar charts and column charts

Power BI gives you several flavors of bar and column charts, and they're workhorses for comparing data. Think of them as your go-to charts when you want to line up different categories and see which one's bigger, smaller, or somewhere in between. Bar charts run horizontally, and column charts stack up vertically — but they both do the same job of making comparisons crystal clear at a glance.

Stacked bar charts and stacked column charts

Stacked charts are perfect when you want to compare categories while also showing what makes up each category. Think of them like walls made of different colored bricks — each color represents a different type, and you can see both how long each wall is overall and how many of each color brick went into building it.

With stacked bar charts, these brick walls stretch horizontally. With stacked column charts, they build up vertically like towers. Either way, you get two stories in one chart: how the categories compare overall, and what's inside each one.

Start simple with just two variables, but don't worry — Power BI can handle more complex breakdowns when you need them. For example, Figure 11-7 shows a basic stacked bar chart that examines the data of four agencies by PSC code (filtered), specifically DA01, DA10, and DB01. Each colored segment represents the percentage of the total that falls into each category.

Want to dig deeper? Add another layer, such as *"Agency,"* and observe the results (see Figure 11-8). Now, each agency gets its bar, and you can see how the award statuses break down differently for each one. Some agencies may submit awards in all four categories, and others may submit awards in only one or two.

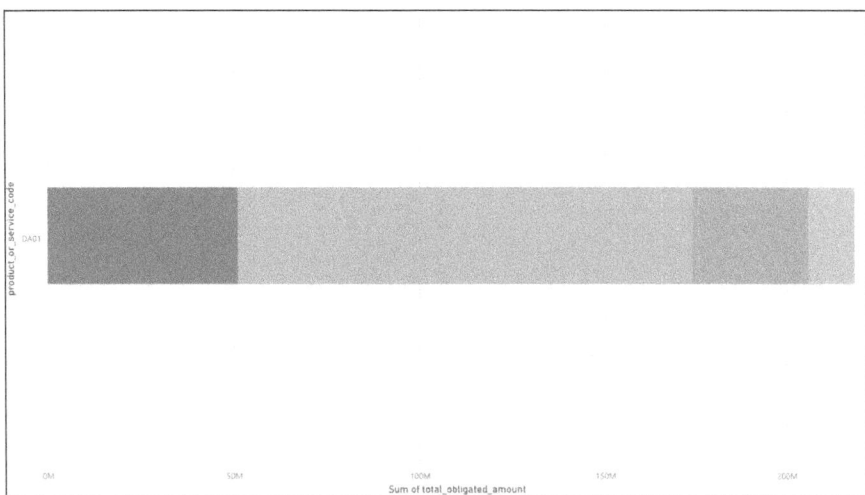

FIGURE 11-7:
A stacked
bar chart.

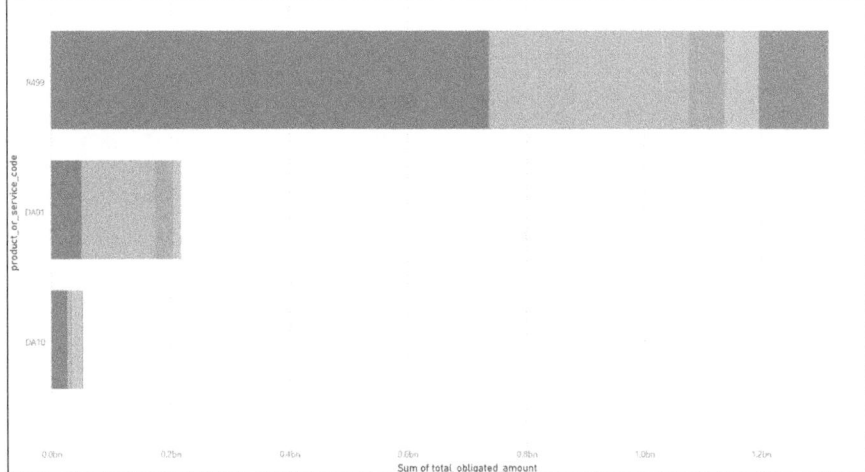

FIGURE 11-8:
Using multiple
dimensions in a
stacked bar chart.

A stacked column chart does the same thing as a stacked bar chart — it just goes up instead of sideways. You're looking at the same data and getting the same insights whether your bricks stack horizontally or stack vertically. Figure 11-9 shows the same data as in Figure 11-7 but in an upright orientation. The same applies to Figure 11-8 and Figure 11-10.

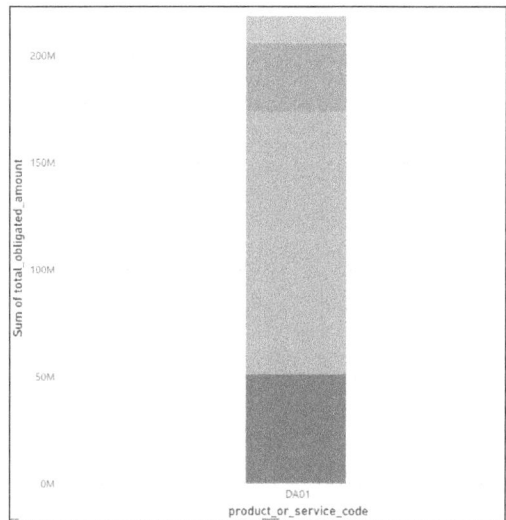

FIGURE 11-9:
A stacked
column chart.

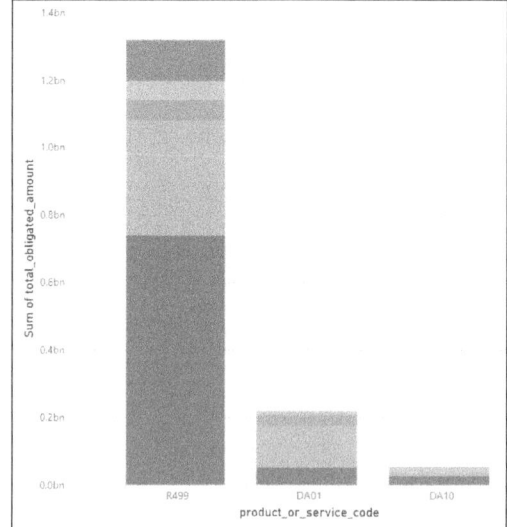

FIGURE 11-10:
Using multiple
dimensions
in a stacked
column chart.

Clustered bar charts and clustered column charts

Clustered charts take a different approach than stacked charts. Instead of piling everything into one big bar, a clustered chart spreads the data out side by side (or up and down). Think of it like parking cars — stacked charts are like a multi-level garage where cars stack on top of each other, and clustered charts are like a single-level parking lot where each car gets its own space, but everything is on the same level.

This side-by-side setup makes it much easier to compare individual values. Figure 11-11 shows a clustered bar chart, and Figure 11-12 shows the same data as a clustered column chart. Notice how you can quickly see that the four agencies have spent varying amounts on the specific PSC Code DA01. In this case, the Department of Health and Human Services outspends the other three agencies by a significant margin. The second-largest agency spender is the Department of Defense, followed by the Department of the Treasury, and then the Department of Veterans Affairs.

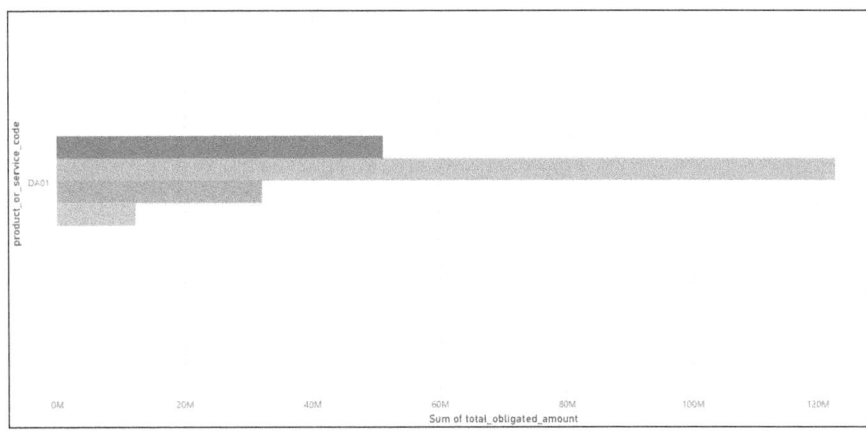

FIGURE 11-11: A clustered bar chart.

100% stacked bar charts and 100% stacked column charts

The 100% stacked charts put everything on a level playing field, allowing you to compare proportions instead of actual numbers. Using the charts shown in Figure 11-13 and Figure 11-14, for example, you can compare the distribution of government IT contracts between large companies and small businesses.

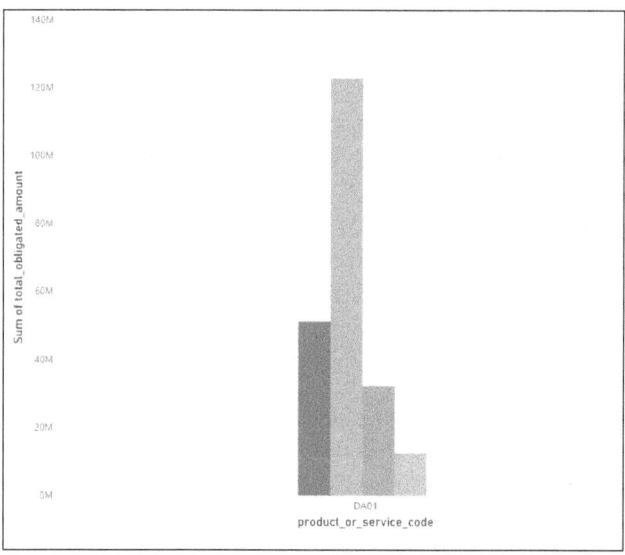

FIGURE 11-12:
A clustered
column chart.

Here's how to interpret the visuals: Companies with revenue over $35 million (considered large contractors) versus those under $35 million (small business contractors). I filtered the data to focus on specific IT-related industry codes (NAICS 541511, 541512, 541513, and 541519 — these cover computer programming, systems design, and related services) and compared two types of contract awards: regular "open competition" contracts versus those specifically "set aside" for small businesses. Even though large companies may win more total contract dollars, the 100% stacked chart lets you see what percentage of the total goes to each group for each NAICS code. This helps you spot patterns in how government contracting works. For instance, you may notice that small businesses capture a higher percentage of contracts for a specific NAICS when they are specifically set aside for them, compared to when they compete directly with large companies under other categories.

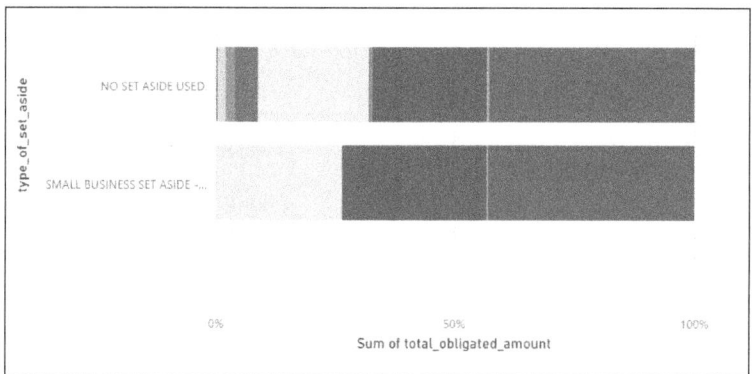

FIGURE 11-13:
A 100% stacked
bar chart.

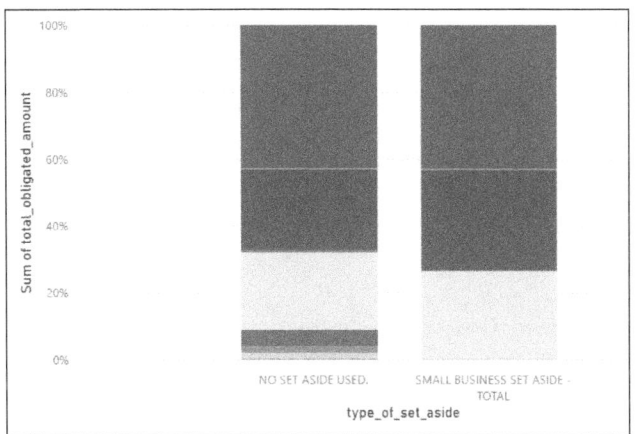

FIGURE 11-14:
A 100% stacked
column chart.

Using basic line charts and area charts

Line charts and area charts are your best friends when you want to show how something changes over time. Both work the same way — time goes along the bottom (x-axis), and your numbers go up the side (y-axis), but the data is presented differently. Line charts just connect the dots with a line, and area charts fill in the space below the line with color. I recommend using area charts when you want to emphasize the overall volume or when the area under the curve is essential.

Figure 11-15 and Figure 11-16 show the same data — the number of awards won over time. You can quickly spot that some years had more awards for analytics projects than others. In this case, you evaluate two data points: *award_latest action_date* in the X-axis and *awarding_agency_name* in the Y-axis.

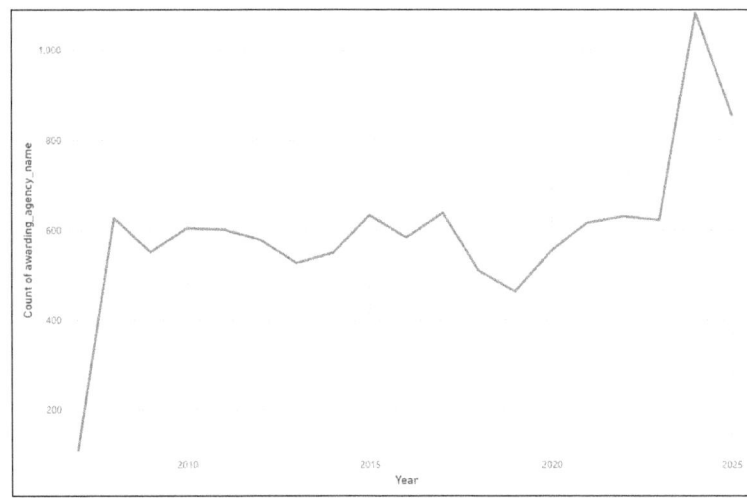

FIGURE 11-15:
A line chart.

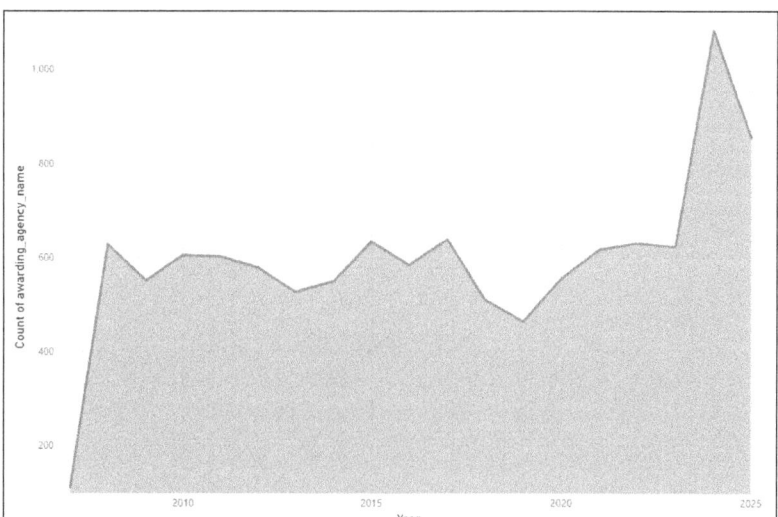

FIGURE 11-16:
An area chart.

Combining line charts and bar charts

Sometimes, you need to tell two stories on the same chart. One example may be displaying both sales revenue (in large numbers) and the number of customers (in smaller numbers) over time. That's where combo charts shine — you can mix a line chart with either stacked or clustered columns.

Figure 11-17 shows a perfect example. The line chart examines different types of government contract set-asides and tracks two key metrics: the amount of money committed (obligated) for each type (displayed as columns) and the actual expenditure (outlay), which is displayed as the line. Looking at the chart, you can see that 8A Sole Source Awards and Small Business contracts had both the highest commitments and the highest actual spending compared to other contract types. The combo chart lets you spot this pattern immediately — without it, you need two separate charts to see the whole picture.

Working with ribbon charts

Ribbon charts are helpful when you want to visualize trends and compare different categories against each other. The chart creates flowing bands that make it easy to follow how values change and compare across your data.

In Figure 11-18, you can see trends in funding across different states, with Virginia showing the highest dollar amounts and the District of Columbia showing the smallest. The different-colored ribbons represent the difference between what was allocated and what was spent, allowing you to track both overall funding trends and spending trends on a state-by-state basis over time.

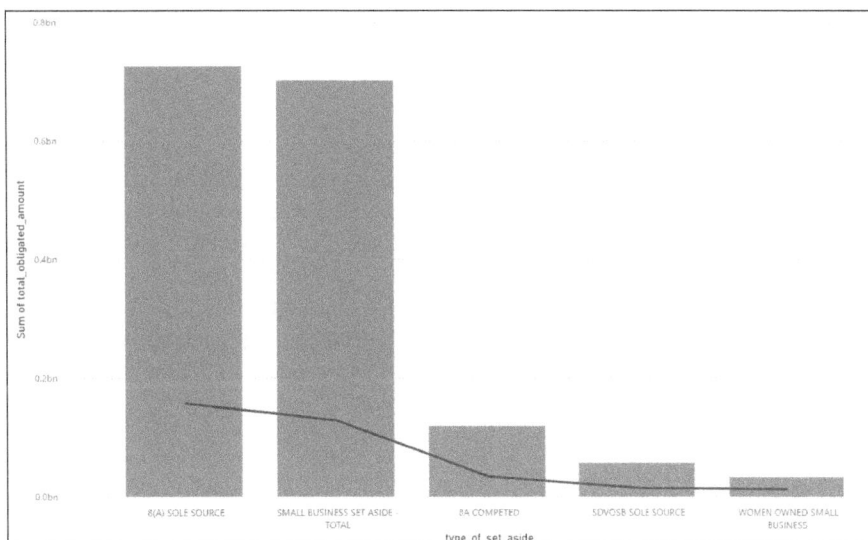

FIGURE 11-17: A line chart and a stacked column chart.

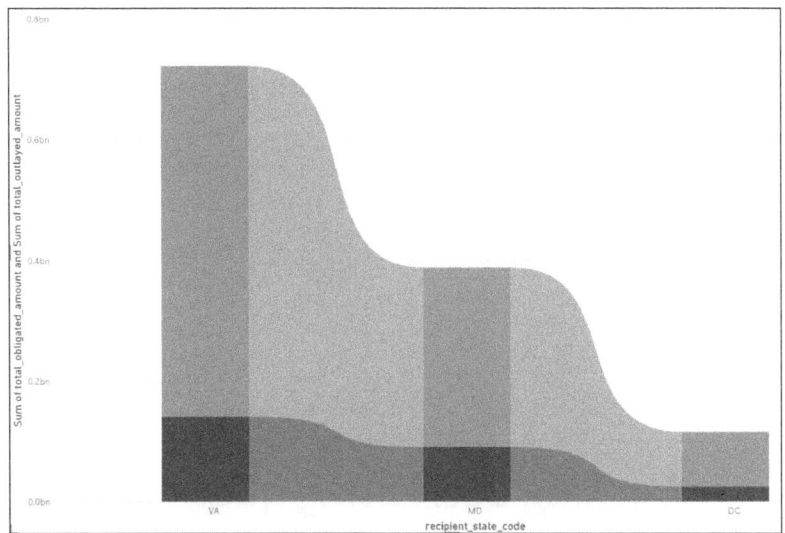

FIGURE 11-18: A ribbon chart.

Visualizing progressions with waterfall charts

Waterfall charts show how you get from point A to point B by breaking down all the steps in between. Think of them like tracking your bank account — you start with $1,000, add your $500 paycheck, subtract $200 for rent, and subtract $50 for groceries, ending up with $1,250. Each step up or down is visible. Waterfall charts are ideal for illustrating changes in budgets, profit and loss breakdowns, or any scenario where you want to visualize the progression from your starting point to your outcome.

Figure 11-19 shows how funding is distributed across three states and various industry types (as defined by NAICS codes). The chart shows how the total funding amount gets allocated, with each bar representing either an addition or subtraction to reach the final totals for each state. In this example, MD, VA, and DC account for the total spend on analytics in NAICS 541511, 541512, 541513, and 541519, as shown with the bar on the right. Virginia got the lion's share of that spending, with $1.32 billion compared to Maryland's $311 million and DC's $8 million.

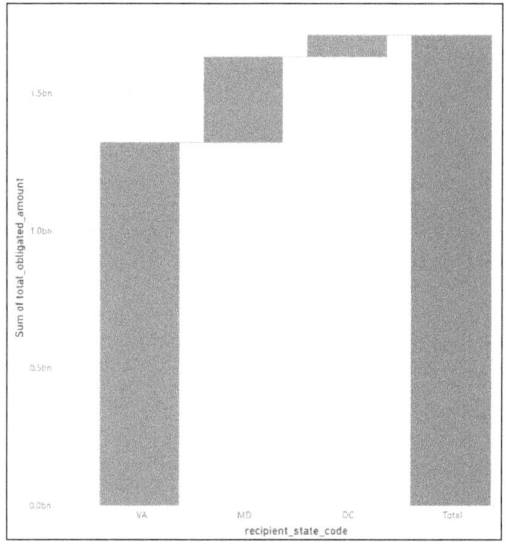

FIGURE 11-19:
A waterfall chart.

Tracking decreasing quantities with funnel charts

Funnel charts are ideal for illustrating how quantities decrease at each stage of a process, or for comparing different-sized items within your data. Think of an actual funnel — you pour a lot in at the top and less comes out at each level. The classic example is a sales funnel: You may start with 1,000 leads; 500 become prospects, 100 become quotes, and 20 become actual sales. Each stage gets smaller and smaller, which is precisely what a funnel chart shows.

Figure 11-20 shows total contract values by state, arranged in a funnel format. Each bar represents all contracts awarded to a different state, with the states ranked from highest total value (at the top) to lowest (at the bottom). You can immediately see which states received the most contract dollars and how they compare to each other. The percentages show what portion of the total contract spending each state represents.

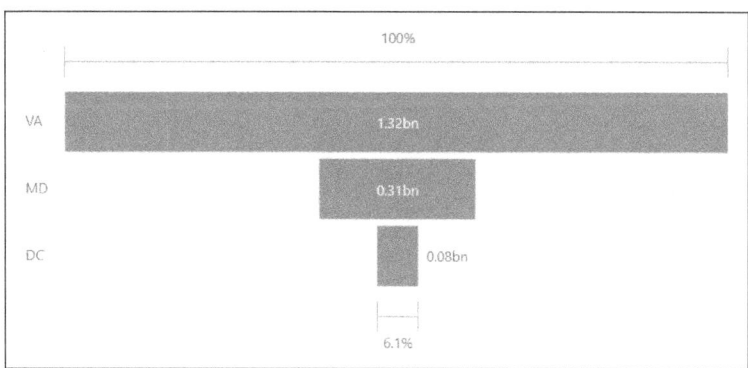

FIGURE 11-20:
A funnel chart.

TECHNICAL STUFF

Many charts in this chapter offer detailed data filtering options. That's because each chart type has different options that you can customize in the Visualizations pane. No matter which chart you're building, you'll likely work with these key areas in the formatting section:

>> **Categories:** What goes along your horizontal axis (like months, states, or product names). You can add multiple categories to create more detailed breakdowns.

>> **Breakdown:** Lets you split your data into smaller groups to compare them (such as showing sales by region and by product type).

>> **Values:** The actual numbers you want to display (like sales amounts, quantities, or percentages).

>> **Tooltips:** Those helpful pop-up boxes that appear when you hover over parts of your chart, giving extra details about that specific data point.

Identifying relationships with scatter charts

Do you have two sets of numbers and want to see if they're related? A scatter chart, also known as a scatterplot, is ideal for this purpose. They plot dots on a grid to show whether your data points have a relationship — do higher values in one area tend to go with higher values in another? With scatter charts, when dots cluster together in a line or pattern, there's probably a relationship. When they're scattered all over the place, there may not be much connection.

Figure 11-21 illustrates an excellent example in which I've filtered the data to display all obligations and outlays exceeding $5 million. Most states cluster together in the lower quadrants of the chart. Still, a few stand out as outliers — Maryland, Virginia, California, Oklahoma, and Colorado obligations are the most predominant, hence they are at the top of the scatter chart for a majority of the commitments.

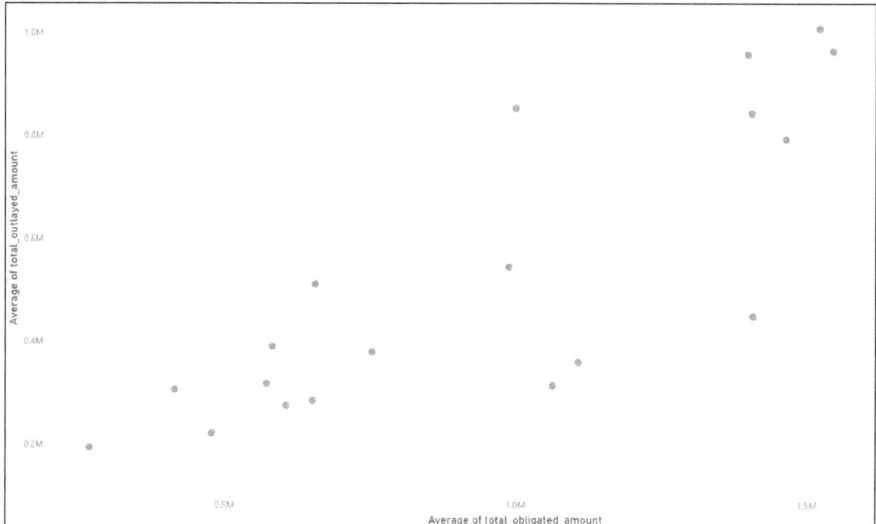

FIGURE 11-21:
Scatterplot.

Eyeing percentages with pie charts and donut charts

Pie charts are the classic "slice of the pie" visualization — they take your data and divide it into wedges that show what percentage each piece represents. Everything adds up to 100 percent, just like cutting up an actual pizza. Donut charts do the same thing but with a hole in the middle (think of it as a pie chart that's been turned into a bagel). The data is identical — it's just a style preference. Some people find donut charts easier to read, and others prefer the classic pie chart look.

Figure 11-22 and Figure 11-23 show how many awards for the states of Maryland and Virginia were distributed against the set-aside field *type_of_set_aside*. You can see how the different set-aside statuses break down as percentages of the total. Whether you choose pie or donut style, you get the same insights about your data.

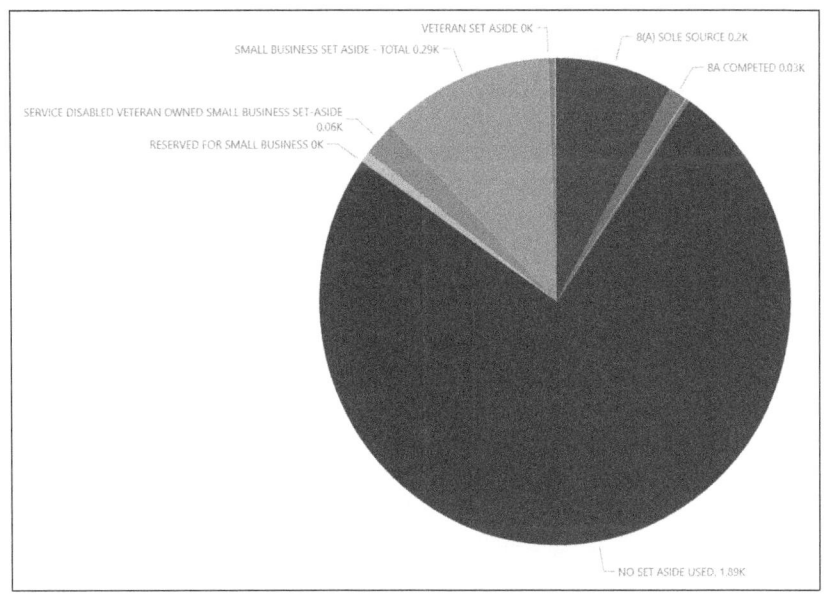

FIGURE 11-22:
A pie chart.

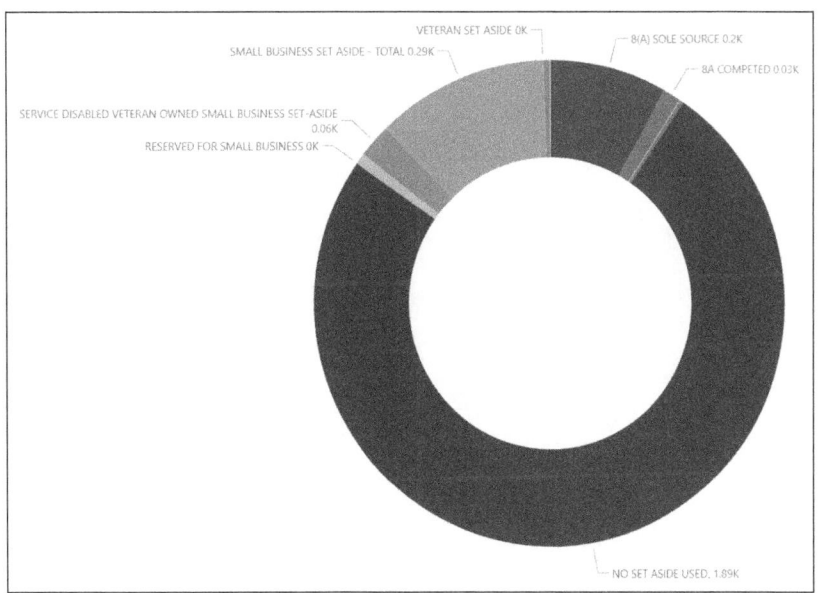

FIGURE 11-23:
A donut chart.

Branching out with treemaps

Treemaps are great for showing "big picture" data where size matters. Think of them like a floor plan where bigger rooms represent bigger values. Each rectangle's size is proportional to the data it represents — the bigger the number, the bigger the box. Treemaps organize data in a hierarchy similar to a family tree, but instead of names, you get boxes of varying sizes. The layout flows from left to right, with the most significant values typically appearing on the left side and smaller ones filling in the remaining space.

Figure 11-24 shows how different agencies allocated their business intelligence tool budgets, specifically comparing the purchases of IBM Cognos and Tableau. The bigger the rectangle, the more money the agency spent on these tools. You can immediately see which agencies made the most significant investments in premium licenses. Keep in mind that to see these results, I had to filter using the following fields: *prime_award_base_transaction_description* contains either Cognos or Tableau. For values, Category should be *awarding_agency_name,* and both Details and Values should be *total_obligated_amount.*

TIP

You can add more fields to the treemap to show additional layers of detail. For example, beyond just showing agencies and dollars obligated, you may add sub-agencies, PSC, or NAICS Codes to create a more detailed breakdown of how money is being spent across different organizations.

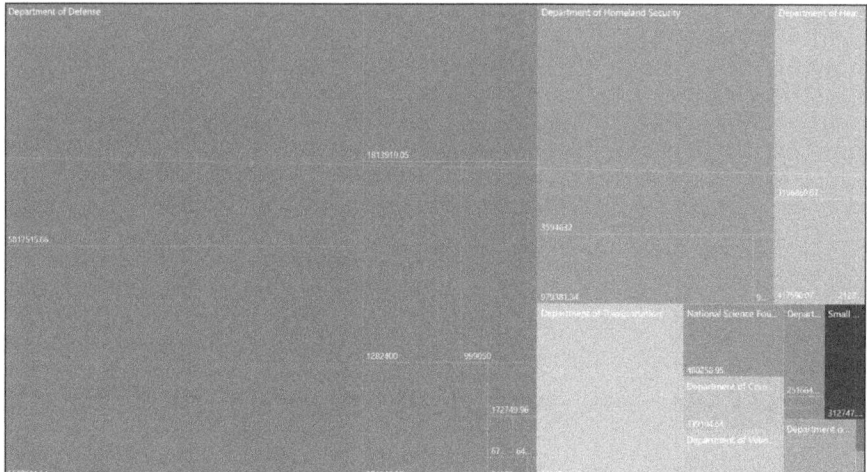

FIGURE 11-24:
A treemap.

Representing where data occurs with maps

Power BI has some solid mapping capabilities that may surprise you. You can create maps using location data, addresses, or even latitude and longitude coordinates to visually represent where your data is occurring. Maps are perfect when you want to see patterns across different locations, like which regions are spending the most, where your customers are concentrated, or how programs are distributed across the country. Power BI automatically adjusts the zoom and focus to show your data clearly, and you can choose between regular maps (showing data points) or filled maps (coloring entire regions).

Figure 11-25 shows where government agencies are spending the most on analytics and AI initiatives across the United States. You can immediately spot the hot spots — certain states have much larger investments in these technologies than others. The map reveals geographic patterns that would be difficult to discern in a long laundry list of data points or a raw dataset.

Figure 11-26 shows a filled map that colors entire regions based on the data. Here's where it gets interesting — you can zoom in for a closer look at specific areas. From far away, you can spot the major hot spots where spending is concentrated. Still, when you zoom in closer, you'll discover more detailed patterns that tell a richer story about how analytics investments are distributed.

FIGURE 11-25:
A map.

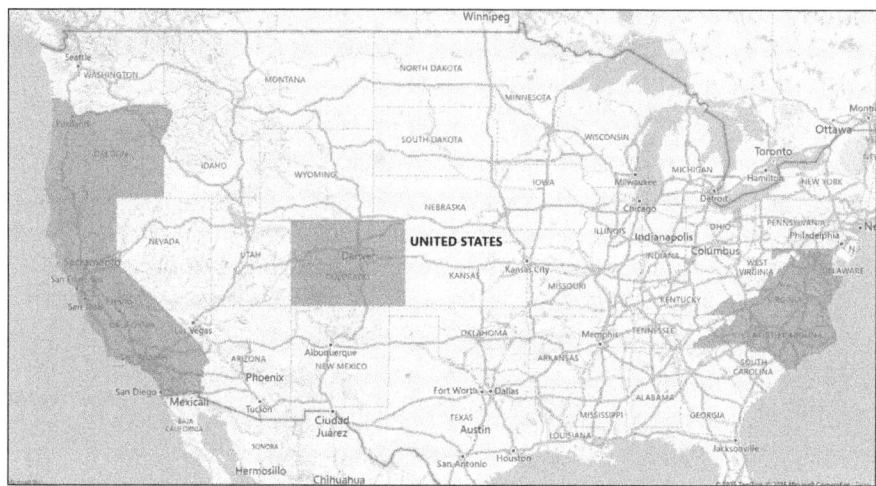

FIGURE 11-26:
A filled map.

Showing progress with indicators

Sometimes you need to show how you're doing against your goals — are you on track, ahead, or falling behind? That's where indicator visuals come in handy. They're perfect for displaying key metrics at a glance, much like dashboard lights in your car that indicate that everything is running smoothly. In the following sections, I describe indicator visuals you may consider using in your Power BI visualizations.

Gauges

The first indicator type you want to consider is the gauge. A gauge looks just like the speedometer in your car — it shows where you stand compared to your target. Gauges are ideal for tracking items such as budget spending, sales goals, or project completion rates.

In Figure 11-27, you see small business contract spending. The government budgeted $184.4 million for Fiscal Year 2024 for analytics contracts but spent only $92.2 million, or just under 50% of the obligated amount. The gauge indicates that government spending is in the safe zone — spending is on track without exceeding the budget. You need to define two values: the minimum value and the maximum value. In this case, the minimum value is *total_outlayed_amount,* and the maximum value is *total_obligated_amount.*

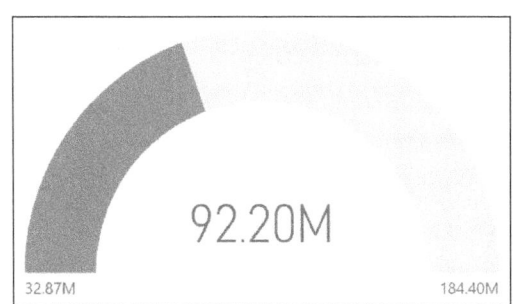

FIGURE 11-27:
Using a gauge.

Cards and multi-cards

Sometimes, you need just one number to tell your story — such as total sales, the number of customers, or the percentage of work effort completed. That's where cards are a handy tool. They display a single key metric, making it impossible to miss the most important number on your report. Figure 11-28 shows a simple card indicating the number of contracts awarded. Clean, simple, and to the point. And better yet, you only need a single column to generate a result. In this case, I used the *total_obligated amount* to identify that between Fiscal Year 2022 and Fiscal Year 2025, $4.23 billion was obligated for analytics projects.

Want to show multiple key numbers together? Use a multi-card visual. Just add more fields to create additional cards that sit side by side. Figure 11-29 shows three cards together — set-aside, obligated amount, and total obligated — providing a quick snapshot of the key metrics for how money was spent versus what was obligated based on the set-aside.

4.23bn

Sum of total_obligated_amount

FIGURE 11-28:
A card visual.

SMALL BUSINESS SET ASIDE - TOTAL	
352,726,973.87	125,995,521.69
Sum of total_obligated_amount	Sum of total_outlayed_amount

8A COMPETED

65,114,918.23	33,759,002.69
Sum of total_obligated_amount	Sum of total_outlayed_amount

FIGURE 11-29:
A multi-card visual.

Key performance indicators

Key performance indicator (KPI) visuals are perfect when you want to show not just a number, but how that number compares to your goal. Think of it like a sales scorecard — it shows your current performance and whether you're hitting your target or falling short.

To create a KPI visual, you need three key elements: your actual number, your target number, and a time frame to illustrate the trend. The visual will display your current status and show a small trend line in the background, allowing you to see whether you're moving in the right direction.

Figure 11-30 illustrates KPI tracking of obligations versus outlay over time. You can view the current average, compare it to the target, and determine whether the trend is increasing or decreasing. In this case, the average spend is 65.46% less than the obligated amount. The average analytics contract value for the period from fiscal year 2022 to 2025 was $240.87K

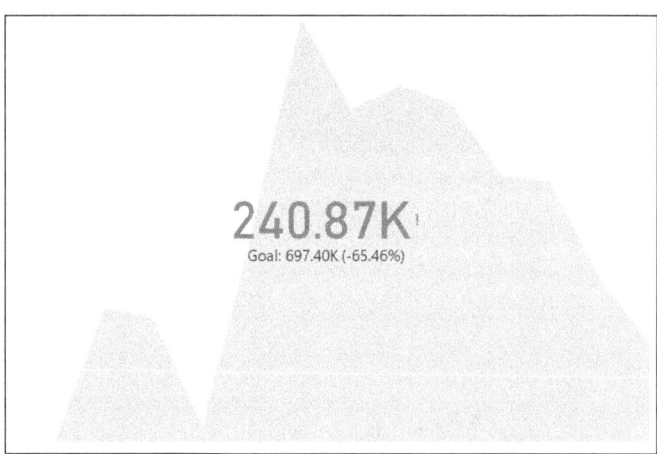

FIGURE 11-30:
A KPI example.

TECHNICAL
STUFF

Although there may be many indicators you are interested in evaluating, you can only assign a single value as your KPI. The same is true for the target and trend axis. You need to adjust the data category parameters to precisely calculate the output, whether you're looking for average, sum, distinct (single instances), or another measure.

TIP

Use the card visual only if there's a single value to display. If you need to compare a value against more than one target, use the KPI visual — it offers users the ability to add trends in the background. Though it has limited information, the data is nonetheless focused. The multi-card option can fulfill the business requirement for those looking to compile unrelated metrics on a single page.

Dealing with Table-Based and Complex Visualizations

Even though a picture may be worth a thousand words, you may need a bit of textual context. That's when you would still want to sort through detailed records, compare multiple dimensions at once, or let users filter the data themselves. That's where the Power BI table-based visuals and advanced analysis tools come in.

These tools include everything from simple data tables and interactive slicers to sophisticated visuals, such as decomposition trees, that help you drill down layer by layer to identify what is truly influencing your numbers. Think of them as your detective tools for when you need to investigate the story behind the story in your charts.

Laser focusing on data with slicers

Would you like to let users filter your report themselves? Slicers are perfect for this. Think of them like the filters on an online shopping site — users can click to select exactly what they want to see (size, color, price range, brand) and the results update instantly to show only items that match their choices.

Slicers sit right on your report page, so users can easily narrow down to the specific data they care about. Figure 11-31 shows a typical slicer in action, reducing a dataset to just a few targeted records.

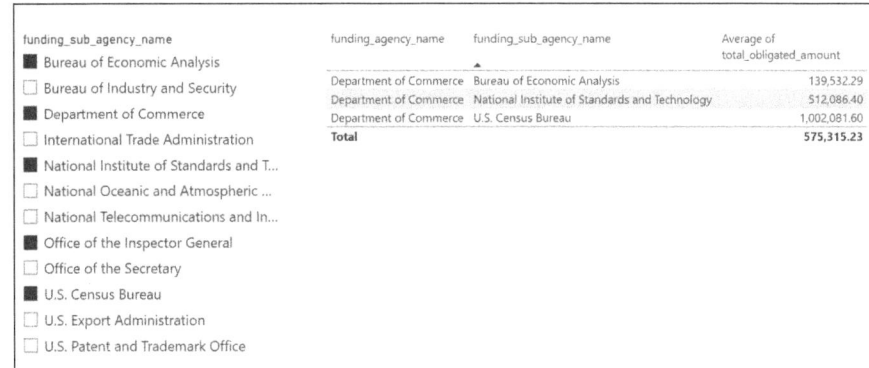

FIGURE 11-31:
A slicer tied to a table.

Digging into data with table visualizations

You may wonder, "Why not just look at my raw data if I want to see it in table format?" Good question! The difference is that Power BI table visuals provide a quick fix that raw data doesn't, such as instant sorting, filtering, and the ability to summarize information in a handy table format on the fly. A chart may show you the big picture, but tables let you drill into the details. Some conditions you may want to use a table visual for include evaluating exact numbers, patterns of high to low values, or determining whether a record meets a specific criterion. That's where table visuals are your go-to visual option.

Figure 11-32 shows a table that's been filtered to display only contract award values tied to the Department of Commerce. The values have been aggregated to display the average award obligation amount for each agency within the Department of Commerce. If you combine this table with the slicer shown in Figure 11-31, you can focus down to a specific line item.

funding_agency_name	funding_sub_agency_name	Average of total_obligated_amount
Department of Commerce	Bureau of Economic Analysis	139,532.29
Department of Commerce	Bureau of Industry and Security	1,835,224.64
Department of Commerce	International Trade Administration	484,224.47
Department of Commerce	National Institute of Standards and Technology	512,086.40
Department of Commerce	National Oceanic and Atmospheric Administration	455,178.05
Department of Commerce	National Telecommunications and Information Administration	5,761,639.57
Department of Commerce	Office of the Secretary	441,372.10
Department of Commerce	U.S. Census Bureau	1,002,081.60
Department of Commerce	U.S. Patent and Trademark Office	943,376.31
Total		**726,027.74**

FIGURE 11-32: Table visualization.

Combing through data with matrices

Matrices let you compare data across multiple categories at the same time. Unlike regular tables that show data in simple rows and columns, matrices create a grid where you can see how different factors relate to each other. Use matrices when you need to break down data by more than one dimension, such as contracts by multiple regions, or perhaps by product versus service type, or performance across different periods and agencies. You can expand and collapse different sections to focus on specific details.

Figure 11-33 shows a matrix that compares different agencies with the types of IT contracts they award (using industry codes 541511, 541512, 541513, and 541519, which cover computer programming and systems design services). The matrix is expanded to show details for the Department of Health and Human Services, revealing that only the Food and Drug Administration and the National Institutes of Health awarded contracts across all four types of IT services.

funding_agency_name	541511	541512	541513	541519	Total
⊞ Corps of Engineers - Civil Works		1		1	2
⊞ Council of the Inspectors General on Integrity and Efficiency	1			1	2
⊞ Court Services and Offender Supervision Agency		1			1
⊞ Department of Agriculture	10	14		16	39
⊞ Department of Commerce	4	7		21	30
⊞ Department of Defense	60	49	6	84	174
⊞ Department of Education	6	4		7	17
⊞ Department of Energy	2	1		8	11
⊟ Department of Health and Human Services	28	31	4	50	103
Administration for Children and Families		1			1
Agency for Healthcare Research and Quality	1				1
Centers for Disease Control and Prevention	4	8		3	
Centers for Medicare and Medicaid Services	6	9		4	17
Department of Health and Human Services				2	2
Food and Drug Administration	6	5	2	20	30
Health Resources and Services Administration	1	2		2	5
Indian Health Service	1	1			2
National Institutes of Health	10	4		15	27
Office of Assistant Secretary for Preparedness and Response		2		1	3
Office of the Assistant Secretary for Administration	3	4	2	3	12
Office of the Inspector General				1	1
Substance Abuse and Mental Health Services Administration		1		1	2
⊞ Department of Homeland Security	16	23		25	62
⊞ Department of Housing and Urban Development	2	2	1	1	6
⊞ Department of Justice	6	9		22	34
⊞ Department of Labor	1	3		7	11
Total	191	187	21	268	581

FIGURE 11-33: A matrix.

Breaking down data with decomposition trees

Decomposition trees help you break down your data step by step, like peeling an onion to see what's inside each layer. Start with your big number at the top, then drill down to see what's driving that total — maybe a program, a service provider, or an agency. Think of it like asking "what's behind this number?" and getting to click through the answers. You may start with aggregate value and then see how that breaks down by state, then by customer type within each state, and so on.

Figure 11-34 shows a decomposition tree that begins with the total number of analytics contract recipients. Click down one level to see how this breaks out across the four different types of IT services (NAICS codes 541511-541519). Dig even deeper and you'll discover which agencies are funding every kind of contract. The final layer shows which specific office within each agency is writing the checks. In this example, you can see that most of the systems design contracts (NAICS 541512) at the Department of Health and Human Services are funded by the Center for Medicare and Medicaid Services.

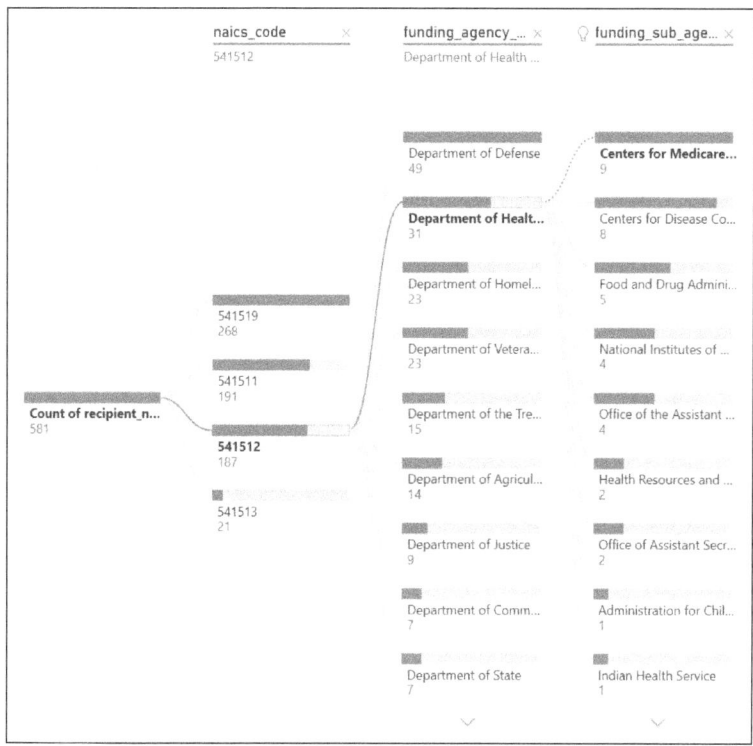

FIGURE 11-34:
A decomposition
tree.

Focusing in on key influencers

Ever look at a chart and wonder, "What's driving these results?" The Key Influencers visual is designed to answer that question. It uses AI to analyze your data and identify the factors that have the most significant impact on the outcome you're measuring. Key Influencers provides a comprehensive view of both the big picture and the details. You'll see which factors matter most, along with a scatter plot that shows how all your data points relate to one another. It's like having a data detective that automatically finds the most important patterns.

Figure 11-35 shows Key Influencers analyzing what drives high 8A Sole Source contract awards by state. The analysis reveals that Alabama (AL) has an unusually high percentage of these specialized small business contracts (8.62%) compared to the national average. Key Influencers identified this as significant because only Virginia (28.98%) and Maryland (13.32%) have higher rates of 8A Sole Source awards. This suggests that certain states have factors that make them more likely to use this specific type of contracting approach. In this case, that factor is the high density of government agencies located in these states.

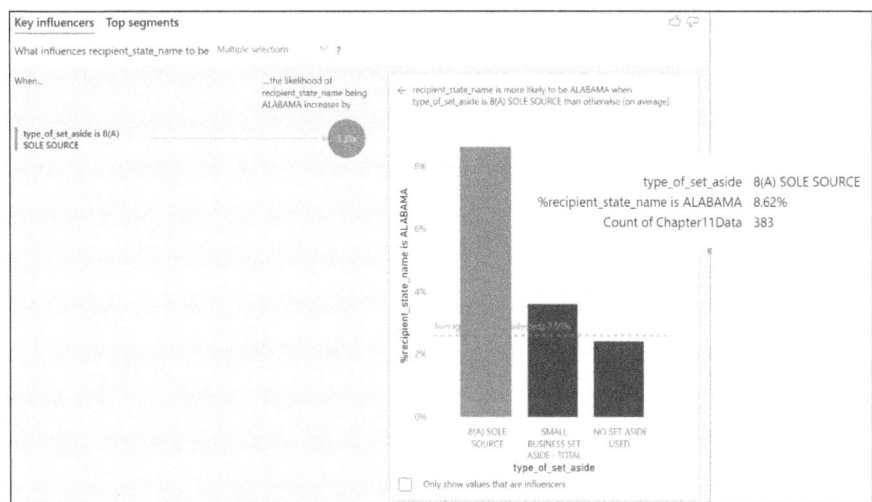

FIGURE 11-35: Working with key influencers.

Creating Charts with the Q&A Feature

Power BI's Q&A feature enables you to ask questions about your data using everyday language, eliminating the need to create charts manually. Type something like "show me all awards for a company," and Power BI will create a chart for you. The feature analyzes your data and suggests relevant questions based on which fields you have available. You can either use these suggestions (shown in Figure 11-36) or enter your questions (see Figure 11-37). If Power BI doesn't understand your question, try rephrasing it or using simpler terms, as if you were speaking to someone.

In Figure 11-37, I entered the question: How many HUBZONE SET-ASIDE? In the Chapter 11 Data, 13 distinct companies were found.

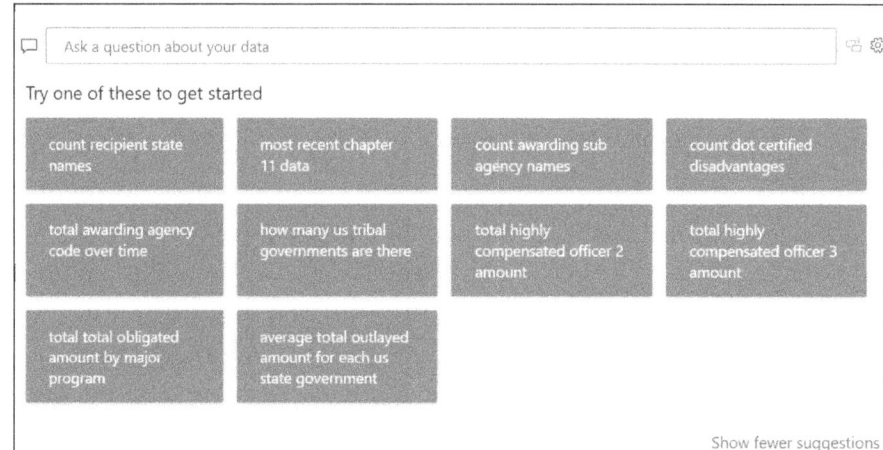

FIGURE 11-36:
Prescribed
questions
and answers.

FIGURE 11-37:
Self-created
questions
and answers.

Adding Smart Narratives for Busy People

Sometimes you need to explain what your charts show in plain text, especially for busy executives. Smart Narratives can help with this. If your organization has Fabric capacity, you can add a Smart Narrative visual to your report and tell it what you want it to focus on, and Power BI will generate a written summary based on the other visuals on your page. For the example shown in Figure 11-38, I created a table with about twenty data fields on a separate report page. Using Smart Narratives, I asked it to make an executive summary of key takeaways from that table. After I clicked Update, Power BI generated the text-based report shown on the left side of the window in Figure 11-38.

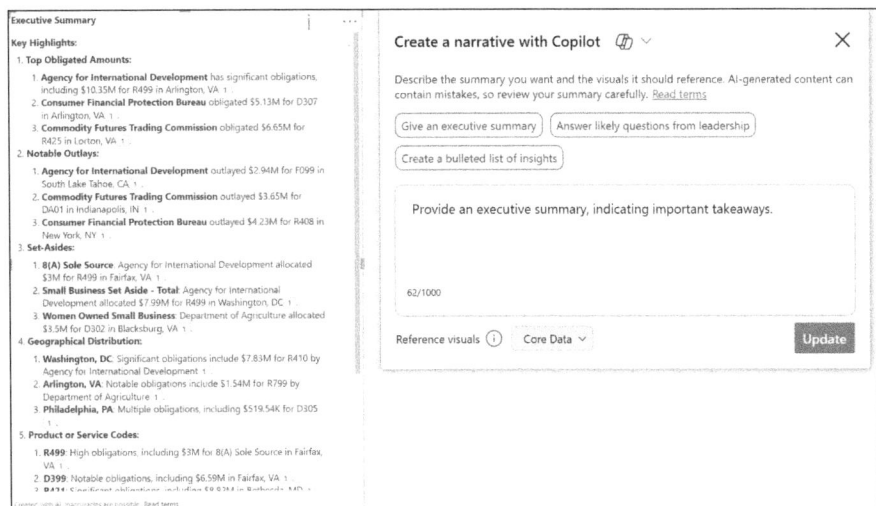

FIGURE 11-38:
Smart Narratives.

WARNING

As of mid-2025, Smart Narratives requires Fabric Capacity (F2 or higher) licensing. This feature is not available with Pro, Free, or Trial licenses. These enterprise-level licenses are significantly more expensive, so check your organization's licensing availability before building reports that depend on this feature.

TECHNICAL STUFF

ADVANCED OPTIONS FOR DATA SCIENCE

For users with programming experience, both Power BI Desktop and Service support Python and R scripting to create custom visualizations and advanced analytics. You can find these options in the Visualizations pane alongside the standard charts. These script-based visuals are ideal for specialized statistical analysis, custom charts, or advanced data science work that exceeds the built-in capabilities of Power BI. If you're interested in exploring these advanced options, see the Microsoft documentation for the latest supported packages and capabilities at https://learn.microsoft.com/en-us/power-bi/connect-data/desktop-python-scripts.

Chapter **12**

Pumping Out Reports

hink of each visualization you can create using Power BI as offering a different set of insights for a dataset. Visualizations can be used stand-alone or combined with other visuals to create your report. Whether simple or complex, the output of a visualization is an end-state deliverable: a report. Although it's not uncommon for a report to include a single visualization, having multiple visualizations can offer a tremendous perspective to an organization. Depending on the user's role, the report can also take on many different lives. Some users may be the report's designer, and others may be the consumer of report data. This chapter uncovers how to configure visuals and report settings for end-user consumption using Power BI Desktop and Power BI Service.

Formatting and Configuring Report Visualizations

All visuals in Power BI are configurable in some shape or form. Although some visualizations have report-specific configurations based on their predefined criteria, many formatting options are common across all visuals. Regardless, you can format a visual by selecting the item and clicking the handy Paint Roller icon in the Visualizations pane (see Figure 12-1) to access the formatting tools.

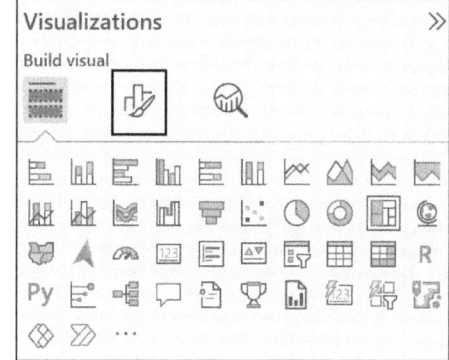

FIGURE 12-1:
Formatting features found in the Visualizations pane.

Here's a description of some common formatting choices:

>> **General formatting:** Here's where you can select the *x*-position, *y*-position, width, height, and *alt text* — the description used for accessibility options.

>> **Title:** Format the title text, word wrapping, color (font and background), and text features (alignment, font size, and font face).

>> **Background:** Set the page and visualization background.

>> **Lock aspect:** Lock a visual element based on the proportion of the specific object on the canvas.

>> **Borders:** Format the border colors and radii of your visuals.

>> **Shadow:** Set the shadow color and position.

>> **Tooltips:** Format any default or report-specific tooltips (descriptors).

>> **Headers:** Hide or show headers based on conditions.

Many other options are available, depending on the visualization. The list I came up with here covers only the ones you see across all visualizations.

Working with basic visualization configurations

Don't confuse *visualization* configurations and *report* configurations. The difference is that each time you include a visualization in a report, you're free to configure that particular visualization with specific settings. A *report* configuration affects the layout and design of all your visualizations on a single page.

You need to have one or more visualizations on a page in order to generate a report. Each time you want to configure the visualization, you select the particular visualization in the Canvas window and click the Visualizations pane's Paint Roller icon. That action brings up the visualization formatting settings.

When trying to configure the position and size of a visualization, go to the General section (see Figure 12-2) and choose from the following:

>> **Responsive:** This allows for the visualization to be adjustable based on the canvas size. It automatically adjusts on your behalf.

>> **X-Position:** The visual will be positioned from the left edge of the canvas at this coordinate.

>> **Y-Position:** The visual will be positioned from the top edge of the canvas at this coordinate.

>> **Width:** The horizontal size for the visualization.

>> **Height:** The vertical size for the visualization.

>> **Maintain layer order:** Selecting this option automatically brings the visualization to the front, above other overlapping visuals. Deselecting pushes the visualization backward.

>> **Alt-Text:** The ability to textually describe the visualization for those requiring help using adaptive technologies.

Many visualizations include a legend to help differentiate elements, such as boxes, lines, or plot points, depending on the visualization. You can position the legend in several regions of a page as well as custom-format the presentation of the legend based on its location on the page, as shown in Figure 12-3.

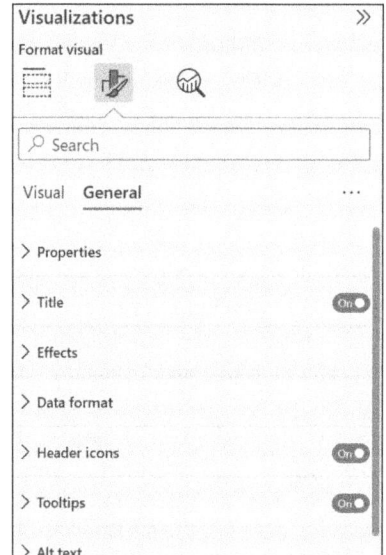

FIGURE 12-2:
The General
settings for
formatting a
visualization.

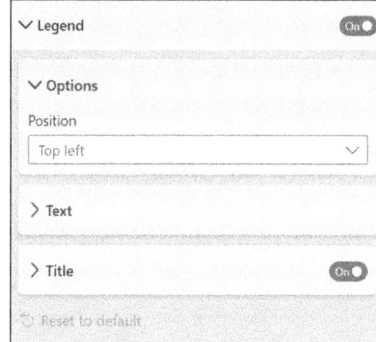

FIGURE 12-3:
Configuring
the legend.

The Data Colors, Data Labels, and Total Labels options vary from visualization to visualization. For example, if you have a bar chart, you can change the colors of each bar beyond the Microsoft suggestion for the default. Similarly, you can change the text color for any data labels, as shown in Figure 12-4. This is particularly useful when using dark background colors — you'll want to change data labels to a light color, such as white or yellow, for better readability.

Visualizations have their title separate from the report header title. You can update the title text to change what Microsoft automatically assigns to a visualization. You can also change the font size using the Title Heading option. You can adjust positioning, color, alignment, and title background color as needed. These features are shown in Figure 12-5.

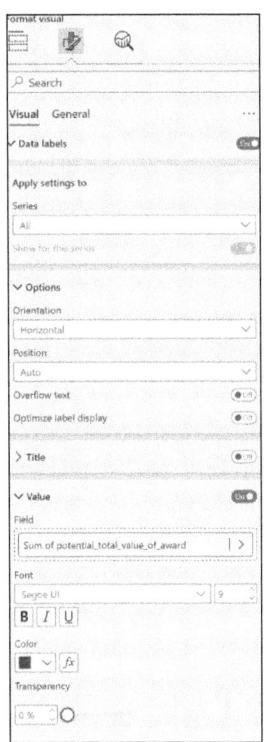

FIGURE 12-4:
The Data Colors and Data Labels options.

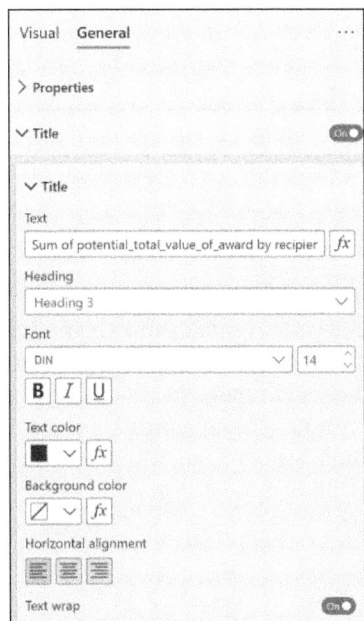

FIGURE 12-5:
The title settings.

If you want to make the background color of a visualization stand out, you can opt to change the color and apply transparency to other objects on the page, as shown in Figure 12-6. Examples of items that may require transparency are the legend, header, and x- and y-axis text.

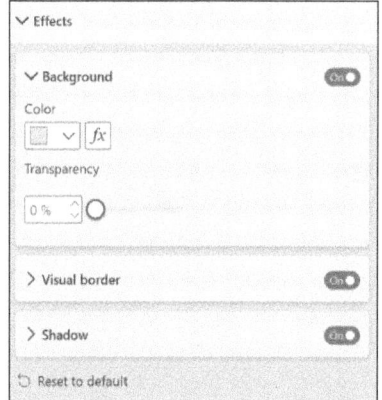

FIGURE 12-6:
Setting the
background color.

Here are some other formatting features that can be configured on a case-by-case basis:

» **Lock aspect:** Visualizations can scale based on size and position.

» **Border:** A visualization border can be configured based on its thickness and color.

» **Shadow:** A visualization border shadow can be configured based on color, direction, and position.

Figure 12-7 shows these options.

Another configuration to consider for each visualization concerns Visual Header settings, as shown in Figure 12-8. Every visualization enables users to transform the visual experience through action-based controls. You have the option to hide or show the header of each visual in a report. As you design your visualizations, you can turn the visual header on or off and configure the aesthetics, including the filter functionality. Visual indicators include the Visual Warning icon, Visual Error icon, from more than 10 drilling options. For each option, you can turn it on or off individually.

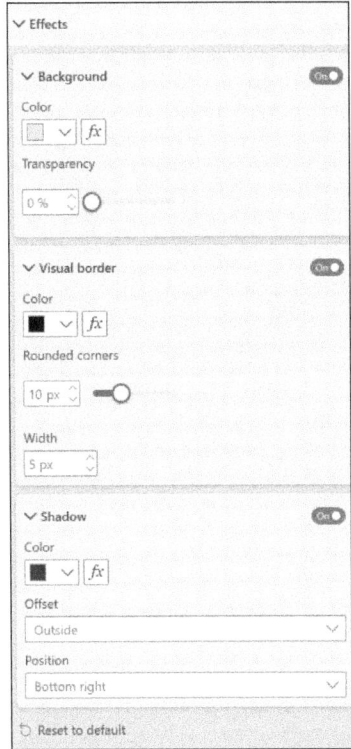

FIGURE 12-7:
Integration of
lock aspect,
background,
and border.

Here are some of the icons included in the Visual Headers field that you can configure:

>> **Drill On icon:** Explores specific data points within a report.

>> **Drill Up icon:** Shows a higher-level perspective of a current view.

>> **Drill Down icon:** Provides a more granular view of the current view.

>> **Expand To Next Level icon:** Displays an additional hierarchy level to the current view.

>> **Filter icon:** Lets user filter when fields are configured for filtering.

>> **Focus Mode icon:** Allows a user to see the report data exclusively.

>> **More Options icon:** Gives a user access to additional options for visualization and report customization.

>> **Pin icon:** Allows you to pin an item to a canvas.

FIGURE 12-8:
Visual Header
configuration
options.

>> **See Data Layout icon:** Lets you review the data in a tabular format, if available.

>> **Show Next Level icon:** Assuming a hierarchy exists, the user can use this icon to display the next level of the hierarchy.

>> **Visual Header Tooltip icon:** Allows the user to provide custom tooltips to the user, assuming you've configured them.

Applying conditional formatting

You may notice the Conditional Formatting (*fx*) button on certain formatting areas within the Visualization pane. When you see this button you can customize one or more aspects of the visualization experience at any time. Figure 12-9 shows the Conditional Formatting (*fx*) button as it appears under the Data Labels heading.

FIGURE 12-9:
The Conditional
Formatting
button.

Conditional formatting
Make this property change under different conditions that you define.

Color

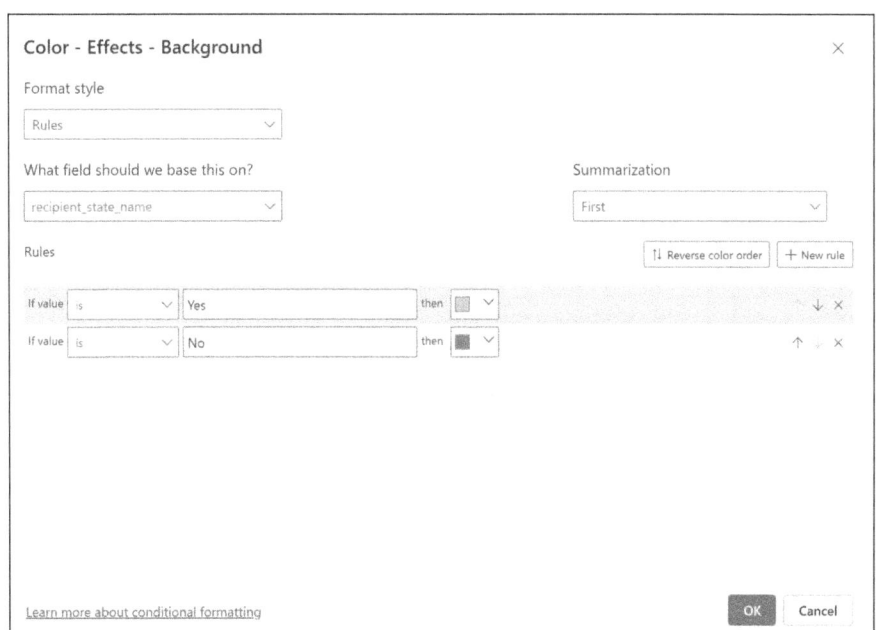

A configuration screen appears whenever you click the Conditional Formatting (*fx*) button, allowing you to configure one or more aspects of the visualization under certain conditions (see Figure 12-10). For example, for Data Labels you can format by color scale, rules, or field value. After selecting the preferred choice, you can select the condition based on options including Field, Summarization, Minimum, and Maximum. Of course, there is a Default formatting parameter that is considered the user baseline.

Color - Effects - Background

Format style

Rules

What field should we base this on?

recipient_state_name

Summarization

First

Rules

⇅ Reverse color order   + New rule

If value   is   Yes   then   ↓ ✕

If value   is   No   then   ↑ ↓ ✕

Learn more about conditional formatting

OK   Cancel

FIGURE 12-10:
The Conditional
Formatting
interface.

Filtering and Sorting

You can filter data based on the visual element itself, across an entire page, or across all pages for every visualization. Most users filter based on a visual because a report with multiple visuals often has different behaviors.

Regardless of the filtering-and-sorting option you choose, you need to select Filter On This Visual, Filter On This Page, or Filter On All Pages. For Figure 12-11, I selected and placed particular fields into the area-specific visuals under Filters On this Visual heading.

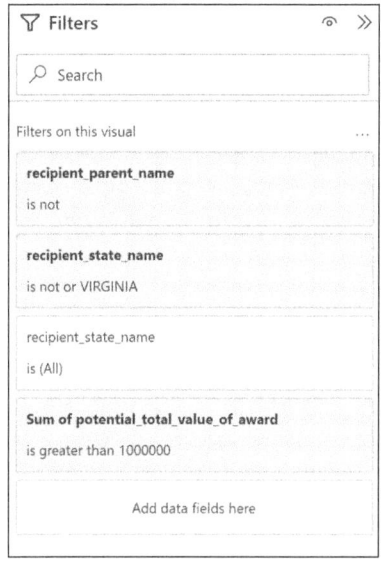

FIGURE 12-11: Configuring fields for a specific visuals example.

Here's how you manage it:

1. **In Report view, drag one or more fields from the Data pane to one of the Add Data Fields text boxes in the Filter pane.**

2. **Expand (or collapse) the fields you just brought over from the Data pane.**

   Each field creates an object called a *filter card* — a visual way to filter the dataset.

3. **Configure the filter according to the required condition.**

   Text-based conditions are different from numerical conditions.

REMEMBER
A user can choose between Basic Filtering, Advanced Filtering, and Top N Filtering. Figure 12-12 shows an example of advanced filtering:

>> **Basic filtering:** Limits the user to those fields in the dataset.

>> **Advanced filtering:** Integrates the use of Boolean conditions such as AND, OR, or NOT in addition to the value meeting a particular condition.

>> **Top N filtering:** Associated with the rank order of items.

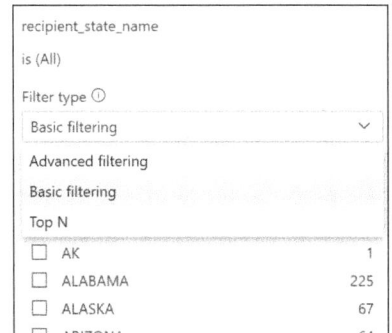

REMEMBER

Over-filtering can be a problem for reports, so avoid adding too many fields. As reports become more complex, it's tempting to add more filters. If you filter across multiple fields, limit the number of conditions unless your report requires precise granularity. Use the Search box at the top of the Filter pane to find fields and values more easily.

Configuring the Report Page

Formatting a report page isn't much different from formatting a visual element, except that a report may have multiple visuals. To configure page formatting, go straight to the Visualizations panel. Once there, click the Paint Roller icon. On the screen that appears, you see many options to change the layout and design of your report page, as shown in Figure 12-13. Most of your options focus on positioning, alignment, and color of the overall report experience.

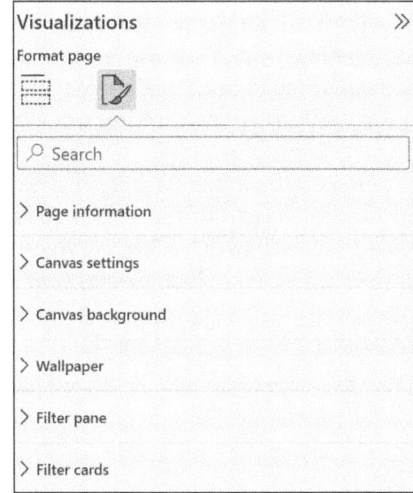

FIGURE 12-13:
Configuring a
report page.

A user can format the following page-related features:

>> **Page information:** Modify the report's name, turn tooltips on and off, and enable Q&A across an entire page, not just a specific visual.

>> **Page size:** Pick the size or paper type based on how you plan to share the report.

>> **Page background:** Configure the background color of the report page.

>> **Page alignment:** Choose whether to center the content or align it to the top-left of the page.

>> **Wallpaper:** Brand a report with specific colors or perhaps a logo to take advantage of the Wallpaper option.

>> **Filter pane:** To change the Filter pane, an integral part of online-based report viewing, a user can configure the user experience to match the paper-style interface with color, transparency, borders, and specific text.

>> **Filter cards:** Like the Filter pane, Filter cards are specific to a given field (a column found in a table, for example). They let a user highlight one or more objects in a report using various aesthetic tools.

REMEMBER

The best way to ensure consistency in report formatting is to create a page once and duplicate the page configuration multiple times. This approach saves you the wasted effort of re-creating the wheel.

Refreshing Data

Power BI offers you several ways to import data. Although some methods require manual updating (such as Import), others can be automatically refreshed. If you're using DirectQuery to connect to data, for example, you want to have your data automatically refresh, especially when monitoring real-time data.

You can set automatic page refresh by enabling Page Refresh in the Visualizations pane of a report page. You need to toggle to the Page Refresh section and set the option to On. Once activated, Power BI refreshes all visuals on a page at the interval you select: either a fixed interval or change detection.

REMEMBER

You can configure Page Refresh in Power BI Desktop, but the automatic refresh functionality only works when the report is published to Power BI Service.

Working with reports

It may seem that there's *so* much to get done using Power BI Desktop for a report to be shared with the masses, but the truth is that I have described only a fraction of what can be done. Your hard work in preparing a report aesthetically for distribution over the Internet using Power BI Desktop will save you time later.

REMEMBER

If your business goal is to create reports at the Desktop client and distribute PDF versions of your outputs, you likely don't need to use Power BI Service. The catch: Your audience can't interactively manipulate or view data in real time. A piece of paper is only a snapshot in time.

The very moment that you decide that more than one user must manipulate your data, even if it's basic filtering or sorting online, you need to publish your datasets and visualizations to Power BI Service. If the scope of your sharing is limited to view-only access, a free Power BI license with appropriate capacity is adequate. If, however, you want users to collaborate in your workspace, you need to use a paid version of Power BI. For enterprise deployments with advanced features and larger datasets, Microsoft Fabric capacity is the most comprehensive solution for accommodating report viewing and distribution.

To publish a report, follow these steps:

1. **Go to the Home tab on the Power BI Desktop Ribbon.**

2. **Click the Publish button, found on the right end of the Ribbon.**

   You're prompted to save all your Desktop work.

3. **Save your work by clicking Save.**

4. **In the new dialog box that appears, select the location where you want your dataset and visualizations to be housed.**

   The assumption is that you've created one or more workspaces on Power BI Service. If you haven't, you're prompted to create a workspace or save it to My Workspace (see Figure 12-14).

5. **After choosing a workspace as your Save location, click Select.**

6. **If this is the first time you've saved it to the workspace, click Save. If you've already saved an item to the workspace, you're asked to replace the item because it already exists, as shown in Figure 12-15.**

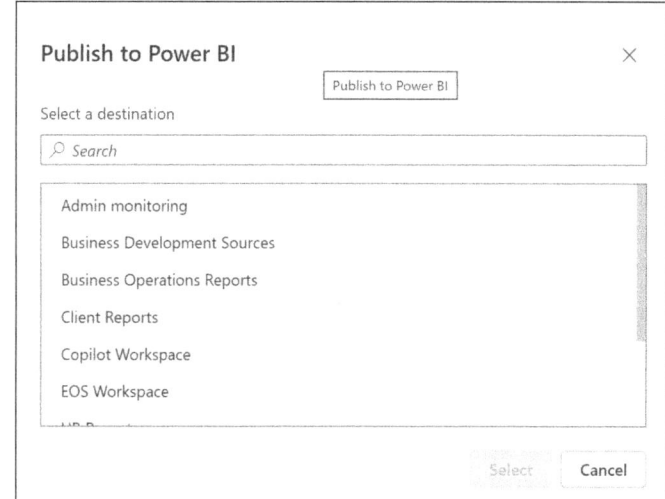

Finding migrated data

You have two ways to gain access to the data you have just published to Power BI Service. First, you can find all your data by clicking the Home button on the left-side navigation bar, where you can find all your most recent items in chronological order under Recent (see Figure 12-16). After you find the file you imported, click to continue making modifications online.

The second possibility is to go directly to the Workspace section of Power BI Service where you've imported the data after initiating the publishing process. In this case, I saved the Examples.pbix file to the Client Reports Workspace. Once there, select the imported items in the list you want to review, as shown in Figure 12-17.

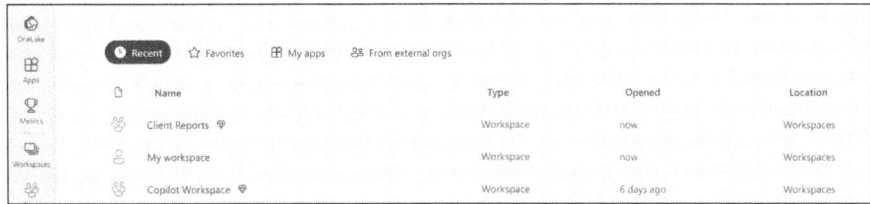

FIGURE 12-16:
The Recent menu
under the Home
button in Power
BI Service.

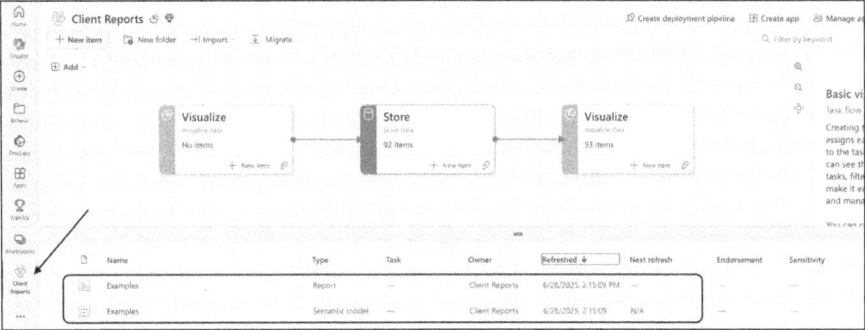

FIGURE 12-17:
Selecting an item
from the selected
Workspace in
Power BI Service.

Exporting reports

Suppose that you don't want to save the report you've created to Power BI Service. Your singular aim is to print a snapshot in time by saving the data to a PDF file. That is entirely possible using Power BI Desktop. To export a report without saving to Power BI Service, follow these steps:

1. **Choose File ⇨ Export from the main menu.**

2. **Choose Export from the menu that appears.**

3. **Save the file either as a Power BI template by providing a description and pressing OK or selecting a PDF file, which automatically generates an Adobe Acrobat PDF in your Web browser, as shown in Figure 12-18.**

   The export is saved to the desktop.

A user who selects the Power BI template option receives a file equivalent to a PBIT file. A Power BI template is based on an existing desktop report template. It features a report layout, report pages, visuals, schema, relationships, measures, datasets, and pre-built data models. Additionally, a definition file may include queries and query parameters. The PDF file, on the other hand, has only static copies of the visualizations accumulated across all tabs.

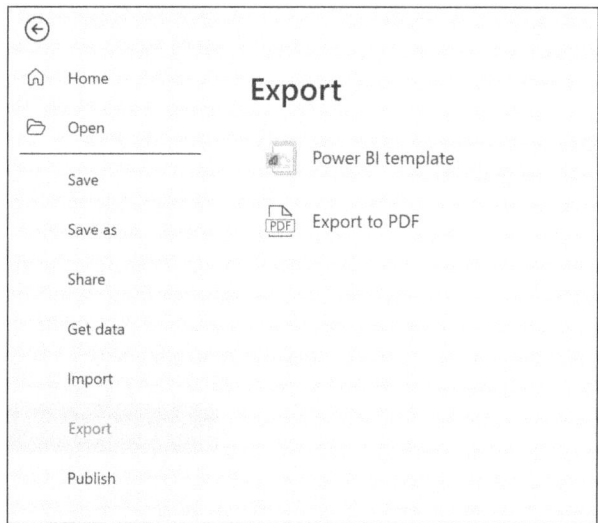

FIGURE 12-18:
Your export
choices.

Perfecting reports for distribution

Power BI paginated reports are perfect for creating pixel-perfect, print-ready documents that display data in a structured format. These reports work exceptionally well for invoices, statements, regulatory reports, and other formal documents that require consistent formatting across multiple pages and need to be distributed beyond the screen of an Internet browser. In this case, you can think of good ole printing. To create a paginated report, use Power BI Report Builder and then publish it to Power BI Service.

1. **Navigate to a workspace.**

    Open Power BI Service in your web browser and navigate to the workspace where you want to create your paginated report. Workspaces help organize your reports and datasets by project or department.

2. **Start a new paginated report.**

    In the top-left corner of your workspace, click the New button, and then select Paginated Report from the drop-down menu (see Figure 12-19). This opens the paginated report creation wizard.

3. **Select a data source.**

    Choose the semantic model that contains the data for your report. For this example, I selected the Example dataset located in the Client Reports workspace. This semantic model serves as the foundation for all the information that will appear in your report.

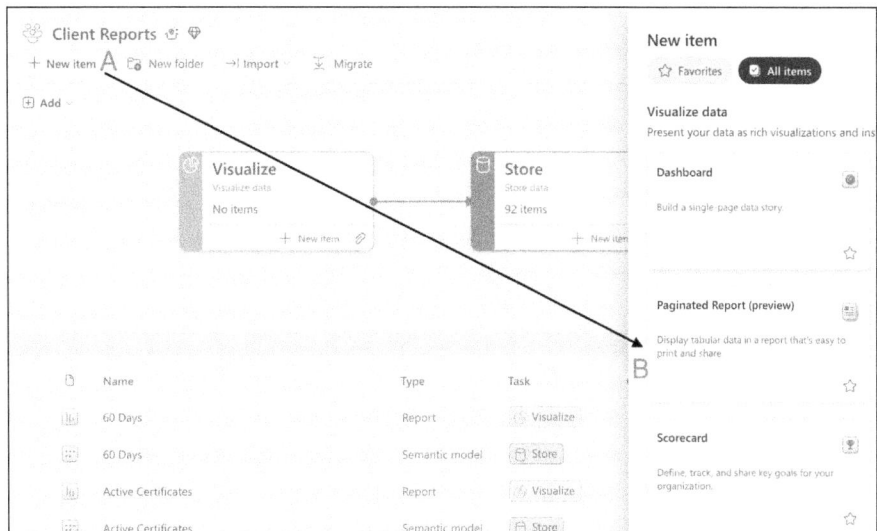

FIGURE 12-19:
Create a new
paginated report.

4. Create the report.

Click the Create Paginated Report button at the bottom of the screen (see Figure 12-20). Clicking this button launches the Power BI Paginated Report Builder, which is your design environment for creating the report layout.

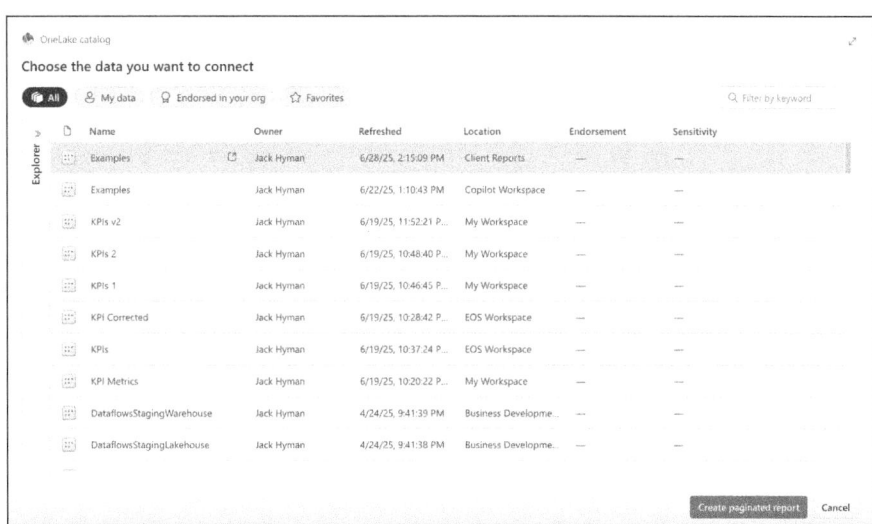

FIGURE 12-20:
The Create Power
BI Paginated
Report button.

5. Add data fields.

The Report Builder interface has a Data pane on the left side. From this pane, select the fields you want to include in your report by clicking on them. These may include customer names, dates, amounts, or any other relevant information from your dataset.

6. Configure the report layout.

As you select fields, they automatically appear in three locations:

- *The Filters pane:* You use this pane to control what data appears in the report.

- *The report canvas:* You design the layout of the report on this canvas.

- *The report preview:* You can use the report preview to see how the final report will look.

You can drag and drop these fields to arrange them exactly how you want them to appear in your finished report (see Figure 12-21).

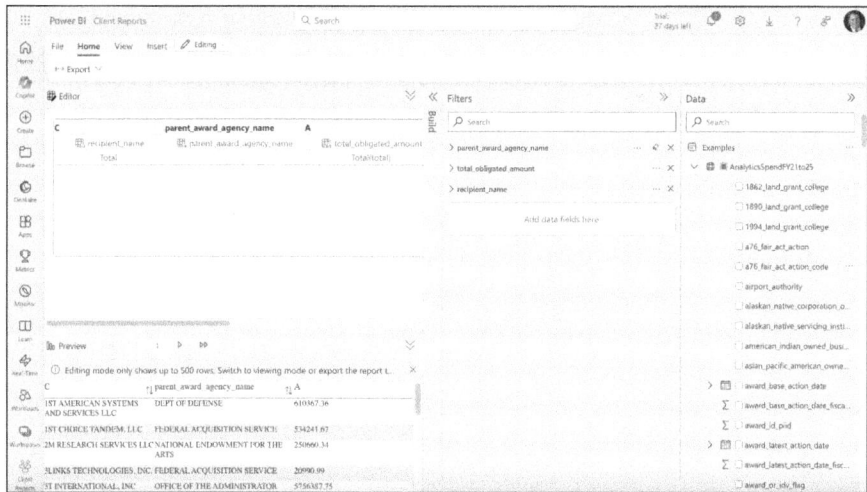

FIGURE 12-21:
The Report
Builder interface.

7. Switch to Viewing mode.

Once you're satisfied with your report design, change from Editing mode to Viewing mode by using the toggle in the toolbar (see Figure 12-22). This allows you to see exactly how your report will appear to end users.

FIGURE 12-22:
Switching from
Editing to Viewing
mode in the Power
BI Paginated
Report Builder.

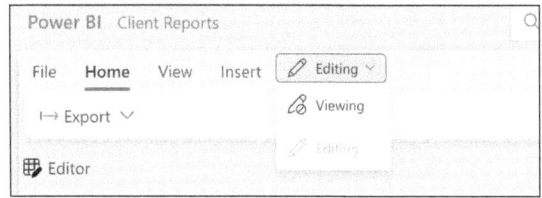

8. Export the report.

To share your report, open the Home tab in the Ribbon, click Export, and then select PDF (see Figure 12-23). This creates a downloadable PDF file that maintains your report's formatting perfectly.

9. Share your report.

Your paginated report is now saved as a PDF file that you can easily share via email, upload to a shared drive, or distribute through any other method your organization prefers.

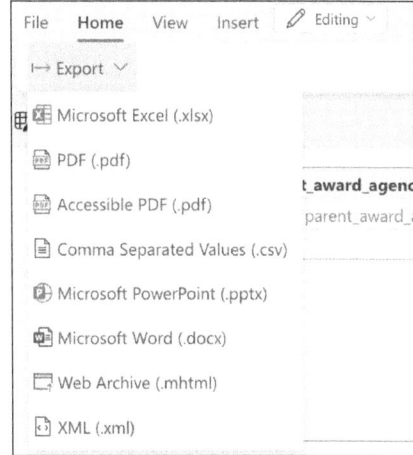

FIGURE 12-23:
Exporting a
Report as
a PDF file.

REMEMBER

If you've come to the end of this chapter and you want to know how to format visualizations for reporting, you should remember that Power BI Service offers a virtually identical experience to Power BI Desktop, including the user experience. The primary difference is that collaboration is possible online when using the Desktop client, whereas only one user can manage the application simultaneously. What you know about configuring a report is consistent across all user experiences.

Chapter **13**

Diving into Dashboarding

Think of your Power BI dashboard as a digital command center that helps you track whether your business is operating smoothly. One visual on this command center changes color, and your eye is drawn immediately to it, alerting you that an issue requires attention. A Power BI dashboard doesn't just display data; it delivers insight.

With the introduction of Microsoft Fabric, Copilot, and real-time capabilities that Microsoft has added to Power BI, you can do even more with dashboards. In this chapter, I show you how to create, customize, and get the most from dashboards, which you access through Power BI Service.

REMEMBER

To work with Power BI dashboards as I describe in this chapter, you need the following:

>> **Power BI Service:** You can only create a dashboard using Power BI Service. In fact, to truly experience the full breadth of dashboarding, you need to use the web version, not Desktop.

>> **A Pro license:** You need a Pro license or a workspace assigned to Premium or Fabric capacity to share dashboards.

Creating a New Dashboard

A dashboard provides a single-screen view of your most important business metrics, designed to facilitate quick decision-making and monitoring. In Power BI, dashboards consist of tiles — visual representations of data pinned from reports, Q&A queries, and other sources. Unlike reports, dashboards can combine data from multiple datasets and workspaces, giving you a consolidated view of key performance indicators that update in real time.

If you're logged into Power BI Service, you should ensure that you have a dataset and some visuals that can be placed on a dashboard. To create your first dashboard, follow these steps:

1. **In Power BI Service, navigate to My Workspaces.**

2. **Click New Item at the top of My Workspaces.**

3. **Choose Dashboard from the menu that appears, as shown in Figure 13-1.**

4. **Enter the name of the new dashboard (see Figure 13-2) and then click Create.**

   A blank canvas is set up for you, as shown in Figure 13-3.

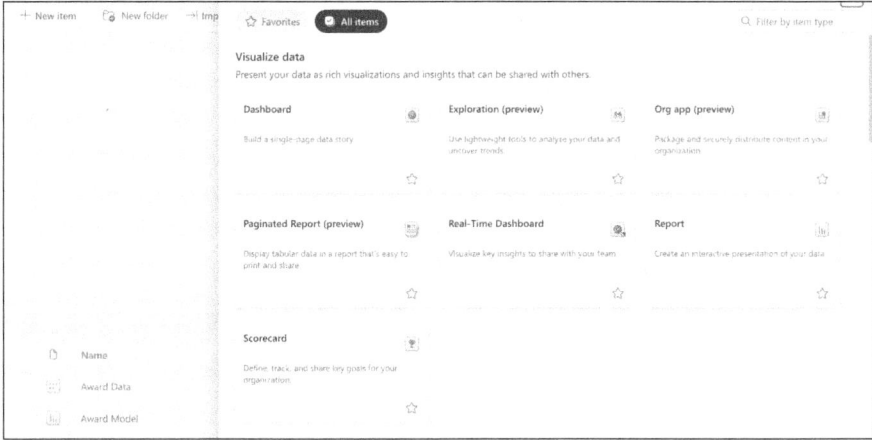

FIGURE 13-1:
Creating a dashboard.

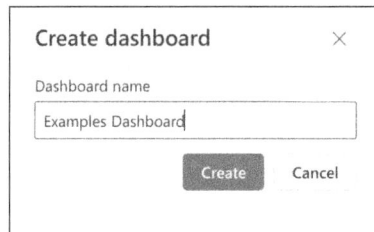

FIGURE 13-2:
Naming a new dashboard.

FIGURE 13-3:
A blank dashboard canvas.

Enriching Your Dashboard with Content

You need to keep a couple of points in mind when trying to integrate an object on your dashboard canvas. The first thing to consider is what type of objects will make the dashboard meaningful. The second has to do with the layout and number of objects you intend to pin to the canvas. You have only so much real estate per dashboard canvas, so pick wisely.

At this point, you can add a few different items beyond reports:

» **Web content:** HTML-based web content

» **Images:** Publicly accessible images exclusively

» **Text boxes:** Static text that can be formatted

» **Video:** Videos that can be embedded either on YouTube or Vimeo

» **Custom streaming data:** Real-time data coming from an API, Azure Stream, or PubNub source

TECHNICAL STUFF

You are probably familiar with most of the content sources listed above, but if you are interested in extremely large datasets being presented in a dashboard, consider using Azure Streams or PubNub. Azure Stream is the abbreviated name for Azure Stream Analytics, a real-time analytics and complex event-processing engine designed to analyze and process high volumes of (usually live) data from multiple sources simultaneously. PubNub, like Azure Streams, is another real-time analytics streaming service focused on delivering content using a real-time publish/subscribe messaging process, primarily for Internet of Things (IoT) devices.

To add content-based objects to the canvas — *tiles*, in Power BI-speak — follow these steps:

1. **From the dashboard canvas, open the Edit menu.**

2. **Choose Add a Tile, as shown in Figure 13-4.**

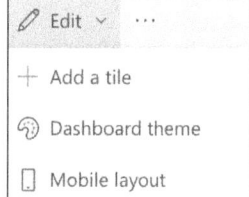

FIGURE 13-4:
Accessing the Add
a Tile menu.

3. **From the new menu that appears, choose one of the listed object types. (See Figure 13-5.)**

    Notice that the menu does not have a Report option.

    WARNING

    All content placed on a dashboard must be publicly accessible. Even if authentication or uploading is necessary for a user to view the data, Power BI doesn't presently support such features.

4. **After choosing an option, use the option's customizing features to place your content the way you want it.**

    For example, if you were to choose the Text Box option, a new screen would appear (see Figure 13-6) in which you can add titles, subtitles, and text. You can even tweak whatever you've added by using any of the displayed formatting commands. When you finish, click Apply. Any changes you've made show up on your dashboard, as shown in Figure 13-7.

Once the tile is on the dashboard canvas, you can move it to any location you prefer. By default, it sits flush left top unless other tiles are in the region. In the earlier example, I moved the tile to the upper-right corner so that I could add other tiles later.

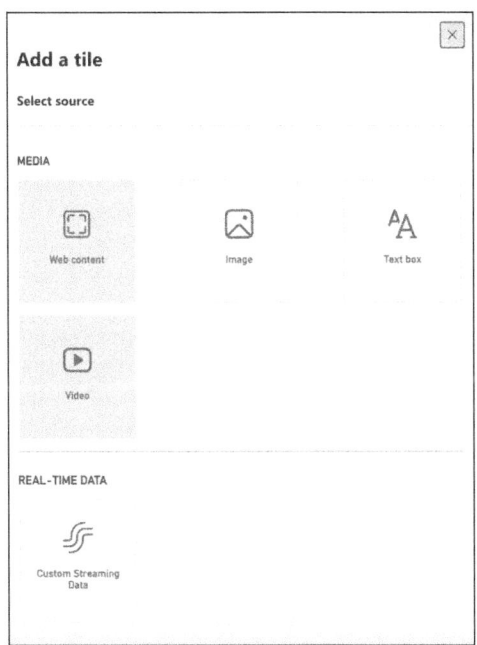

FIGURE 13-5:
Selecting a
tile type.

Add a tile

Select source

MEDIA

Web content

Image

Text box

Video

REAL-TIME DATA

Custom Streaming
Data

Add textbox tile

* Required

Details

Display title and subtitle

Title

Examples Dashboard - Awards Dataset

Subtitle

Content
Fill in the details.

Segoe UI Light | 10.5 | A | B | I | U

The examples below are a compilation of awards data extracted from
www.usaspending.gov as of June 30, 2025.

Restore default

Technical Details

Back | Apply | Cancel

FIGURE 13-6:
Configuring a tile.

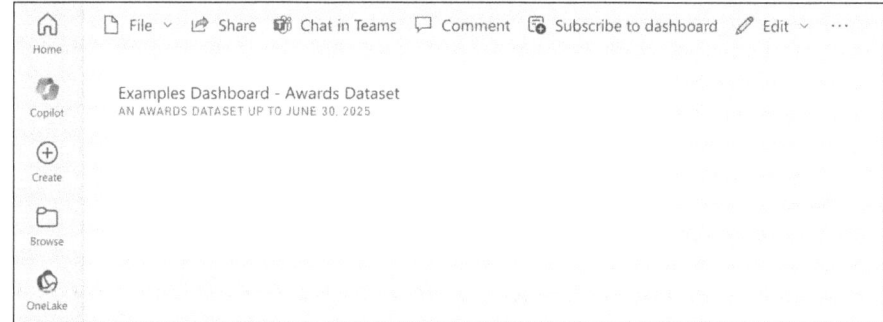

FIGURE 13-7:
Customizing a
content tile on
the dashboard
canvas.

Pinning Reports

Because you create visualization reports within Power BI, creating a report visualization tile is a slightly different process from adding other content. Basically, you pin the existing report visualization to the dashboard rather than create a new tile — the asset is already stored in Power BI, so you don't have to "create" anything. To pin a report visualization, follow these steps:

1. **Open a workspace that contains a report that includes one or more visualizations you'd like to include in a dashboard.**

2. **Locate the Pin button in the Visual header (see Figure 13-8).**

FIGURE 13-8:
The Pin button.

3. **On the new screen that appears, click a radio button to specify whether the visualization will be part of a new dashboard or added to an existing one (see Figure 13-9).**

   You'll add the visualization to a new dashboard, so you should choose that option. You then add the name of the new dashboard. For this example, I called it the Examples Dashboard.

4. **After making your selections, click Pin.**

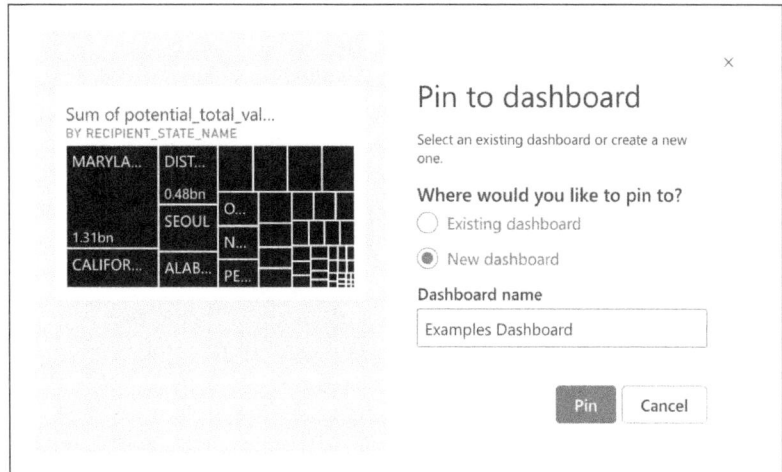

FIGURE 13-9:
Opting for a
new or existing
dashboard.

Repeat Steps 1–4 for as many visualizations that you want to include on your dashboard. The result is a dashboard similar to the one shown in Figure 13-10. Keep in mind that this dashboard incorporates a combination of slicers, headers, and pinned visualizations along with a theme, which I cover in the next section. To find out more about the types of visualizations available in Power BI, see Chapter 11.

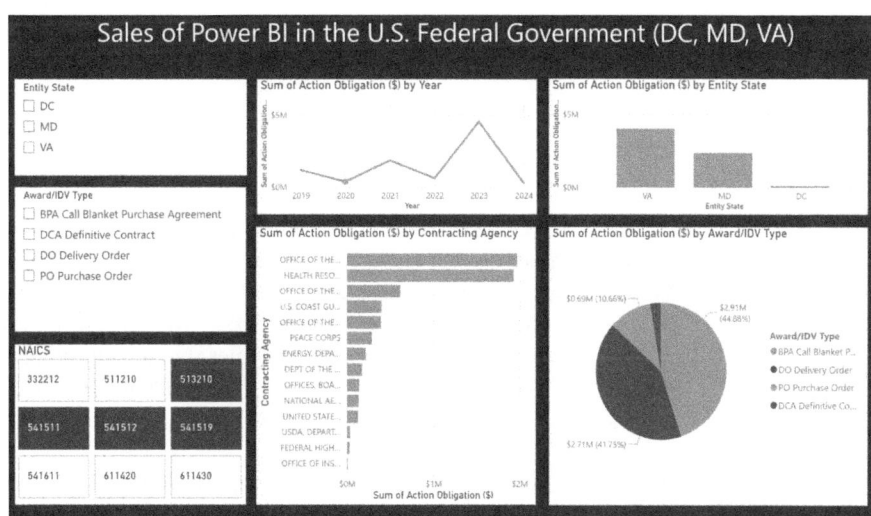

FIGURE 13-10:
A finished
dashboard
with tiles.

REMEMBER

Pinned visualizations aren't interactive. Updates are visible only after you refresh the dataset from which the visualization was derived. If you're looking for real-time data, you must use the Custom Streaming Data tile.

Customizing with Themes

Users who like a unified look often add a theme to a Power BI visualization. You can do the same thing to a dashboard. In fact, the need for an overarching theme is greater in a dashboard. Just think about it: Suppose that you must integrate several reports, each of which has a different look and feel, into one dashboard. By developing a dashboard theme, you maintain a consistent user experience that not only looks cohesive but also makes it easier for users to spot changes, recognize patterns, and interpret visuals across different tiles.

Configuring a dashboard theme is like adding a tile. To add a theme to a dashboard, open the dashboard you want to add the theme to. Just above the dashboard in the menu, select the Edit menu. Then choose Dashboard Theme from the list of options, as shown in Figure 13-11.

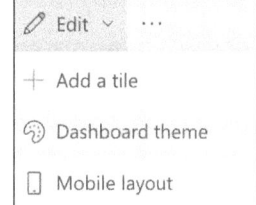

FIGURE 13-11:
Choosing the
Dashboard
Theme option.

As the dashboard creator, you can apply a prebuilt theme such as Dark, Light, or Color Blind Friendly from the Dashboard Theme screen, as shown in Figure 13-12, or develop your own custom theme. When you choose Custom from the drop-down menu, you gain complete control over the images, colors, font color, and tile background. Then you can fine-tune the look to your heart's content. Figure 13-13 shows the Custom Theme menu choices.

TECHNICAL STUFF

You may have noticed a choice labeled Upload JSON theme. If you want to add more complex theme designs, you can do so by selecting this option. To download additional themes created by Microsoft that apply the JSON theme schema, go to `https://community.powerbi.com/t5/Themes-Gallery/bd-p/ThemesGallery`.

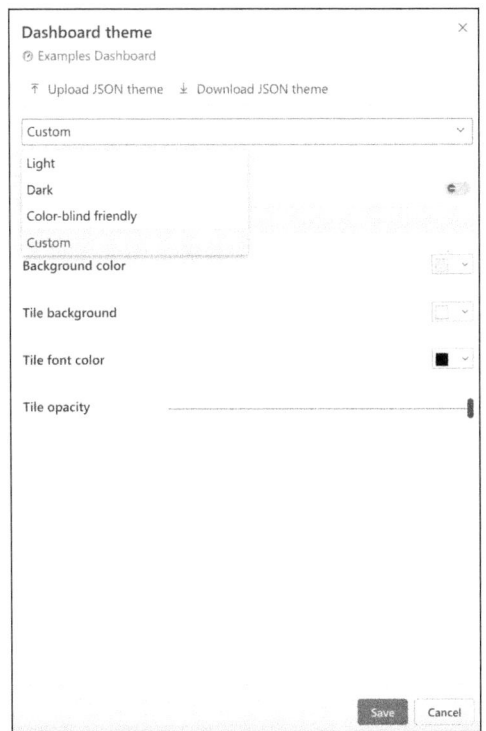

FIGURE 13-12:
Choosing a
prebuilt theme.

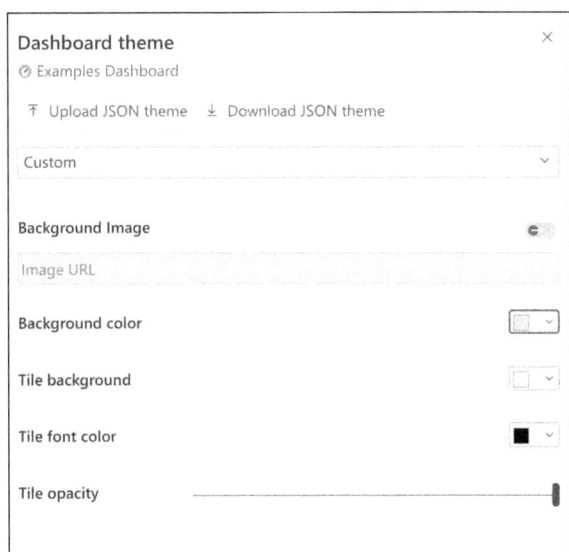

FIGURE 13-13:
Customizing
a theme.

Working with Dashboard Layouts

Like Power BI reports, dashboards also offer different layout options to accommodate various device form factors. For dashboards, a web view and mobile view are available — a web layout occupies far greater screen real estate than a mobile layout. Figure 13-14 shows an example of a web layout.

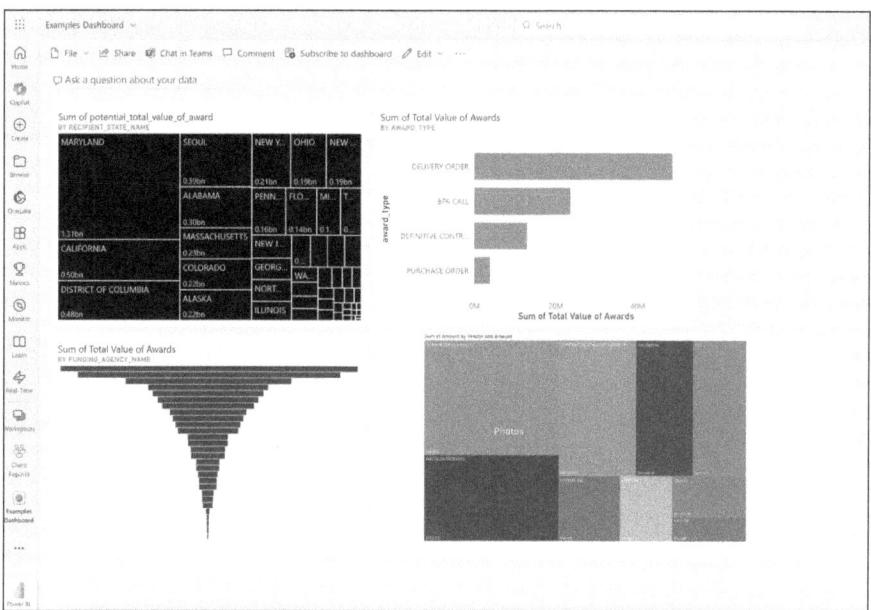

FIGURE 13-14:
The web layout for a dashboard.

The mobile layout organizes each visual as a stacked asset. Only one pinned visual appears horizontally, by default. You can change the layout of a dashboard for the mobile design and add more than one horizontal pinned visual. The mobile layout shown in Figure 13-15, for example, has several unpinned visuals. If you want to add a visual to the mobile layout, you click the pin and the visual is added to the mobile simulator. This example has two visuals plus the header. You can add two additional visuals to the mobile dashboard in this example.

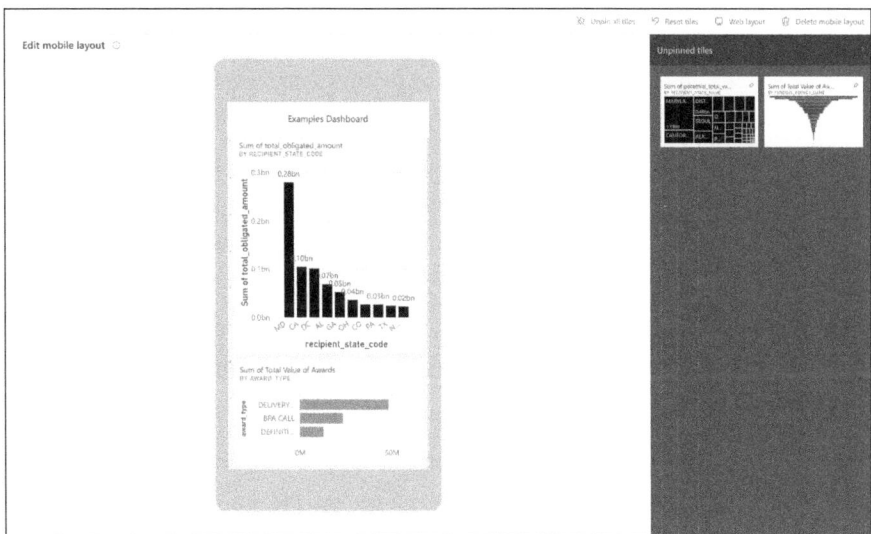

FIGURE 13-15:
A dashboard's
mobile layout.

Setting Alerts and Establishing Subscriptions

Think of your Power BI dashboard as a digital command center dashboard. As a digital command center, your dashboard provides signals to indicate whether things are okay or, perhaps, that a five-alarm fire may be brewing. Instead of sitting by the computer clicking your mouse to refresh the screen again and again, you can configure Power BI to send an alert to your device when something hits an acceptable or unacceptable threshold. In this way, Power BI alerts and subscriptions are like your assistant who never sleeps.

Alerts are like having a watchdog for your data. You set up rules like "tell me when sales drop below $10,000" or "notify me if more than 100 new users come to the website in an hour." When these conditions are triggered, assuming that the data is available in your data source and the system has been refreshed, Power BI sends you an email immediately. It's perfect for monitoring KPIs (key performance indicators) that need immediate attention. In other words, alerts are tied to managing unusual events.

Subscriptions work more like a newspaper delivery service. These are scheduled notifications that inform you about the status of your data. You can schedule these notifications hourly, daily, weekly, monthly, or any other interval that makes sense to you or your organization. You can assign a schedule for Power BI to email snapshots of entire reports or specific dashboard pages. Scheduling notifications ensures that you and your team stay informed about business performance without having to actively log into Power BI every time you want to check the numbers.

The beauty of both features is that they work in the background. You set them up once, and Power BI handles the rest, keeping you informed whether you're in the office, working from home, or even on vacation.

To set up a data alert, follow these steps:

1. **Navigate to your dashboard in Power BI Service.**

2. **Find the tile you want to monitor.**

3. **Click the tile so that only that tile is in focus.**

4. **In the toolbar, click the Set Alert button (see Figure 13-16).**

   The Alerts pane appears on the right side of the screen (see Figure 13-17).

   The parameter is defined based on what needs to be changed, as specified in the previously set report configuration title.

FIGURE 13-16:
The Set
Alert button.

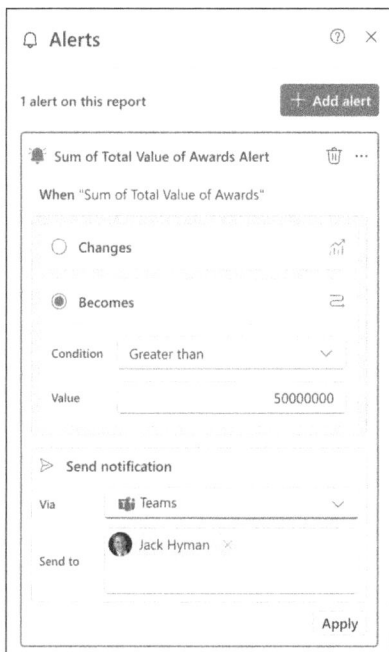

FIGURE 13-17:
The Alerts pane.

5. **Decide whether you want the alert to trigger based on changes that occur *by a certain threshold,* as shown in Figure 13-18, or when a change *meets a specific value threshold,* as shown in Figure 13-19.**

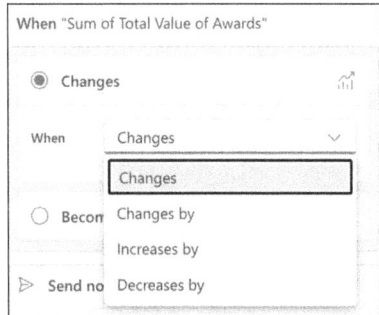

FIGURE 13-18:
Change conditions for alerts.

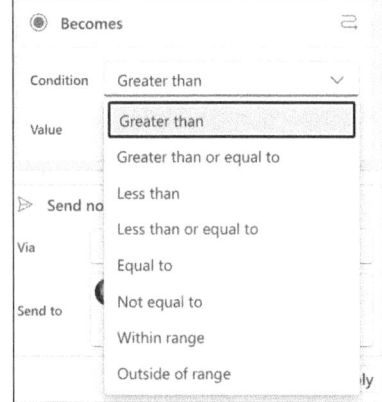

FIGURE 13-19:
Becomes conditions for alerts.

For the example in this section, I established that assuming the value is greater than $50 million, I want an alert to be triggered. Otherwise, I will not be notified. Notice that I set the alert to trigger in Teams. You have two options: using Teams or using Outlook (email).

6. **Once you are okay with the conditions of your alert, click Apply.**

Your alert is then tied to the specific tile within the dashboard. This is evident when you return to the Alert panel, as shown in Figure 13-20.

If you choose to use Teams as your notification method, you'll receive a verification notice, similar to the one shown in Figure 13-21, indicating that the alert is now active.

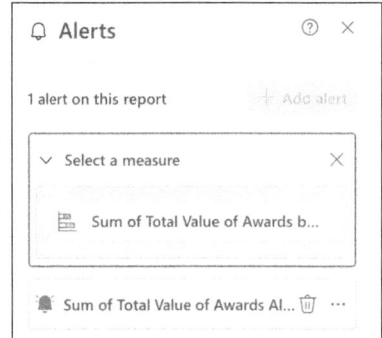

FIGURE 13-20:
Active alert in the Alerts pane.

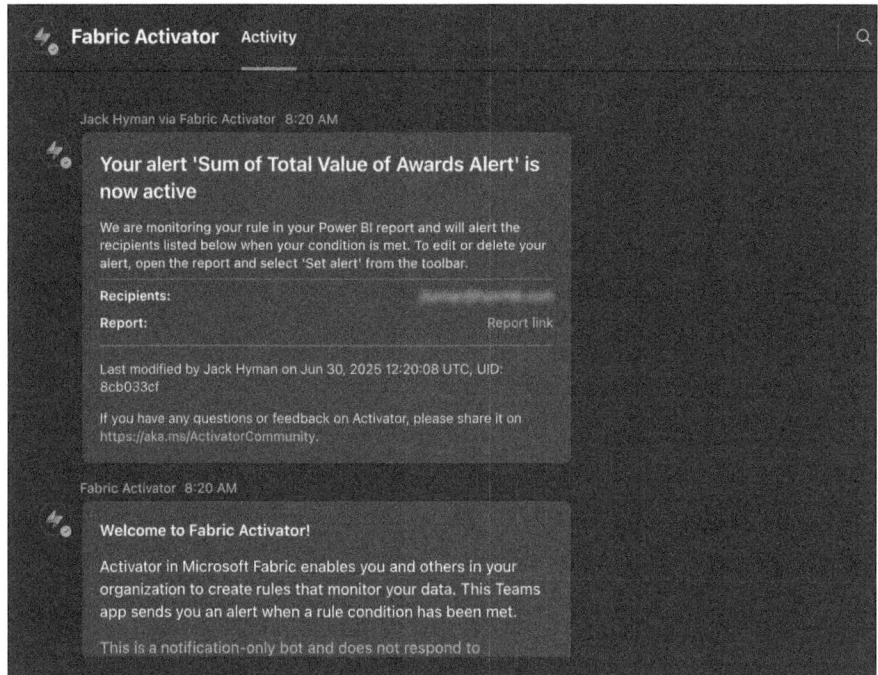

FIGURE 13-21:
Alert notification in Microsoft Teams.

Subscribing to Reports and Dashboards

You can set up a subscription for a specific tile or for an entire dashboard. When you subscribe to a tile, you receive point-in-time updates for that single visual on the dashboard. When you subscribe to a whole dashboard, you receive a snapshot that includes all tiles on it, which may come from one or more reports. In this example, the dashboard contains four tiles.

To subscribe to a dashboard, follow these steps:

1. **From the toolbar of your dashboard, click Subscribe to Dashboard (see Figure 13-22).**

FIGURE 13-22:
The
Subscription
button.

2. **Click Create a Subscription**

   On the right side of the screen, a Subscription pane appears (see Figure 13-23).

3. **Name the Subscription in the Subscription Name field.**

   In this case, I named my subscription *Example Subscription.*

4. **Add the recipients who should receive the subscription.**

   Each recipient must have a Power BI Pro or higher license to receive this report.

WARNING

5. **Schedule the frequency, which includes the start and end dates, repeat interval, scheduled delivery time, and time zone.**

   For this example, I set the report to run daily at 9:00 AM from October 1, 2025, to October 31, 2025, in the Eastern Time Zone.

6. **Expand the More Options menu.**

7. **Add the email subject and message you want to include each time the subscription is sent.**

   For example, your subject may be something like *Daily Examples Dashboard – October 1, 2025 to October 31, 2025.* In the message board, you may want to indicate the purpose of the dashboard you are distributing to the user.

8. **Configure whether you want the user to have access to the dashboard via email, see a link in the email directly to the Power BI dashboard, or preview the dashboard data in the email.**

FIGURE 13-23:
Configuring a
subscription.

9. **When you are satisfied with your selections, click Save.**

The dashboard now appears as part of the list within the specific Dashboard subscription pane. You can turn the subscription on and off at any time, as shown in Figure 13-24.

TIP

You can test that a subscription works by clicking Send Now.

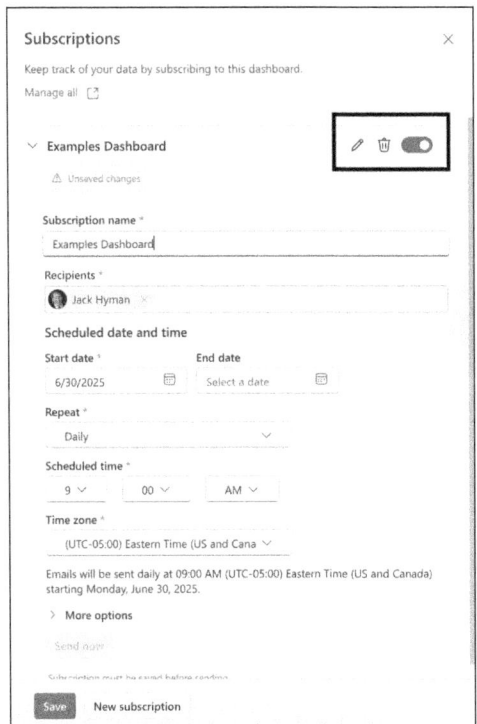

FIGURE 13-24:
Turning
subscription on/
off and testing a
subscription.

Chapter **14**

Sharing and the Power BI Workspace

E ventually, as a power user of Power BI, you'll want to share the data from your desktop with everyone who is a stakeholder in your business. When you do this, you shift from working within Power BI Desktop and work instead from the web, with Power BI Service. To prevent other users from mangling your Power BI Desktop data, the users you share your work with carry out activities using a workspace, a feature that is designed for collaboration and sharing and available only in Power BI Service.

In this chapter, I discuss collaboration tools available exclusively in Power BI Service. You find out about workspaces and how you can use them to collaborate and share your work. You also discover how you can use the monitoring and performance tools available in Power BI Service to accelerate your business operations.

Working Together in a Workspace

Picture yourself in an art museum. You can explore visuals and read anecdotal tales about each work by yourself or with others by your side. A Power BI workspace, available in Power BI Service, is analogous to curated content for a museum, except that the content on a dashboard represents data. Power BI designers create workspaces to manage collections of dashboards and reports. Designers share a workspace with users based on user roles, responsibilities, and permissions.

Designers can also build apps by bundling together targeted collections of dashboards and reports and distributing them to their organization, whether that involves just a few users or an entire community. These apps, called *template* apps, are distributable on a variety of devices, including desktops and smartphones.

Defining the types of workspaces

The idea behind a Power BI workspace is that it should contain all content specific to your business objective. When designers create a targeted workspace, they bundle all the content assets necessary for use and deployment and make them available in the workspace, where the purpose is singular. You don't scour data across workspaces. Instead, the data is stored in a single container, like documents in a file cabinet, organized into drawers and folders. The content may include datasets, dashboards, and reports.

REMEMBER

A workspace doesn't need to include all content types. It may contain reports, datasets, or dashboards exclusively. Designers choose the type of content based on the business purpose the content serves, and how they want to share and collaborate with other users.

The workspaces shown in Figure 14-1 are intended for sharing and collaboration using a collaboration scheme with others. You access them via your My Workspace (see Figure 14-2), as this workspace serves as your online desktop for Power BI.

You can publish data from Power BI Desktop to Power BI Service. Then you can organize, store, and share those assets just published online to one or more workspaces that you may intend to use for collaboration. In Figure 14-3, you find assets that were originally created in Power BI Desktop that are now available in a workspace associated with the Pipeline Identification project.

It may be challenging at first to understand why it's necessary to transition from Power BI Desktop to Power BI Service. The key selling point is often the workspaces and sharing and collaboration features in Power BI Service. Workspaces provide many benefits and enable you to do the following:

>> Sustain focused collaboration among a small or globally dispersed team

>> Use workspaces to house reports and dashboards for one team or multiple teams

>> Streamline the sharing and presentation of reports and dashboards by housing them in a single environment

>> Maintain security by controlling access to datasets, reports, and dashboards

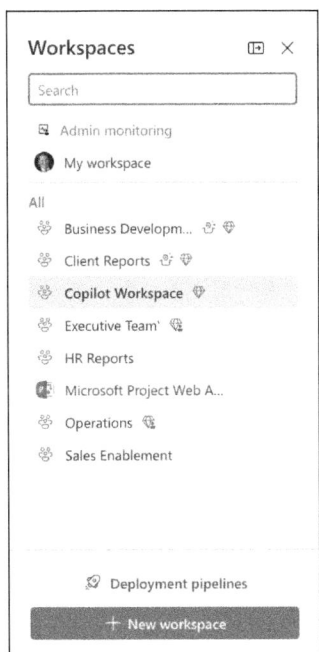

FIGURE 14-1:
A list of workspace apps.

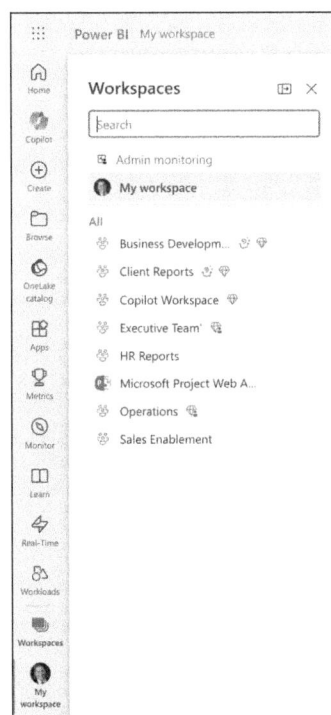

FIGURE 14-2:
The My Workspace interface.

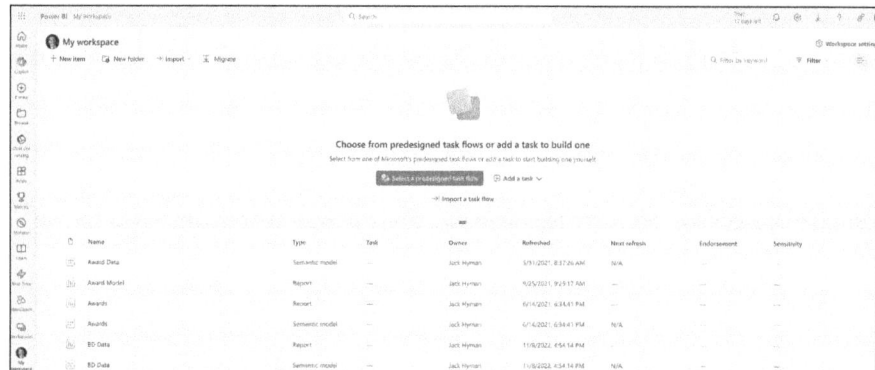

FIGURE 14-3:
The content of a workspace in Power BI.

Getting started with workspaces

When you go into Power BI Service, you're introduced to the Power BI Service navigation menu (see Figure 14-4). To no one's surprise, data ingestion and access are a big part of Power BI Service.

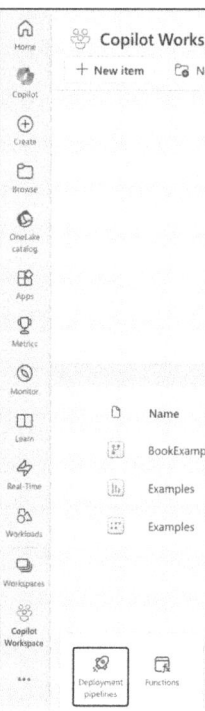

FIGURE 14-4:
The navigation menu in Power BI Service.

At the bottom of the list, you find workspaces-related features. Power BI Service provides you with a single My Workspace, but you can create many workspaces within My Workspace. However, you can remain active and have only one workspace open at a time — the one highlighted in the navigation.

Creating and configuring the workspace

Creating a workspace requires configuring several items, including its branding, name, description, access, storage, license mode, app type, and security settings. To complete this configuration, follow these steps:

1. **Click the Workspace button on the Power BI Service navigation menu.**

2. **On the menu that appears, click the +New Workspace button (see Figure 14-5).**

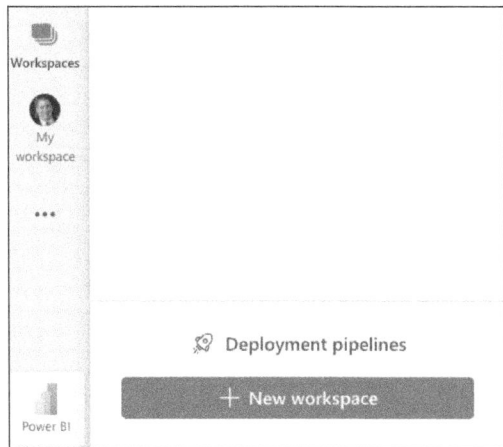

FIGURE 14-5:
The +New Workspace button.

3. **In the new window that appears on the right side, use the settings to configure the new workspace.**

   Some of the key features that you must enter when configuring a new workspace in the Standard setup (see Figure 14-6) and Advanced setup (see Figure 14-7) include

   ● *Workspace Image:* Save a photo from your desktop to customize the workspace experience.

   ● *Workspace Name:* Name the workspace based on its content and datasets. Treat this name as you would for a file collection.

   ● *Description:* Describe the purpose of the workspace.

- *Domain:* Select the domain to align the workspace with a specific business area or function, ensuring proper governance, ownership, and data access within that organizational context.

- *Contact List:* Workspace admins or assigned users receive notifications about updates in each Power BI workspace.

- *License Mode:* Select the license type assigning the right to access content in the workspace. An organization may have access to one type (Pro) or more than one type (Premium-based).

- *Fabric Capacity:* Select the Fabric capacity to allocate the compute and storage resources needed for optimal performance, scalability, and data refresh within the workspace.

- *Semantic Model:* Select the semantic model to define how data is structured, related, and measured, allowing reports and dashboards to deliver consistent, business-ready insights. You can choose from two options: a small or a large semantic model.

- *Template Apps:* Select the option to allow for the creation of template apps in a workspace. This lets you quickly deploy a prebuilt Power BI solution that includes reports, dashboards, and semantic models, accelerating setup and standardizing analytics across your organization.

4. **When you finish, click Save.**

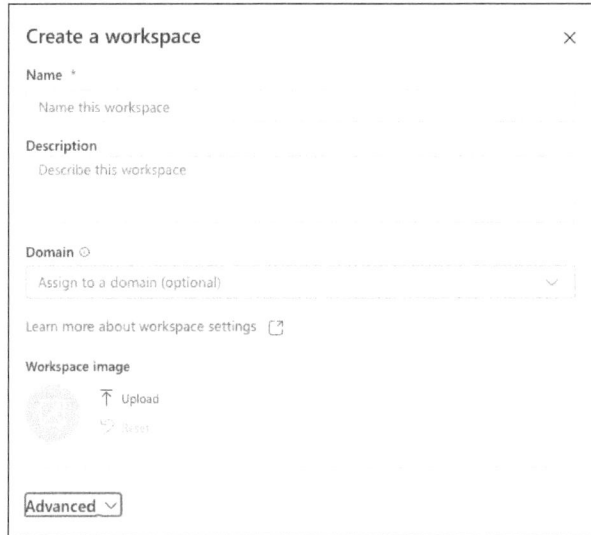

FIGURE 14-6:
Configuring the standard features of a workspace.

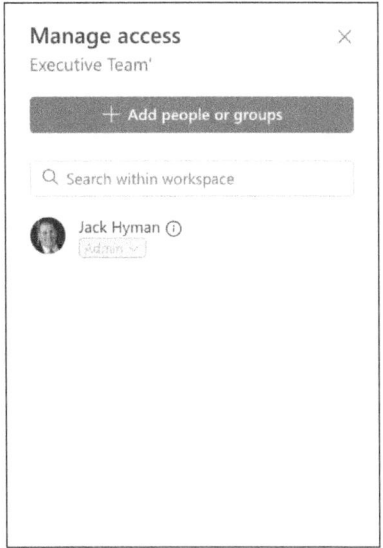

FIGURE 14-7:
Configuring the
advanced
features of a
workspace.

TIP

For a refresher on license types and the difference between Pro and Premium-based licensing, see Chapter 3.

Wandering into access management

A big part of sharing and collaborating starts with access management. You must configure who has access to workspaces and to each content asset within them. You, as the designer, can assign four distinct role types: admin, member, contributor, or viewer. To change access rights for a group of users, follow these steps:

1. **Click the Workspace button on the Power BI Service navigation menu.**

2. **Choose the workspace you want to modify from the menu that appears.**

3. **On the right side of the workspace label, select the three dots.**

4. **Click Workspace Access from the menu that appears, as shown in Figure 14-8.**

   Doing so brings up the Workspace Access pane on the right side of the screen.

5. **Enter the email addresses or group accounts for those whose access you want to control, along with the workspace roles you want to assign them.**

6. **When you finish, click Close.**

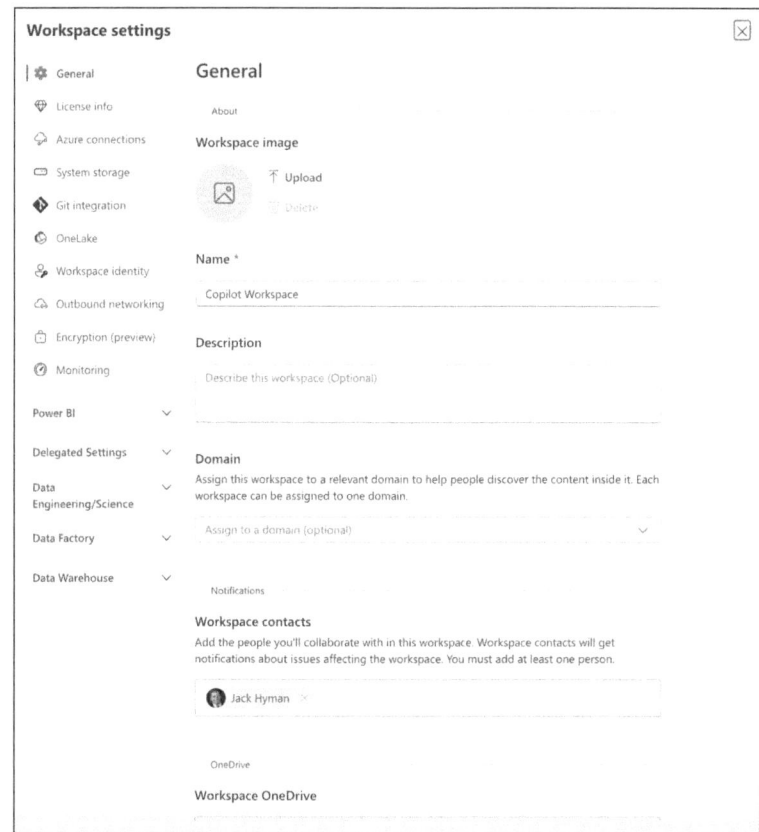

FIGURE 14-8:
Assigning
workspace
access.

REMEMBER

When you create a user group, everyone in that group is assigned to it. Assuming that a user is a part of several user groups, that person is assigned the highest permission level based on their assigned role. However, if you embed the user groups, all contained users inherit the permissions.

WARNING

Your ability to interact with data in workspaces is significantly limited unless you have a Pro or Premium license. You can either view and interact with items or read data stored in workspace dataflows — nothing less, nothing more.

Dealing with settings and storage

Remember all those settings you configured when you first created a workspace? You can modify them at any time, including changing the storage type from Pro to

Premium per User, Premium per Capacity, or Embedded. Also, if you're looking to delete a workspace, you can do so under Premium. To make these changes, follow these steps:

1. **Click the Workspace button on the Power BI Service navigation menu.**

2. **Choose the workspace you want to modify from the menu that appears.**

3. **On the right side of the workspace label, click the three vertical dots.**

4. **Click Workspace Settings.**

   Doing so brings up the Workspace Settings pane on the right side of the screen.

5. **Open the Premium tab.**

6. **Select the capacity choice that best reflects your need.**

7. **When you finish, click Save.**

TECHNICAL STUFF

What exactly does the Embedded option involve? Suppose that you've used an enterprise application or visited a website and seen analytics features embedded. In that case, Power BI Embedded may be the solution behind the application or website. The Embedded option lets you build an app so that a customer does not need to authenticate.

Creating and Configuring Apps

Unlike a Power BI workspace, which is intended for a finite number of users for collaboration, an app is intended for a broader number of users after it's published. An *app* is a published, read-only view of data. Apps provide mass distribution to those who want access to analytic insights. There is a catch, though; you must have, at minimum, a Pro license to consume and view an app. Alternatively, the app must be supported by one of the two Premium capacity types in an organization.

Before creating and configuring an app for distribution, a workspace must contain content. Once the workspace is set up, you can bundle its assets — such as reports, dashboards, datasets, dataflows, and files — into a single deployable application. After that, assign collaborator roles and permissions to manage who can edit, view, or distribute the content.

To add any type of content into an app workspace once set up, select the New button and then choose the content you want to add (see Figure 14-9).

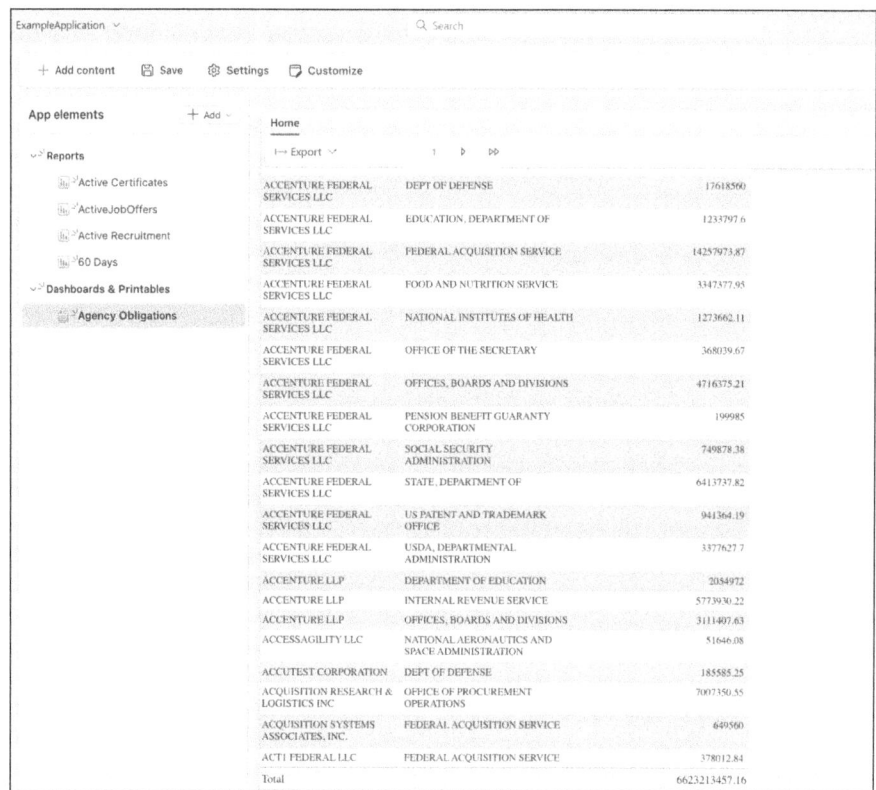

FIGURE 14-9:
Adding new content to an app workspace.

Each time you add content, the content is added to the Workspace list. You can then choose to include the item in the app and assign users to it by granting access, as shown in Figure 14-10. Select the slider to show whether it should be included, and when you're ready to package the app for distribution, click the Create an App button in the upper-right corner.

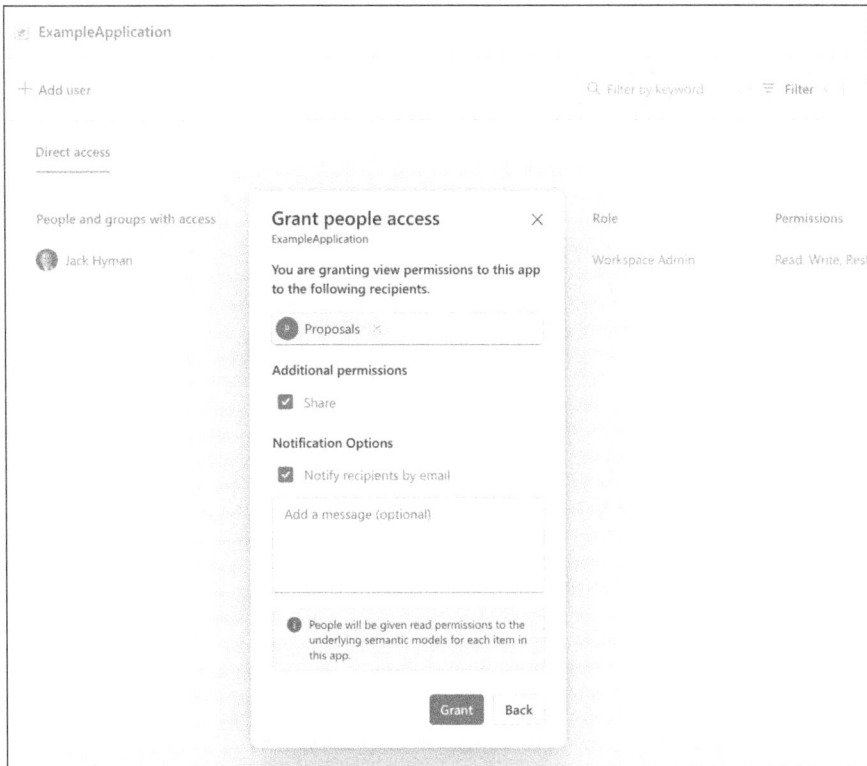

FIGURE 14-10:
Granting
permissions as
part of the app
creation process.

Slicing and Dicing Data

As users consume your reports, dashboards, and datasets, you may want to know *how* they consume these content assets. This is why Microsoft has integrated monitoring and alternate data analysis tools within Power BI for those users who have Pro and Premium licensing to evaluate such metrics.

You can slice and dice usage data in several ways. Options include analyzing data in Excel as well as accessing a high-level view of your data with the Quick Insights report. You can also use metrics reports to understand who is accessing and viewing your reports and dashboards. Click the three vertical dots next to any reports or dashboards within a workspace to access these capabilities. You see two options: one for dashboards (see Figure 14-11) and another for reports (see Figure 14-12).

FIGURE 14-11:
The Dashboard
menu under
Workspaces.

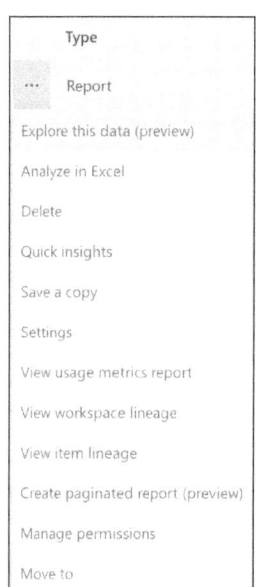

FIGURE 14-12:
The Report
menu under
Workspaces.

Analyzing in Excel

Sometimes, Power BI is too much for a user to evaluate enterprise data comfortably. Users may want to review a subset of data, so they return to Microsoft Excel. With the Analyze in Excel option, you can import Power BI datasets into Excel. Then you can choose to view and interact with the dataset side-by-side or independently. Whether your business goal is to create a PivotTable, chart, table, or Excel output, you need to have downloaded the Excel add-on feature from Power BI. Don't be alarmed when you see a prompt the first time you try to analyze in Excel (like the one you see in Figure 14-13). Once the add-on is downloaded to the computer, you can begin evaluating your datasets.

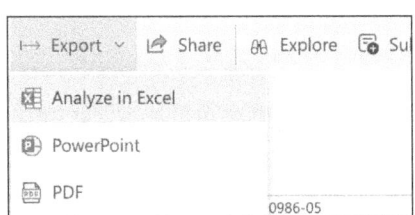

FIGURE 14-13:
The Download
prompt for the
Excel add-on.

Benefiting from Quick Insights

Perhaps you want a quick snapshot of a dataset. Or maybe you're looking for patterns, trends, and ambiguities in your data. The anomalies in the data can be challenging to find if you're first starting out and don't know where to start looking. However, Power BI at least attempts to do the hard work for you. Its artificial intelligence engine finds critical trends, patterns, indicators, and anomalies in your data. With Quick Insights, Power BI automatically produces the top trends it believes are essential in each dataset for a user to consider evaluating. In the example shown in Figure 14-14, you have one federal agency, the State Department, obligating the lowest dollar amount for COVID 19–related projects relative to other federal agencies. Similarly, for counties in Virginia, a greater allocation of dollars was given to Fairfax and Stafford relative to others.

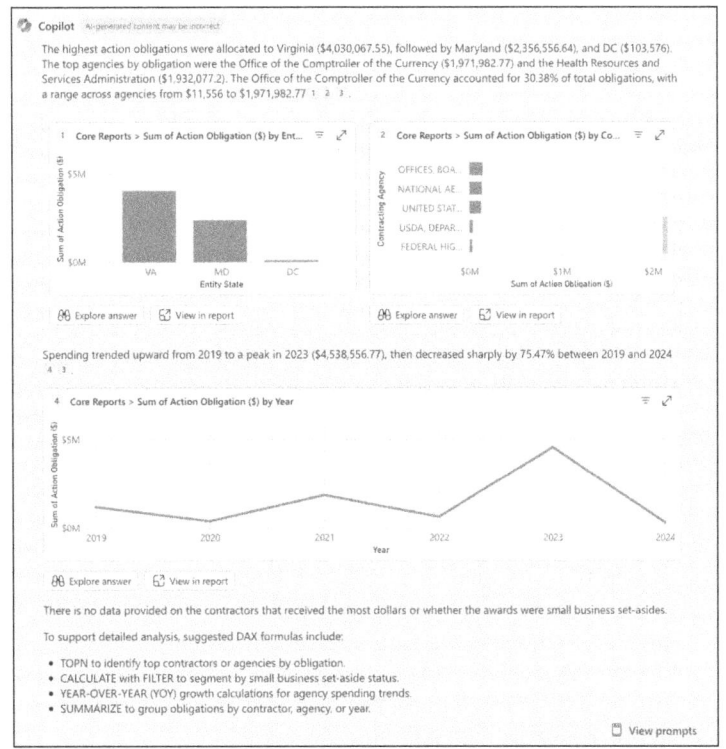

FIGURE 14-14:
The Quick
Insights feature.

Using Usage Metric reports

Ever want to know how popular a report or dashboard is? Or perhaps who accessed an item in a workspace today, this week, or over time? Microsoft recognized that data access metrics help improve a designer's ability to deliver best-in-class analytics. The Usage Metrics report can help users analyze data points, including distribution types, views, viewers, viewer rank, views per day, and unique views per day, as shown in Figure 14-15.

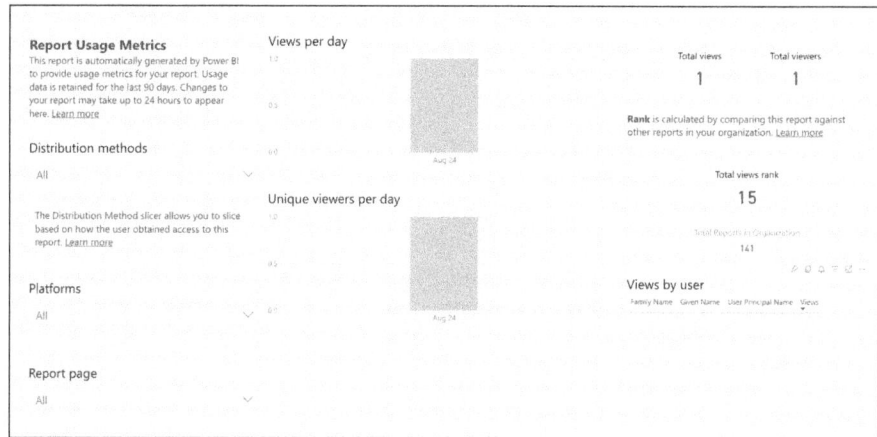

FIGURE 14-15:
A usage
metrics report.

Troubleshooting the Use of Data Lineage

Business intelligence projects can get complex pretty quickly. Following the flow of data from one source to its destination may even be a challenge. Suppose that you've built a relatively complex, advanced analytical project that contains several data sources and maintains numerous reports and dashboards. Each of these assets clearly has a variety of dependencies. As you review these assets, you may come upon questions such as, "What will happen to this report if I make a change to this data point?" Or you may want to better understand how a change you might make will reflect in a dataset.

Data lineage simplifies many complex processes by breaking down processes into more manageable steps. Think of it as your little detective! With data lineage, you can see the path your data takes from start to completion, which is crucial when you're scratching your head, having hit many roadblocks. Whether you're managing a workspace with a single report or dashboard or one with many, make sure that the impact of a single change in a dataset is recognized by referring to the data lineage to track those changes. A bonus is that you can resolve many data-refresh concerns with data lineage as well.

To access data lineage information, follow these steps:

1. **Go to the workspace you're targeting.**

2. **Click View.**

3. **Choose Lineage from the menu that appears (see Figure 14-16).**

   Lineage view appears, as shown in Figure 14-17.

FIGURE 14-16: Gaining access to data lineage.

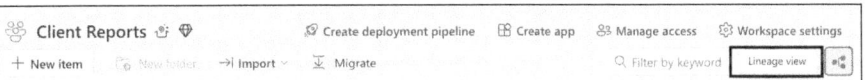

FIGURE 14-17: An example of data lineage.

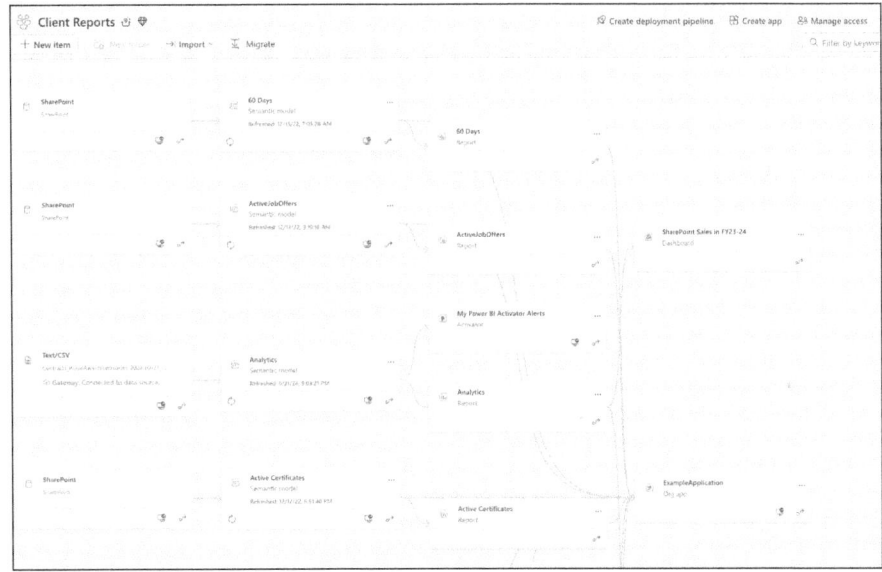

As with other workspace features, only specific roles can access the Lineage view. You must be an admin, a contributor, or a member to see the Lineage view. Also, you must have a Power BI Pro or Premium license using an app-based workspace to make use of the view.

Once you select Lineage, all items in the workspace appear on the canvas. Figure 14-17, for example, shows the data lineage for the Pipeline Identification workspace.

The Lineage view provides a synopsis of all artifacts in your workspace — datasets, dataflows, reports, and dashboards, for example. As shown in Figures 14-18 through 14-21, each of the cards on the canvas, as represented in Lineage view, is a separate asset. The arrows between each of the cards explain the data flows among assets. Data flows from left to right, allowing you to observe it as it moves from the source to the destination. Generally, the flow tells a story, such as the one in this list:

>> A source produces one or more datasets (see Figure 14-18).

>> Reports are generated from datasets (see Figure 14-19).

>> A collection of reports presenting a snapshot in time results in the creation of a dashboard (see Figure 14-20).

>> Data flows in particular directions (see Figure 14-21).

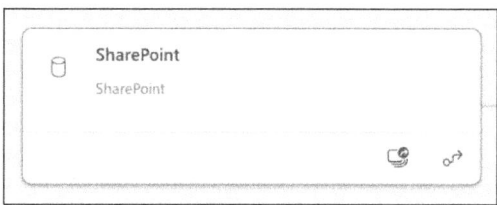

FIGURE 14-18: Example of a Dataset card.

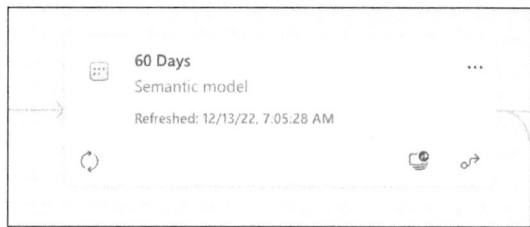

FIGURE 14-19: A Report card.

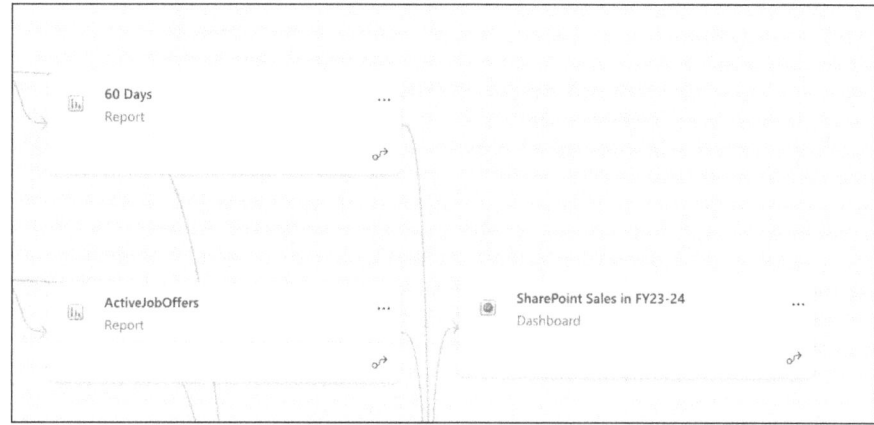

FIGURE 14-20: A Dashboard card.

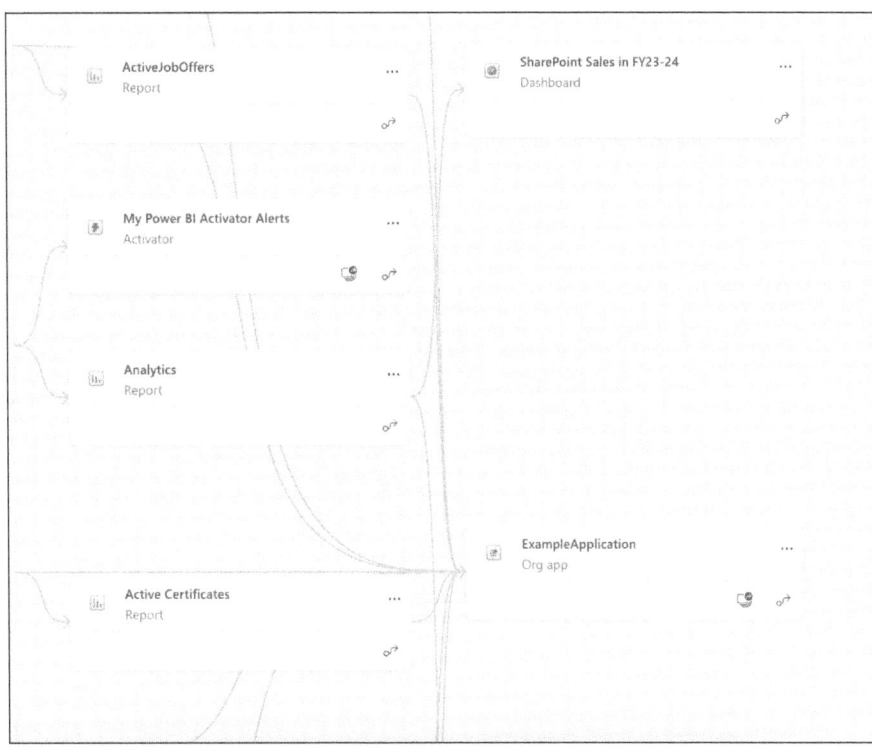

FIGURE 14-21:
Arrows between
each asset in a
workspace.

Datasets, Dataflows, and Lineage

It's not uncommon for datasets and dataflows to be associated with external sources. Some examples may include databases or datasets found in external workspaces. When reviewing the Dataset card, as shown in Figure 14-22, you see that a user can drill down to evaluate different factors by choosing one of these three commands. Each command reveals a different aspect of the dataset:

» **View Details and Related Reports:** This command displays all reports tied to the associated datasets or dataflow.

» **Show Impact Across Workspace:** This command provides you with an impact analysis of how the dataset or dataflow impacts workspace activity (see Figure 14-23).

» **Show Lineage**: This command provides you with a micro-level view of the dataset.

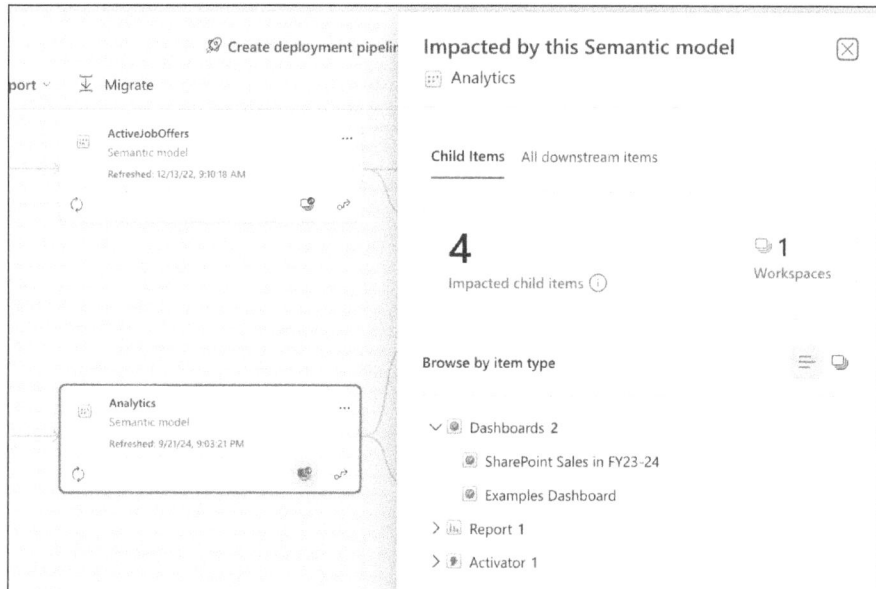

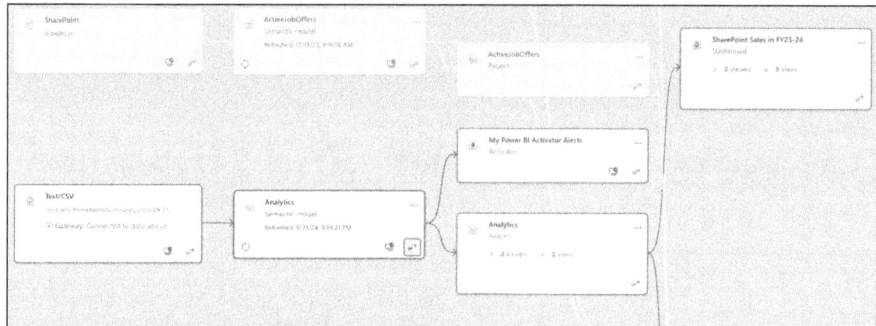

Defending Your Data Turf

Can you imagine a sensitive report or dashboard being exposed to an unauthorized user group in your organization? That won't go over too well, because global exposure can compromise your data and information security practices. Microsoft integrated a way to codify protection for your data analytics assets. Called *sensitivity labels,* this feature (which is available across the Microsoft 365 product family and integrates with Power BI) allows users to apply labels to reports, dashboards, datasets, dataflows, and `.pbix` files. Such labels guard sensitive content against unauthorized access. It is incumbent on you to label your data correctly to ensure that only authorized users access your data.

Though information protection may seem nonnegotiable, your organization must have a few implementation prerequisites in place first, such as a Power BI Pro or Premium per User license. For sensitivity labels to work, edit permissions must be enabled for all content you want to label in the workspace. Before edit permissions can even be accessed, a systems administrator must enable sensitivity labels in Settings for users to apply such permissions in the Power BI workspaces (see Figure 14-24).

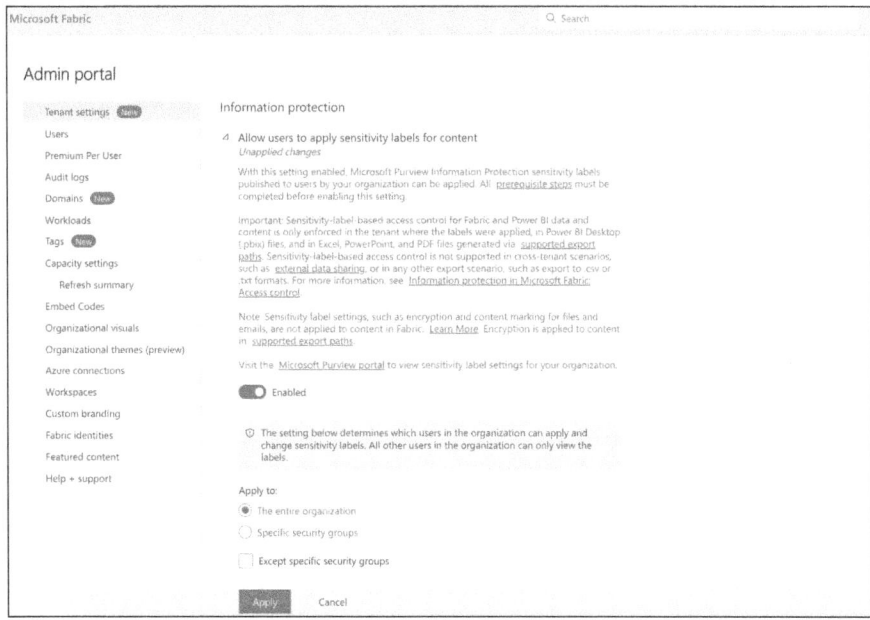

FIGURE 14-24: Enabling sensitivity labels in Power BI.

You must be part of the security group authorized to apply the sensitivity labels; otherwise, access is disabled.

Data protection must be enabled for your instance of Power BI so that sensitivity labels can appear. Otherwise, you won't find any sensitivity labels in the Sensitivity column in List view of dashboards, reports, datasets, or dataflows with your workspace.

WARNING

Your systems administrator must configure sensitivity labels in the Microsoft Information Protection Admin console, separate from the Power BI Admin console. This step must be completed before sensitivity labels can be enabled and usable by any user.

To make changes to a sensitivity label on a report or a dashboard, follow these steps:

1. **Open the report or dashboard you want to edit.**

2. **Click the three vertical dots.**

3. **Choose Settings from the menu that appears.**

4. **Locate the Sensitivity Label section in the Settings pane that appears.**

5. **Choose the appropriate sensitivity label.**

6. **When you finish, click Save.**

   In your workspace, the sensitivity label appears in the column under the appropriate report or dashboard.

ON THE WEB To learn how to configure sensitivity labels in the Microsoft 365 information protection admin console, go to https://docs.microsoft.com/en-us/microsoft-365/compliance/create-sensitivity-labels.

4

Oh, No! There's a Power BI Programming Language!

IN THIS PART . . .

Manipulate datasets with Data Analysis Expressions (DAX) in Power BI.

Work with the key components of the DAX language.

Discover ways that DAX can help you complete complex data analysis activities.

Quickly debug and optimize your DAX code using tools and coding-based techniques.

Chapter **15**

Digging into DAX

In Part 3 of this book, you discover how to build Power BI visualizations that become a part of reports and dashboards. I am confident that you will encounter a moment where the standard drag-and-drop features fall short, whether that happens because a data format doesn't meet your needs or a custom calculation is required. Moments like these are when Data Analysis Expressions (DAX) can come in handy.

DAX is the programming language that runs behind the scenes in Power BI. Sure, you can create basic reports without writing a single line of DAX code — Power BI's built-in features handle plenty of scenarios. However, when stakeholders request complex business logic, custom time intelligence, or performance-optimized solutions for large datasets, DAX will inevitably be required. Consider the following, though: DAX is not limited to use in Power BI. If you have used Excel's Power Pivot, SQL Server Analysis Services, and Azure Analysis Services, you already have a head start in the Power BI programming race.

In the next two chapters, you get the technical foundation you need to build reports, debug performance issues, and create advanced analytics products.

Discovering DAX

Data Analysis Expressions (DAX) is a formula language that uses expressions to manipulate data in analysis tools such as Power BI. Functions, formulas, constants, and operators combine to create expressions that calculate results across your entire data model. DAX shares Excel's formula approach but operates on entire data models rather than individual cells, giving it sophisticated data manipulation capabilities for business intelligence and data modeling.

Throughout many chapters of this book, I demonstrate how to complete tasks without writing code. So why introduce programming now? The built-in features of Power BI handle many common calculations automatically through pre-programmed tools. However, you'll encounter scenarios where standard features can't deliver what you need, whether you need custom business logic, complex time calculations, or advanced filtering that goes beyond basic aggregations. The results from drag-and-drop features may not meet your requirements. That's when DAX becomes essential.

Peeking under the DAX hood

At its core, DAX combines three fundamental concepts: syntax, context, and functions. When combined, these concepts work together to create expressions that produce results that yield the desired results, as I describe in this list:

>> **Syntax** refers to the rules and structure for writing DAX formulas. It includes how you reference tables and columns, use operators, and organize expressions. For example, Sales[Revenue] follows DAX syntax rules for referencing a column in a table.

>> **Context** refers to the data environment where your calculations occur. Context determines which rows DAX considers when performing calculations. You need to understand two types: row context (the row being evaluated) and filter context (the rows included based on applied filters).

>> **Functions** are predefined operations that perform specific calculations or data manipulations. DAX includes functions for aggregation (like SUM), time intelligence (like SAMEPERIODLASTYEAR), and logical operations (like IF).

ON THE
WEB

I provide a complete reference for key DAX functions on this book's Cheat Sheet. To find the Cheat Sheet, go to www.dummies.com and enter **Power BI For Dummies** in the Search box.

Establishing syntax

The very first thing you need to learn about DAX is the composition of a formula. In Figure 15-1, you find a sample formula for a measure.

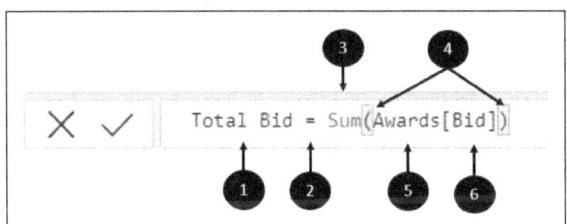

FIGURE 15-1:
A syntax
example.

I've numbered these six components of note in Figure 15-1:

1. **The measure name is** `Total Bid`.

2. **The equal-sign operator (=) indicates the beginning of the formula.**

   After the formula is calculated, the result is returned.

3. **The DAX function** `SUM` **is used in this formula, which adds all numbers in the** `Awards[Bid]` **column.**

4. **A parenthesis ( ) almost always surrounds an expression containing one or more arguments.**

   Arguments handle passing values to functions.

5. **The reference table is** `Awards`.

6. **The specific reference column** `[Bid]` **is found in the** `Awards` **table.**

   Using the specified argument, the `SUM` function aggregates all data for this specific column.

A calculated measure returns the total value of all awarded bids. The formula also includes a *function* — a predefined formula. Formulas make it easier to complete complex calculations and manipulate large datasets, especially when various numbers, dates, times, and text are involved. One column name is Award Amount. Now, the column does belong to the Award Data table, but including the table name along with a column name — *fully qualifying* a column name, in other words — is nonetheless a best practice.

TIP

When a table name has spaces, reserved keywords, or words with disallowed characters, be sure to use single quotation marks to enclose the table name. Also, be sure to enclose any table in quotation marks if the table name has any non-ANSI alphanumeric characters.

WARNING

Power BI catches syntax errors, but typos that create valid but incorrect column names won't trigger warnings. For example, a table and column reference such as `Award Data[Revenue]` may look fine to Power BI but can return blank results because that column doesn't exist or the wrong column is being called. Use the DAX editor's IntelliSense feature — the drop-down suggestions that appear as you type — to ensure that you're referencing the correct tables and columns.

Conceiving context

Context is a critical concept in DAX because it determines which data your calculations consider. You need to understand two types of context: row and filter.

>> **Row context** is evaluated each time an expression is repeated in a table. That means that for each individual row, there's a different context. Row context exists either as a calculated column or a DAX function. Sample functions may be `SUMX`, `AVERAGEX`, or `FILTER`.

Suppose that a calculated column has been previously created. In that case, you can assume that the row context consists of the values in each individual row. That means, then, that the values in columns are related to a current row. Figure 15-2 shows an example of a row context.

>> **Filter context** is the application of those filters during the evaluation of measures or expressions. A filter can be applied directly to a column, like a filter on the funding_agency_name column in the Award Data table. In the case of Figure 15-3, the filter is applied to just those opportunities that are in process. The table transitioned from multiple agencies to a single agency because a slicer filter was used.

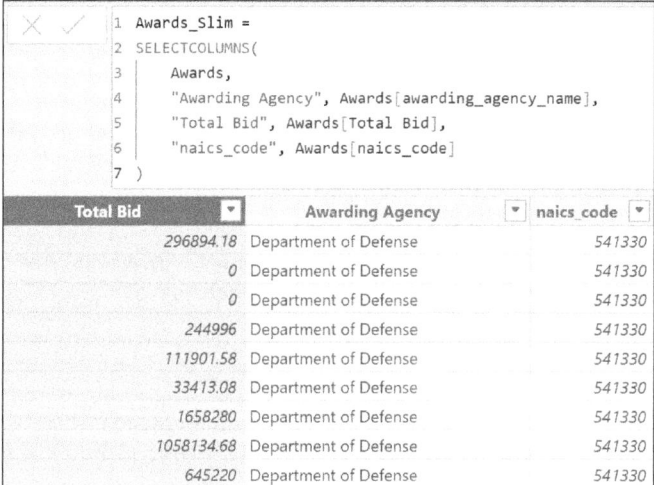

FIGURE 15-2: A row context example.

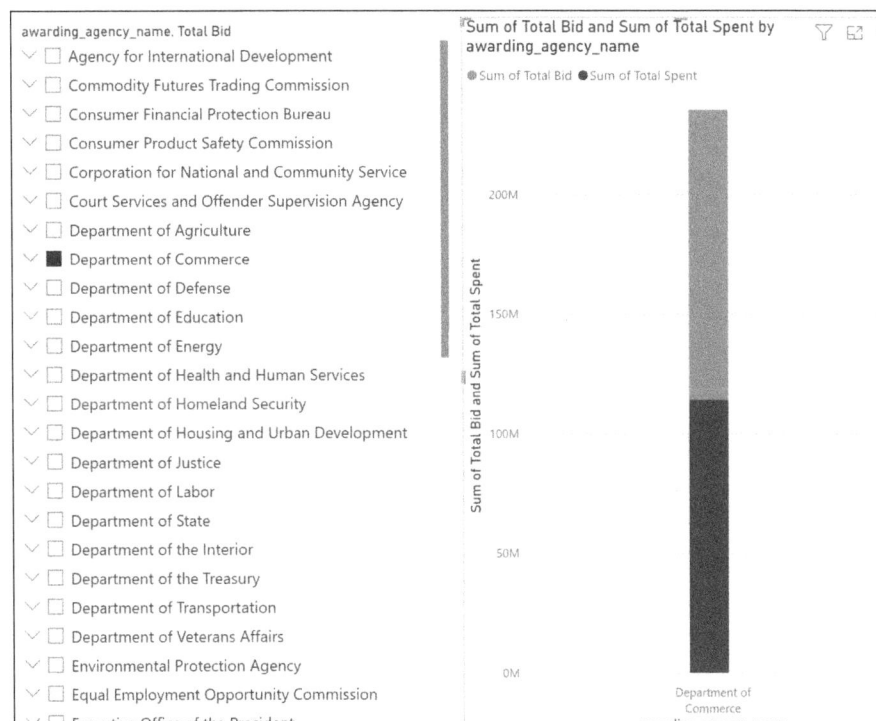

FIGURE 15-3:
A filter
context
example.

Formulating functions

Functions are predefined operations that perform specific calculations and manipulate data. Each function accepts inputs called *arguments* and returns a *result*. Arguments can include column references, numbers, text values, logical expressions, or even other functions nested within each other.

DAX offers an extensive function library organized into categories like aggregation (SUM, AVERAGE), time intelligence (SAMEPERIODLASTYEAR, DATESYTD), logical operations (IF, AND), and text manipulation (CONCATENATE, LEFT). With over 250 functions available, you'll find tools for virtually any calculation scenario you encounter in business intelligence.

Working with calculations

DAX formulas are used in measures, calculated columns, calculated tables, and row-level security. To create new calculations, switch to Table view in Power BI Desktop. In the Ribbon, find the Table tools tab, which contains the calculation tools. You have four options, as shown in Figure 15-4, and this list describes what you can do by choosing them:

>> **New Measure:** Write a DAX expression from your data.

>> **Quick Measure:** Choose from a list of predefined calculations in Power BI.

>> **New Column:** Write a DAX expression that creates a new column in the selected table and calculates the values for each row.

>> **New Table:** Create a DAX expression to create a new table.

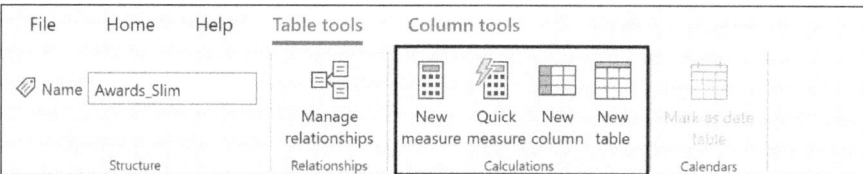

The following sections present all four options, allowing you to better understand how to create measures, quick measures, calculated columns, and calculated tables.

Measures

Measures help users gain insights into their data by performing calculations that respond dynamically to user interactions. Examples include aggregations (sum, average, minimum, maximum, count), ratios, percentages, and time-based comparisons. Unlike calculated columns that store values in your data model, measures calculate results on demand based on the current filter context. Each time users apply filters, select different time periods, or interact with slicers, a measure recalculates the results of the current selection. Such behavior is useful when creating interactive dashboards and reports.

You can create measures in either Report view or Table view in Power BI Desktop. After they have been created, measures appear in the Fields pane with a calculator icon (*fx*). You can name measures descriptively and add them to visualizations like any other field.

For the example shown in Figure 15-5, I created a discount calculation that applies an 8 percent reduction to all award amounts. The DAX formula is: `DiscountRate = CALCULATE('Award Data'[Total Bid]* 0.92)`. Figure 15-6 shows the new measure, now available in the Fields pane.

FIGURE 15-5:
A calculated
measure in the
DAX editor.

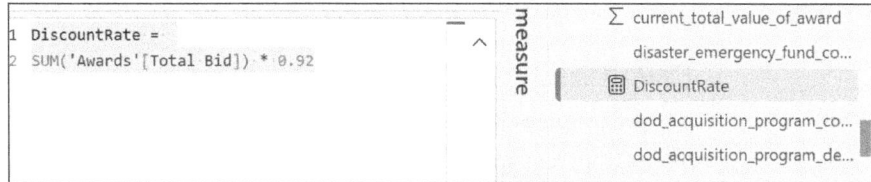

```
1  DiscountRate =
2  SUM('Awards'[Total Bid]) * 0.92
```

FIGURE 15-6:
A calculated
measure
added to the
Fields pane.

If you prefer to generate measures automatically, see Chapter 8 for details on Quick Measures.

Calculated columns

Suppose that you already have a model, and you want to add data to it. Sometimes, you can't simply load new data into a table and consider the task complete. That's why you should consider using *calculated columns,* a type of DAX formula that defines the values of the columns. You can use the Calculated Columns feature to add new data to a table in your existing model. Rather than load the data using a data source, you create a DAX formula to do the work. Calculated columns are created using the New Column feature available under Report view (Modeling Tab) or Table view (Table Tools).

Don't confuse calculated columns with custom columns — they're created in different places and serve different purposes. Custom columns are created in Power Query using the Add Column tab in the Power Query Editor, typically before the data is loaded into your model. In contrast, a calculated column is created after the data has already been loaded, usually in Table view or Model view, using a DAX formula. When you create a calculated column, the resulting product appears in the Data pane. You'll find that the calculated column has an icon showing that its values are the result of a formula. As with measures, you can name the column however you want. Once the column is added to the list of fields found in the Data pane, you can integrate the resulting column into a report visualization, as you would others.

In Figure 15-7, you can see a calculated column created in Table view. In this case, the column calculates *Profit Amount* as 10% of the *Award Amount*. The Formula bar appears at the top of the view, and the calculator icon signals that the column is derived from a formula. After it's created, the column behaves like any other field and can be used throughout your report. The column appears the farthest to the right in this image (10%) of each award.

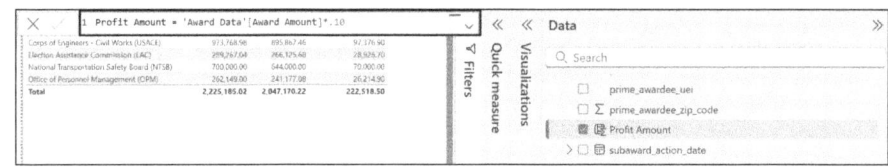

FIGURE 15-7:
Calculated
columns in
Report view.

Calculated tables

When you use Power BI, you usually create tables by importing them into your model from an external data source. You can also create tables programmatically, however, by using *calculated tables*. These are tables built using DAX formulas based on data already loaded into the data model. The idea here is to create a DAX formula to define the table's values, rather than querying and loading the values into the table's columns from a source.

TIP

Calculated tables work best for more complex calculations and data you want to store as part of a data model rather than with the help of ad hoc calculations. In fact, combining tables using statements such as UNION, INTERSECT, or CROSSJOIN is a great use case for calculated tables because they can have relationships with other tables.

Calculated table columns typically include data types and specific formatting, and they often belong to a specific category. As with other Power BI elements, you can name a column however you see fit and add it to a report. Power BI recalculates the table whenever the underlying data changes; the results are then recalculated, assuming that a data refresh has occurred. The exception is with the use of DirectQuery. In that case, tables reflect changes only after a dataset is refreshed in its entirety. For DirectQuery models, it's best to create calculated tables within the source system. It's best to have the calculated table in the DirectQuery instance for assured data freshness.

To create a calculated table, follow these steps:

1. **Choose Table View in the navigation bar on the left side of the Power BI Desktop screen.**

2. **Choose New Table in the Calculations area of the Ribbon's Home tab.**

3. **In the new screen that appears, click the New Calculations button, which allows you to create a DAX-based calculation.**

4. **Enter the DAX expression that you want associated with the calculated table in the field, as shown in Figure 15-8.**

    As you are entering the expression, you'll see the calculated tables pre-populate on the screen. In this case, I've used the existing Awards Data dataset to replicate a new calculated table, called *Vendor Data*.

5. **After you are satisfied with your DAX entry, press Enter.**

The expression is now committed as a new table to the existing dataset tables.

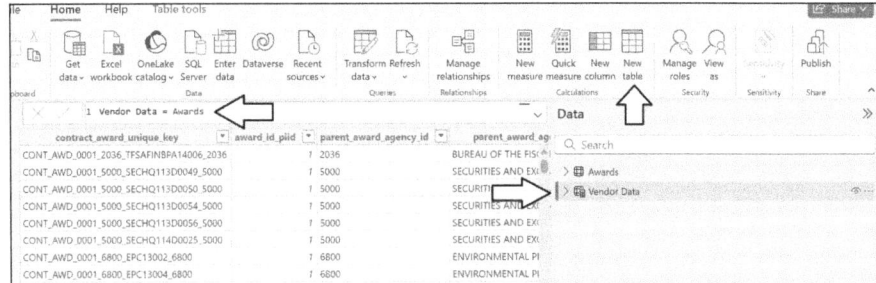

FIGURE 15-8:
Creating a calculated table from Table view.

Dealing with Data Types

DAX supports a range of data types like Power Query, but it uses a different system than Power Query. With DAX, each source can also support various data types, though the range is limited compared to Power Query. Figure 15-9 and Figure 15-10 compare the differences between data types in DAX and Power Query. With DAX, when you import data into a model, the data is converted into a model-specific data type used by DAX.

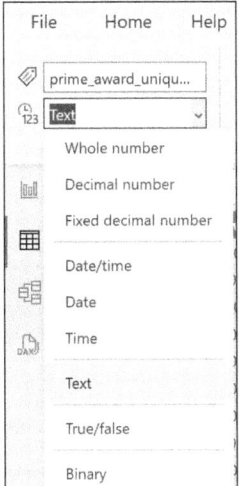

FIGURE 15-9:
DAX data types.

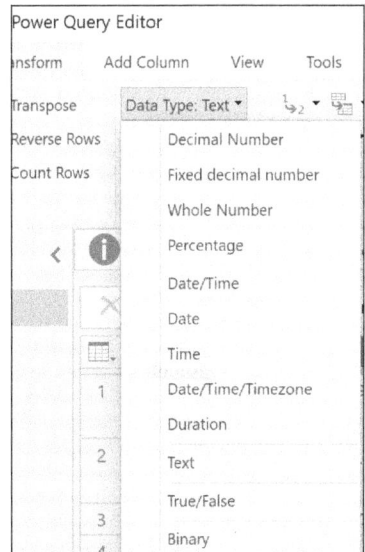

FIGURE 15-10:
Power Query
data types.

Each time model data is used as part of a calculation, the data is transformed into a DAX data type that is most suitable based on what Microsoft assumes is accurate. Sometimes this may be wrong, though. A classic example is when Power BI perceives all values to be a whole number, but you know later on that there may be values requiring decimals, such as 10.0 (whole number) versus Decimals or Fixed Decimals (10.123). When you create a DAX formula, the terms you use determine which data type is returned. Table 15-1 illustrates the DAX data types.

REMEMBER

Like importing data using Power Query, data types are set automatically. You should be familiar with how data types apply to DAX formulas. The most common reason for errors in a formula or result set is an improper data type. An example is using the wrong operator with a data type in an argument.

TABLE 15-1   **DAX Data Types**

Model Data Type	Data Type in DAX	What It Means
Whole number	64-bit (8-byte) integer	Numbers without a decimal place. The number can be an integer with either a positive or negative value. The negative range starts at 9,223,372,036,854,775,808 (–2^63) to a positive range not to exceed 9,223,372,036,854,775,807 (2^63-1).
Decimal number	64-bit (8-byte) real number	Real numbers with a wide range of parameters. Negative values can range from –1.79E +308 through –2.23E –308. Positive values range from 2.23E –308 through 1.79E + 308. The limit is 17 decimal digits.

Model Data Type	Data Type in DAX	What It Means
Fixed decimal number	64-bit (8-byte) real number	Representative of monetary values. The range of values can be from −922,337,203,685,477.5808 to 922,337,203,685,477.5807. Four decimal digits can be used to ensure precision.
Date/Time	Date/Time	Date/time representation. The range begins after March 1, 1900, at 12:00 a.m.
Date	Date	Just the date (no Time part). Upon conversion, the date value is the same as a Date/Time value without the digits to the correct placement.
Time	Time	Just the time (no Date part). Upon conversion, the time value is the same as a Date/Time value without the digits to the left placement.
Text	String	Unicode character data string. It can be an alphanumeric string represented in a text format. The maximum string length is 268,435,456.
Boolean	True/False	A Boolean value that is either TRUE or FALSE.
Binary	Binary	Used to represent any other data with a binary format not included on this list.
Blank	Blank	Considered the equivalent of a NULL value in SQL. It can use the BLANK function. To query, you can use the ISBLANK( ).

Operating with Operators

Arithmetic operators return numeric values based on performed arithmetic calculations. You can use five different arithmetic operator types to create formulas in DAX. Table 15-2 describes these operators and provides examples for each one.

TABLE 15-2 **Arithmetic Operators**

Operator	What It Means	Example
+	Addition	4+2
−	Subtraction	4−2
*	Multiplication	4*2
/	Division	4/2
^	Exponent	4^2

Comparison operators return a TRUE or FALSE value based on comparison values. Table 15-3 shows you the DAX comparison operators.

TABLE 15-3 ## Comparison Operators

Operator	What It Means	Example
=	Equal to	[State] = "CA"
>	Greater than	[Close Date] > "June 2000"
<	Less than	[Close Date] < "June 2000"
>=	Greater than or equal to	[Price] >= 500
<=	Less than or equal to	[Price]<= 100
<>	Not equal to	[County] <> "CANADA"

Logical operators allow you to combine multiple conditions into a single result. You can use them in calculated columns, measures, and conditional logic. Table 15-4 shows you the DAX logical operators.

TABLE 15-4 ## Logical Operators

Operator	What It Creates	Example
&&	An AND condition	([State] = "NJ") && ([Visitor] = "yes"))
||	An OR condition	((([State] = "NY") || ([Visitor] = "yes"))
IN	A logical OR condition or BETWEEN condition	'Product'[Size] IN { "Square", "Box", "Circle" }

REMEMBER

Note the ever so slight difference between an OR and AND comparison operator and OR and AND logical operator. With the comparison operator, you are evaluating numbers. With logical operators, you are evaluating text.

Text operators return a value based on concatenated operators that join two or more string values. Table 15-5 shows you the single DAX text operator.

TABLE 15-5 ## Text Operator

Operator	What It Does	Example
&	Connects two values to make a single text string	[City] & "," & [State]

Ordering operators

Ordering operators, formally known as *operator precedence* in DAX, help manage the order in which calculations are performed, which affects the value that's returned. In this context, operator precedence in DAX follows the traditional mathematical rule of PEMDAS (Parentheses, Exponents, Multiplication, Division, Addition, and Subtraction), which specifies the order of operations required to achieve the desired outcome from left to right.

All expressions evaluate a specific operation order. An expression always starts with an equal sign, which is meant to indicate the characters constituting the expression. After the equal sign, you find the elements that are calculated. Calculated elements are referred to as *operands.* Each operand is separated by the calculation operators. Though expressions are always read from left to right, the order in which elements are grouped can be fully manipulated if you use parentheses. Table 15-6 shows the operator order for a DAX equation.

TABLE 15-6

Operator Order

Operator	Description
^	Exponentiation
–	Sign (as in negative)
* and /	Multiplication and division
!	NOT (unary operator)
+ and –	Addition and subtraction
&	Connects strings (concatenation)
=,==,<,>,<=,>=,<>	Comparison

TECHNICAL STUFF

Frequently, you use multiple operators in the same DAX formula. When operators have the same level of precedence — such as multiplication and division, or addition and subtraction — Power BI evaluates them from left to right, based on the order they appear. However, when different types of operators are combined, DAX follows a specific operator order, where exponentiation happens before multiplication or addition. To make your formulas easier to read and ensure that they calculate as expected, you can use parentheses to override the default order of operations, as I describe in the next section.

Parentheses and order

In DAX, like in old school math, a simple bracket can change how a calculation turns out. Let's take a look at this equation. What's the difference between these two items?

= 2+2*3

= (2+2)*3

The first equation orders the data differently from the way the second equation does. The parentheses change the order in which the equation is calculated. In the first equation, 2×3 is calculated first. Then you add two, which equals 8. On the other hand, the parentheses in the second equation change the calculation order because 2+2 equals 4. You then multiply 4 times 3. The result is 12.

Making a Statement

There are several types of statements used when writing full DAX queries throughout Power BI. Common query statements include DEFINE, EVALUATE, ORDER BY, and VAR. These statements help you structure complex DAX queries by allowing you to define variables, set up measures or tables, and control the output of your query results. Although you may not use these in everyday formulas for measures or calculated columns, they are useful for testing and exploring your data model in a more advanced, flexible way. Table 15-7 shows the four types of statements.

TABLE 15-7 Statements

Statement Type	What It Does
DEFINE	Defines one or more entities that exist for the duration of a DAX entry exclusively
EVALUATE	Required to execute any type of DAX query
ORDER BY	Used, for one or more expressions, to sort results in a DAX query
VAR	Stores the result of an expression as a named variable and can be passed to just about any argument, including other measure expressions

Ensuring Compatibility

The DAX language shares many similarities with Excel, particularly in its handling of calculations. However, DAX also includes more advanced features. Unlike Excel, DAX supports a broader set of data types and is designed to work with relational data models, making it more powerful for building dynamic reports in Power BI Desktop.

One important concept in DAX is *type coercion*, which occurs when two values in a formula don't share the same data type. DAX will try to convert the values — called operands — to a common type before performing the operation. This allows calculations, such as addition or multiplication, to work correctly, even when one value is a number and the other is a text string that resembles a number.

For example, imagine a formula like `=[Cost] * 0.50`, where `[Cost]` is stored as text but contains a numeric value. DAX will automatically convert the string to a number, allowing it to complete the multiplication. In most cases, DAX will use the largest compatible numeric type to preserve accuracy.

A common case that trips people up involves leading zeros. For example, a value like `0123` is considered text, not a number. If combined with numeric data, DAX may attempt to coerce it to a number, such as `123`, omitting the leading zero. However, if the value also contains non-numeric characters, such as `0123A`, it cannot be converted and will either cause an error or be treated as text. These situations highlight how data type mismatches can lead to unexpected results, hence compatibility challenges.

Not all operations allow coercion. In particular, comparison operators such as `=`, `<`, or `>` may return errors or incorrect results if the data types can't be matched. That's why it's best to keep data types consistent — or use functions like `VALUE()` to convert text to numbers or `FORMAT()` to control output types explicitly.

Chapter **16**

Digging Deeper into DAX

I n Chapter 15, I show you how to create DAX formulas that perform the sophisticated calculations required to drive meaningful insights for your organization. This chapter helps you better understand the technical elements behind coding and debugging your DAX formulas in Power BI. You explore the core principles that remain constant as Power BI evolves, and you see how you can take advantage of error message management, use AI-based autocomplete features, and explore testing capabilities to make writing DAX easier.

Working with DAX Parameters and Naming Conventions

Like any programming language, DAX has a standardized parameter naming convention that helps facilitate language usage, especially when incorporating prefixes in the parameter name. (In fact, some DAX parameters allow you to use the prefix exclusively for names.) The enhanced Power BI IntelliSense and autocomplete features can also help you follow these conventions by suggesting parameter names as you type. Table 16-1 the standardized parts of parameter names used across DAX functions. It defines what each parameter name represents, how it behaves in evaluation, and whether it refers to a value, table, or constant.

TABLE 16-1   Parameter Naming

Part	Description
Expression	A DAX expression that returns a single value; may be reevaluated multiple times depending on row context (for example, based on filters and iterations).
Value	A DAX expression returning a single value but evaluated once before being used often for constants or single evaluations.
Table	A DAX expression that returns a full table; used in functions like FILTER( ) or SUMMARIZE( ).
tableName	A direct reference to an existing table (not an expression). It's written in standard DAX syntax 'Sales'.
columnName	A direct reference to an existing column, typically fully qualified 'Sales'[Amount]. It can't be an expression.
Name	A string literal that names a new object, such as SUMMARIZECOLUMNS("Total Sales", SUM(Sales[Amount])).
Order	An enumerated value that determines sorting order using ASC or DESC.
Ties	An enumerated parameter that controls how ties are handled in ranking or ordering such as the RANKX( ) tie-breaking options.
Type	An enumeration specifying data types or path positions, which are used in functions like PATHITEM( ) and PATHITEMREVERSE( ).

Prefixing parameter names

Each time you qualify a parameter, you may want to include a *prefix* — a specific unique value to differentiate a given parameter. An example may be adding the initials of a state in front of a parameter name. To qualify a parameter with a prefix, ensure that the prefix is descriptive based on the argument. Also, leave no ambiguity reading a parameter — for example:

Hide_ColumnName references a column used to hide values in the DAX LOOKUPVALUE ( ) function.

Seek_ColumnName references a column used to show a value in the DAX LOOKUPVALUE( ) function.

TIP

Parameter names can sometimes be omitted. You would use only the prefix, assuming that it's clear enough to describe the parameter. Following this strategy may help avoid confusion later while reading the code. An example following this approach is `DATE (Year_value, Month_value,Day_value)`.

Playing with parameters

To start out this chapter, I show you how DAX function parameters work in practice. Chapter 15 covers the different types of functions available; this chapter focuses on the basic rules for naming and using function parameters. Figure 16-1 shows a sample function with fully qualified parameters.

```
1  AwardByRegion =
2  CALCULATE(
3      SUM(AnalyticsSpendFY21to25[total_outlayed_amount]),
4      FILTER(
5          ALL(AnalyticsSpendFY21to25
            [recipient_state_name]),
6          AnalyticsSpendFY21to25[recipient_state_code] =
            "MD"
7      )
8  )
```

FIGURE 16-1:
A sample
function.

Each DAX function has a distinct parameter structure. In Figure 16-1, you notice that each parameter for a specific DAX function is incorporated as part of the table with a description. For the example provided, the DAX function `SELECTCOLUMNS` has the following attributes:

>> **Table:** The expression returns a table.

>> **Name:** The name given to a column; it requires double-quotes.

>> **scalar_expression:** It returns a scalar value, such as an integer or string.

TECHNICAL STUFF

Keeping a strict naming convention is essential with DAX functions, especially when it comes to the values for parameters. A table name is specific to what appears in a data model, as is the column name. Still, you find square brackets enclosing the column. An example is a `Purchase [Purchase Amount]`. That said, as you type, Power BI guides you in correcting your syntax. If you make a mistake, you know right away.

Using Formulas and Functions

If you've ever used formulas in Excel, you're likely familiar with DAX to some degree. Even though Excel has some power features like dynamic arrays and improved data handling, the structure and design of Excel and DAX formulas are still similar in nature, with a few caveats:

» **DAX functions reference complete columns and tables.** To reference a specific value in a table or column, you need to incorporate a filter.

» **DAX has a variety of functions that return a table full of data instead of just a value.** The table isn't present in a report, but you can use it to input other functions. The idea is similar to the way Excel's dynamic array functions work.

» **DAX includes more than just numeric functions.** In fact, you have features that include time intelligence and string-based data. Such formulas allow you to define or select data ranges and even perform calculations against one or more data ranges.

» **DAX supports customized calculations, even for a single row of data.** You can use DAX for a current row or a series of rows by applying a parameter to perform calculations assuming a known context.

Because DAX is a functional language, any complete code sample including a formula contains a function. DAX formulas may be a combination of conditional statements, functions, and references. Further, DAX formulas come in two flavors: numeric and non-numeric variations. Numeric data includes values such as integers, decimals, and currency-based values. Non-numeric is composed of strings and binary objects.

To review 250+ DAX based functions across numerous categories, head over to the Cheat Sheet for this book. Go to www.dummies.com and enter **Power BI For Dummies** in the Search box.

ON THE WEB

When reading a DAX expression, be sure to evaluate from the innermost function to the outermost. Expressions follow the operator rules, which I also discuss in Chapter 15, making crafting a DAX formula a task that demands precision.

TECHNICAL STUFF

Working with Variables

One of the first things you learn in Programming 101 is how to use variables. Well, guess what? Variables are also a fundamental construct in DAX. You can declare DAX variables in your formula expressions. As long as you declare at least one variable, a RETURN clause is used to define the expression. The result then refers to the variable.

For many reasons, you want to use variables as you begin programming, whether for syntax, context, or functionality. Here are a few:

» Improves readability and maintenance of formulas

» Increases performance by allowing the user, developer, or observer to evaluate code once, as needed

» Supports design-time testing of easy, targeted strategies for complex formulas, only returning *key variables* — those being called upon, in other words

Writing DAX Formulas

Whether you're creating a calculated column, calculated table, or measure in Power BI, you follow a standard convention for writing formulas.

Every DAX formula has the same basic structure: a name, followed by an equal sign, followed by the DAX expression. Here's the pattern:

```
<Name> = <DAX Formula>
```

For the following calculated table example, I created a new table called Awarded Status that duplicates all data from the existing Awarded table.

```
Awarded Status = 'Awarded'
```

When it comes to Calculated Columns, the behavior is similar, but the syntax varies slightly. In this example, two columns are aggregated into one: First Name and Last Name. Notice that these are strings, not numbers. Don't be fooled by the word *calculated*; strings being concatenated also constitute being called a calculation.

```
Full Name = Customer[First Name] & " " & Customer[Last Name]
```

Measures allow a user to calculate the values in a column of a table. In the following example, the measure sums all the values in the Amount column of the Sales table. The beauty of a measure is that its value is dynamic — the value can and will change if you place it in a chart and then apply a filter. For example, if you want to see just the sales for a country (United States) versus all the countries in

North America, the filter adjusts without you having to make any adjustments. In other words, a measure adapts to the context in which you place it, making it an extremely powerful tool for creating dynamic reports.

```
Total Sales = SUM(Sales[Amount])
```

Understanding DAX formulas in depth

DAX formulas consist of a bit more than a few variables and an equal sign. Quite the contrary! Most important, a DAX expression is meant to return a result — either a table object or a scalar value. I can break it down a bit further. If you have a calculated table formula, the result is a returned table object. In contrast, both calculated columns and measure formulas return singular values.

Now take a step back for a moment. What can a formula have? A formula may have all the elements, as shown in Table 16-2.

TABLE 16-2   **Elements of DAX Formulas**

Element	What It Does
Function	Functions carry out specific goals. A function has an argument that allows the passing of a variable. The formula may use a function call and often needs functions inside one another. Function names are a type of formula with conditions that should always be followed by parentheses. Within each parenthesis, you have a variable passed.
Operator	Operators perform arithmetic calculations, compare values, work with strings, and test conditions of varying states.
Variables	Formulas may use variables to store results as part of a calculated expression.
Whitespace	With DAX, some characters can help users format formulas to make it easier to understand expressions. Different whitespace characters include spaces, tabs, and carriage returns. You don't necessarily need to include whitespace as part of your formula logic. It won't hurt performance. It will, however, have a positive impact on format style and consistency.
References to model objects	Formulas reference tables, columns, and measures. A formula cannot reference a hierarchy or a hierarchy level. Therefore, for a table reference, a table name must be enclosed within a single quotation mark. Likewise, a column reference requires an enclosure within square brackets. Under specific conditions, a column name can be preceded by its table name. Finally, measure names must always be enclosed within the square brackets.

Extending formulas with measures

It's all fine and dandy to understand the *concept* of functions, formulas, and measures, but at some point, you need to bring the three together in Power BI Desktop to create extended calculations. That time is now.

One way to extend calculations is to use measures. DAX uses two types of measures: implicit and explicit. Most users prefer to begin by creating simple measures that summarize a single column or table. Then, over time, they realize that as their data grows, they need to create more detailed measures based on other measures in their model.

Implicit and explicit measures

Implicit measures are automatic behaviors that allow visuals to summarize model column data. *Explicit measures* are calculations you can add to a model.

Anytime you see the sigma symbol (Σ) in the Data pane, that should alert a user or data modeler that

>> The data is numeric.

>> The data will use the summarized column value in visualizations and fields to support summarization.

In Figure 16-2, the table includes only fields that can be summarized, including the AwardByRegion calculated column.

FIGURE 16-2:
The Data
pane, showing
a calculated
column.

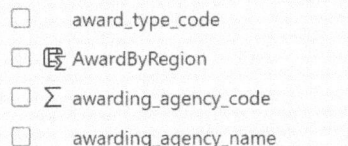

REMEMBER

You control how the column summarizes data by setting the Summarization property either to Don't Summarize or to a specific aggregation function (such as Sum, Average, Count, or something else). When you set the Summarization property to Don't Summarize, the sigma symbol (Σ) disappears from that column in the Data pane. You can access these settings by right-clicking on any field in the Data pane.

As an example, I created a new Power BI report that includes a table containing three columns from the Awards table: total_obligated_amount, total_outlayed_amount, and award_type.

The output of the table, shown in Figure 16-3, indicates that I am keeping track of various award types and corresponding obligations and outlayed spending patterns.

To decide how the column has been summarized, go to the Data pane and choose the either the total_obligation_amount or total_outlayed_amount fields. Then right-click the field under Columns within the Visualization pane to open the Summarization options menu. From this menu, select Sum (as shown in Figure 16-4) to aggregate the field's values in your table. The figure displays the pop-up menu with the Sum command selected, confirming that Power BI is summing the column values.

You can see that the pane now displays the award_type field data as summarized, as shown in Figure 16-4. The data can be tabulated in other ways, but it will likely not provide an optimal response to the reader of the table.

award_type	Sum of total_obligated_amount	Sum of total_outlayed_amount
DELIVERY ORDER	4,828,715,714.71	896,278,841.30
DO	1,210,458,660.98	0.00
DEFINITIVE CONTRACT	1,191,151,292.36	276,802,911.91
BPA CALL	1,190,732,113.07	461,040,198.05
PURCHASE ORDER	301,920,782.21	95,820,700.72
DCA	237,817,664.52	0.00
BPA	73,153,500.17	0.00
PO	71,351,863.20	0.00
Total	**9,105,301,591.22**	**1,729,942,651.98**

FIGURE 16-3:
The table output.

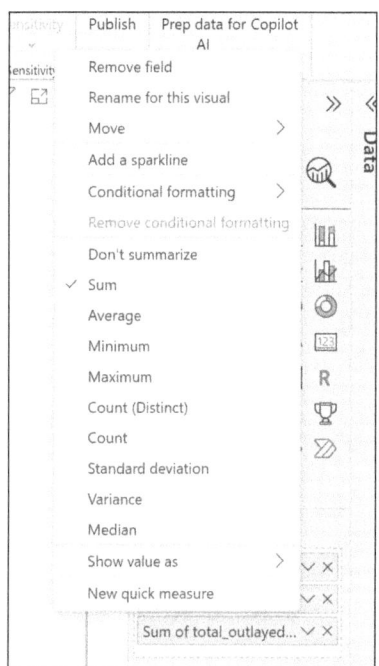

FIGURE 16-4:
Setting a column's calculation type.

Numeric columns utilizing DAX functions provide a wide range of aggregation functions. You can program these programmatically or use a drop-down menu. The most often used numeric column options include these:

>> Sum

>> Average

>> Minimum

>> Maximum

>> Count (distinct)

>> Count

>> Standard deviation

>> Variance

>> Median

REMEMBER

When you format DAX calculations, you may see a phrase containing the word *distinct* now and again. Then there may be another choice that looks almost identical. What's the difference exactly? Take, for example, the difference between COUNT and COUNT DISTINCT. The Count Distinct option shows only unique instances of a given value, whereas COUNT shows results of all records.

Summarization of non-numeric data

Don't assume that only numeric data can be summarized — non-numeric data can be summarized, too! Text columns don't have the sigma symbol (Σ) next to them in the Data pane, but they still offer useful aggregation options:

>> First (alphabetical)

>> Last (alphabetical)

>> Count (Distinct)

>> Count

Date and Boolean (True/False) columns also offer aggregation options that make sense for their data types. For example, date columns can show earliest/latest dates, and Boolean columns can count True values. Take a look at how this works with a practical example using customer data:

>> **First (alphabetical):** "Washington, George"

>> **Last (alphabetical):** "Adams, John"

>> **Count (Distinct):** 8,675 unique customers

>> **Count:** 309 total records (some customers appear multiple times)

Given the data provided in the preceding list, you use the following aggregation options to satisfy the corresponding queries:

>> **Count (Distinct):** "How many unique customers do I have?"

>> **Count:** "How many orders were received during a given month?"

>> **First/Last:** "Who is the most recent or oldest customer in my system?"

The reason this is important for reporting is that when you drag a text field like Customer Name into a visual, Power BI needs to know how to handle multiple values. Should it count unique customers? Count total transactions? Show all names? Selecting the appropriate summarization setting tells Power BI what makes sense for your analysis.

Reasoning for implicit measures

You may argue that explicit measures are better for Power BI because they're calculation-driven — period. However, the truth is that implicit measures are somewhat easier to learn and use. They provide far more flexibility because report authors can use implicit measures to quickly visualize data. It requires a bit more effort with explicit measures when creating calculations.

Of course, every positive has its negative counterpart. Implicit measures allow the report author to create sloppy report designs, if they choose. That means aggregation can be done incorrectly. The aggregated data may not be proper or suitable, based on the representative columns.

Simple and compound measures

You can write just about any DAX formula to add a measure to any table in your model. The only constraint you have is that a measure formula must return a single value (like a number, text, or date).

TECHNICAL STUFF

Measures don't store values in the data model. Instead, measures are used at query time to return summarization instances of model data. Additionally, a measure cannot reference a table or column directly. That's why they must be passed to a table or column using a function to produce a summarization.

Measure complexity boils down to how many columns are aggregated. A simple measure aggregates the value of a single column. It performs the same function as implicit measures do automatically. In the following steps, you add a measure to the Awards table:

1. **In the Data pane, select the** Awards **table.**

2. **In the Calculations area of the Ribbon's Table Tools tab, click the New Measure button, which allows you to begin creating a new DAX formula.**

3. **In the Formula bar, enter the following measure definition:**

   ```
   AwardedOppty = SUM(Awards[total_outlayed_amount])
   ```

4. **When you finish, press Enter.**

   After you press Enter, the Home Ribbon switches to the Measure Tools Ribbon so that you can format the formula.

TIP

Change the formatting as soon as possible. In this case, you change the number format to currency and set the decimal position to two. This helps create consistent values.

The measure is now properly structuring financial data by changing the formatting type to currency and the decimal position to two spots. Now, whenever you add financially oriented data such as total_obligated_amount to a report, the same structure follows suit. To prove this statement, I created a new measure, TypicalBid:

```
TypicalBid = AVERAGE(Awards[total_obligated_amount])
```

As soon as the new formula, TypicalBid, was entered into Power BI Desktop, the formula was recognized based on its context. Changes that occurred included the switch to the currency format, given that the table was Awards and the column was Bids. You can see the results of a modified format type (currency) in Figure 16-5. Note that Power BI recognized the change automatically.

FIGURE 16-5: Power BI automatically recognizes a modified format type (currency).

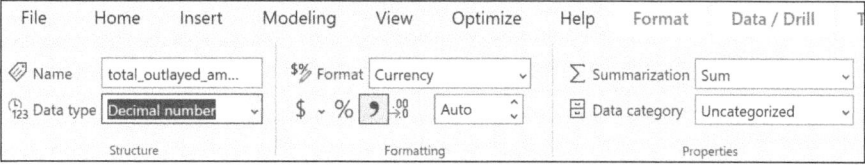

REMEMBER

If more than one measure is involved in the formulaic equation, such as Profit = Bid - Earned, it's known as a *compound measure*.

Comparing measures and columns

This chapter covers both calculated columns and measures. This section helps you determine which to choose and when. Consider the following:

>> Both calculated columns and measures allow you to add data to models.

>> Both are defined by using DAX formulas.

>> Both are referenced in DAX formulas by enclosing their names with parameters.

The differences, however, lie in their purpose, evaluation, and storage criteria. Table 16-3 explores the differences.

TABLE 16-3 **Calculated Columns versus Measures**

	Calculated Columns	Measures
Purpose	Extends a table with new columns	Summarizes data models
Evaluation point	Row context at data refresh	Filter context at query time
Storage	Stores values for each row	Never stores values
Visualizations	Filters, groups, and sorts data	Designed for summarization

Syntax and context

DAX expressions analyze critical data for use in Power BI reports. These expressions must use specific syntax and context as a result. DAX expressions accept tables and columns as references. Keep these points in mind:

>> DAX operators don't require users to repeatedly enter functions to create different expressions across tables.

>> DAX operations apply to the entirety of selected data columns, not just a subset.

>> With DAX, you can return the value of an entire table instead of returning a single value.

>> DAX supports calculating date, time, and year variables from column data.

>> With DAX, you can create as many as 64 nested functions in a single DAX expression.

The syntax of an expression

If you look at the following formula, you can see that there's a specific architecture to the equation taken from a table of data:

```
Profit = SUM(Sales([Earned])
```

The equation has the following syntactical elements:

>> Profit is the name of the measure or the calculated column.

>> The equal sign (=), also known as the operator, marks the start of the function.

>> SUM is the DAX function that adds all the numbers in the Sales([Earned]).

>> Sales refers to the name of the table being analyzed.

>> Earned is the column in the table that the SUM function will analyze.

>> The parentheses ( ) enclose at least one argument.

When you craft equations and formulas, be sure that you adhere to a strict syntax that's in line with these principles.

Best Practices for DAX Coding and Debugging in Power BI

Power BI extends the use of DAX beyond what other Microsoft applications do — for a good reason! With DAX, your ability to visualize and augment data is increased exponentially. This chapter, along with Chapter 15, walks you through the basics of syntax, context, and functions. At the end of the day, however, you need to be laser-focused on optimization first because you don't want the code to become clunky.

Testing DAX Queries with DAX Query view

To test your DAX Queries as a stand-alone effort, you can use DAX Query view in Power BI. DAX Query view is a dedicated workspace where you can test and refine your DAX formulas before adding them to your reports. Think of it as a sandbox (self-contained) environment where you can experiment with calculations without affecting your actual semantic model.

Unlike measures that you create in the Data pane, DAX queries in DAX Query view follow a specific syntax. Every DAX query must start with the EVALUATE keyword, followed by a table expression that defines the data to be returned. The reason for this is that DAX Query view solves a common problem that DAX beginners face: You write a complex measure, add it to a visual, and discover that it doesn't work as expected. Instead of troubleshooting within your report (and often panicking that you've made your report unusable), you can now test formulas in isolation and see exactly what they return with your model.

To open DAX Query view, click the New DAX Query button in the Home Ribbon of Power BI Desktop. This opens a separate tab where you can write and execute DAX queries directly against your semantic model without the risk of unintended changes affecting your data as you work.

In Figure 16-6, notice that the DAX button is on the left and the formula being tested in the DAX editor produces a single answer. As shown in this example, you can evaluate the difference between the obligated and outlayed funding for this dataset. The DAX editor uses SUM the total of both *total_obligated_amount* and the *total_outlayed_amount*. Then it applies the formula to determine the difference in the value.

As shown in the DAX editor (see Figure 16-6), the formula entered was:

```
EVALUATE
ROW(
"Difference",
SUM(AnalyticsSpendFY21to25[total_obligated_amount])-
    SUM(AnalyticsSpendFY21to25[total_outlayed_amount]))
```

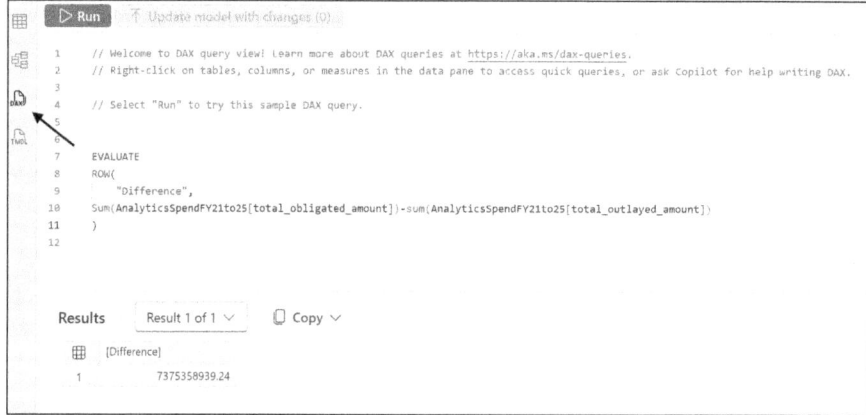

FIGURE 16-6:
DAX editor
query testing.

Using error functions properly

Anytime you're writing DAX expressions, there's a chance you may write evaluation-time errors. It's inevitable. Consider these two DAX functions to reduce any nerves:

» Use the ISERROR function to take a single expression and return a TRUE statement when the expression results in an error.

» Use the IFERROR function when there are two or more expressions. Should the first expression result in an error, the second expression is returned.

WARNING

The ISERROR and IFERROR expressions can definitely be beneficial because they can contribute mightily to writing easy-to-understand expressions. Here's the downside: They can quickly degrade the performance of calculations. It can happen because the functions increase the number of hits to the system concurrently. Many of these errors are caused by unexpected BLANKs or zero values, so it's essential to know the data type conversion errors processing through the system.

Although you may be inclined to use the ISERROR and IFERROR functions, it's often better to use defensive strategies when developing your models and writing expressions. Consider the following:

» Ensure that the data incorporated into the data model is of a high quality.

» Use the IF function when you are looking to test a logical test expression that can decide whether an error result occurs.

» It is better to use IF rather than ISERROR and IFERROR as a defensive approach because it ensures that quality data is loaded into a model and supports error handling more efficiently. Although IF may result in added scans to a dataset, performance is better because of the added error handling built in.

» Use error-tolerant functions.

Avoiding converting blanks to values

You may be tempted to just leave things empty from time to time because there's simply no value realized from the expression. In these instances, where you encounter a value such as zero, you should reconsider before giving up. Consider the following measure, which explicitly turns a BLANK result into a 0:

```
Bid (No Blank) =
If (
ISBLANK ([Bid]),
0,
[Bid]
)
```

Here's another measure that converts BLANK results into zeroes:

```
Commissions =
DIVIDE([Commissions], [Sales], 0)
```

First, the DIVIDE function takes Commissions and measures it by the Sales measure. Should the result be zero or BLANK, the third argument — the alternate result, in other words — is then returned. In this example, the measure is guaranteed to always return a value because zero is passed as the alternate result. As you can see, both measure designs are inefficient and lead to poor report designs.

Power BI tries to retrieve all groupings within the filter context, even when these items are added to report visualizations. The problem is that the result is a significant query leading to a slow report. Each example measure effectively turns a sparse calculation into a theatrical production, causing Power BI to sputter because the mundane tasks become a memory hog. The groupings, frankly, overwhelm the report user. That's why you want to be highly efficient with your use of the filter context, groupings, and variables. An example formula supplying more efficiency and appropriate use of variables includes this line:

```
Commission Payable = DIVIDE ([Commissions], [Sales])
```

TIP

In certain circumstances, you must configure a visualization to display all groupings. That means you should return values or BLANK within the filter context by enabling the Show Items with No Data option.

With DAX, there's only one condition when it's permissible to return a BLANK. That condition is when your measure is forced to return a BLANK because no meaningful value can be returned. This is an efficient approach, allowing Power BI to make reports faster.

Knowing the difference between operators and functions

Once upon a time, you learned basic mathematical formulas in school. Remember the difference between numerators and denominators? With DAX, it's a bit more technical. You need to know the difference between the function DIVIDE and the usage of the operator divide.

When using the DIVIDE function, you pass the numerator and denominator expression to get your result. You can also pass in a value that gets an alternate result:

```
DIVIDE(<numerator>, <denominator> [,<alternateresult>])
```

The DIVIDE function was deliberately created to handle division by zero. If an alternate is not passed in and the denominator is either zero or BLANK, the function should return a BLANK. The secondary use case is when an alternate result is passed in — it's returned instead of BLANK.

Referring to the IF, ISBLANK, or BLANK functions that I discuss in Chapter 15, these do not stand on their own. You need a minimum of four DAX functions to complete the function properly. Such coding requirements are quite inefficient. Here's an example of an inefficient (and erroneous) code sample:

```
Bid Margin =
IF (
OR (
ISBLANK([Bids]),
[Bids] == 0
),
BLANK (),
[Bids] / [Sales]
)
```

The reason why this code is inefficient is because the [Sales] is the denominator. Using [Bids], a numerator, will result in an infinite result of BLANK. As you can tell, the code is improperly formatted, causing unnecessary errors.

Here's an example using DIVIDE, which offers a far more efficient way of producing exactly the same formula:

```
Bid Margin =
DIVIDE([Bids], [Sales])
```

Given what you know from the review of these two equations, you should be in a position to follow these rules:

>> Use the DIVIDE function whenever the denominator is an expression that can return 0 or BLANK.

>> When the denominator is a constant value, use the divide operator, not the DIVIDE function. The division is 100 percent foolproof, and your expressions can perform better because no testing is needed.

>> Before you use the alternate value, think twice. You're often better to return a BLANK than anything at all.

>> Carefully consider whether the DIVIDE function should return an alternate value.

>> BLANK is often better for report visualizations because it helps eliminate groups when summarizations are BLANK. You can also focus your attention on groups in which data exists.

>> When in doubt, you can configure visuals to display all groups that return values or BLANK within the filtered complex, by enabling the Show Items with No Data option.

Getting specific

A few letters with DAX make all the difference. You may need to write a DAX expression that tests whether a column can be filtered using a specific value. Over the years, DAX has used specific values, including IF, HASONEVALUE, and VALUES. For example, if you need to determine the sales tax for a customer in California, you may decide to use the following code:

```
CA State Tax =
IF (
HASONEVALUE (Customer [State Tax]),
```

```
IF (
VALUES (Customer [State Tax]) = "California",
[Sales] * 0.0725
)
)
```

As presented here, the HASONEVALUE function returns a TRUE condition only if a single value of the STATE TAX column is visible in the current filter context. When it's TRUE, the VALUES function must be compared to the specific text "California". If the text condition is TRUE, the Sales measure is multiplied by 0.0725, or 7.25 percent, which is the state sales tax rate in California. If the HASONEVALUE function returns FALSE, which may be the case because there's more than one value filter column, the first IF function returns BLANK.

Using the technique as structured here is entirely defensive and prickly. It's needed because it can produce multiple value filters for the State Tax column. The VALUES function can return a table that produces a multi-row table. That said, when you compare a table of multiple rows to a scale value, the results yield a significant error.

Rather than use the trifecta of functions, why not just use a single filter, the SELECTEDVALUE function? Sometimes, simplicity, elegance, and efficiency do win the race. The same code equation using one function versus three can be written this way:

```
CA Sales Tax =
IF (
SELECTEDVALUE (Customer [State Tax]) = "California",
[Sales] * 0.0725
)
```

It's clean, simple, and pretty, indeed!

Knowing what to COUNT

You may need to write DAX expressions that count table rows periodically. You can carry this out in a few ways. Your first choice is to use the COUNT function to count the values in a column. Another is to use the COUNTROWS function to count the rows in a table. Both alternatives achieve the same result. There's one caveat: As long as the counted columns have no BLANKs, both will work.

In the first use case:

```
Bids Processed =
COUNT(Bids[BidDate])
```

This counts only rows where `BidDate` contains a value. If some rows have blank dates, they won't be counted.

```
Bids Processed =
COUNTROWS(Bids)
```

This example counts every row in the table, regardless of `BLANK` values in any column.

Again, efficiency and elegance prevail for a variety of reasons. `COUNTROWS` is usually better because it's more reliable and self-descriptive. It doesn't miss rows due to missing data. Use `COUNT` only when you specifically want to exclude records with blank values.

TECHNICAL STUFF

Anytime you look to review a pair of tables in Power BI, you can find many relationships. You may have many inactive relationships. However, only one active relationship can be evaluated at a time using DAX. DAX code uses the active relationship by default. DAX can use a specific inactive relationship when associated with the `USERELATIONSHIP` function.

Preferring measures over columns

Earlier in this chapter, I discuss the differences between measures and columns. (See the section, "Comparing measures and columns.") But here's the truth — measures always produce better DAX results in Power BI. Why? A measure is like a virtual calculation that resides on top of your model. A measure executes only when it needs to be used, whereas calculated columns are heavily integrated into the model.

Here are a few other reasons to use measures over calculated columns:

>> Measures are lightweight and deployed when needed, whereas calculated columns are deployed unnecessarily when you run an equation that includes code.

» Though a calculated column can be used in a slicer, the column size increases along with the data model each time you run an operation. That isn't the case with the use of a measure. You see a measure executed only when called upon.

» One of the most powerful techniques for complicated calculation measurement is to measure branching and measure groups. Measure branching allows you to start with a core calculation and then build more complicated calculations from the base calculation, like a tree branch. Measure groups are like folders. Like-kind calculations are grouped to perform a task.

Suppose that you intend to perform nested calculations that require complex calculations. In that case, measure branching cuts out a significant chunk of the code, which improves calculation performance. Calculated columns don't improve calculation performance.

Measure groups keep reports clean and organized, helping you locate data quickly and more efficiently.

Seeing that structure matters

REMEMBER

If there's anything I should be reiterating countless times as you reach the end of this chapter, it's the simple truth that structure matters. If you don't need something in your code, remove it. If an internal column is in use, hide it rather than expose it in Power BI so that you don't need to expose it with DAX. If you want to call out a column using DAX as a variable, rename it so that it makes sense because all names should be user-friendly. And, whenever possible, use explicit measures because you'll be thankful for code readability and accelerated performance.

5

Enhancing Your Power BI Experience

Transition from Power BI Desktop to Power BI Service to share and collaborate with organizational stakeholders using workspaces.

Gain insights from your data by using the Power BI Service prebuilt reporting and dashboarding solutions.

Establish best practices and approaches to ensure that your datasets are always secure and up-to-date for the most relevant experience.

Explore ways to extend Power BI with other Microsoft 365 and applications, including Power Apps, Power Automate, OneDrive, Teams, SharePoint 365, and Dynamics 365.

Enhance your data experience with the use of artificial intelligence and big data analytics capabilities that integrate with Power BI.

Chapter **17**

Making Your Data Shine

Old data is of no use to an organization if newer, more relevant data is available. And, let's be honest, if the data is stale and lacks integrity, will the analysts who actively use Power BI to crunch numbers be able to create new compelling reports, observe dashboards, and craft complex calculations? I doubt it. Ensuring that your Power BI semantic models are second to none and are performing like the workhorses you dream of for your teams is what every data professional aims for. That's why Microsoft has integrated several data refresh and security features into Power BI. In this chapter, you see how to design, configure, and deploy enterprise Power BI semantic models for data freshness and fine-grain security.

Establishing a Schedule

What good is data if it's not kept clean and up-to-date? Some data analysts may prefer to refresh data manually in Power BI Desktop and Service. Still, this approach is illogical when you need to ensure that data is periodically updated to maintain data relevance.

Rolling out the scheduled refresh

When you have your data ducks all in a row and want to craft an online refresh schedule, you set up that activity in Power BI Service. (This capability is integrated into Fabric as well.) To create a schedule update, follow these steps:

1. **In Power BI Service, navigate to the workspace you want to refresh.**

2. **Find your semantic model in the workspace.**

3. **Click the More options menu (three dots) next to the semantic model name.**

4. **Select Schedule from the drop-down menu.**

   The Schedule Refresh interface appears (see Figure 17-1).

5. **Click the Refresh Now button (optional).**

   Clicking Refresh Now before setting the schedule acts as a verification step to confirm that everything works properly and that the data model is fresh and functional before automating the refresh process. It's not strictly required, but doing so is strongly recommended as a best practice for model reliability, credential validation, and data freshness.

6. **Click the Add Schedule button.**

7. **Set your refresh frequency.**

   You can change the frequency, time zone, and time of your scheduled refreshes using the Scheduled Refresh settings. Any schedule notifications can then be sent to a specific email address or an Entra (Active Directory) group.

8. **Choose the specific conditions that are appropriate for your refresh.**

   Use this step to specify any conditional settings, such as incremental refresh policies, refresh triggers, gateway options, or retry behavior, depending on your semantic model and source configuration.

9. **Click Save.**

REMEMBER

Power BI is your little corner of the world, whereas Power BI Service is for sharing.

Note: The preceding example assumes that you've already established a data gateway. If you haven't, pay close attention to the next section.

Refreshing on-premises data

To access and refresh on-premises data, you need to use a *data gateway* — a type of bridge that supports connection details and credentials. You download and install a data gateway from Power BI Service by going to the Download area on the top menu of the Power BI Service home page. (You know, our friend the Download icon.) Once there, choose Download⇨ Data Gateway, as shown in Figure 17-2.

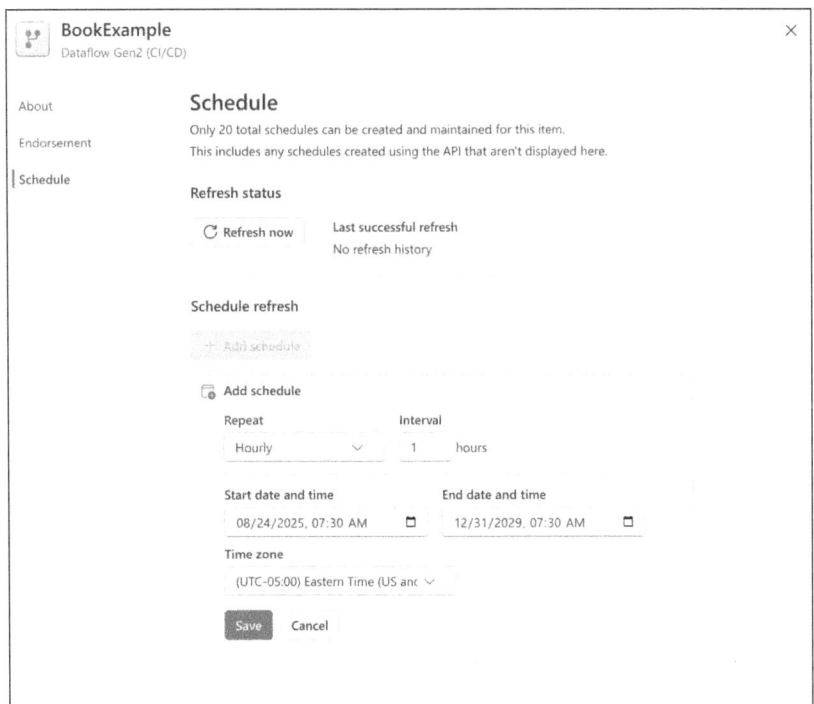

FIGURE 17-1:
The Schedule
Refresh interface.

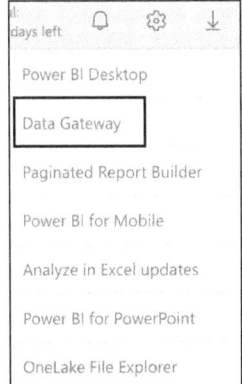

FIGURE 17-2:
Downloading a
data gateway.

There are two gateway modes: standard and personal. Here's how they differ:

>> **Standard mode:** Multiple people can access the gateway. You can also use Standard mode with other Microsoft services, such as Power Platform and Azure. Standard mode is ideal for organizations.

>> **Personal mode:** One person, one dataset. Personal mode only works for Power BI and use of this mode is generally discouraged.

TIP

Microsoft strongly recommends Standard mode because it integrates with Fabric monitoring, governance, and Purview data policies.

Assuming that you've installed the gateway or that the Power BI Service group administration has granted you access as a gateway user, you're now authorized to use the gateway to refresh datasets that use on-premises datasets.

For each gateway, you can select a different dataset in the Datasets settings menu. To make these changes, follow these configuration steps:

1. **Go to the Datasets tab in a workspace.**

2. **Select a semantic model to review.**

3. **Hover the cursor over the semantic model in the list.**

4. **When the settings for the semantic model you've selected appear in the pane on the right, as shown in Figure 17-3, click the Gateway Connection option on the right.**

   You will then see a list of data sources along with associated data gateways.

5. **For each data gateway, select a data source that you'd like to map to, as shown in Figure 17-4.**

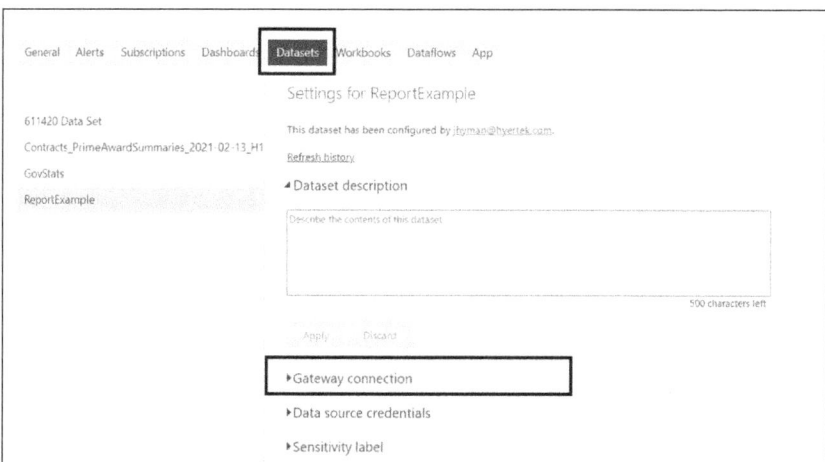

FIGURE 17-3:
Data gateway
options.

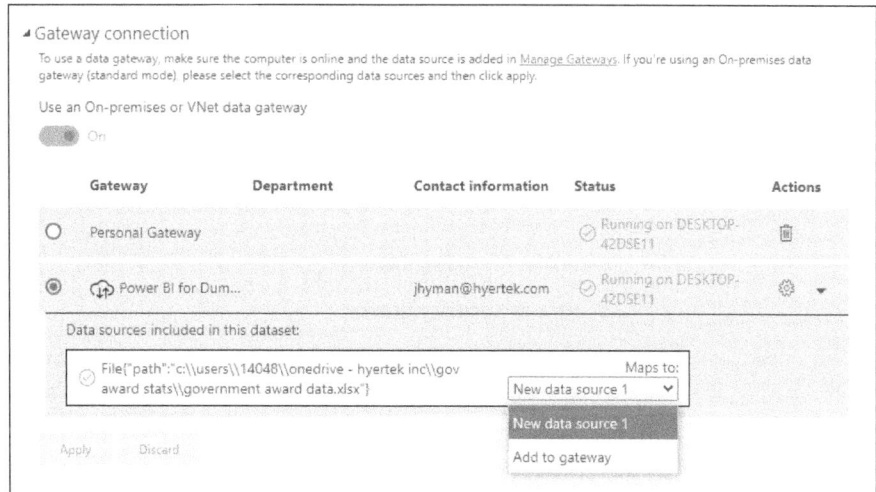

Each time you create a data source, you need to provide data source credentials in the Data Source section. This means that you need to edit the credentials securely so that they can be cached in the Power BI Service.

REMEMBER

Protecting the Data Fortress

Data is precious. Not everyone should gain access to it. If it's on your desktop, it's generally restricted to you unless you share your computer. As soon as the data hits the Internet, though, all bets are off. You need to protect the crown jewels of your organization. That means that datasets, reports, and dashboards may need focused security settings. That's why you want to implement row-level security (RLS) with Power BI to restrict data access, ensuring that unauthorized users don't gain unauthorized access to sensitive data. With RLS, filters restrict data access at the row level. You can define the filters within a role. Members of an assigned workspace have access to the Power BI Service datasets, assuming that you're within the provisioned security group.

Configuring RLS can occur in several different locations. You can configure RLS in Power BI Desktop or by using DirectQuery with SQL Server, for example. When using Analysis Services or Azure Analysis Services live connections, you configure RLS in your model. Try to avoid configuring security with Power BI Desktop — your configurations won't appear in the live connection dataset.

**TECHNICAL
STUFF**

Configuring for group membership

To create group memberships, you must first define roles and rules within Power BI Desktop. When you publish the data model, those details are associated with the published data model. To configure these roles and rules, start in Power BI Desktop and follow these steps:

1. **Select the Modeling tab.**

2. **Locate the Security button.**

3. **Select Manage Roles and then determine the name for your new role, the table to apply the role to, and the columns that should be filtered (see Figure 17-5).**

   Repeat this process until you've added the number of roles, tables, and columns you feel are sufficient.

4. **Click Save.**

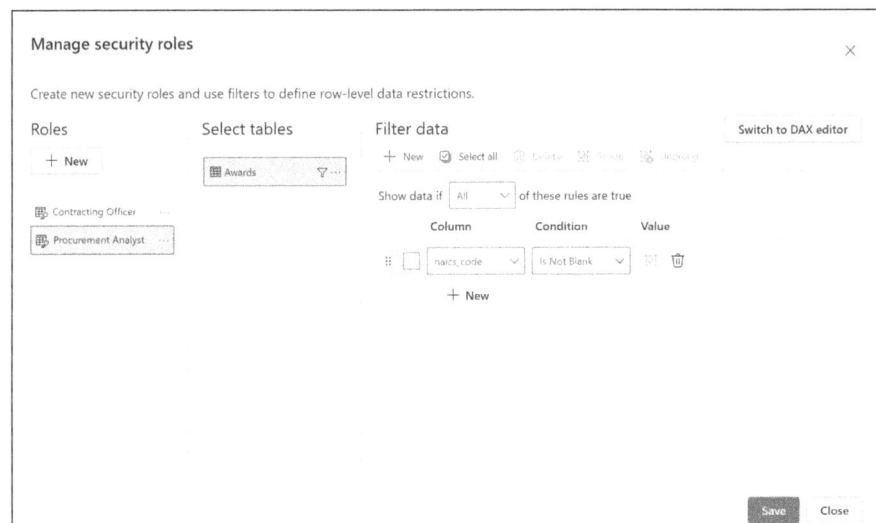

FIGURE 17-5:
Configuring security roles for group membership in Power BI Desktop.

REMEMBER

You don't assign users roles within Power BI Desktop. That happens in Power BI Service.

Beyond RLS, you can configure Object-Level Security (OLS) to hide entire tables or columns. Together with Fabric's integration with Purview and sensitivity labels, you now have enterprise-grade governance.

Object Level Security requires the use of the Tabular Editor, which is beyond the scope of Power BI Desktop or Service. To learn more on how to configure your models to meet such data granularity, head over to `https://learn.microsoft.com/en-us/fabric/security/service-admin-object-level-security?tabs=table`.

Unlike RLS filters, OLS is absolute. If you deny a table or column, the user is unaware that it exists.

Making security role assignments in Power BI Service

You can't just "set it and forget it" when it comes to security role assignments in Power BI Desktop. In Desktop, you're only creating the blueprint for security — the actual enforcement happens once the model is published to the Power BI Service. Think of Desktop as your drafting table and Service as the construction site.

When you publish to Power BI Service, that's when you assign users and groups access to semantic models, reports, and dashboards in a workspace for sharing and collaboration. Over time, your job in Service isn't just creating reports; you also must manage security to ensure that the right people have proper access.

You can assign two types of access: workspace access and access to specific models, reports, or dashboards.

To provide access to the workspace, follow these steps:

1. **Open the Workspaces section of the Power BI Service.**

2. **Find the workspace you want to manage and then click the three dots (More options) next to its name to open the menu.**

3. **Select Workspace Access (see Figure 17-6).**

   The Manage Access panel opens on the right side of the screen.

4. **Click Add People or Groups.**

   Enter individuals or groups that are part of your Azure Entra ID Directory. Remember, you need to be licensed to share and collaborate within Power BI Service or Fabric.

5. **After you add the users, click Apply.**

6. **Set each user's individual access level. You have the choice of Viewer, Member, Contributor, or Admin (see Figure 17-7).**

   In the Manage Access pane, locate each person or group and use the role drop-down menu next to their name to choose the access level you want to grant. After you apply the permission for each user, close the window. Your changes are saved automatically as selected.

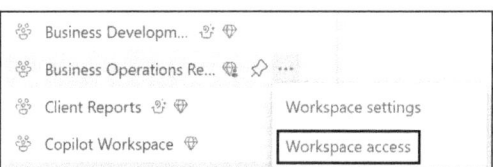

FIGURE 17-6:
Managing
workspace
security.

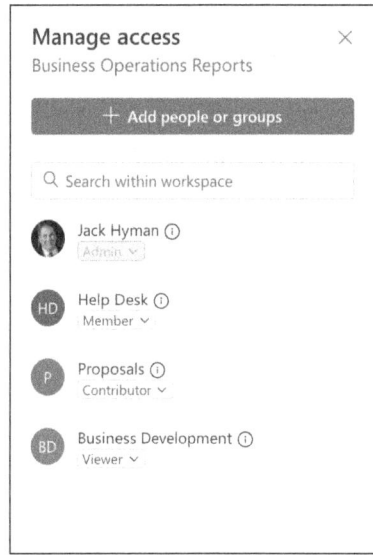

FIGURE 17-7:
Configuring
workspace
security.

When you set up report, dashboard, or semantic model-level security, you first must set up security roles in Power BI Desktop. If you don't configure the security in Power BI Desktop, you will see an error message reminding you that no security roles exist when you try to publish and enforce security in Power BI Service (see Figure 17-8). After you configure the roles, the roles are listed in the Security pane. On the left are the role names. In the right pane, you are asked to enter the user or group that should be assigned to the security groups you created in Power

BI Desktop. For the example shown in Figure 17-9, a single user was added to the Contracting Officer, and two groups were added to the Procurement Analyst.

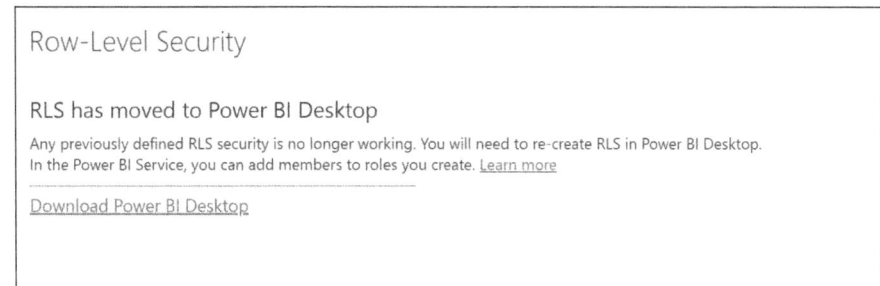

Row-Level Security

RLS has moved to Power BI Desktop

Any previously defined RLS security is no longer working. You will need to re-create RLS in Power BI Desktop. In the Power BI Service, you can add members to roles you create. Learn more

Download Power BI Desktop

FIGURE 17-8:
RLS error.

Row-Level Security

Contracting Officer (1)

Procurement Analyst (2)

Members (2)

People or groups who belong to this role

Enter email addresses

Add

Government Contracts & Sales ×

Help Desk ×

Save   Cancel

FIGURE 17-9:
Assigning users
and groups to a
semantic model
in Power
BI Service.

Keep in mind that taking care of one or two users is relatively straightforward, but how about a few hundred or several thousand users? The reason is simple. The same users may be using the same row-level security settings for various semantic models, which means assigning those users to the same security groups as members within an assigned row. Under these conditions, you can create a single security group once, and then your work is done.

Sharing the Data Love

Power BI Service enables collaboration among various users and groups. It's not just about sharing datasets — it's also about sharing reports, dashboards, and apps. You can share data at scale in several ways, including the ones described in this list:

>> **Workspaces:** When you publish to Power BI Service, you publish to a workspace. You automatically have access to the content you publish, and you can assign others access by setting their workspace roles (Viewer, Contributor, Member, or Admin). These roles determine what each person can do with the content in that workspace.

>> **Apps:** You can bundle up reports and dashboards into an app to make them easier for others to find and use. To make a semantic model available through an app, you need to grant users the Build permission, which allows them to create new reports from that dataset. App permissions can be assigned to individuals or, more commonly, to security groups.

REMEMBER

Revoking app access doesn't automatically remove a user's access to the underlying dataset. Always manage dataset permissions directly if you want to completely remove access.

TIP

For larger enterprises, remember that Power BI Service is now part of Microsoft Fabric. In Fabric, workspaces and apps connect directly to OneLake storage, use Microsoft Entra ID groups for access, and integrate with Purview for governance. That means you can manage security and compliance at scale, while providing thousands of users with consistent, trusted access to data.

Refreshing Data in Baby Steps

Semantic models come in all shapes and sizes. You find some that are minuscule and others that weigh in at several gigabytes, even as Power BI attempts to compress the data in real time. Power BI does its best to mitigate speed, resource usage, and reliability issues. One way around all three of these issues is to use incremental refresh.

An *incremental refresh* enables you to refresh a subset of data, resulting in a quicker and more reliable refresh with lower resource utilization and consumption. Suppose that you know your data will scale well into gigabyte territory. In that case, consider planning for an incremental refresh as part of your deployment strategy from the outset. For an incremental refresh of that kind to work in Power BI Service, it must be configured in Power BI Desktop. In broad steps, here's what needs to be done:

1. **Create a RangeStart and RangeEnd parameter.**
2. **Filter by using the RangeStart and RangeEnd parameters.**
3. **Define an incremental refresh policy.**

The following sections dig a little deeper into each step of the process.

Creating RangeStart and RangeEnd parameters

Creating the incremental refresh parameters in Power BI Desktop for filtering is the first step in ensuring that your data always sparkles and shines. Those two parameters that need to be created are RangeStart and RangeEnd. Like DAX parameters, these parameters are case-sensitive. If you try to use other parameter names, you will be unsuccessful.

Here's what you need to do:

1. **Open Power Query.**
2. **Click Manage Parameters on the Power BI Ribbon's Home tab and choose New Parameter from the menu that appears.**
3. **In the Parameters pane, enter** RangeStart **in the Name field.**
4. **Choose Date/Time from the Type drop-down menu and Any Value from the Suggested Value drop-down menu.**
5. **Enter the following date in the Current Value field:** 01/01/2023.

   Power Query may change the format of this value later, depending on your system settings. Don't panic! Also, the dates you enter are based on your personal needs — they aren't set in stone.

6. **Repeat Steps 3 through 5 for RangeEnd.**

   The Current Value field date should be 12/31/2024. Your date format may vary, depending on your system formatting scheme in Power BI.

Figure 17-10 shows the parameters from the preceding steps entered into Power Query.

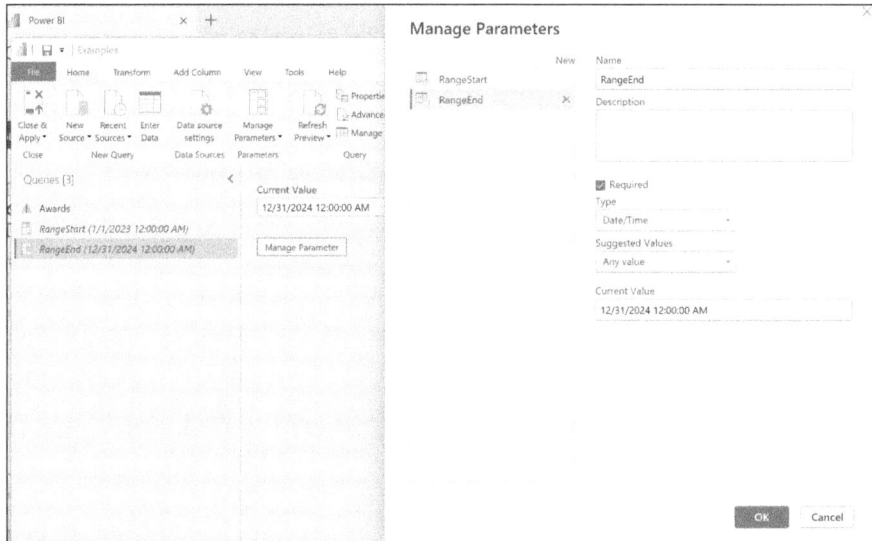

FIGURE 17-10:
Managing
parameters.

Filtering by RangeStart and RangeEnd

To support an incremental refresh, you first must configure a filter using the RangeStart and RangeEnd parameters. Suppose that each time a file is updated with a new award date, you want to know whether a win, a loss, or an update to details has occurred. Using the data in the file, your team will be able to recognize these changes. From Power BI Desktop, follow these steps to configure the filter:

1. **Open the Power Query Editor.**

2. **Click to select the Awards table from the list of queries.**

3. **Select the** period_of_performance_start_date **column header and then choose the Date/Time Filter option from the menu that appears.**

   You will initiate a filter for the Awards column.

4. **Drill down to the Custom Filter option.**

   You will now set the Incremental Refresh parameters. You will need to make a few modifications from the previous section, though.

5. **When the Filter Rows interface appears, make sure that Basic is selected, and then choose the Is After or Equal To option from the first drop-down menu.**

6. **Click the Calendar icon.**

   Doing so brings up a Date, Parameter, or New Parameter menu.

7. **Choose the New Parameter option.**

8. In the new pane that appears, click RangeStart.

9. Change the Date type from Date/Time to Date, and then click OK.

You've now established the first parameter for the filter.

10. Choose the Is Before or Equal To option from the bottom drop-down menu.

11. Click the Calendar icon.

Doing so brings up a Date, Parameter, or New Parameter menu (again).

12. In the new pane that appears, click RangeEnd.

13. Change the Date type from Date/Time to Date, and then click OK.

You've now established the second parameter for the filter.

At this stage, you have successfully created the filter conditions that should mimic those in Figure 17-11.

14. Click OK.

15. Click the Ribbon's Close & Apply button to exit the Power Query Editor.

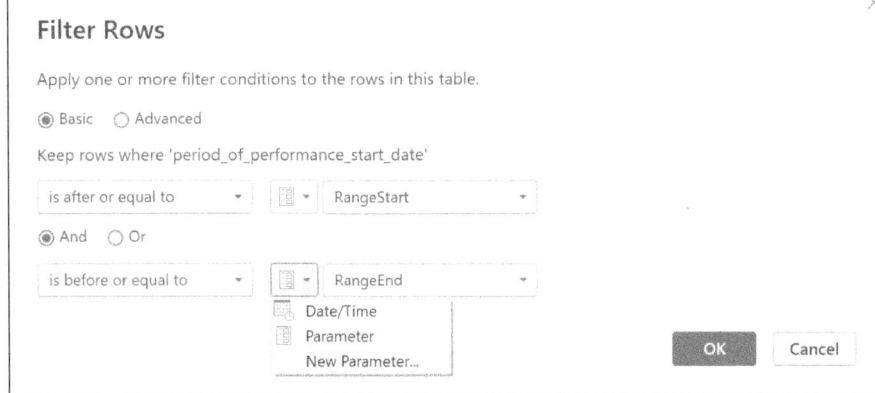

FIGURE 17-11: Filtering rows using the RangeStart and RangeEnd parameters.

Establishing the Incremental Refresh policy

Whenever you put a filter in place for an incremental refresh, you must complete one additional step: defining the execution policy. Continuing with the example presented in the preceding section, where you have a column Due Date in the table Awards, you can create the policy by following these steps:

1. Go to the Data pane of Power BI Desktop and right-click the table you want to refresh incrementally.

2. **Select Incremental Refresh from the menu that appears (see Figure 17-12).**

   Be sure to select the correct table from the drop-down menu.

3. **In the new screen that appears, switch the Incremental Refresh toggle to On.**

4. **Select the periods in which data must be stored and refreshed.**

REMEMBER

   Storing data means keeping it housed permanently; updating it for relevancy is a *refresh*.

   You can select the check boxes to detect data changes or only refresh during complete days.

5. **Select the Apply All button when complete.**

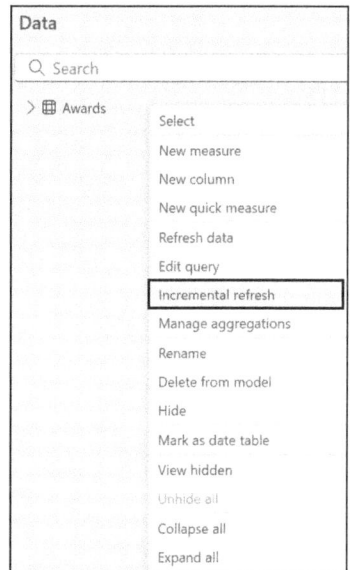

FIGURE 17-12: Setting up an incremental refresh.

Treating Data Like Gold

Have you been in a situation where you've worked on building the semantic model into a reliable dataset for a very long time, and now, when it's ready for prime time, you want to tell the world that it's ready for showtime? Sure, you won't win any gold, silver, or bronze medals. Still, you can increase your dataset's visibility for others to access by using endorsement techniques.

To an analyst, a semantic model is just another dataset. An analyst wants to be assured that a dataset is reliable, practical, and accurate. Some datasets may be created as a test, whereas others are intended for production and are considered authoritative sources of truth.

Data at the end of the day translates back into code when it's searched, no matter which business intelligence tool you may be using, including Power BI Desktop or Power BI Service. That's why you enforce the use of dataset endorsements. In other words, let the report's creator know exactly which semantic model is reliable and ready for consumption.

You can endorse several content assets in Power BI, including semantic models, dataflows, reports, and apps. You can implement endorsements in two ways:

>> **Promoting:** When content is designated as promoted, it receives a badge signifying that the content is ready for use by other users. Contributing members of a workspace who have access to the content where it resides can promote the content. The goal of content promotion is reusability.

>> **Certifying:** Certification shows that a content asset is recommended for usage because it's highly reliable, curated, and well-maintained. A Power BI admin must assign users the designation to certify content within a group.

REMEMBER

Regardless of the content type, the endorsement process remains the same.

To configure an endorsement, follow these steps:

1. **Open Power BI Service.**

2. **Locate the workspace that includes the content asset (semantic model, dataflow, report, or app) that you want to promote.**

3. **Click the three vertical dots on the left side of the content type.**

4. **Choose Settings.**

   A Settings pane appears on the right side of the screen.

5. **Scroll down the pane to the Endorsement section.**

   Under Endorsement, you have four options to pick from: None, Promoted, Certify, and Feature on Home, as shown in Figure 17-13.

6. **Pick the appropriate choice for promoting your data.**

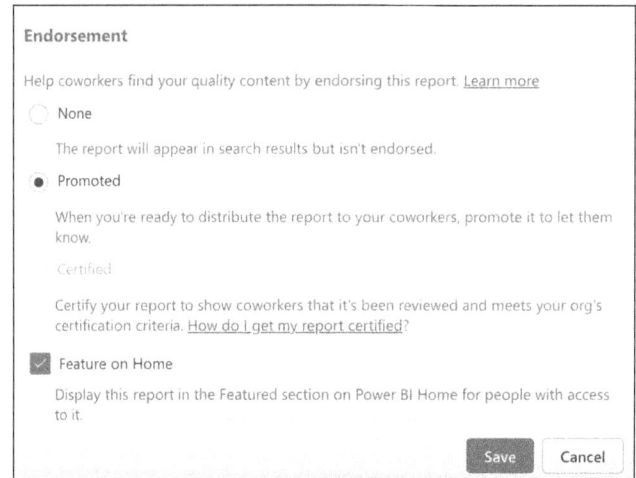

FIGURE 17-13:
Configuring
endorsements.

Notice that, in Figure 17-13, the Certified option is grayed out. That's because the system administrator must enable endorsements for the specific user or group before they're allowed to configure any content within a given workspace. A promoted and featured endorsement called *Examples* is now shown on the Power BI Service home screen (see Figure 17-14).

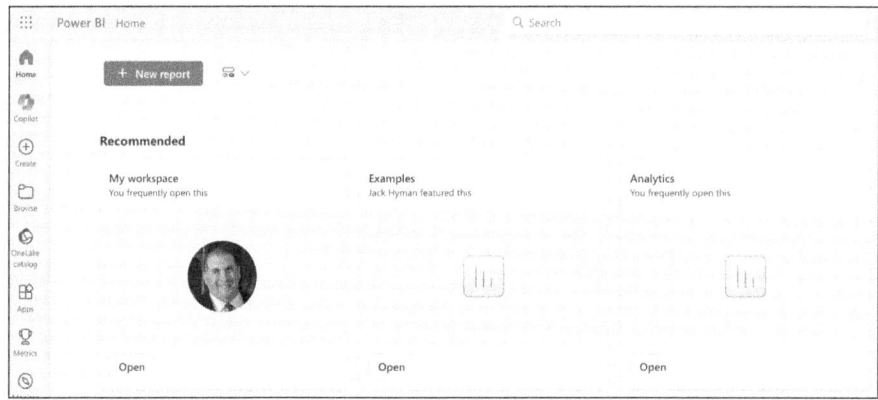

FIGURE 17-14:
Endorsements
listed in a Power
BI workspace.

TIP

If you're using Microsoft Fabric with Power BI Service, endorsed content can also be marked as *Featured*, which places it directly on the Power BI home page for maximum visibility. Fabric admins can also integrate endorsements with Microsoft Purview, making promoted and certified content automatically searchable and governed across the enterprise.

Configuring for Big Data

Power BI has come a long way from its early days, when datasets were capped at 10 GB. For enterprise users working with Big Data, those limits quickly became a barrier. Today, with Microsoft Fabric and Power BI Premium, dataset scalability extends into the hundreds of gigabytes, depending on your capacity SKU. Features such as Direct Lake, hybrid tables, incremental refresh, and V-Order storage formats (specific to Fabric) ensure that models can efficiently handle modern enterprise-scale data.

For users on Premium Per User (PPU) or some legacy Premium capacities, you may still need to enable the Large Dataset Storage Format setting as follows:

1. **In Power BI Service, navigate to the workspace that includes your dataset.**

2. **Open the dataset's Settings menu.**

3. **Under the Large Semantic Model Storage Format option, toggle the option to On and click Apply (see Figure 17-15).**

If this setting is unavailable, it is possible that you do not have the correct license or workspace permissions.

At the workspace or capacity level, Fabric automatically manages dataset support. Workspace admins can confirm capacity mode in Settings by going to the Premium/Fabric Capacity settings, where storage defaults are controlled.

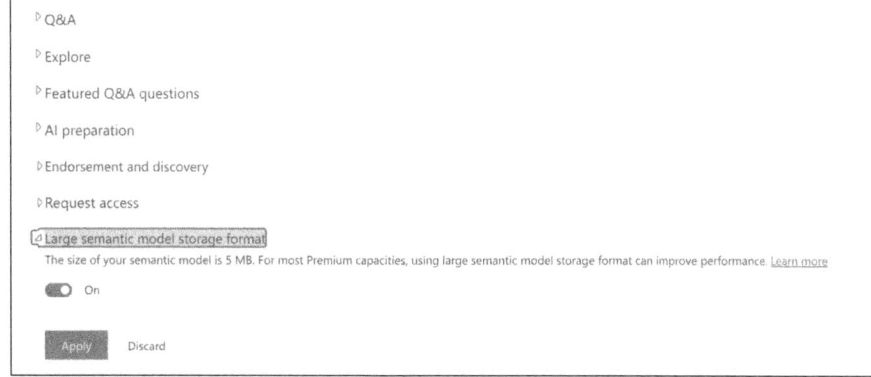

FIGURE 17-15:
Large Semantic Model Storage Format configuration.

TECHNICAL STUFF

You rarely need to think about hard limits anymore. Instead, focus on using the right Power BI Service or Fabric storage modes and refresh strategies to strike a balance between cost, performance, and scale.

Governing Your Power BI Data

When you start sharing and publishing reports across your organization, you're no longer just building cool dashboards or reports; you're managing assets that other people rely on to make decisions. That's where *data governance* comes in. Think of governance as the laws that govern your business, or in this case your Power BI environment. Without it, you risk confusion, duplicate reports, or even compliance issues. And if you have too many assets that make no sense to users who are working in the environment, you are bound for problems, including data being erased or a security vulnerability eventually.

Here are the key parts of governing your Power BI data:

>> **Data ownership and access:** Every semantic model in Power BI should have a clear administrator. This is the person or team responsible for keeping it accurate and up to date. Power BI lets you control who can view, edit, or share reports so that sensitive information doesn't end up in the wrong hands. You can manage permissions at the workspace, models, or even row level (through Row-Level Security).

>> **Data quality and trust:** Governance isn't just about locking things down; it's about making sure people trust what they see. Use reliable data source or promoted content to tell your colleagues, "This is the official source." That way, users won't waste time wondering if a version is just another document sitting in the proverbial filing cabinet.

>> **Compliance and security:** Many organizations have regulations governing the storage and use of data. Power BI connects to Microsoft Purview and contains features like sensitivity labels, data loss prevention (DLP), and audit logs. These tools help your business stay compliant with privacy and security requirements.

>> **Lifecycle management:** Just like old files on your computer, reports and datasets in Power BI can pile up. Governance means having a process for retiring outdated content based on retention policies whether it is archiving historical data or even deleting the data completely.

>> **Self-service with oversight:** One of the biggest strengths of Power BI is that anyone can build reports as Microsoft aims to empower everyone to be a citizen (an everyday) developer, but in terms of governance, self-service can turn into chaos. A good approach is to let people explore and create while keeping official data models and reports under IT oversight.

REMEMBER

Governance isn't about taking control away from users; it's about creating a balance between security, data quality, and responsibility. With a little planning, you can keep your Power BI environment clean, secure, and trusted, while still giving users the flexibility they need.

Chapter **18**

Extending the Power BI Experience

M icrosoft positions Power BI as the data analytics centerpiece of its Power Platform — the low-code/no-code suite that combines Power Apps, Power Automate, Power Pages, and Copilot Studio. Together, these tools allow organizations to build applications, automate business processes, deliver analytics, and create AI-powered experiences with minimal development effort. Within this ecosystem, Power BI provides the analytics foundation: turning raw data into interactive reports, dashboards, and insights. Each of these applications heavily relies on Power BI to deliver the presentation layer for reporting, dashboarding, and data analysis. In this chapter, you see how Microsoft has woven Power BI into the broader Power Platform and Microsoft 365 suite so that collaboration, automation, and data-driven decision-making work seamlessly across apps, workflows, and pages.

Linking Power Platform and Power BI

Microsoft Power Platform is a suite of low-code/no-code applications that empower users to build solutions, automate workflows, analyze data, and create AI-driven experiences. At its core, Power BI provides the analytics foundation — transforming data into insights that connect seamlessly across the rest of the platform. Power Platform includes four major components:

>> **Power BI:** Enterprise-grade analytics and visualization

>> **Power Apps:** Rapid application development for building low-code/no-code apps across web and mobile

>> **Power Automate:** Workflow automation for connecting systems, streamlining processes, and reducing manual effort

>> **Copilot Studio (formerly Power Virtual Agents):** A conversational AI builder for creating chatbots and copilots that extend business processes

These components are designed to work together, giving organizations a single ecosystem to build, automate, and analyze — without heavy coding or complex integrations.

REMEMBER

With Power Platform, you can connect to over 1,000 prebuilt data connectors — and Microsoft continues to expand that list with every major release. These connectors allow you to integrate data from cloud services, on-premises systems, and third-party applications into a single workflow. At the center of this ecosystem is Microsoft Dataverse (formerly Common Data Service), the secure and scalable data platform that underpins all Power Platform applications. Dataverse provides standardized tables, relationships, and governance so that applications and analytics share the same trusted foundation. As shown in Figure 18-1, the breadth of connectors available makes it possible to extend Power Platform solutions across nearly every system your organization uses.

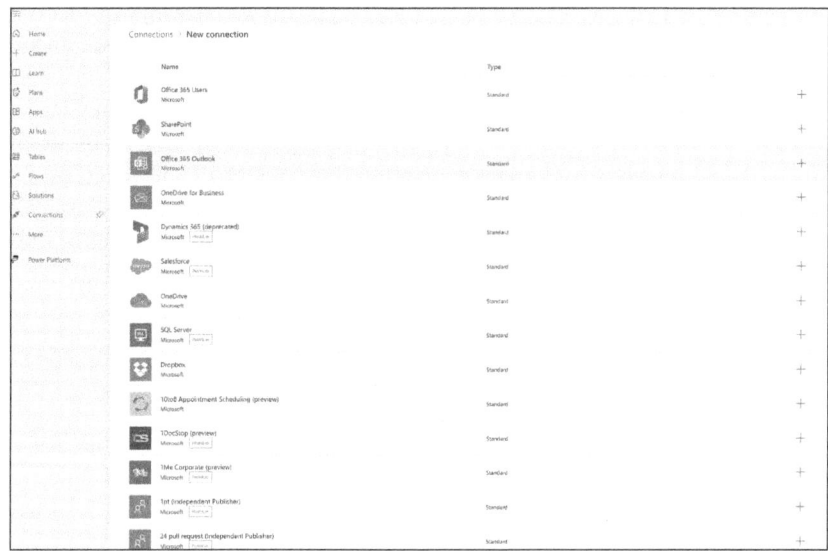

FIGURE 18-1:
Data connector options in Power Platform.

Powering Up with Power Apps

Power Apps is Microsoft's low-code/no-code development tool, which means you can create apps by dragging, dropping, and connecting building blocks rather than writing long programs, similar to how you create reports in Power BI. Even beginners can build apps that pull data from multiple systems, add logic, and run on phones, tablets, or the web. You can use Power Apps to build two styles of apps:

» **Canvas apps:** You start with a blank canvas and design the app exactly how you want. This is ideal for task-specific solutions, such as expense reports, inspections, or customer check-ins. The data that you pull in and out of these apps is often smaller in size.

» **Model-driven apps:** These apps are built on top of Dataverse, the Microsoft secure data platform. You don't need to worry much about layout, as Power Apps generates the interface automatically based on your data and business rules. This is ideal for enterprise users as the apps maintain a more structured process, such as case management or HR onboarding.

Because Power Apps often connects to sensitive business data, security is baked in. Access is controlled through Microsoft Entra ID, allowing you to enforce policies such as multi-factor authentication.

Here's how this relates to Power BI: Many Power BI dashboards rely on data that comes from apps and flows created in Power Apps or Power Automate. The rules you set for these apps, such as where data lives, who can access it, and what connectors are allowed, directly affect how Power BI can use and display that data. That's where admin portals come in:

» **The Power BI Admin Portal** is your home base for BI-specific settings — things like who can share dashboards, how workspaces are governed, and how much Dataverse capacity is being used.

» **Power Platform Admin Center (PPAC)** is where you manage everything else in the Power Platform: creating or working environments (such as sandboxes for testing and production for live apps), applying data loss prevention (DLP) policies that block risky connector combinations, and monitoring usage and storage across apps and flows.

» **The Microsoft Purview compliance portal,** part of the Microsoft 365 Admin Center, enables you to access audit information for all activities across your entire Microsoft 365 environment, commonly referred to as your *tenant*. This portal stores the audit logs that provide a detailed record of actions and changes within your organization.

Together, these tools provide a complete suite of tools to build apps quickly with Power Apps, analyze the results with Power BI, and ensure that, behind the scenes, your administrators can maintain security, compliance, and control. If you want to learn more about Power Apps, several chapters in my other book, *Microsoft Power Platform For Dummies* (Wiley), discuss the app-building and administration process.

ON THE WEB

To access each of these consoles, visit these websites:

>> **Power BI Admin Portal:** https://app.powerbi.com/admin-portal? experience=power-bi

>> **Power Platform Admin Center:** https://admin.powerplatform. microsoft.com/home

>> **Purview Admin Portal:** https://purview.microsoft.com/home

REMEMBER

Power Platform can connect to almost any data source. Although Dataverse is the preferred option for security and governance, you don't have to use it. Your data can remain in apps like SharePoint Online, and Power Automate, Power Apps, and Power BI can work with your data directly through connectors.

Creating Power App visuals with Power BI

Power BI is designed to deliver insights for better decision-making, and Power Apps enables you to build low-code apps that interact directly with your business data. When combined, you can embed a Power Apps visual into a Power BI report. This allows users to pass context-aware data from the report to a canvas app, creating a two-way, real-time interaction between reporting and app functionality.

Follow these steps to add and configure a Power Apps visual in Power BI:

1. **Confirm your setup.**

   You work in Power BI Service to complete this integration. Head to an existing report and make sure that you can add the visual from the Visualizations pane.

2. **Add the Power Apps visual to your report.**

   From the Visualizations pane, select the Power Apps visual and drag the fields you want to use into the visual's data fields (see Figure 18-2). You can then choose to link an existing app or create a new one.

REMEMBER

   For the app to function, the report must be published to Power BI Service and opened in a browser.

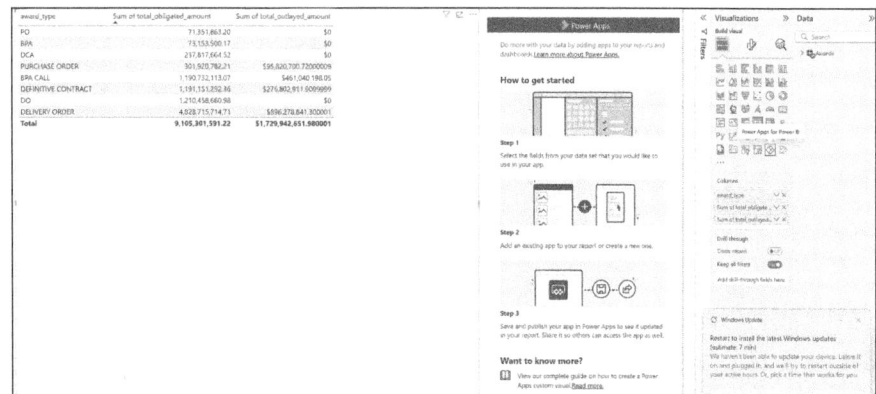

FIGURE 18-2:
Placing a Power
App in a Power
BI Report.

3. **Connect to an existing or new app.**

When you select the embedded visual, Power BI prompts you to do one of two things (see Figure 18-3):

- *Use an existing app:* Choose an app from your environment.

- *Create a new app:* Power BI generates a new app shell inside Power Apps Studio based on the fields you select.

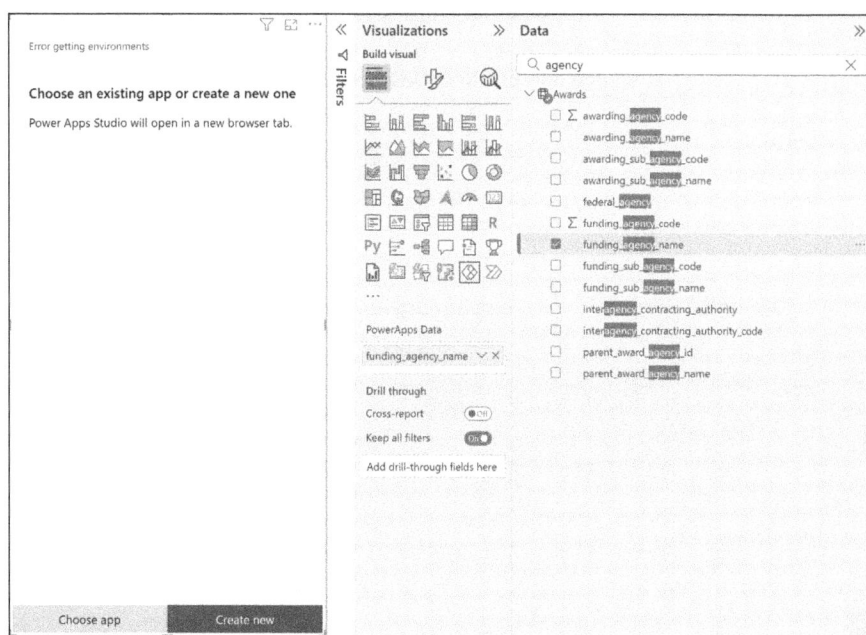

FIGURE 18-3:
Select an existing
app or create a
new one within
the Power
BI Report.

4. Select the correct environment.

If your organization has multiple Power Platform environments (for example, sandbox and production), choose the correct one before proceeding. Small organizations often have only a single environment. Otherwise, Power Apps Studio launches and scaffolds the app automatically — no heavy coding required.

TECHNICAL STUFF

If you choose to use an existing app, the required integration components are added so that the app can receive data from Power BI. If you choose to create a new app, Power Apps automatically wires up the integration in a grid format. Your main task afterward is to connect any additional external data sources and update the layout as you desire.

5. Configure live data integration.

Power BI and Power Apps now share a live connection. You can filter or update report data and immediately see changes reflected in the embedded app.

TIP

Use the `PowerBIIntegration.Refresh()` function to ensure the app refreshes correctly as report data updates. Without it, the app may not respond to user interactions. For example, to pull a field into Power Apps from the embedded data, you may use a formula like:

```
LookUp(Agency, Agency_Name = First(PowerBIIntegration.
    Data).Agency_Name)
```

6. Save and publish the app.

At the right side of the Power Apps Studio Ribbon, click the floppy disk icon. Then choose the name and where you want to save the app. After the location and name are determined, click Save (see Figure 18-4).

FIGURE 18-4:
Saving the App within Power Apps.

7. Test the integration.

Return to your published Power BI report. The embedded Power Apps visual should now display your app and interact with report data in real time (see Figure 18-5). Users can explore, filter, and drill into the report while simultaneously interacting with the app.

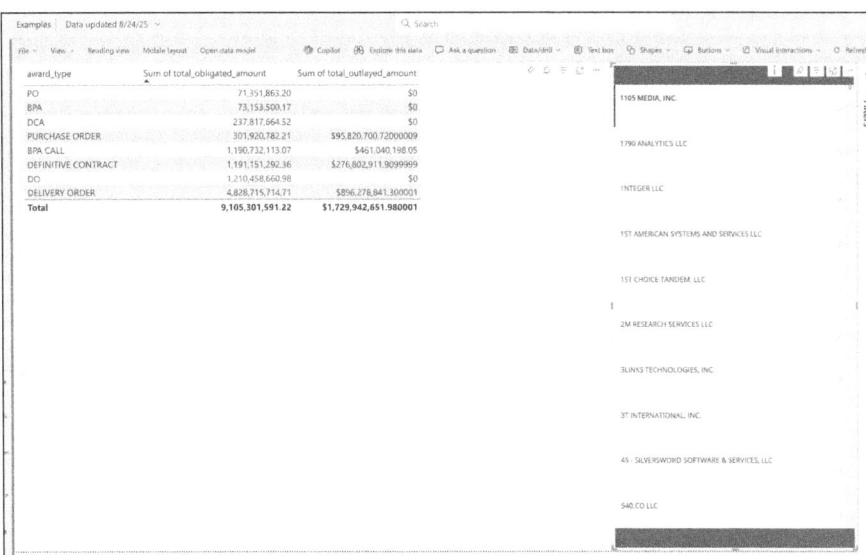

Acknowledging the limitations of Power Apps/Power BI integration

Like any integration, the combination of Power Apps and Power BI comes with a few limitations. These limitations aren't deal breakers, but if you don't know about them ahead of time, they can cause unnecessary frustration. Understanding these limits will help you design your reports and apps so they work smoothly together.

Here are the key limits to keep in mind:

» **Row limit:** A Power Apps visual within a Power BI report can only pull in *up to* 1,000 rows of data from Power BI at a time. This is a hard limit; therefore, you can't override it. If your dataset is larger, filter or summarize the data in Power BI before passing it to Power Apps.

» **No Report Server support:** Power Apps visuals work only in the Power BI Service. If you're using Power BI Report Server, the integration isn't available.

>> **Separate data sources:** When you embed a Power BI report that includes a Power Apps visual (for example, in Teams or SharePoint), the two pieces don't share a single dataset. The Power BI report uses its own semantic model, and the app connects to its own data source. What is shared, however, is *context*; for example, the row you select in Power BI can be passed into the app.

>> **Field changes require updates:** If you make changes to fields in your Power BI report, like renaming or removing them, you may need to reconfigure the Power Apps visual in the Power BI Service. Otherwise, the app might stop functioning as expected.

>> **Refresh is limited:** A Power Apps visual doesn't trigger a dataset refresh in Power BI. If your app writes data back to the same source as your report, the changes won't show up in Power BI until the dataset refreshes on its own schedule.

>> **App sharing is separate:** Publishing your Power BI report doesn't automatically share the Power App inside it. Users need to have permission to access both the report *and* the app for the integration to work.

These limits aren't designed to restrict how you use Power Apps and Power BI together. Instead, they're there to help ensure reliable performance. By planning for them, you can avoid issues. A bit of design up front can save you a lot of troubleshooting later.

Integrating OneDrive, SharePoint, and Teams with Power BI

OneDrive is like your dedicated desk in the cloud. The storage solution is excellent for personal files. SharePoint, by contrast, is more like the office library or main workspace, with richer collaboration tools, governance, and team visibility. Power BI works well with OneDrive — especially for simple scenarios — but SharePoint offers more advanced options for structured collaboration.

Integrating files from OneDrive

When you establish a connection with OneDrive, you must apply the same rigor as when connecting to other files (see Chapters 4 and 5). Here are the steps:

1. **In Power BI Desktop, choose Get Data ➪ Excel (or CSV/TXT, depending on your file type).**

   The file picker window appears.

2. **Locate your file in OneDrive.**

3. **Select your file (XLS, CSV, or TXT) and click Open.**

   Power BI connects to the file and displays the Navigator dialog box.

4. **Choose the tables, sheets, or ranges you want to import.**

   Click Load to bring the data directly into Power BI, or click Transform Data to clean it in Power Query first.

5. **Publish your report to Power BI Service.**

   This allows you to save the recently imported data from the XLS, CSV, or TXT file into the PBIX file.

6. **Post the file into your OneDrive location of choice (see Figure 18-6).**

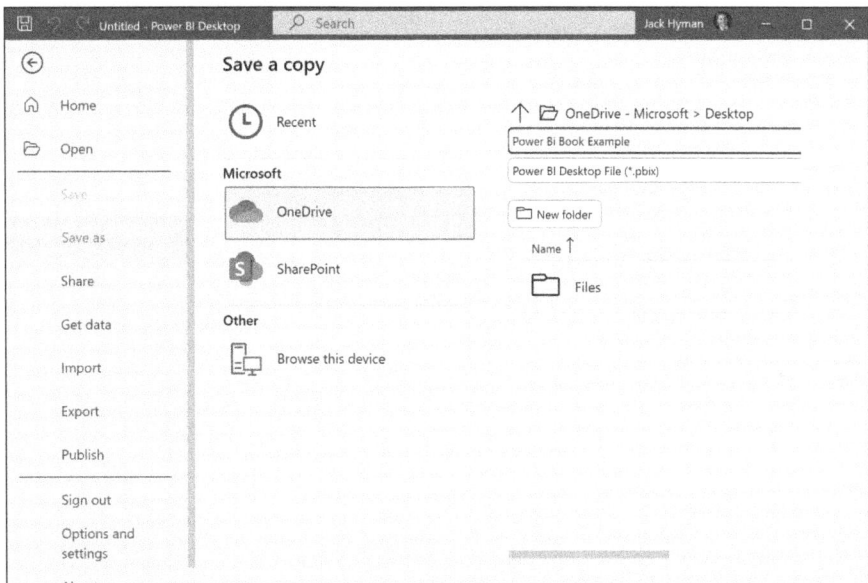

FIGURE 18-6:
Saving a PBIX File
to OneDrive.

Integrating files from SharePoint and Teams

Integrating files from SharePoint can be a bit trickier than integrating files from OneDrive. First, you must be aware of the document library where your data file is stored. If you intend to use a SharePoint list, you must know the URL for that SharePoint list as well.

If your Excel, CSV, or TXT file is stored in a SharePoint document library (including a Teams file library), follow these steps:

1. **In Power BI Desktop, click Get Data ⇨ SharePoint Folder, not SharePoint List (see Figure 18-7).**

2. **In the dialog box that appears, paste the SharePoint site URL (not the full file path). For example, using this fictional SharePoint site:**

   `https://powerbifordummies2ed.sharepoint.com/sites/Finance`

3. **Power BI lists all files in that site. Use the search or filter options to locate your file.**

4. **Select your file and click Combine ⇨ Combine & Transform Data to open it in Power Query.**

5. **Clean and shape the data as needed, and then click Load to bring it into Power BI.**

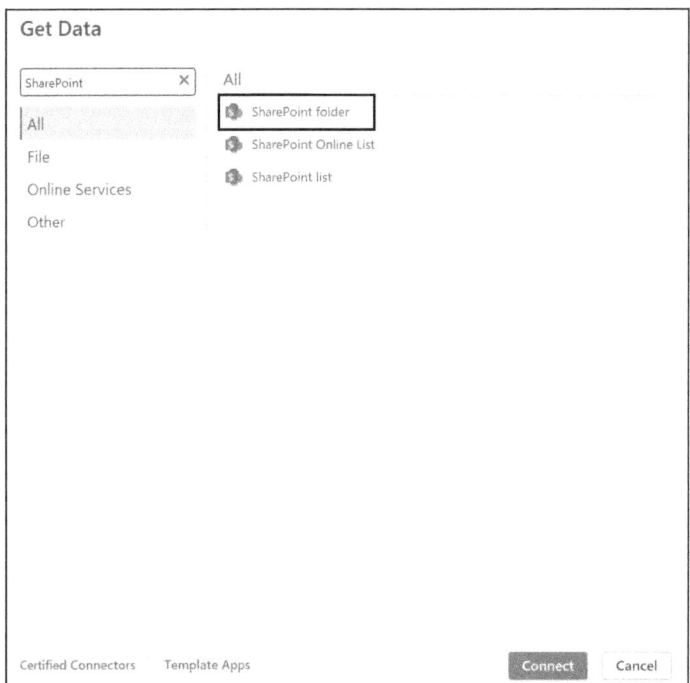

FIGURE 18-7:
Choosing between a SharePoint folder and Share-Point list.

Integrating with a SharePoint and Teams list

To integrate data that lives inside a SharePoint list, follow these steps:

1. **In Power BI Desktop, choose Get Data ⇨ More.**
2. **Choose Online Services ⇨ SharePoint Online List, and click Connect.**
3. **Enter the full URL of the list. For example:**

   https://powerbifordummies2ed.sharepoint.com /sites/Projects/Lists/ ProjectTasks

4. **Authenticate with your Organizational Account (OAuth2) if prompted.**
5. **In the Navigator, select the list you want, and then click Load or Transform Data.**

TECHNICAL STUFF

If you're using Teams, SharePoint powers Teams file storage, too. Connecting to the SharePoint site backing your Team folders works the same way as connecting to any other SharePoint library. Table 18-1 compares the differences among the three platforms.

TABLE 18-1   Comparing OneDrive, SharePoint, and Teams

Feature	OneDrive	SharePoint	Teams
Best for	Personal storage, small-scale sharing, quick prototyping	Team projects, structured collaboration, intranets, governance	Collaboration hub that combines chat, meetings, and files (backed by SharePoint)
Data type support	Excel, CSV, TXT files stored in your OneDrive	Excel, CSV, TXT in document libraries; SharePoint lists	Same as SharePoint (files are stored in the Team's SharePoint library)
Integration with Power BI	Connect via Get Data ⇨ Excel/CSV or OneDrive URL	Connect via SharePoint Folder (for libraries) or SharePoint Online List	Connect to the underlying SharePoint site that stores Teams files
File ownership	Tied to individual users	Owned by the site (team-based)	Owned by the Team (through its linked SharePoint site)
Collaboration	Limited. File sharing is user-driven	Full team collaboration, permissions, workflows, and versioning	Real-time collaboration around files, reports, and conversations
Refresh in Power BI Service	Supports scheduled refresh with OAuth2	Supports scheduled refresh with OAuth2	Supports scheduled refresh with OAuth2 (through SharePoint backend)
Typical scenario	An analyst working solo or needing a central file	A department managing shared datasets or business processes	A team working together daily on reports, chats, and meetings with shared context

TIP

If you're working on your own, OneDrive is usually all you need. But if you're collaborating with a team, store the file in SharePoint or a Teams document library instead. This way, everyone can contribute without version chaos.

Embedding Power BI Reports in SharePoint Online

I discuss earlier how to pull data into Power BI to create visualizations. Now, you will likely want to expose the data source to the world. One way to accomplish this is by using the Power BI web part for modern SharePoint pages. You need to configure the report in Power BI Service, grab the correct link, and drop it into SharePoint. This is a two-step process, as I describe in the following sections.

Preparing your report in Power BI Service

Before SharePoint can display your report, you need to configure it in the Power BI Service. Follow these steps:

1. **Go to Power BI Service in your browser.**

2. **Locate the report you want to share. Reports are stored inside your workspaces.**

3. **Open the report and choose File ⇨ Embed Report ⇨ SharePoint Online (see Figure 18-8).**

4. **Copy the link from the Embed Link for SharePoint Online dialog box.**

    You'll paste this link into SharePoint.

Add the report to a SharePoint page

To switch over to your SharePoint site where you want the report to appear, follow these steps:

1. **Navigate to a modern SharePoint page. (Classic pages don't support the Power BI web part.)**

2. **Click the plus (+) sign in the section where you want to add the report (see Figure 18-9).**

3. **From the list of available web parts, select Power BI (see Figure 18-10).**

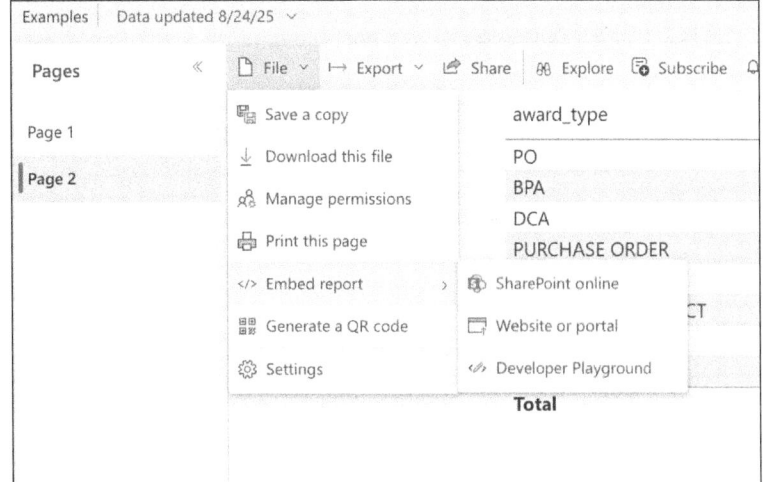

FIGURE 18-8:
Accessing the
Power BI Embed
functionality for
SharePoint.

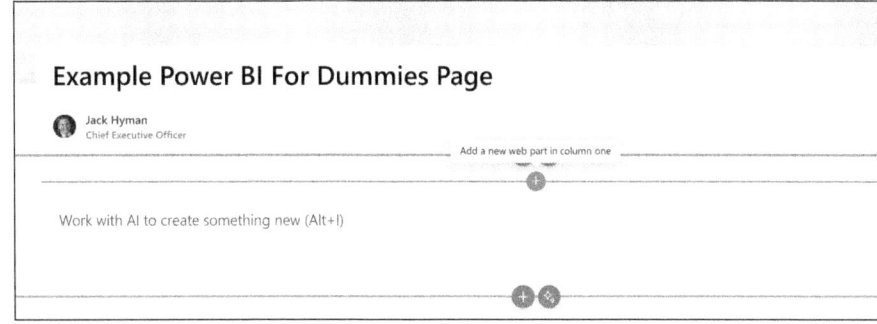

FIGURE 18-9:
Adding a web
part in
SharePoint.

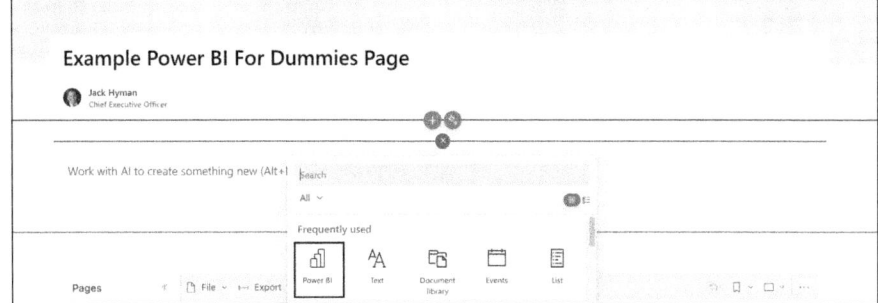

FIGURE 18-10:
Locating the
Power
BI web part.

4. **When the Power BI web part is added, click Add Report (see Figure 18-11).**

   A configuration panel opens on the right-hand side of the screen (see Figure 18-12).

5. **Paste the link you copied from Power BI Service into the Power BI Report Link field.**

6. **Press Enter to confirm your changes.**

   The report now appears live in your SharePoint page, complete with its page tabs, filters, and interactivity (see Figure 18-13).

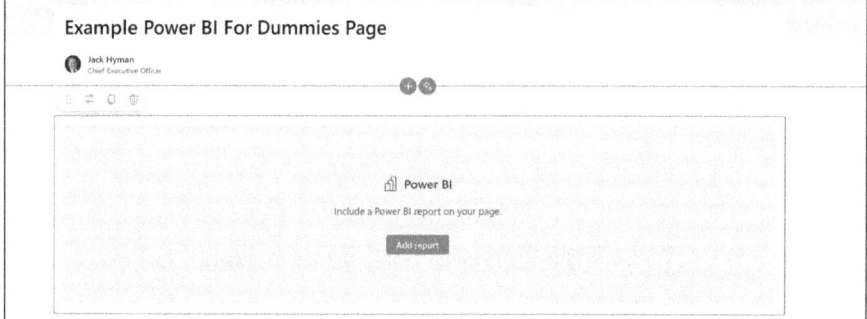

FIGURE 18-11:
Adding the report to the SharePoint page.

FIGURE 18-12:
Copying the link into the URL bar to present the Power BI report.

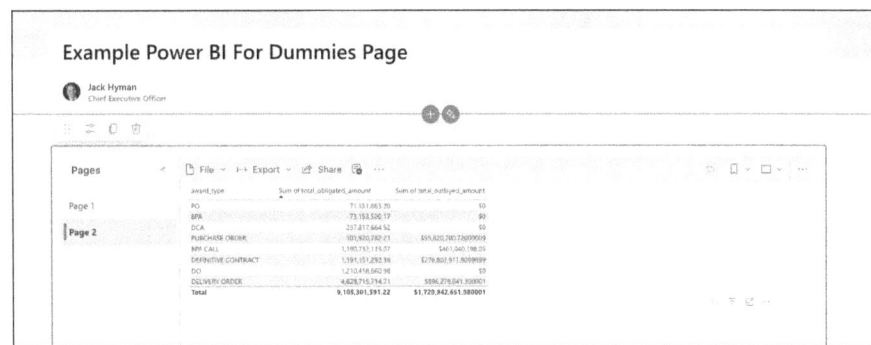

FIGURE 18-13:
Complete
integration of
Power BI within
the SharePoint
page.

Automating Workflow with Power Automate and Power BI

Power Automate (formerly called Microsoft Flow) is Microsoft's workflow automation tool. It helps organizations reduce repetitive, manual tasks by connecting different systems. One reason many users prefer Power Automate instead of manual data ingestion is that Power Automate eliminates the need to move data using laborious techniques. Instead, you can create an automated "flow" to handle those jobs for you.

Think of Power Automate as the bridge: It doesn't store your data, but it makes sure information moves between systems quickly, accurately, and consistently. When paired with Power BI, you can turn insights into actions — for example, send an alert when a KPI falls below target, update a SharePoint list when a new record appears, or even start an approval workflow directly from a report.

Using prebuilt flows with Power BI

The easiest way to get started is with Microsoft's prebuilt templates. These templates save you from building a flow from scratch. The following steps demonstrate how you may integrate Power Automate between Power BI and Excel:

1. **Open the Power Automate app from the Microsoft 365 console.**

2. **Go to Templates.**

3. **In the Search box, type** Power BI.

   A list appears of prebuilt templates designed for common BI scenarios (see Figure 18-14).

4. **Select a template, such as Update an Excel Table from Power BI.**

5. **Sign in and authenticate your Power BI and Excel accounts.**

6. Map the fields from your data sources, as well as the dataset, to the corresponding Excel columns in the Action (second box in flow).

7. Make sure that the Trigger (first box) is configured to the appropriate Power BI data source.

8. Test the flow to make sure everything works once all items are filled out completely, and then select Save.

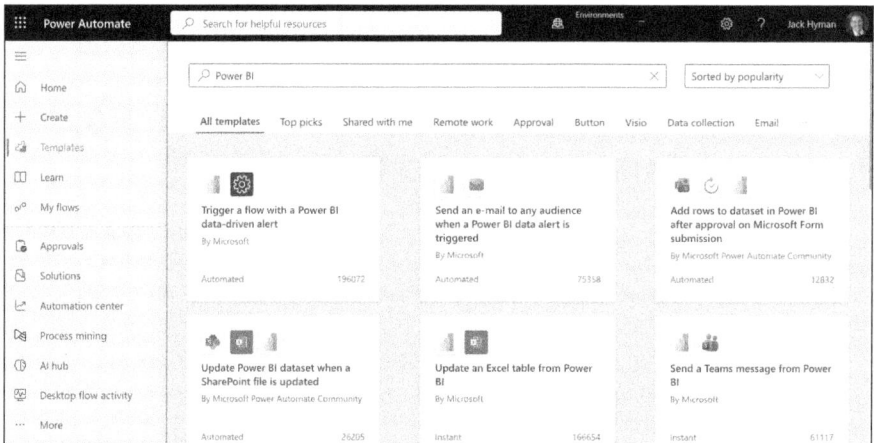

FIGURE 18-14: Configuring your Power Automate Flow with Power BI.

Adding the Power Automate visual in Power BI

Power BI also includes a special Power Automate visual that enables you to trigger flows directly from a report. This way, users can act on insights without leaving Power BI. To integrate the flow within your Power BI Report, follow these steps:

1. In a Power BI report, open the Visualizations pane and add the Power Automate visual to the canvas (see Figure 18-15).

2. Choose the field you want to use as the trigger (see Figure 18-16).

3. Select the visual, click the More Options menu, and choose Edit (see Figure 18-17).

   Power Automate launches in your browser.

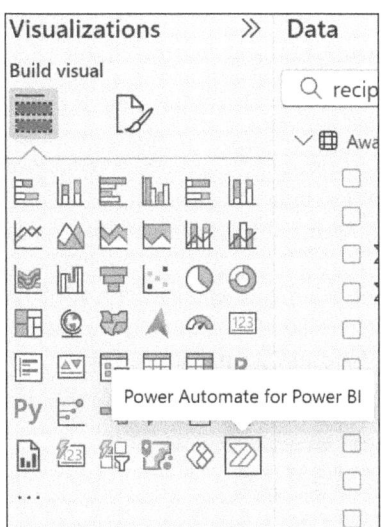

FIGURE 18-15:
Accessing the
Power Automate
Visualization.

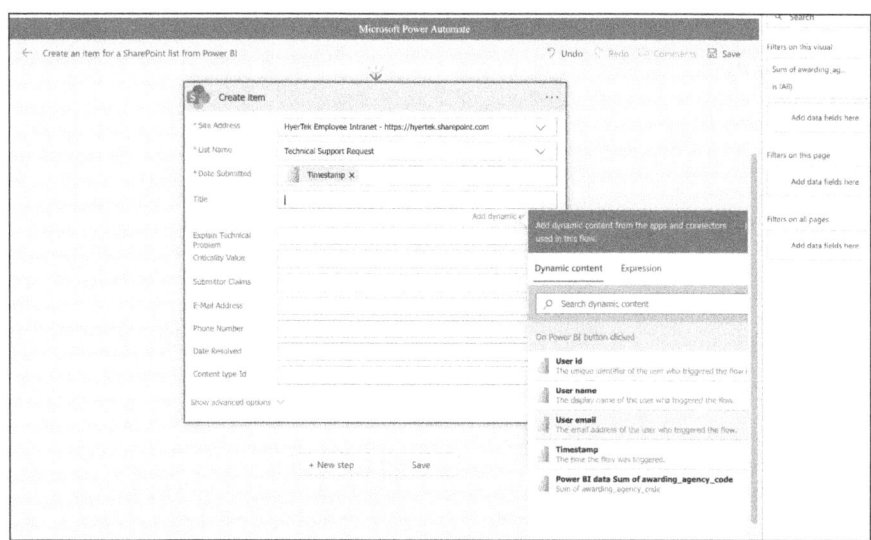

FIGURE 18-16:
Configuring the
Power Automate
Visualization.

4. **Pick a prebuilt flow, such as Create a SharePoint List Item from Power BI, or design your own.**

5. **Authenticate Power BI and SharePoint, map the fields, and click Save.**

6. **Close the window to Power Automate and head back to Power BI.**

   You need to perform this action manually; it does not occur automatically.

7. **In Power BI, admire the new Run Flow button that is added to your report (see Figure 18-18).**

When users interact with that visual, the flow can run automatically by updating a list, sending a message, or initiating an approval without ever leaving the report, each time the Run Flow button is triggered. By adding this functionality, you avoid manual data entry, including copying and pasting datasets.

WARNING

If you are not going between Microsoft applications with Power Automate, you will require a premium license. So, for example, Power BI to Salesforce CRM requires a Power Automate Premium license.

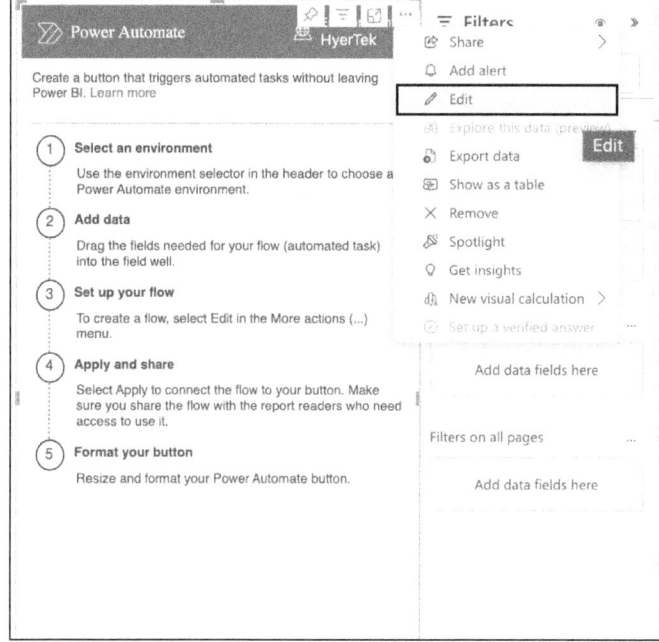

FIGURE 18-17:
Selecting the Power Automate template to support the dataset.

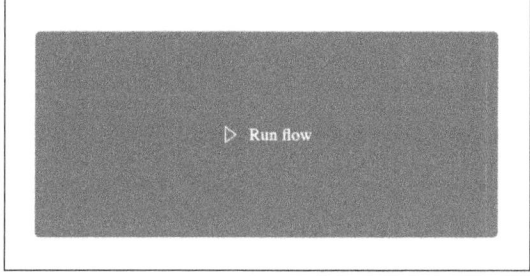

FIGURE 18-18:
A Run Flow trigger button.

Unleashing Dynamics 365 for Data Analytics

Dynamics 365 comes in many flavors. Whether you're a user of Dynamics 365 CRM, Sales, Finance, Operations, HR, Business Central, or another module, Power BI can help you evaluate your data with greater depth than Dynamics 365 alone. Embedded in Dynamics 365 are countless ways to slice and dice your data based on available industry metrics. Still, many organizations need to compare data outside of what Dynamics 365 offers. Often, the data must be aggregated with third-party systems. Regardless of the circumstances, the way to ingest data into Power BI Desktop for evaluation and analysis is exactly how it works in Chapter 6. All the options for Dynamics 365 are found under Online Services (see Figure 18-19). Select the application you want to ingest data from into Power BI and follow the prompts after clicking Connect.

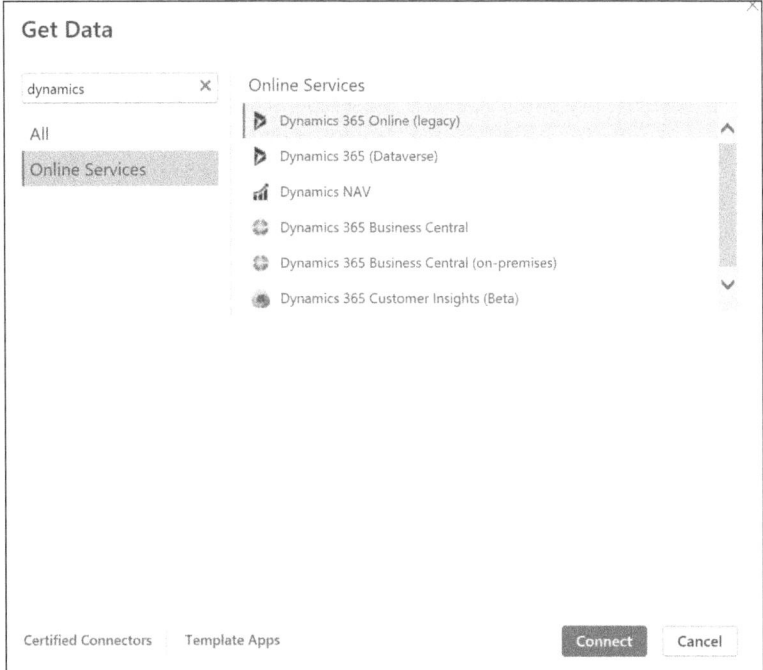

FIGURE 18-19: The menu for selecting a Dynamics 365 Instance.

Here's what happens after you select a Dynamics application:

1. **You're either asked to enter the URL for your organization's instance of Dynamics CRM or asked to log in for Dynamics 365 (all other applications).**

   In this case, login credentials are provided.

2. Once you're logged in, select which tables from the Production instances you want to transform and load by checking each item on the left.

3. When ready, select Transform Data.

    Keep in mind that you are pulling data from Dataverse, which is where all Dynamics 365 data is stored. There is no difference in the process that we've covered in previous chapters.

4. Your Dynamics 365 application data has been imported into Power BI for evaluation using Power Query Editor.

Now you can create reports using the tables and data just imported into Power BI without having to depend on Dynamics 365.

Collaboration with Microsoft Teams and Power BI

Microsoft Teams is where most organizations collaborate, chat, and share information. Instead of asking a member of a team to open a browser and go to Power BI every time they need a report, you can bring Power BI directly into Teams. This makes insights part of the daily conversation. You can integrate the report as part of the Teams Channel.

Here's how you can embed a report right inside a Teams channel:

1. Open the Teams app and navigate to the channel where you want to share the report.

2. At the top of the channel, click the + (Add a tab) button (see Figure 18-20).

3. In the list of apps, choose Power BI (see Figure 18-21).

4. Select the report you want from your available workspaces.

5. Click Save.

A new tab appears in your channel with the Power BI report fully interactive (see Figure 18-22). Everyone who has permission to view the report in Power BI will be able to see it in Teams.

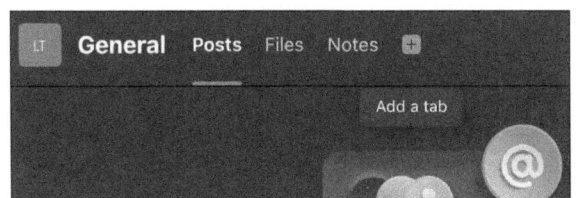

FIGURE 18-20:
Integrating Power
BI into Teams
Configuration.

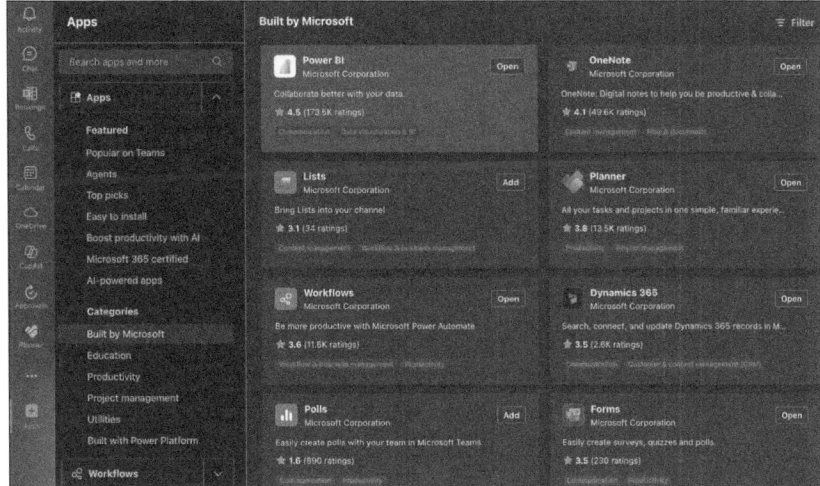

FIGURE 18-21:
Selecting Power
BI from the
Teams
App Gallery.

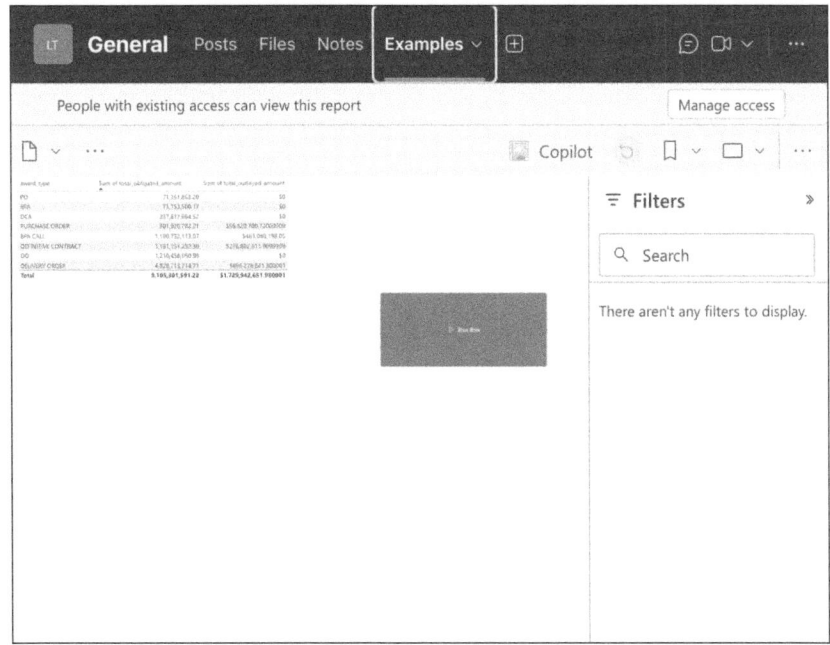

FIGURE 18-22:
A report
integrated into
Teams from
Power BI Service.

IN THIS CHAPTER

» Seeing the value of Microsoft Fabric
as part of the Power BI story

» Standardizing and sharing your data
preparation across Power BI reports
by using Dataflows in Fabric

» Using OneLake, Lakehouse, and
Direct Lake Mode to increase the
capacity and performance of your
Power BI reports

» Determining when to use Fabric
versus using Power BI alone

» Making complicated tasks easier with
Copilot in Power BI and Fabric

Chapter **19**

Enhancing Power BI with Fabric and Copilot

Working in Power BI is great for building charts and dashboards, but anyone who's done it knows the slow part isn't the visuals; it's getting the data ready to support visualization. That's where Microsoft Fabric comes in. Fabric provides you with shared tools to clean, store, and manage your data, ensuring that everyone works from the same trusted source, rather than each person reinventing the wheel. And if you incorporate Copilot for Power BI, your AI helper can suggest formulas, build models, and even draft reports for you. In this chapter, you see how Fabric and Copilot extend what Power BI can do, when they make sense to use, and how they can help keep your reports running smoothly without adding extra headaches.

Knowing When to Introduce Fabric and Copilot

Fabric and Copilot provide stronger foundations for preparing, managing, and analyzing your data as your data analysis becomes more complex or the storage volume exceeds gigabytes. If you've worked with Power BI for any length of time, you know the routine: Every analyst cleans and shapes the same data slightly differently, leading to inconsistent results and wasted effort. Tasks like writing DAX formulas or creating the perfect chart can also eat up hours of trial and error. Fabric addresses these problems by centralizing data preparation and storage for collaboration, not just for one-off usage. Centralizing data preparation and storage also ensures that all teams are working from the same semantic models.

When you use Fabric and Copilot, nothing in Power BI goes away. You still build models, write measures, and create visuals the same way. What's different is that Fabric introduces various ways to collaborate, store, and process datasets at scale. Capabilities such as OneLake, Lakehouse storage, and shared dataflows become fundamental requirements, allowing everyone to use the same trusted data. Copilot adds an AI layer that can generate suggestions, formulas, and even first-draft visuals, all while you stay in control within seconds, versus having an analyst take hours or days to pore over datasets.

REMEMBER

Not every project needs extra horsepower. If you're analyzing a small dataset or creating a one-off report, Power BI Desktop and Power BI Service on their own are more than enough. Fabric and Copilot excel when you're working at scale, enabling activities such as preparing data for teams, building enterprise-grade reports, or automating repetitive tasks.

Getting to Know Fabric for Power BI

Before diving into transformations and reports, it is essential to understand how Fabric integrates into your Power BI environment. Power BI excels at the last mile of analytics, which involves transforming raw data into visuals and actionable insights. However, much of the work leading up to that point, such as cleaning, shaping, and sharing data, has often been done in silos by folks like you and me. No two data experts prepare data in the same way, which can lead to mismatched reports and wasted time. Microsoft Fabric steps in to provide the necessary foundation as your organization transitions from handling small datasets to managing large datasets. You gain features such as shared storage, more powerful workspaces, and a familiar environment in which everyone starts with the same clean data.

Fabric removes many of the limits you hit when working with large or complex data in Power BI. In traditional Power BI, datasets reside within reports or Power BI Service, which works well until the volume grows and performance starts to lag. Fabric introduces OneLake, Lakehouse storage, and Direct Lake mode (which I describe in the upcoming section, "Storage options in Fabric"), which allow you to handle millions or even billions of rows at speed, without workarounds or slow refreshes.

Microsoft Fabric also makes collaboration easier for large organizations (not just a few people, think one hundred or more). Shared dataflows ensure that colleagues across departments, such as finance and sales, work from the same clean dataset. Because OneLake serves as a single hub for storage, no one needs to wonder which version of the data is correct.

Power BI Desktop and Service remain the primary tools for building reports and dashboards. When you pair these tools with Fabric, those dashboards can scale bigger, run faster, and deliver more consistent results.

Fabric Workspaces versus Power BI Workspaces

In Chapter 14, you read about the Power BI Service as a workspace. In the context of Power BI, a *workspace* is a shared location where you and your teammates can store datasets, reports, and dashboards. The Power BI workspace doesn't manage the earlier steps in the data pipeline. Fabric takes the workspace concept a bit further.

If your goal is to manage the entire data analytics lifecycle, the Fabric workspaces are designed to be the home for all your analytics assets from the minute the cycle starts. In addition to reports, dashboards, and semantic models, a Fabric workspace can contain dataflows (for data preparation), Lakehouses (for big data storage), warehouses (for structured data storage), pipelines (for data movement), notebooks (code workspaces), and assets that include AI learning models. Having everything under one roof makes collaboration for data analysts easier than scattering it across multiple systems. Figure 19-1 shows the Fabric home page (https://app.fabric.microsoft.com). Table 19-1 describes the key differences between the two workspace types.

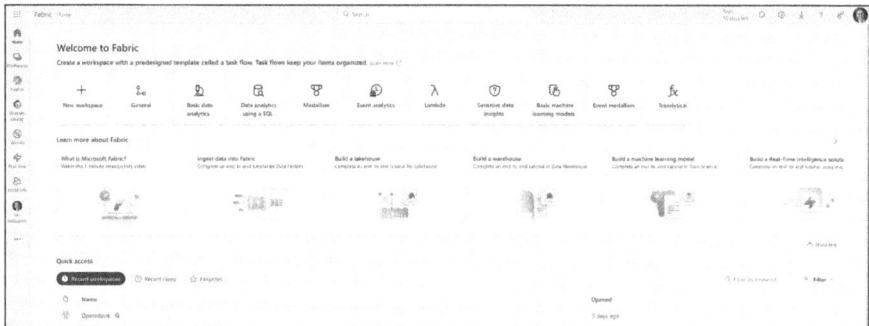

FIGURE 19-1:
Microsoft Fabric
capabilities.

TABLE 19-1   Contrasting Power BI and Fabric Workspaces

Feature	Power BI Workspace	Fabric Workspace
Primary purpose	Store and share reports, dashboards, and datasets	Manage full analytics lifecycle: data prep, storage, and reporting
Dataflows	Limited focus on Power BI Dataflows within Power BI Service	Full Fabric Dataflows with broader integration
Storage	Dataset-centric, within Power BI Service	Centralized via OneLake; supports Lakehouse and Warehouse
Collaboration scope	Report authors and data consumers	Data engineers, analysts, report builders, and admins
Assets supported	Reports, dashboards, and semantic models	Reports, dashboards, datasets, dataflows, Lakehouses, warehouses, pipelines, notebooks, and more
Best for	Small-to-medium scale requirements	Enterprise-scale data and analytics with Power BI integration

Storage options in Fabric

Power BI needs a place to keep your data. With Power BI Desktop, you can store it on your local hard drive, a SharePoint document library, or a third-party data system. Once you move to Power BI Service, the semantic model and all its data attributes are stored in one or more workspaces. This type of storage works well for smaller projects, but as your data grows, things can start to slow down and even come to a halt. Microsoft Fabric steps in with storage choices to make life easier. Table 19-2 breaks down your storage options in Fabric.

TABLE 19-2 **Storage Options in Fabric**

Storage Option	What It Is	How It Works
OneLake	A big data storage drive for your datasets	OneLake is the "OneDrive for big data." Every asset in Fabric connects back to a single place, and that place is OneLake.
Lakehouse	A home for all the unstructured data	Lakehouse is great for storing huge amounts of data, whether clean or messy. Use it to store anything from logs, text, or large exports from apps.
Warehouse	A home for all the structured data	When you have a system that must follow a stringent process, containing the same rules of the road for each record, your data is generally stored in a warehouse. Examples include your ERP, HCM, or CRM systems.
Direct Lake Mode	Fast, live analytics pulled directly from OneLake.	Direct Lake mode enables Power BI to read data directly from OneLake without copying it into a dataset. This reduces refresh time, improves performance, and allows reports to work with large amounts of data efficiently.

Fabric provides options for working with data of any size or complexity. If you have a small dataset, such as a few thousand records or a handful of tables, or only need to create a few small to moderately complex reports, Power BI alone is usually sufficient. However, when your data grows larger, involves complex transformations, or needs to be shared across multiple teams, OneLake, Lakehouse, and Warehouse offer the flexibility and structure to keep everything organized and performing efficiently.

Preparing and Managing Data with Fabric

Getting solid results in Power BI isn't just about building charts and dashboards; it starts with clean, well-prepared data. If the data going in is messy, the reports coming out will have little value. This is where Microsoft Fabric comes into play. Fabric provides you with tools to prepare, shape, and share your data, ensuring that everyone on your team works from the same reliable foundation. Whereas Power BI is meant for slicing and dicing the data alone and Power BI Service is primarily meant for sharing and collaboration, Fabric brings the entire data life-cycle together in your web browser.

Meet Dataflows in Fabric

Dataflows are the foundation of data preparation in Fabric. You can think of them as recipes. Each time you make a meal, you follow a set of steps to prepare it before serving. Similarly, once you define the steps to clean and shape your data, you don't have to rewrite them every time you need to analyze it.

In Power BI Desktop, these preparation steps typically live inside individual reports, meaning each report maintains its own version of the transformations. Fabric streamlines this by allowing you to create a shared dataflow that multiple analysts can use. For example, each analyst can connect to the same source and apply their own filters or naming conventions as needed. The dataflow becomes a single, trusted source for everyone in your organization.

To create a new dataflow in Fabric, follow these steps:

1. **Open your Fabric My Workspace.**

   Navigate to My Workspace or another workspace where you want to create the dataflow.

2. **Click New ⇨ Dataflow (Gen2). (See Figure 19-2.)**

3. **Name your dataflow and click Create.**

   If you also want to integrate with a Git repository, check the box.

4. **Select a data source and click Next.**

   Examples of data sources include Excel, SQL Server, or SharePoint. For this example, use the data file downloaded from Kaggle.com.

5. **Preview the data file before committing and then click Create.**

   Change any of the column names or data types as needed and then click Create.

   The loaded data appears in the Power Query Editor.

6. **Apply at least one basic transformation, such as Remove Column under Home (see Figure 19-3).**

   An example of a basic transformation might be removing a column from a dataset that you no longer need.

7. **Go to Save, located under the Home Ribbon. Click Save and Run.**

   Your dataflow is now saved and will refresh automatically whenever changes are made to the underlying data source.

   Return to Workspace assets, where you'll see your newly created dataflow listed as active (see Figure 19-4).

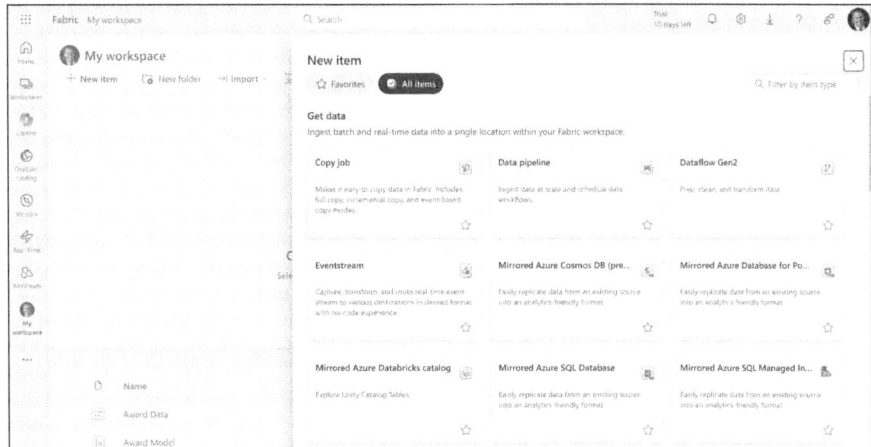

FIGURE 19-2:
Creating a new dataflow.

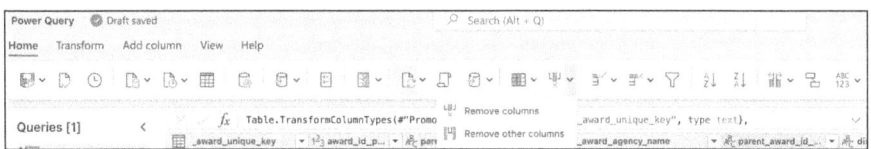

FIGURE 19-3:
Removing a column by using the Fabric Power Query Editor.

FIGURE 19-4:
An active dataflow in the Fabric My Workspace.

Cleaning and transforming data

After you set up a Dataflow in Fabric, your next step in optimizing your data for distribution is to clean and transform it. Think of this as tidying your kitchen before you cook: You don't want stale ingredients, mislabeled jars, or duplicate items cluttering the recipe. Clean data means reliable reports. Fabric uses the same Power Query Editor that you may know from Power BI Desktop, but here, the changes are stored in the cloud. That means everyone who connects to the Dataflow receives the same version, rather than each analyst having to reinvent the wheel. Table 19-3 describes data cleansing and transformation activities that users commonly perform in Fabric.

REMEMBER

The Power Query experience remains the same; the difference is that you are not the sole pilot on the journey. Others can collaborate with you in managing the semantic model and related assets in your workspace.

TABLE 19-3 **Cleansing and Transformation Activities in Microsoft Fabric**

Transformation	What It Does
Remove Duplicates	Keeps you from counting the same item more than once if you are looking for a one-to-one relationship
Replace Values	Fixes inconsistent entries, such as turning "N/A" into blanks
Rename Columns	Swaps technical names (like recipient_state) for business-friendly names (State)
Change Data Types	Converts text to numbers or dates so that calculations work correctly
Split or Merge Columns	Breaks apart combined values (like "First Last") or join tables for richer analysis
Add Calculated Columns	Creates new fields, like multiplying Quantity × Price to get Order Value

Here's an example of how you can cleanse and transform a Dataflow with Microsoft Fabric:

1. **Open your Fabric Dataflow, such as** `Awards_Dataflow`.

2. **In the Power Query Editor, pick a column such as** `parent_award_agency_name`.

3. **Right-click and choose Replace Value.**

   Change a value such as `DEPT OF DEFENSE` to `DEPARTMENT OF DEFENSE`.

4. **Select the** `naics_code` **column and change the type from Whole Number to Text (see Figure 19-5).**

5. **In the Query Settings pane, verify that you've made all the necessary data changes (see Figure 19-6).**

6. **Click Save & Close to commit your changes.**

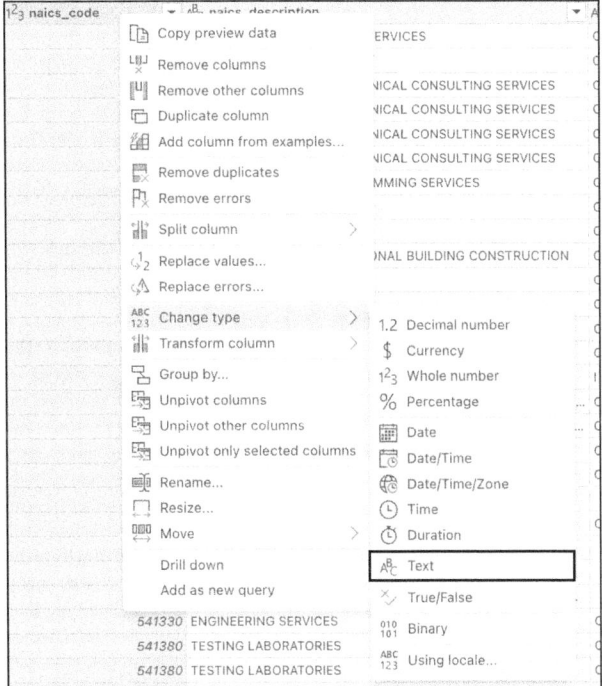

FIGURE 19-5:
Changing a
numeric value to
a text value in the
Fabric Power
Query Editor.

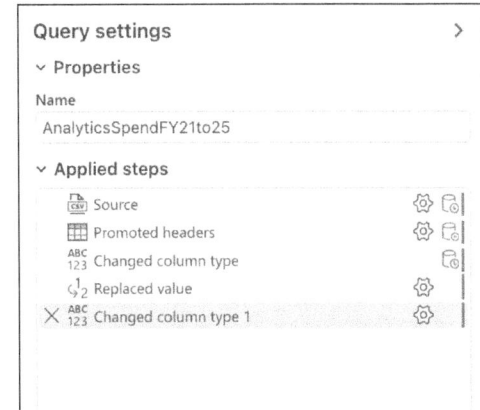

FIGURE 19-6:
Evaluating
changes made
in the Query
Settings pane.

Sharing and Refreshing Dataflows

Creating a Dataflow is just the tip of the iceberg. What makes data valuable is keeping it refreshed so that your reports always show the latest information. Fabric doesn't automatically update Dataflows when you create them; they need to be configured. Therefore, you need to set up a refresh schedule that matches the frequency at which your source data changes. For instance, if your HR system updates once a night, there's no point in refreshing every hour.

To create a refresh schedule for a Dataflow in Fabric follow these steps:

1. **Open your Fabric workspace and open the Dataflow you created.**

2. **From the More Options (. . .) menu, choose Schedule (see Figure 19-7).**

3. **Click +Add Schedule button.**

4. **Enter the parameters on how often you want to refresh the environment (daily, multiple times per day, or weekly), as shown in Figure 19-8.**

    When setting up the refresh schedule, choose how often and when the Dataflow should run. You can select a frequency, which can be daily, multiple times per day, or weekly, based on how frequently your source data changes. You can also specify the time zone, define start and end dates for the schedule, and enable notifications to alert you if a refresh fails. These options help ensure that your Dataflow runs reliably and aligns with your organization's data update cycles.

5. **Click Save.**

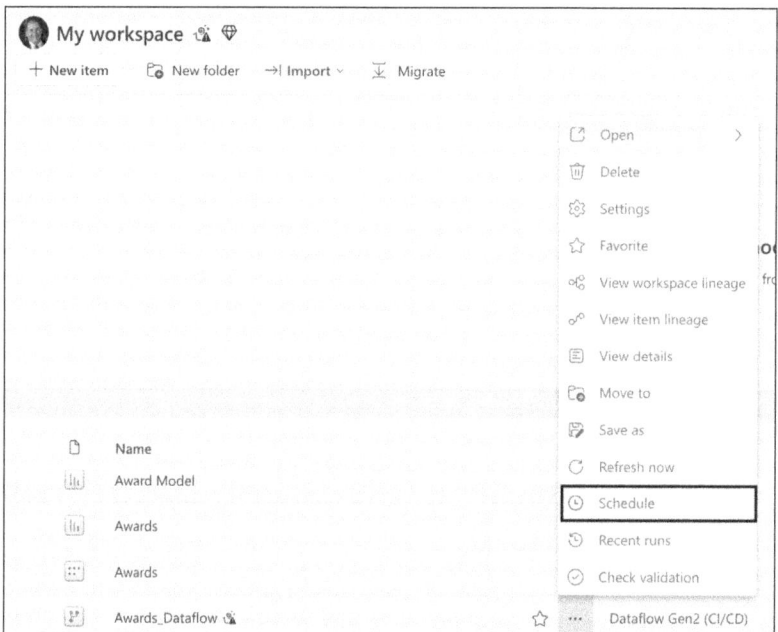

FIGURE 19-7:
Accessing schedule for a Dataflow.

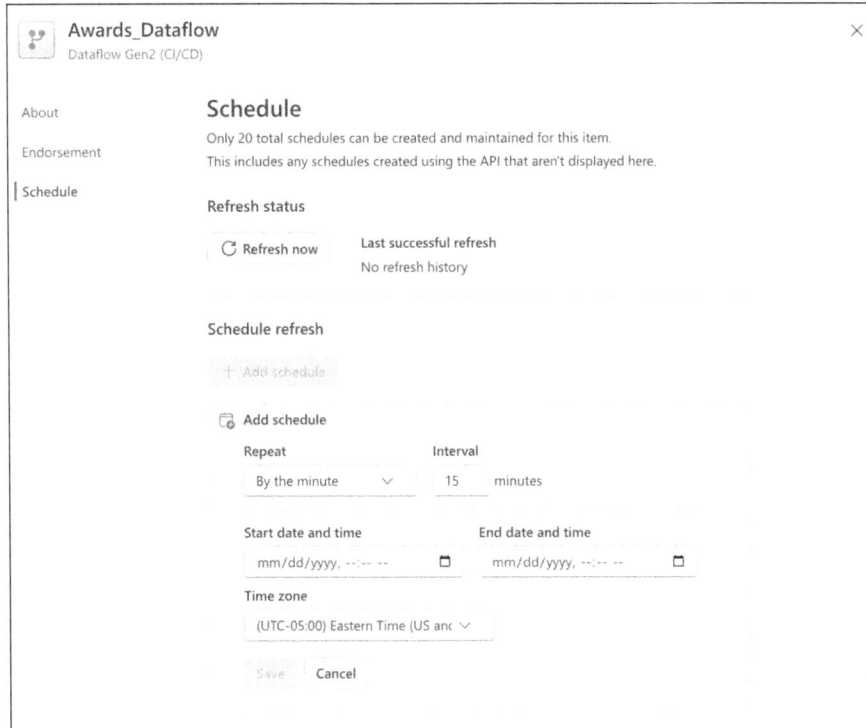

FIGURE 19-8:
Creating a
Dataflow
schedule.

By automating refreshes, you ensure that reports reflect current data without constant manual effort. The key is to align the schedule with your data's update cycle; updating too frequently wastes resources, and updating too infrequently risks outdated insights.

From time to time, you may need to force a refresh out of cycle. Navigate to the same More Options (. . .) menu and click Refresh.

TIP

Instead of reprocessing the full dataset each time, incremental refresh targets just those recent rows, keeping the data fresh while dramatically improving performance. To find out more about incremental refresh, go to https://learn. microsoft.com/en-us/fabric/data-factory/dataflow-gen2-incremental-refresh.

ON THE WEB

Connecting to Power BI Reports

After you prepare and store your data in Fabric, regardless of whether it's using Dataflows, a Lakehouse, or OneLake, you'll want to bring that data into Power BI so that you can build reports and dashboards. The process is straightforward, but the method you choose depends on the type of Fabric asset you're working with.

Using Dataflow data in reports

Dataflows are reusable building blocks for reports. Instead of cleaning and shaping the same dataset multiple times across users, the goal is to prepare a model once in Fabric and then connect to it from Power BI Desktop. To use a Fabric Dataflow in a Power BI report across a team rather than create one-off instances, follow these steps:

1. **Open Power BI Desktop.**

2. **From the Ribbon, click Get Data ⇨ Dataflows or Get Data ⇨ Power Platform ⇨ Dataflows.**

3. **Sign in with your Microsoft account, and then select the workspace and Dataflow you want to connect to.**

4. **Pick the table or tables you need, and then click Load to bring them into your semantic model.**

Once you establish a connection to a Dataflow, you can build visuals, measures, and dashboards on top of that shared dataset. Because the Dataflow refreshes in Fabric, all changes are reflected directly in your reports.

Building from Lakehouse data

The Fabric solution for storing large volumes of semi-structured or unstructured data, such as logs, text files, or app exports, is the Lakehouse. Lakehouses combine the flexibility of a data lake with the usability of a warehouse, making them ideal for both raw and centralized data storage. To connect a Lakehouse to Power BI Desktop follow these steps:

1. **In Power BI Desktop, choose Get Data ⇨ Microsoft Fabric.**

2. **Under the Microsoft Fabric category, choose Lakehouse.**

3. **If you haven't already signed in, log in with your Microsoft credentials and navigate to the Fabric workspace that contains your Lakehouse.**

   The OneLake Catalog appears with a data discovery tool that points to all available Lakehouse data sources (see Figure 19-9).

4. **Select the table or files you want to import.**

5. **Click Connect to bring them into your report.**

From here, you can model the Lakehouse data the same way as with any other dataset. Because Lakehouses can store massive amounts of data, they are handy for combining multiple source files into a single trusted hub.

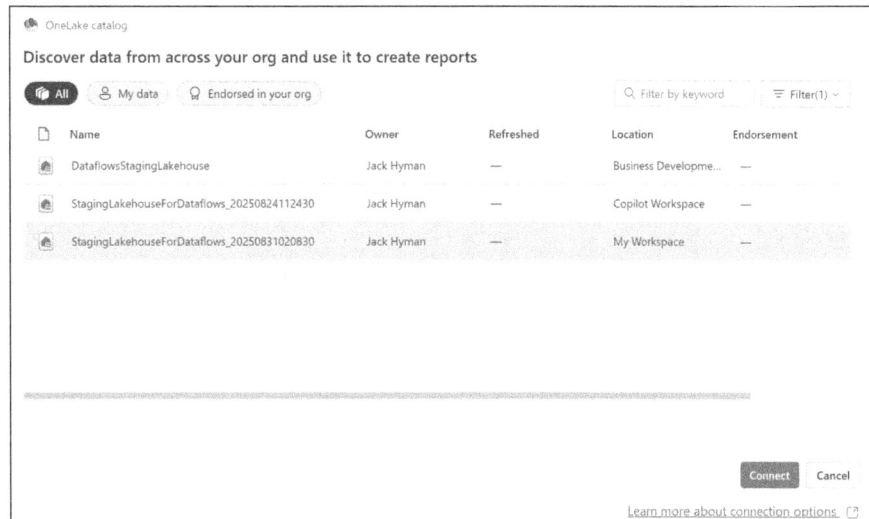

FIGURE 19-9:
Connecting to Lakehouse data in the OneLake storage catalog.

Exploring Direct Lake Mode

When you use Direct Lake Mode, you're not copying data down to your computer. Instead, Power BI works directly with the data sitting in OneLake. This differs from the usual Import mode, in which data is downloaded into a PBIX file, or from DirectQuery, in which every query is sent back to the source system. With Direct Lake, the data remains in OneLake but behaves as if it were already local to the report and semantic model. The data is fast, responsive, and capable of handling large datasets.

A key difference is how you work with your semantic models. Typically, you create a model in Power BI Desktop and then publish it to the service. With Direct Lake, the model lives in the Fabric workspace, so when you open it in Desktop, you're editing it live right where it sits. There is no need to keep clicking Publish for each change you make. If you've ever edited a semantic model directly in the Fabric web interface, the experience is the same as in Desktop. Version control is a key feature within Fabric. Each time you make an edit and save, a version history cycle is created. That means you can roll back to an earlier version if you make a mistake.

Building reports works just as you expect. From Power BI Desktop, you can connect to a semantic model in the OneLake catalog and start creating visuals. Or, if you prefer, you can make a report right inside the Fabric workspace itself. Either way, you're working on top of Direct Lake data that's fast, centralized, and always up to date.

TECHNICAL STUFF

Direct Lake doesn't require a refresh schedule. Your data is always live.

Table 19-4 compares Dataflows, Lakehouse, and Direct Lake Mode.

TABLE 19-4 **Comparing Dataflows, Lakehouse, and Direct Lake Mode**

Option	What It Is	When To Use It
Dataflow	A reusable, cloud-based Power Query pipeline that cleans/shapes data once for everyone.	Multiple reports or teams need the same cleaned tables. You're working with small–to–medium data volumes. You want to standardize prep.
Lakehouse	Fabric storage that blends data lake flexibility with warehouse structure; holds very large structured & semi-structured files/tables in OneLake.	You're landing lots of files/logs/exports at scale that you will later model for business intelligence or machine learning. You need a central hub.
Direct Lake Mode	Feature that enables Power BI to read directly from OneLake-backed Lakehouse/Warehouse without importing so that models feel "live" and fast.	You're using enterprise-scale reports that require near-real-time data and import-like speed without refresh windows.

WARNING

Direct Lake Mode requires that you create a Lakehouse or Warehouse in Fabric first. To use Direct Lake, first set up a Lakehouse or Warehouse in Fabric. Then turn it on in Power BI Desktop by going to File ⇨ Options & Settings ⇨ Preview. Be sure to check the box "Create semantic models in Direct Lake storage mode from one or more Fabric artifacts."

ON THE WEB

Getting into the weeds of Fabric architecture and development is beyond the scope of *Microsoft Power BI For Dummies*. To find out more about building your own Lakehouse, go to https://learn.microsoft.com/en-us/fabric/data-engineering/create-lakehouse.

Getting Smarter with Copilot

AI offers significant productivity gains through data analytics platforms like Power BI. With Copilot, you aren't just saving a few steps; you also can instruct the system to do the heavy work I cover in Chapters 4 through 13. Instead of memorizing formulas like people used to do with telephone numbers before cell-phones (maybe some still do) or spending hours experimenting with tweaking data to make the perfect visual, you can describe what you need in plain language and let Copilot do the rest.

What makes Copilot powerful is that it's conversational. You don't just fire off one prompt and hope for the best. You can have a back-and-forth conversation, guiding Copilot the way you'd guide a team: "Make this a bar chart in red and blue," "Filter it to 2025," or "Add profit margin." The more you interact, the closer the result gets to exactly what you want. And there are times it gets exactly what you wish to correct on the first go-around. Copilot helps you move faster, reduce repetitive work, and focus on the story your data tells.

Prepping a semantic model with Copilot

The semantic model is the brain of your Power BI project because it connects the dots between all the tables, columns, and measures you use. Without the semantic model, your data is just a collection of spreadsheets with little meaning. A well-designed semantic model instructs Power BI on how tables relate to one another, defines the calculations that are relevant to your business, and ensures consistency across reports. For example, if you always calculate "Year-to-Date Sales" or "Profit Margin," the semantic model makes sure that those numbers follow the rinse, repeat, recycle mentality.

Copilot accelerates the model-building process by leveraging conversational AI. Instead of manually dragging lines between tables or trying to guess the relationships between columns among tables, you can describe what you need in plain English. Within the Copilot editor, you can ask to create a relationship between two different columns in a given table or suggest the structure of a measure. If you are satisfied with the output, you just click the Update button and Copilot appends the model. Small helping hands like this in the creation of a semantic model not only expedite the build process but also make it easier to maintain. Copilot can also help you standardize the model and your naming nomenclature if one of your goals is to enforce data governance.

Follow these steps to simplify your existing semantic modeling. Keep in mind that you need to load both the Primary and Secondary Awards tables to create a relationship. The following instructions assume you have already made a report visual:

1. **Open the Report view in Power BI Desktop.**
2. **Click the Prep Data for AI button, located next to Copilot in the Ribbon.**
3. **Select the Simplify the Data Schema option (see Figure 19-10).**

4. **Unselect all fields except for** `naics_code`, `recipient_name`, `recipient_city_name`, `recipient_state_code`, and `awarding_agency_name`.

5. **Click Apply and then click Close.**

6. **Load both the Primary and Secondary Awards tables into the semantic model.**

   Adding both tables ensures that the relationship exists before you move to Verified Answers. Without both tables loaded, Copilot can't correctly infer or test relationships.

7. **Select a visual that you've already created in a report and then click the Verified Answers option (see Figure 19-11).**

8. **Pick one or more of the recommended model conditions.**

   Notice that the report has changed drastically based on the columns applied in the model.

9. **Click the menu option on the left and select AI Uses Instructions.**

   Provide explicit instructions on what you expect the model to do in terms of relationships and output (see Figure 19-12).

10. **Click Apply and then click Close.**

The result is a modified visualization that focuses solely on the specific columns you selected and the requested filtering conditions. Ultimately, your model was reduced from over 275 fields to less than 10, which accelerates data delivery.

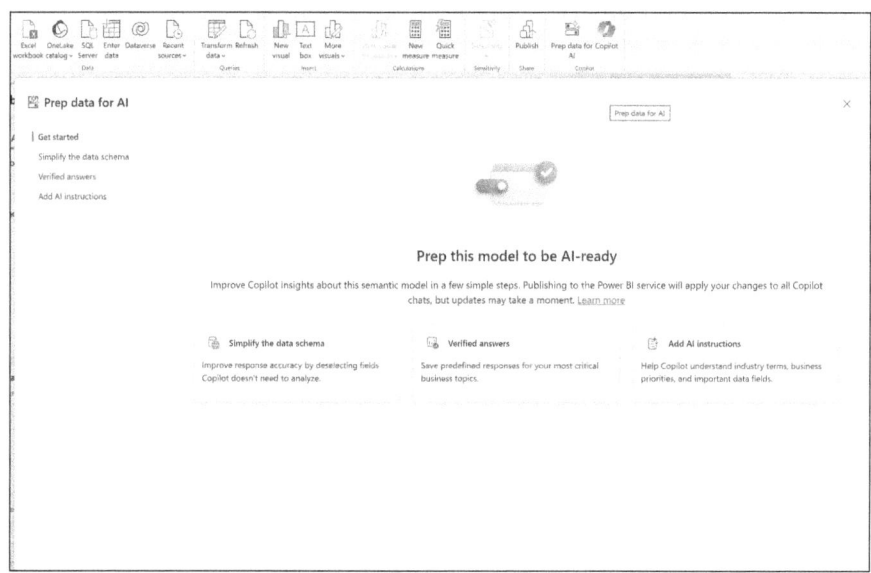

FIGURE 19-10:
Simplifying the data schema with Copilot.

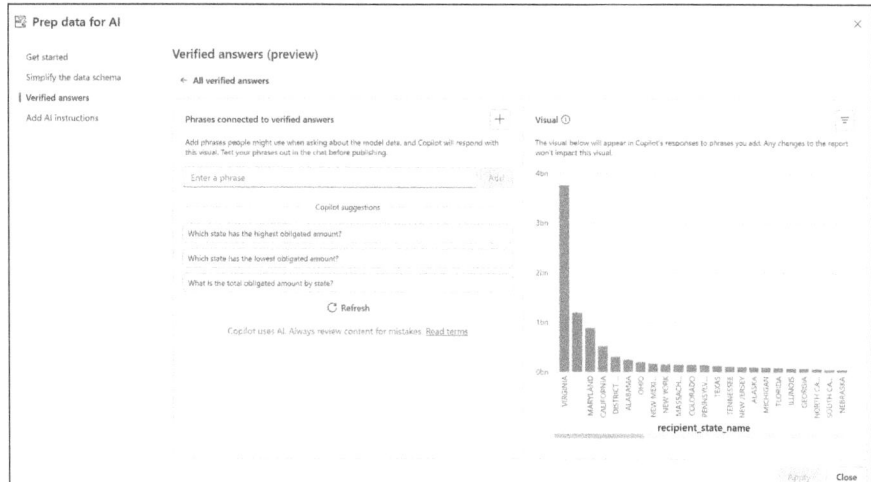

FIGURE 19-11:
Selecting queries to validate model changes.

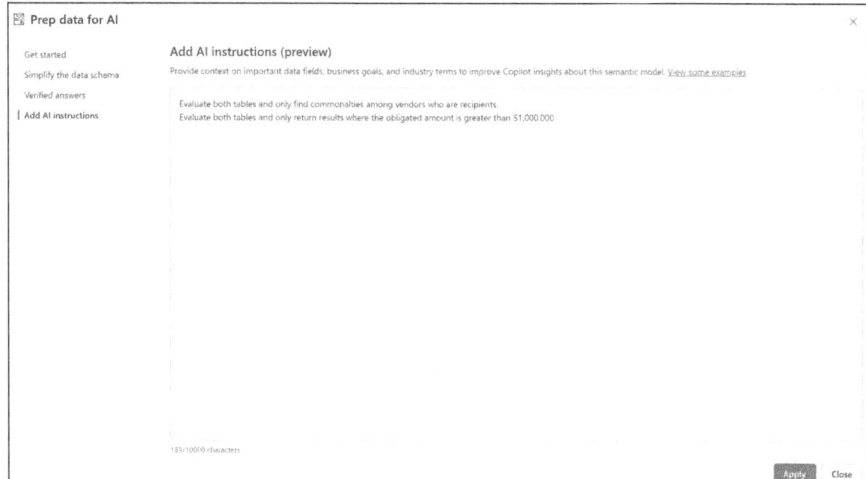

FIGURE 19-12:
Applying conversational instructions into the semantic model.

Writing DAX with Copilot

DAX is the language that powers calculations in Power BI. If you've ever tried to write a DAX measure from scratch, you know it can feel intimidating as you are typing your formula. This is where Copilot comes in. By using plain language that you understand, not computer or complex mathematical speak, you can ask Copilot to suggest the correct DAX queries, saving you time and reducing errors.

Power BI Desktop includes four main views: Report, Table, Model, and DAX Query. In DAX Query view, you can find Copilot on the Ribbon, ready to translate your natural-language prompt into usable DAX code. Imagine that you want to view the total spending for each federal agency by NAICS code. Instead of writing the formula manually, you can tell Copilot the following prompt in the box:

PROMPT: Calculate the total spend per awarding agency based on the NAICS code

COPILOT OUTPUT: SUMMARIZECOLUMNS(

    // Group by awarding agency and NAICS code

    AnalyticsSpendFY21to25[awarding_agency_name],

    AnalyticsSpendFY21to25[naics_code],

    // Calculate total spend as the sum of the obligated amount

    "Total Spend", SUM(AnalyticsSpendFY21to25[total_obligated_amount])

)

    ORDER BY

    AnalyticsSpendFY21to25[awarding_agency_name] ASC,

    AnalyticsSpendFY21to25[naics_code] ASC

As shown in Figure 19-13, the results of the entered prompt produced the following results in the DAX Query Editor based on your downloaded Kaggle.com file. Notice the code section, prompt editor, and results section.

The process is formulaic, whether just trying to determine the best DAX option or create a complete measure. Here are the steps:

1. **Open DAX Query view in Power BI Desktop.**
2. **Enter a natural language prompt as described.**
3. **Review the query that Copilot generates.**
4. **Select Keep Query to save it.**
5. **Choose Update Model With Changes if you want the new measure added to your model.**

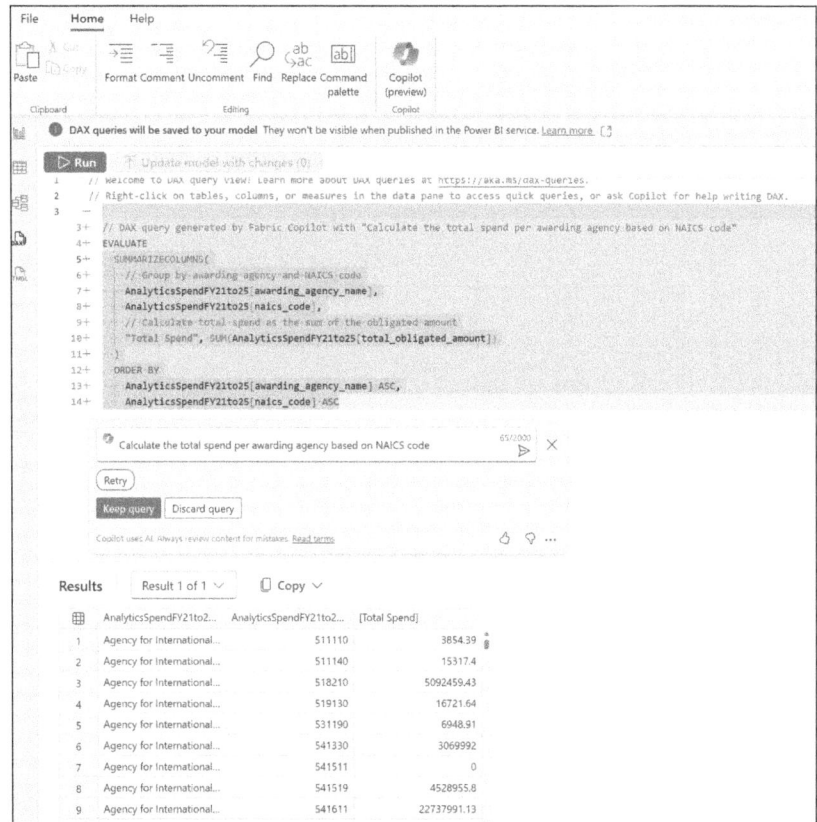

FIGURE 19-13:
DAX Formula
created based
on a prompt.

Creating reports and narrative insights with Copilot

In Chapters 11, 12, and 13, you find out about creating actionable reports and dashboards. Most people scratch their heads, overwhelmed by the choices they have regarding which data visualization type to use based on their dataset. Building a report in Power BI can sometimes feel like staring at a blank canvas where the only way to start is by splattering paint to make a statement. You know the data is there, but where do you start? Copilot helps take away that uncertainty. By using natural language prompts, you can ask Copilot to create draft visuals and even whole pages of a report. You still get to adjust and polish the results, but Copilot gives you a big head start. You can choose from two options:

>> Ask Copilot to recommend its best guess and create a report page, suggest content for a new reports page, or answer questions about the data for you

by pressing the button (see Figure 19-14). Copilot will then engage in a dialogue with you to refine the report before generating an output such as the one shown in Figure 19-15.

>> Build your own prompts without relying on Microsoft Copilot's recommendations, which are based on its evaluation of the data.

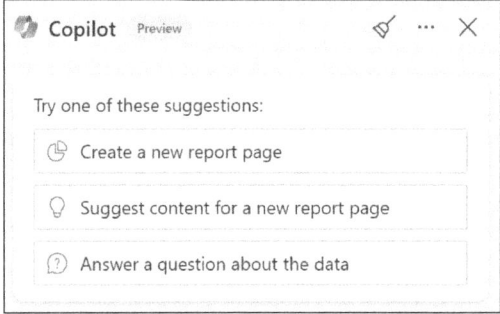

FIGURE 19-14:
Giving Copilot complete control of the report and narrative experience.

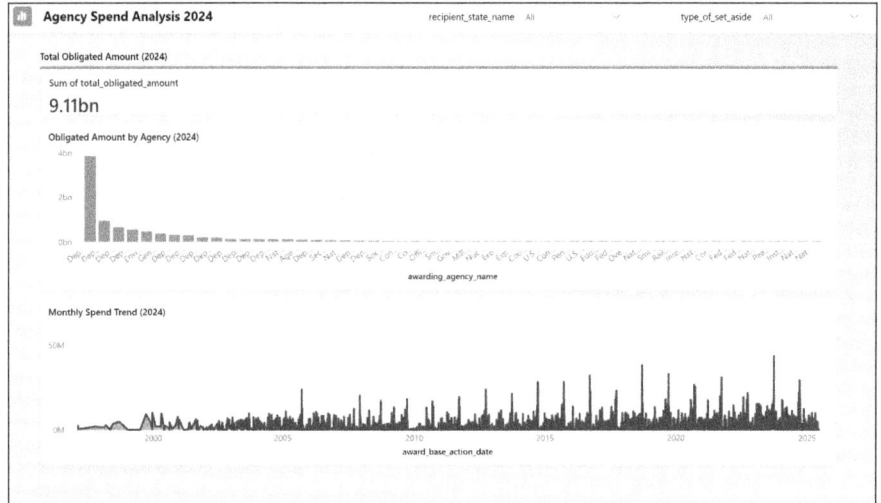

FIGURE 19-15:
Report output based on a conversational dialogue with Copilot.

You can expand the visualization analysis in two ways as well. The first is to ask Copilot specific questions about your dataset, and it will provide you with targeted responses in the agent window (see Figure 19-16). In this case, all that was required once the visualization was produced and filtered using the slicers was

"Evaluate the graphic." Notice that the word graphic is used, not visualization. The conversational engine understands what is being asked and still produces a detailed analysis.

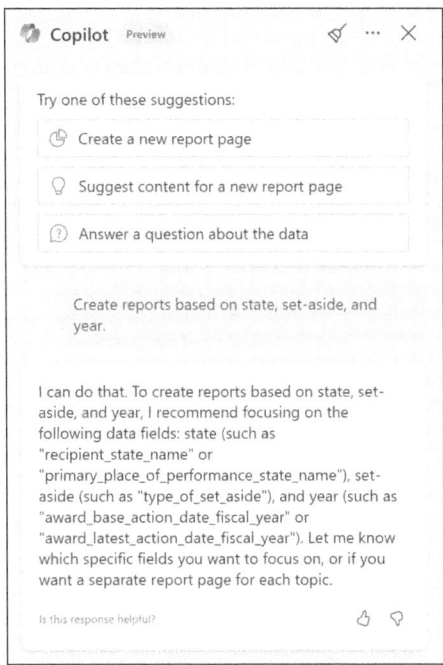

The second way is to use Narrative Visualization, an option found in the Visualizations pane. To summarize the data, follow these steps:

1. **Go to the Visualizations pane.**

2. **Select the Narrative Visualization.**

3. **Place the Narrative Visualization on the Canvas.**

4. **Configure the Narrative Visualization to interact with Copilot. This includes providing a prompt for what you are trying to achieve.**

   The prompt request is: *"Summarize the data on the page."*

5. **Click Update.**

   A concise text summary of the report's key findings appears (see Figure 19-17). As you change the slicers on the report, the text updates in real time.

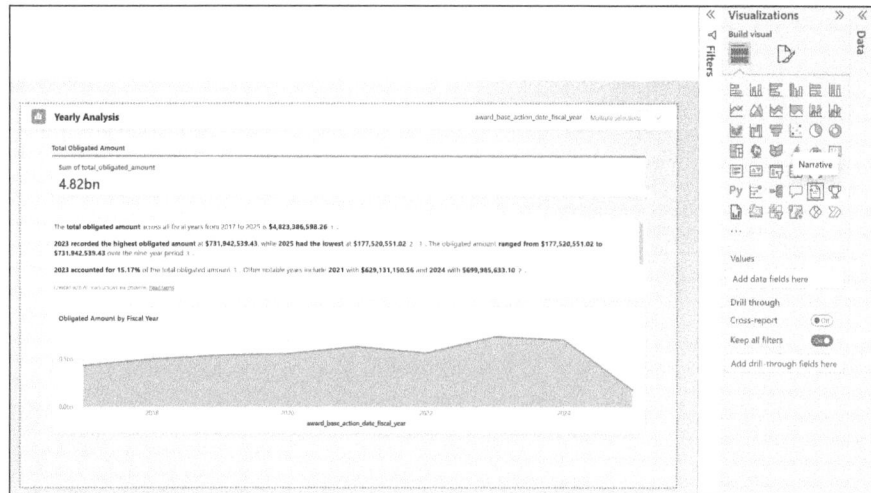

FIGURE 19-17:
A text-based
summarization
of a Copilot-
generated report.

TIP

Copilot is designed to save you from the repetitive work of building reports. When you click the Copilot button, select an option, and provide a natural prompt, you get better results — hands down. Let Copilot guide you through the process. If you fall back on typing formulas and dragging fields manually, you're defeating the purpose of using AI in the first place. Copilot is your conversation partner, not just another tool to complicate your life.

Best Practices and Pitfalls When Using Fabric and Copilot with Power BI

Fabric and Copilot can take your Power BI experience to the next level. These tools make it easier to handle larger datasets, collaborate with your team, and even utilize AI to streamline everyday tasks. But as with any data analytics tool, this combination is not a magic bullet. The tools work best when used appropriately. The trick is to know when to use these tools in conjunction with Power BI, as described in Table 19-5.

REMEMBER

Fabric and Copilot are boosters, not replacements. Use them when they save time or improve collaboration, but don't feel pressured to use them on every project. Power BI, on its own, is still more than enough for most everyday scenarios.

TABLE 19-5   Using Fabric and Copilot with Power BI

Best Practice	What To Consider	Pitfalls To Avoid
Avoid overengineering your data problems	Use Fabric only when the problem justifies it. For a one-off report or a small dataset, stick with regular Power BI.	Don't overcomplicate a simple report with Fabric features you don't need, which adds confusion and slows things down.
Plan for the maintenance and refresh cycle early	Set refresh schedules and assign someone to monitor them. Keep an eye on refresh history and errors.	Assume your data will always update itself without oversight unless you deliberately make it a one-time import. Outdated data kills trust fast.
Keep the human-in-the-loop	Don't automatically trust everything AI produces. Use Copilot to draft formulas, visuals, or insights. A human must still review and adjust.	Blindly trusting Copilot's answers can be problematic. AI can miss context or make wrong assumptions. Trust but verify.
Know when Power BI is enough	If your dataset fits in a PBIX file and refreshes quickly, you probably don't need Fabric.	Don't feel pressured to use Fabric or Copilot for every project, especially when Power BI alone does the job perfectly for some projects. Consider the data, the audience, and long-term objective. Then you can decide whether Power BI is enough, or whether you need to use Fabric.

6
The Part of Tens

Chapter 20

Ten Ways to Optimize DAX Using Power BI

The Data Analysis Expressions (DAX) language is a formula expression language used across many Microsoft products. If you've ever used products such as Analysis Services, Power Pivot in Excel, or Power BI, you already know a smidgeon about DAX. The functions, operators, and values to perform advanced calculations and the queries on data in relational tables in Power BI are, in many cases, the same ones used in other Microsoft products. However, with Power BI Microsoft has created specific niche DAX features that are available only for its enterprise business intelligence product.

In this chapter, I show you how to take into consideration those special features found only in Power BI. I also share ways to perfect your DAX code using Power BI.

Focusing on Logic

Performance optimization is the key to modeling data, database delivery, and data extraction. This is why, when you design a high-quality database layer, you are in effect setting the path for an optimized data model that supports data efficiency with DAX.

When creating the data model and database layer, focus on ensuring that the fields are correctly mapped, have an intended purpose, and lack redundancy. This not only helps you minimize your need for calculated columns, calculated tables, and measures with DAX but also provides a generally faster overall output experience with Power BI. Don't be a glutton for performance challenges by calculating in more complex activity, resulting in a slow DAX environment.

DirectQuery mode with DAX has some significant limitations. In this mode, DAX expressions must be translated to queries executed against the source database, which impacts performance. Specific limitations include restricted use of iterative functions like RANKX and AVERAGEX, no support for calculated tables, and performance degradation with complex expressions. When using DirectQuery, minimize calculated columns and complex measures as these create a significant performance lag.

On the other hand, the Import Model mode brings its own challenges. Because this mode supports in-memory models, you need to avoid business logic that feeds a data model arbitrarily. The random use of feeds slows down the processing speed of a model. You can undoubtedly use filters within a view, but if you do so, minimize the required logic when deploying the filters. (In this context, *minimizing the filter logic* means not implementing the same filter many times across the same environment.)

Whether following the DirectQuery mode or Import Model mode, a solid approach to implementing logic is putting logic in stored procedures that create tables, enabling your models to reuse the logic. By doing this, you can create the same set of tables and a single source of truth. Also, you should implement indexes — ideally, clustered *columnstores,* which store data in a compressed, column-oriented format optimized for analytical workloads when applying large tables.

Formatting Your Code

It's common for you to have your own quirky way of naming code. Everyone has their own system. If your code is only for you, it's probably okay to break a few rules here and there. Notice the word *few,* not *all.* Why is that? Just because the code is for you now doesn't mean you won't share the sample later with someone else.

Throughout this book, you may notice that everything I cite maps clearly to a table, column, or row. Every variable is meaningful and relevant for the code sample. Common courtesy is making sure that others aren't baffled when trying to read your DAX code. You don't want to open your code sample one day and scratch your head while you wonder what you wrote.

Your first goal is to format all your code consistently and document meticulously. Here's an example of well-documented, formatted code:

```
Total Orders =
IF (ISFILTERED ('Date Ranges'[Date Range]),
CALCULATE (COUNTROWS ('Order Data'),
FILTER ('Order Table',
'Order Table'[Submit Date] >= [Commit Date]
&& 'Order Table'[Submit Date] <= [Ship
Date]) ),
COUNTROWS ('Order Data') )
```

Following these best practices can help you keep your code clean:

>> Always indent a new row when referencing a new function or measure.

>> Place spaces before and after open and closed brackets to ensure that the data context is realized.

>> Always place spaces around operators such as +, –, and = for the purpose of readability.

>> Don't overcomplicate your code with unnecessary variables, functions, and formulas.

>> Never create items arbitrarily or give a table the exact name you might call a measure. It just confuses you or other developers.

>> Never include a column name unless you reference the table where it originated.

ON THE WEB

When in doubt, if you ever need to ensure that your code is formatted correctly, use the DAX formatter tool at www.daxformatter.com.

Keeping the Structure Simple (KISS)

You may remember the phrase "Keep it simple" in some incarnation from when you were much younger. That statement also applies to Power BI and DAX: The more complicated you make tables and columns, the more likely you are to experience two problems. First, you see an immediate performance hit when it comes to getting results. Second, deciding what's necessary versus what's arbitrary data is difficult.

Simply put, it's essential to include only those tables and columns needed in your model to explore a business issue. When you add more code than necessary, you're causing excess memory usage and increased user complexity, and you're likely to increase data volume unintentionally. All these factors lead to decreased performance. You're trying to reduce a model's number of columns and rows.

Less is more — your goal is to find precision and accuracy.

As you work through reengineering your data to achieve simplicity, you likely need to rework fact tables where columns have been removed — the tables need to be reaggregated. Under almost all conditions, the smaller the model the better the performance.

One condition that may prohibit data reduction involves unique IDs. An example is a primary key, such as TransactionID or ProductID, which counts items. Although these IDs are necessary, they can impact model size. Consider using integer data types instead of strings to reduce memory consumption. These types of columns create prohibitive circumstances for creating lightweight models. The lesson here is simple: Think twice before using unique data and DAX.

Staying Clear of Certain Functions

Have you heard the old saying, "I wouldn't touch it with a ten-foot pole?" It applies to certain DAX functions when misused because it impacts Power BI performance, and the potential data output can harm your dataset.

A good practice is to use DAX Studio's query plan analyzer or Performance Analyzer in Power BI Desktop to evaluate the efficiency of your DAX expressions. When reviewing your code, critically assess whether complex functions truly add value, as they often lack efficiency and can be cost prohibitive from a performance standpoint. Avoid essential functions such as SEARCH, IFERROR, CONTAINS, and INTERSECT. Here's why.

SEARCH is a potentially costly function for memory and processing load because it requires the system to scan each row for a given value. In other words, there are no search shortcuts. A way to tackle searching with DAX more efficiently is to create a column in your database. Afterward, you bring the column into the model as a data column. SEARCH must perform operations on the fly; therefore, for functions, there's a need to leverage SEARCH when potentially using measures. If you can't create a new column in a database, consider making a calculated column. You need to have the measurements refer to the column.

IFERROR is a benign function in Microsoft Excel. When this function is used in Power BI, however, you'll likely experience performance issues in specific scenarios, particularly with division operations. Using simpler functions, such as DIVIDE, resolves divide-by-zero errors more easily using built-in processes without errors, mitigates many mistakes, and supports faster performance. However, IFERROR helps handle errors in other contexts, such as text manipulations or external data connections.

Using functions that require excessive parsing, especially when virtually mapping relationships, can be highly inefficient. Again, the concern relates to performance concerns. The more you parse data, the higher the performance degradation appears to the user. It's not uncommon to use CONTAINS or INTERSECT for virtual relationships. Both require heavy interaction among table relationships. That's why you should consider using a nimbler function such as TREATAS. Whereas with CONTAINS and INTERSECT, you parse through the entire dataset, TREATAS filters out column data to a finite set of data from a specific set of columns. However, CONTAINS and INTERSECT remain valuable for specific complex filtering scenarios that require particular functionality.

Making Your Measures Meaningful

There is a time and place for using specific DAX features. And the use of measures is no different. Sure, you can compute columns using a calculated column, but it makes more sense to look for data efficiency. Introducing measures into the mix yields no negative performance hit to a data model. Since you can't manipulate data in some cases by using calculated columns on their own, measures are a solid alternative approach. Many mathematical, statistical, and trigonometric calculations require measures, because they can't be completed using a calculated table alone.

Whether you are trying to work with basic DAX functions or are authoring complex DAX function code, you *must* understand that Power BI does allow users to aggregate columns implicitly. In Power BI, implicit measures can be helpful when you want to test how a visualization may perform quickly. Another option is to create an explicit measure by using DAX. In such a situation, you intend to develop focused calculations. Here are reasons why developing repeatable measures for DAX may make sense, even if it's slightly more complex. Consider the dataset by applying *either* of the following schools of thought:

>> **Power BI should behave like Excel.** That means using implicit measures in conjunction with workbook data, which requires heavily using two functions:

SUM for numerical data and COUNT for text data. When you use the Power BI Desktop, any numeric columns can use the Summarize By property.

>> **Power BI should explicitly define all measures.** The model supports data control by explicitly defining measures because the developer is coding the behavior. Though this method may offer more developer flexibility, it may not always yield the exact results you want initially. Revisions may be required but can yield significant results if perfected over time.

When building an enterprise-grade Power BI solution, you need to differentiate between explicit and implicit measures. Explicit measures are recommended when you want the following:

>> Greater control over calculations and business logic

>> Better documentation with business rules, particularly with the use of DAX

>> Consistent results across different visualization types (reports, dashboards, KPIs)

>> Manageable performance optimization

>> Clearer organization using measure groups and display folders

You use implicit measures only for simple aggregations in ad-hoc analysis. After you establish a verified measure, you convert the calculations to explicit measures for production reports.

Filtering with a Purpose

The FILTER function is overused. Though its primary purpose is to filter columns based on measure values, think carefully about why you want to use the filter. If filtering is intended for just a column value, there's no need to use the FILTER function. Your Power BI performance degrades when using the FILTER function when the purpose is unclear. Let's look at a few examples, starting with something you should *not* be doing:

```
BID = CALCULATE ([PROFIT], FILTER ('State', 'State'[Country]
    = "United States"))
```

Avoid the logic used in this example — you're filtering each row unnecessarily. Now, here are two potential options that are more suitable:

Option #1:

```
BID = CALCULATE ([PROFIT], 'State'[Country],
   "United States")
```

Option #2:

```
BID = CALCULATE ([PROFIT], KEEPFILTERS ('State'[Country] =
   "United States"))
```

Both options are solid choices; however, the results are different. Compared with the original query, the second option performs the same way. The difference is that the code is far more efficient because the filter is applied to the column directly rather than to the entire table. The code sample shown in the first option is awkward because it shows profitability in the United States in all areas. You can consider using this option under particular circumstances, such as when you need a value to show regardless of a specific filter having to be applied.

Note that although direct column filtering is more efficient for simple conditions, the FILTER function remains essential under four conditions:

>> When you need to filter based on measure values or complex conditions

>> When you need to perform row context transitions

>> When working with many-to-many relationships

>> When implementing dynamic filtering logic

Referring to the examples, in Option #1, the FILTER is used to replace any condition based on 'State'[Country], whereas in Option #2, using KEEPFILTERS preserves existing filters and adds a new condition. Choose the appropriate filtering method based on your specific requirements for the filter context.

Transforming Data Purposefully

DAX doesn't mean Data *Transformation* Expressions — it's intended for analysis. Keep Power BI capabilities in the proper swim lane, which means if you want to transform your data, spend as much time as possible doing this in Power Query. The more time you spend extracting, transforming, and loading your data in Power Query before you import it into a Power BI model, the less you need to do later. Performing any heavy transformative activities before importing your model helps ensure fast resource processing and optimization.

After you transform your data into the best possible state in preparation before loading it, you can ingest it into Power BI and analyze it. Follow these guidelines before you ingest your data in Power BI, using DAX as a primary utility to transform datasets. Your data should be

>> In a suitable format for analysis

>> Completely loaded into the model using an optimal data model format

>> Cleansed, merged, and split as much as humanly possible, because doing this work in DAX only adds unnecessary steps

It's okay to spend more time preparing your data than analyzing it because getting the best possible format during transformation minimizes later analysis.

TIP

Reserve DAX for time intelligence, running totals, and calculations that depend on user context, and use the query folding capabilities of Power Query for most data transformations.

Playing Hide-and-Seek with Your Columns

By now, you probably realize that filtering an entire table can have profound performance implications, not only with Power BI but also when implementing DAX. The reason is that parsing each table row is incredibly time-consuming and often yields marginal output. Instead, you can choose a better way to manage data in your tables for DAX and Power BI in general. Follow these best practices:

>> **Whatever you do, avoid filtering an entire table.** You run the risk of stalled performance. Suppose you pay for database bandwidth using Azure, AWS, GCP, or IBM Cloud. In that case, you're in for a bit of sticker shock if your transactional volume is significant.

>> **Remove all columns that you know you won't use.** Having columns in a table "just because" adds an unnecessary tax to query performance.

>> **Focus on filtering using a column-based approach.** An even better tactic is filtering only those few columns you know have relevant data. If you can remove the remaining columns from the dataset, do so. You'll likely have high performing results.

Consider these exceptions, as hide-and-seek is not meant to be played under all conditions:

>> Table-level filtering may be necessary when implementing bidirectional cross-filtering.

>> In a complex many-to-many relationship, broader filtering is likely more appropriate.

>> Using a proper star schema data model with dimension and fact tables will improve filtering efficiency regardless of the approach.

>> For those users with Premium Power BI capacity, the large model support and optimization tools of Power BI offer greater flexibility, far more than Power BI Pro licensing, potentially allowing for less aggressive column pruning while maintaining performance.

Optimizing for Large Models

You probably wouldn't bring a massive suitcase on an overnight trip, packing only a single item in that suitcase. That extra load is costly. Think the same way with large model design and development. Large semantic models in Power BI require careful optimization strategies to maintain performance.

Model efficiency depends primarily on thoughtful data architecture and adherence to best practices during development. When working with extensive datasets, the data architect must try to be minimalistic, only adding necessary data selections. This means retaining the required tables and columns to contribute to the analytic requirements. It's not just about less data, which means better performance; it's also about efficiency querying (searchability) and system load (memory consumption). The architect should always keep these five tips in the back of their mind when crafting the large data model:

>> Going back to the preceding section: Less is more. You want to partition large fact tables into smaller, more manageable segments.

>> Whenever possible, replace text-based keys with integer surrogate keys, as performance improves dramatically (think 0's and 1's exclusively).

>> Implement data compression techniques whenever you see a data pattern emerge.

>> Establish clear relationships between the dimension and fact tables.

>> Don't refresh too often if it's not necessary. Instead, let the business need dictate the refresh rate.

Your job is not done after you build the large semantic data model and put it into production, not by any means. You still need to performance tune intermittently. *Performance tuning* requires regularly reviewing usage metrics to identify and optimize frequently executed queries that may cause bottlenecks.

Remember, data optimization is an iterative process, especially for semantic model management. It requires continually monitoring performance as your semantic model evolves and grows and making adjustments to maintain analytical efficiency without sacrificing necessary business insights.

Rinse, Repeat, Recycle

Functions and measures allow you to be incredibly efficient when writing well-written code. That's why there's no reason to write long blocks of code to carry out a menial activity. For example, you're trying to calculate a single value. You're better off splitting your calculations into smaller blocks than creating a long equation, for two reasons:

>> Repetition helps you avoid performance errors.

>> Code efficiency is apparent because you quickly see a pattern after a few equations are written, given that reuse is alive and well.

TIP

One way to ensure that repeatability and code consistency are followed is by using variables. When you use variables, they offer several benefits, such as helping you ensure robust documentation and avoid making unnecessary errors while repeating the coding cycle.

Chapter **21**

Ten Ways to Make Accessible and User-Friendly Reports

The ability to read reports and visualizations in Power BI should not be limited to those people who can distinguish colors or have the ability to read unaided. How about users with color blindness or even those who require assistive technologies to help them interpret data? They should not be left in the dark because they have a unique requirement. With Power BI, you can incorporate numerous capabilities seamlessly with little effort to make reports accessible for multiple audience types.

In this chapter, I describe ten ways to accommodate audiences with special needs when interpreting Power BI data using accessible methods.

Navigating with the Keyboard

Report authors should not worry that users will be limited to using only a mouse to view data in Power BI, thanks to its comprehensive keyboard accessibility features. Report users can also walk through data points in visuals, navigate between report pages and tabular data, and review interactive capabilities, including cross-highlighting data, filtering, and slicing data using their keyboard or mouse.

Users can navigate a report using focus indicators that clearly show their current position within the report. These keyboard navigation capabilities vary across browsers:

» **Microsoft Edge and Google Chrome:** Press Tab to move the focus among report elements, the arrow keys to navigate within visuals, and Enter to select items.

» **Apple Safari:** Use Option + Tab instead of Tab to move between report elements. In some Power BI visuals (such as slicers or dropdowns), focus may not follow the same pattern as in other browsers, and additional arrow or Enter keys may be required to interact with items. Depending on the requirement, the key stroke will vary.

» **All browsers:** Key capabilities regardless of browser include the following:

   ● Press Shift+Tab to move backward through report elements.

   ● Use the arrow keys to move between individual data points in charts and visualizations.

   ● Press Enter to select or drill into a visual for more detailed information.

   ● Use Ctrl + Right Arrow or Ctrl + Left Arrow to move between report pages efficiently.

   ● Press Esc to exit the current focused element and return to the previous navigation level.

   ● To access frequently used keyboard shortcuts, press the question mark (?) key while in Power BI to display a keyboard shortcut dialog list.

TIP

Having a Screen Reader As Your Companion

Microsoft has added support for screen readers to assist users who require visual accommodation. Every object in Power BI with keyboard navigation also has an alternative compatible option for screen readers. Report consumers can navigate all visualizations, including titles, visual types, alt text, and any textual information integrated into the visualizations.

TIP

Popular screen readers like JAWS and NVDA (Windows) or VoiceOver (Mac) work seamlessly with Power BI, announcing chart elements, data values, and filter states in a logical sequence that follows the tab order.

Standing Out with Contrast

Power BI provides built-in support for high-contrast and accessible color themes to improve readability for all users, especially those with visual impairments or working in low-light environments. High-contrast mode limits the color palette and enhances visual separation between text, backgrounds, and data visuals.

When a high-contrast theme is enabled in Windows (such as Black, White, or Inverted), Power BI Desktop automatically detects high contrast mode. It applies the corresponding colors to report visuals, such as charts, tables, and slicers for maximum legibility.

Report authors can also set report themes manually. To ensure accessibility, authors should use the accessible theme options (as shown in Figure 21-1), available from the View tab on the Ribbon.

After publishing to the Power BI Service, the high-contrast or accessible color settings generally carry over to the browser environment. However, results may vary slightly across browsers and custom visuals, so authors should preview their reports to confirm consistent rendering.

REMEMBER

Unlike Power BI Desktop, which automatically detects high contrast settings, Power BI Service does its best to detect the appropriate settings based on the browser being used. You can set the theme manually in Power BI Service by choosing View ⇨ High Contrast Colors from the menu in the upper-right corner of the screen. You can then select the applicable report theme from the choices given.

TIP

Power BI now offers a full high-contrast experience, which extends beyond the visualizations to include the entire application interface. To enable this feature, choose File ⇨ Options and Settings ⇨ Options ⇨ Accessibility, and select the "Apply High Contrast Throughout the Application" check box. This setting enables menus, ribbons, panes, and all UI elements to adopt the high contrast theme, creating a consistent experience for users with visual impairments.

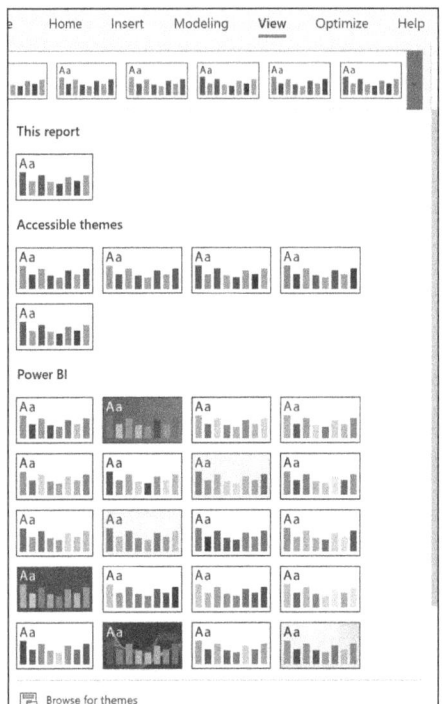

FIGURE 21-1:
Accessing accessible theme options under the View tab.

Recognizing Size Matters (with Focus Mode)

Each visual is set to a default size when generated. Sometimes, you need to increase the size to help those who need to see the finer-grain detail, whether it involves dots on a plot chart or the text size. To improve the readability of a visual in a report or dashboard, you can expand a visual to fill up more screen space by clicking the Focus Mode icon (appearing as a diagonal arrow symbol) that displays when hovering over the top right-hand corner of any visual.

Users can also access Focus Mode by right-clicking on a visual and selecting "Focus Mode" from the context menu or using the keyboard shortcut Alt+F when the visual is selected. This expanded view makes it easier to see details that may otherwise be difficult to see at the default size.

For those who want to see the whole picture, Power BI offers Full Screen mode (accessible from the View menu or by pressing F11), which expands the entire report to fill the screen. Users can combine both approaches by first entering Full Screen mode for the report and then using Focus Mode on individual visuals when needed for maximum readability. Figure 21-2 shows an example of a visual in Focus Mode.

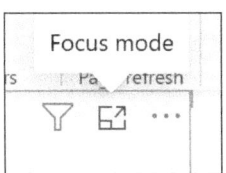

FIGURE 21-2:
Changing
the focus.

Switching between Data Tables and Visualizations

Sometimes, a person who has color blindness or other visual challenges may not perceive nuances in visual data. It may be easier for them to tell apparent differences using textual data. In these cases, having access to tabular alternatives is ideal. You can show tabular data in one of two ways: Press Alt+Shift+F11 to bring up table data, or click More Options and then choose the Show As a Table option on the report. Using the keyboard shortcut (Alt+Shift+F11) displays the data in an accessible format optimized explicitly for screen readers; using the Show As a Table menu option presents the same data in a standard Power BI table that may not provide the same level of accessibility features. Figure 21-3 shows an example of table output.

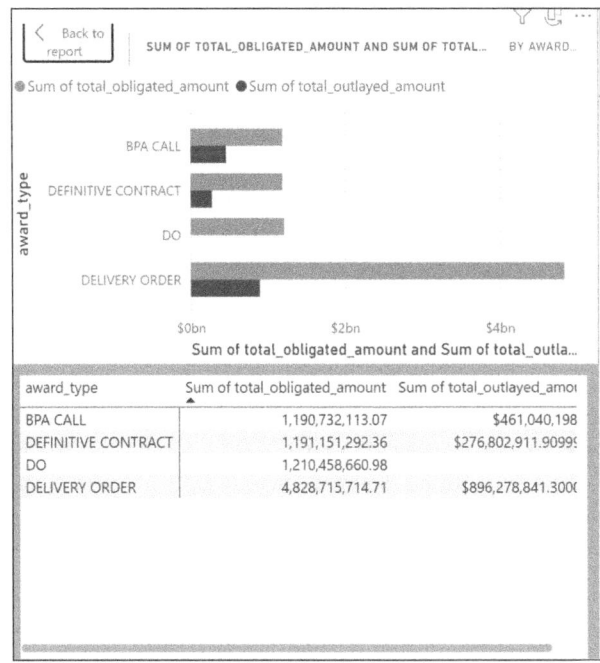

FIGURE 21-3:
Data
table output.

A Little Extra Text Goes a Long Way

Not every feature implemented by a report designer may be readable by a screen reader, especially when created manually by the report designer. When creating visuals and images manually, a best practice is to add alternative text descriptions, called *alt text*. Providing alt text allows anyone requiring assistance to interpret visuals, images, shapes, and text boxes by using textual descriptors.

To provide this alt text, you must create the descriptions for each item by selecting the objects (in Design mode) using Power BI Desktop in the Visualizations pane. Follow these steps:

1. **Go to the Format selection.**

2. **Expand the General tab.**

3. **Scroll to the bottom and fill in the Alt Text box with the text that describes the visual as shown in Figure 21-4.**

   Be aware that Power BI limits how many characters of alt text you can enter: You cannot enter more than 250 characters.

4. **Press Enter.**

TIP

When writing alt text, focus on describing the key insights of the visual rather than just the aesthetic appearance. For example, instead of "A blue bar chart showing sales by region," write "Sales performance across regions shows the Northeast leading at \$1.2M, followed by the West at \$950K." This approach provides more value to screen reader users as the users of alt text frankly are likely not to be able to discern the color; they want the facts exclusively.

You can also create dynamic alt text using DAX measures by clicking the *fx* button next to the Alt Text field. For example, you may include a measure that calculates the percent change from the previous period, allowing the alt text to update when data refreshes automatically.

Be as descriptive as possible when describing your findings in the box while also conserving your use of words. One capability unique to Power BI is that alt text data can be made dynamic. You can include DAX measures and conditional formatting. As values change, the alt text reflects the values to better describe the conditions the user is viewing.

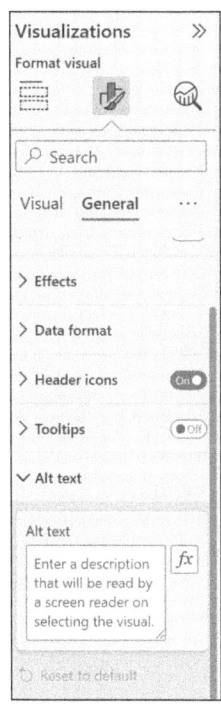

Setting Rank and Tab Order

When you cannot visualize items on a screen and depend on a keyboard or screen reader, you may be at the mercy of the Report tabs. That's why it's also essential that a report designer manipulate the tab order to match how users visually process report visuals. A best practice is to remove any unnecessary decorative elements, such as shapes or images that are only there to add anecdotal asides to a report, as these elements can create confusion and additional tab stops for screen reader users.

To set the tab order, open the View tab from the Ribbon, and click the Selection button in the Show Panes area of the tab to display the Selection pane. When the pane appears, you can reorder items by selecting them and using the up and down arrows to arrange them in a logical sequence that follows your report's narrative flow, as shown in Figure 21-5. The sequence order is what screen readers and keyboard users follow when navigating through reports, so organizing elements in the most logical manner possible is crucial.

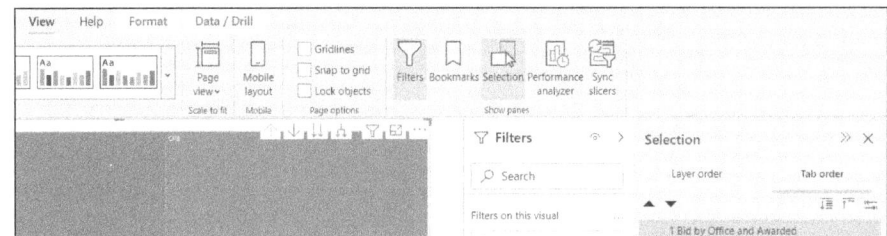

FIGURE 21-5:
Setting the
tab order.

It's All About Titles and Labels

Though a visual is an important asset, the title and labels surrounding the visuals are just as crucial — they're the road signs that orient the reader by describing the context of the content. An excellent visual never includes confusing language, such as acronyms or jargon, even in report titles, legends, headers, footers, or labels. In the example shown in Figure 21-6, the header is explicit in that it describes the specific purpose of the visual. The labels for the bar graph mimic the title that the unit of measurement states, which is thousands for each federal agency bid.

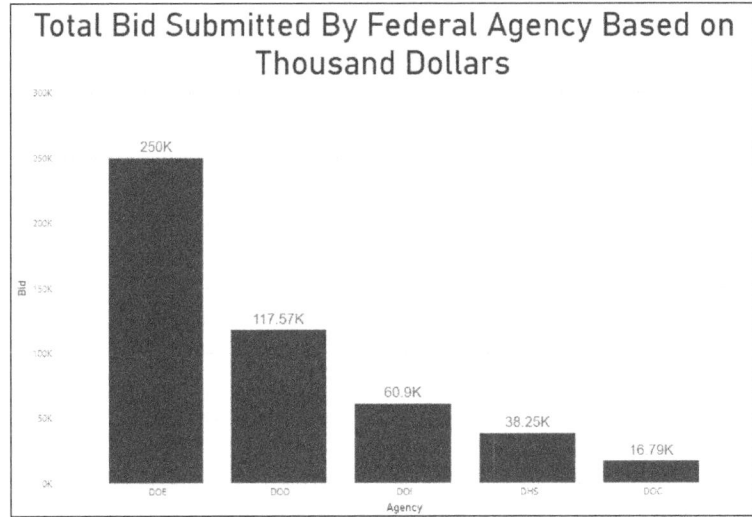

FIGURE 21-6:
Representative
titles and labels
for a visual.

A visual can have a few labels or many. You can turn on and off the labels for each series in your visual. You can even select the position for each label to appear either above or below the series. Labels can be customized for color, size, and contrast, which is particularly important for accessibility. When designing for users with color blindness, ensure that labels have sufficient contrast and don't rely solely on color to convey information. Figure 21-7 and Figure 21-8 are exemplars of quite different approaches.

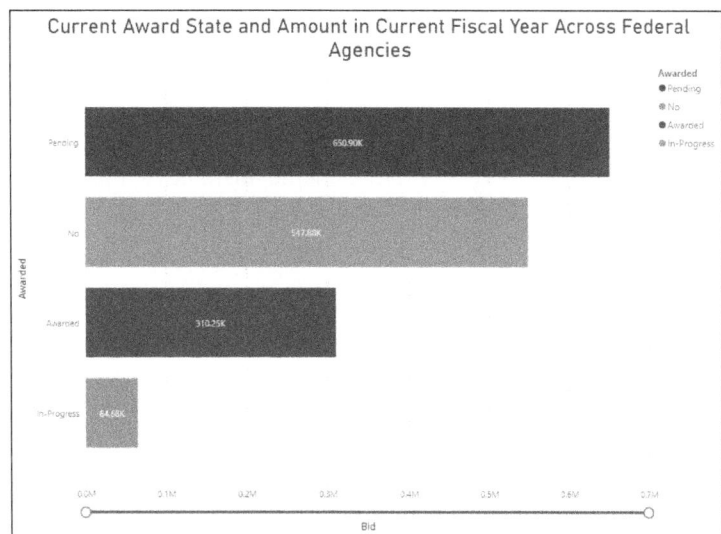

FIGURE 21-7:
Title and labels
that are highly
configured.

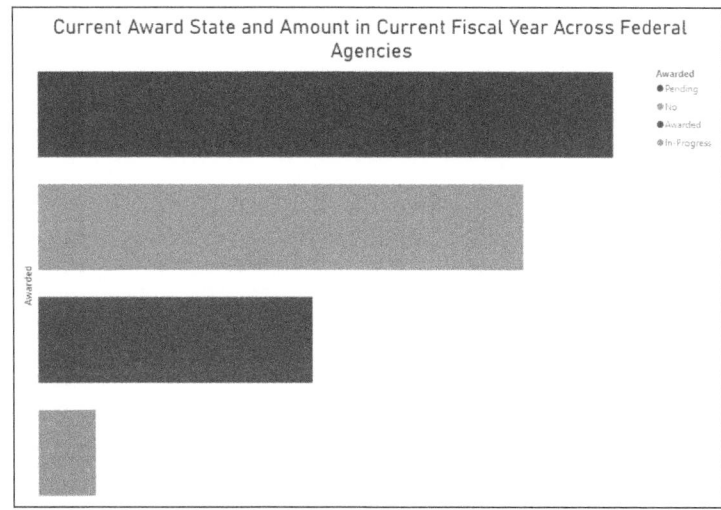

FIGURE 21-8:
Title and labels
with minimum
configuration.

Leaving Your Markers

Some of your report viewers may be color-blind. In these cases, you should avoid using color to express conditional formatting of information points. Instead, markers convey different series-based data, ensuring visual distinction beyond just color differences. A variety of data series, such as line, area, scatter, and bubble visuals, can all convey data markers using shapes as part of each line to break up the data points in a data series. A set of data points helps to decipher values with ease. Figure 21-9 shows an example of implementing markers for three states: awarded, bidding, and lost opportunities over seven months. In Figure 21-10, you can see how you can access the Markers configuration area and the options to configure shapes.

TIP

For maximum accessibility, combine distinctive marker shapes with high-contrast colors, and consider adding text labels at key data points to reinforce the presented information.

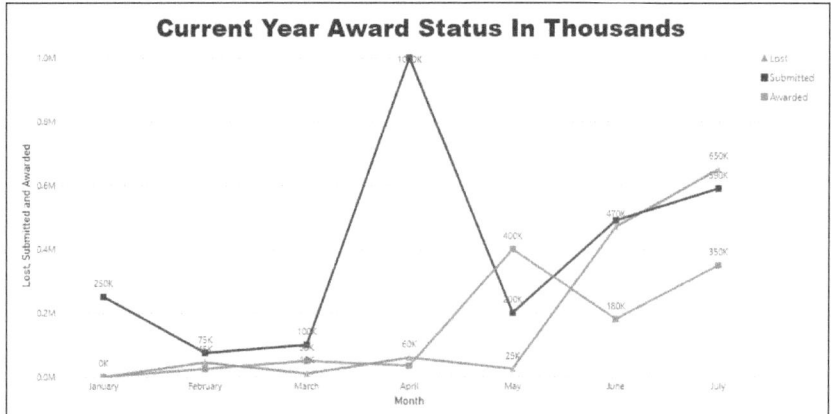

FIGURE 21-9:
Working
with markers.

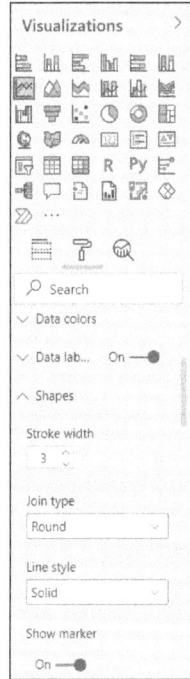

FIGURE 21-10:
Configuring
markers in the
Visualizations
pane.

Keeping with a Theme

Not every theme offered by Microsoft, or for that matter, designed by a report designer, is user-friendly. Sometimes, a consumer of reports may have reverse colors (red/brown, green/orange, blue/purple), whereas others may be color-blind. In other instances, some users may have decoding shading issues, resulting in contrast challenges between text and background colors. Suppose you're familiar with Section 508 Compliance, WCAG 2.0+, or USA Web Design System Guidelines. In that case, they all have certain principles that indicate some level of contrast that mirrors a ratio of 4:5:1. Several tools are available to the public to test for contrast and accessibility on the web for free. That said, there is variation among report reviewers regarding color deficiency.

The best approach is to minimize the use of many colors. That's why Microsoft has developed specific themes that help reduce the creation of inaccessible reports. For example, a user with vision challenges will have difficulty distinguishing between green and red, green and brown, blue and purple, or green and orange. (Bear in mind, these are just a few poor color pairings; there are many more.) When using these combinations, data will likely be misconstrued. Therefore, using a color scheme that is limited to one or two colors that are highly contrast-ing versus a color scheme that is quite similar is the best approach.

To access Microsoft's predefined themes in Power BI (including color-blind-friendly themes), go to the Themes area on the Ribbon's View Tab and click the down arrow. You have several options, including the Power BI themes, theme gallery, browser themes, accessible themes, and current theme customization.

Chapter 22

Ten Useful Power BI Resources

Whether you go on any major search engine such as Google or Bing or head straight to the Microsoft website, you are likely to find a trove of information on Power BI. Or perhaps you are like me and want to have a set of bookmarks that are your handy-dandy references so you don't have to scour the Internet. This chapter highlights the best resources (I think) that can be found online. These sites are often updated with the latest information on Power BI and other Microsoft products.

Microsoft Learn

When starting your Power BI journey, your first stop should be the Microsoft self-instruction portal, Microsoft Learn, found at https://learn.microsoft.com. The site is the official "self-help curriculum" for beginners or those looking to refresh their knowledge about the extensive capabilities of Power BI. The Power BI Learn curriculum is structured using a task-based, interactive learning style that guides you through everything from data connections to DAX formulas to visualization best practices.

Microsoft has organized the Power BI learning path into several courses that build upon each other. You'll begin with "Get started with Microsoft Power BI" to learn the fundamentals of the Power BI Desktop interface, and then progress to more advanced topics like "Implement and manage dataflows in Power BI."

Given the emphasis Microsoft places on certification and role-based tracks, a learner can go down the training path following a specific learning pathway, including the following:

>> Data experts can select the role Data Engineer or Database Administrator.

>> DAX developers can select the role of Developer.

>> Power BI architects may want to review the Solution Architect role.

>> End users have several roles to choose from, including Functional Consultant and education-based roles.

Each learning pathway and its accompanying modules incorporate hands-on labs where you can work directly with Power BI in a controlled environment, allowing you to apply concepts immediately. This structured approach ensures that you build a solid understanding of Power BI capabilities before moving on to more advanced topics like dataflows, composite models, or deployment pipelines.

Microsoft Documentation

If you're looking for the most up-to-date reference on anything Power BI from the vendor, check out the official Microsoft documentation for Power BI, found at `https://learn.microsoft.com/en-us/power-bi`. The official Power BI documentation repository is segmented into four business domains: documentation, training, learning paths, and videos.

The Microsoft documentation is the most comprehensive resource for the Power BI product ecosystem. If you search for help using the Help functionality in Power BI Desktop or the Power BI Service, you'll be right back to the official documentation website. Since Power BI is constantly evolving with monthly updates (maybe even daily or hourly), having access to the official source of truth is invaluable.

The documentation covers everything from basic concepts like connecting to data sources and creating your first visualization, to advanced topics like implementing row-level security, optimizing DAX queries, and configuring enterprise deployment pipelines. The structured learning paths guide you through Power BI

Desktop, Power BI Service, Power BI Mobile, Report Builder, and Paginated Reports — all the key components of the Power BI ecosystem. Even your transition to Fabric appears on this website.

Whether you're a citizen developer building your first dashboard or a professional developer implementing complex enterprise solutions, having this centralized, authoritative reference for all Power BI capabilities ensures that you're following best practices and taking advantage of the latest features in your data visualization and business intelligence projects.

Power BI Social Forums

The Microsoft-sponsored Power BI Forums are the premier global hub for data visualization experts and enthusiasts. This thriving ecosystem connects you with users worldwide who share your passion for transforming data into actionable insights. You can access these forums from the following website:

```
https://community.fabric.microsoft.com/t5/Power-BI-forums/
ct-p/powerbi
```

As part of the broader Power Platform ecosystem, with 5.8 million monthly active users according to Microsoft, Power BI has established itself in 375,000 organizations globally, including 97 percent of Fortune 500 companies. The community continues to expand as more organizations recognize the value of data-driven decision-making.

Whether through online forums, specialized user groups focusing on Power BI techniques, or in-person and virtual events, you'll find resources to accelerate your learning journey. These online user communities ensure that you're never alone in your Power BI development path, allowing you to tap into collective expertise to solve your most complex data challenges.

Power BI Video Channel

The Microsoft Power Customer Advisory Team (Power CAT) represents the company's top technical talent working with their most strategic enterprise customers. This specialized group collaborates with major global organizations to optimize Power Platform implementations, particularly Power BI.

Power CAT embraces a "knowledge sharing first" philosophy, unlike many elite consulting units that guard their expertise. They regularly produce videos (anywhere from weekly to monthly) on YouTube, covering topics ranging from advanced implementation techniques to real customer success stories. The PowerCAT team delivers content to tackle complex issues or explore cutting-edge features.

Anyone interested in enterprise-grade Power BI insights can access this expertise by visiting the official Microsoft Power BI YouTube channel at `https://www.youtube.com/@MicrosoftPowerBI`.

Definitive News Source

Keeping up with the comings and goings in Power BI and related products such as Fabric and Azure can be quite dizzying (literally). The most reliable industry news source outside of Microsoft is Redmond Channel Partners, which can be found at `https://rcpmag.com`. The Redmond Channel Partners website serves Microsoft Partners, or those who sell products and services on behalf of Microsoft. The site provides news analysis, business insights, and product developments, including future roadmap opportunities for Power BI and, more broadly, discussions of Power Platform expansion opportunities. The content ranges from feature updates to strategies on using Power BI technologies in conjunction with others in the Microsoft partner ecosystem. The site lists the most reliable service providers and events to attend worldwide.

WARNING

Redmond Channel Partners is not affiliated with Microsoft. Although most of the information is spot on and has been vetted by the editors, Microsoft is the final source of truth for any product update.

Podcast

Hundreds of podcasts exist on platforms such as Apple iTunes, Spotify, Soundcloud, and YouTube. A podcast, a digital audio or video series, is a streamable or downloadable content series found on the Internet. The content, hosted by one or more subject matter experts, covers a niche topic for a targeted audience. Users subscribe to the topic based on the platform on which the content is made available, and then those users are notified when new content is made available. Some content authors may update the content several times a week, whereas others may update the content once a month. Podcasts have grown in popularity due to their digital portability and the personal touch they offer, as the hosts often build a direct connection with their audience. I've scoured the Internet for you and done the hard work. Look no further than these three sites. You'll find a collection of the best Podcasts on Power BI and Fabric-related topics.

>> **BIFocal:** Covers the latest Microsoft BI changes and Power BI updates with Microsoft MVPs John White and Jason Himmelstein. Find the podcast at `https://bifocal.show`.

>> **Explicit Measures Podcast:** Discusses the "why" behind Power BI features with practical applications for business scenarios. Visit `https://powerbi.tips/explicit-measures-power-bi-podcast`.

>> **Player FM Power BI:** A collection of podcasts focused on Microsoft Power BI tools, data analytics, and business intelligence topics for professionals seeking to improve their data visualization and analysis skills. Go to `http://player.fm/podcasts/Power-BI`.

Learning Platforms for Power BI Skills

Beyond the Microsoft Learning community, thousands of free or low-cost training opportunities are available on platforms such as LinkedIn Learning, Udemy, and Pluralsight. Between those three platforms, you can quickly go from novice to expert developer. Most of these platforms have training to prepare you for Microsoft Power BI certifications or are just great resources to become a rock star in no time. In fact, between Udemy and LinkedIn, you can become certified by some of Microsoft's Most Valuable Players (MVPs) in no time. Remember, though, that each platform requires a premium membership. To access these training solutions, check the following websites. In the search box for each site, type **Power BI**.

>> **LinkedIn Learning:** `https://www.linkedin.com/learning`

>> **Udemy:** `https://www.udemy.com`

>> **Pluralsight:** `https://www.pluralsight.com`

Programming Language Tutorials

As you discover earlier in the book, Power BI has a few programming languages that you may encounter. They aren't complicated, but whoever said Power BI is no-code fibbed a little bit. Power BI leverages multiple programming languages that provide different capabilities throughout the data analytics lifecycle. As a refresher, Power BI supports two primary languages: DAX (Data Analysis Expression) for creating calculations and measures within data models, and M (Power Query Formula Language) for data transformation and preparation. Power BI integrates with traditional data science languages, including R and Python.

WARNING

Data Science languages are well beyond the scope of Power BI. Instead, you use more Azure-centric tooling (think Azure Synapse Analytics) to extend functionality through custom visualizations and complex statistical analysis.

To that end, the multi-language approach of Power BI allows users to handle everything from simple data cleaning to sophisticated predictive modeling within a single platform using an expression-based language rather than object-oriented, long-winded programming techniques of yesteryears. To get a grasp on the language and drill down with exercises and tutorials, head to these websites:

>> **SQLBI:** https://www.sqlbi.com

>> **DAX Patterns:** https://www.daxpatterns.com

>> **DAX Guide:** https://dax.guide

>> **DAX Formatter:** https://www.daxformatter.com

>> **PowerQuery.How:** https://powerquery.how

GitHub Repositories and Sample Templates

The Power BI community has built an extensive collection of open-source resources on GitHub that can dramatically accelerate your development process. Microsoft maintains several official repositories with sample files, including those used in monthly release videos and developer-focused examples. Community organizations like PowerBI.tips offer specialized templates, custom visuals, and Tabular Editor scripts that solve common business issues.

The GitHub repositories provide production-ready Power BI Templates for use across industry verticals. Upon getting access to the GitHub repositories, you can study best practices from experienced developers and then adapt proven solutions to meet your business needs. If you want to contribute to the community, these platforms provide opportunities to share by contributing as a community innovator.

To access these valuable resources, start with:

- **Microsoft Power BI Desktop Samples:** https://github.com/microsoft/powerbi-desktop-samples

- **Microsoft Developer Samples:** https://github.com/microsoft/PowerBI-Developer-Samples

- **PowerBI.tips Resources:** https://github.com/PowerBI-tips

- **Community Dashboards & Templates:** https://github.com/topics/power-bi-dashboard

Annual Events and Conferences

Professional development isn't cheap, but finding the right conferences can significantly accelerate your learning. There are well over 500 events worldwide advertised by Microsoft annually that Power BI users can attend. But if you want to go to just three, the events below are the ones you should consider. The leading Power BI and Microsoft Fabric events provide unmatched access to product team members, MVPs, and industry experts that can't be replicated through online videos or documentation.

Consider these premier events that deliver exceptional value for your investment:

- **Microsoft Fabric Community Conference (FabCon):** Microsoft's flagship data platform event featuring 200+ sessions, workshops, and hands-on labs covering Power BI, Fabric, and AI integration. For more information, go to https://fabriccon.com.

- **Power BI & Fabric Summit**: A multi-day virtual event bringing together Microsoft product group speakers, community experts, and MVPs worldwide. Accessible from anywhere with just an Internet connection. For more information, go to https://globalpowerbisummit.com.

- **Microsoft Power Platform Conference**: The most comprehensive annual event focused on the entire Power Platform ecosystem, including Power BI, Power Apps, Power Automate, and Power Virtual Agents. For more information, go to https://powerplatformconf.com.

TIP

Many of these sessions are eventually published online after the event. The real reason to go is the networking opportunities, hands-on workshops, and the ability to directly question presenters (and the folks from Microsoft) who attend in person. This truly gives you direct access to the experts in Power BI, no questions asked.

Index

publishing

  of data models, 162

  items in Power BI Desktop, 55–56

  reports, 221–222

PubNub, 232

Push mode, 60

Q

Q&A feature, creating charts with, 205–206

queries

  appending of, 110

  combining, 109–110

  configuring of for data loading, 113–114

  data querying, 76–79

  diagnosing, 78–79

  Help queries, 113

  importing of, 146–147

  matching of with capacity, 164

  merging of, 110–113

  optimizing, with Copilot, 118–119

  reducing of, 168–170

  removal of, 114

  segregating of, 113

query cache refresh, 61

Query Diagnostics, 79

query folding, 78

Query Reduction, 168–169

Quick Insights feature, 259

Quick Measure, 131–132, 274

R

RangeEnd parameters, 319–321

RangeStart parameters, 319–321

Reading view (Report view), 18

Recent menu (Power BI Service), 222, 223

Redmond Channel Partners, 400

Refresh button, 67

Refresh icon, 154

refresh schedule, for Dataflow in Fabric, 358

regular maps, 197

relational databases, 83–87

Relationship view, 29

relationships

  creating and editing of, 168

  creating automatic ones, 155

  creating manual ones, 156

  deleting of, 157

  editing of, 140

  managing of, 155–157

  use of term in data modeling, 106

Replace Values, 102–103

Report Builder, 224–227

report canvas, 226

Report card, 262

report configurations, as distinct from visualization configurations, 211

Report menu (Workspaces), 258

report preview, 226

Report tabs, 19, 391

About the Author

Jack Hyman is the founder of HyerTek, a technology and training services firm based in Washington, D.C., that specializes in cloud computing, business intelligence, and enterprise application advisory services for federal, state, and private sector organizations. Before establishing HyerTek, he worked at Oracle and IBM. Jack is the author of *Microsoft Power Platform For Dummies, Microsoft Azure For Dummies,* 2nd Edition, and *Tableau For Dummies,* 2nd Edition. He earned his PhD in Information Systems from Nova Southeastern University.

Dedication

To my children, Jeremy and Emily: I hope you always love learning as much as I do.

Author's Acknowledgments

Many folks were involved in making *Microsoft Power BI For Dummies,* 2nd Edition, become a reality. Thanks to executive editor Steve Hayes for allowing me to write this book (and so many other *For Dummies* projects over the past five years). A great big thanks to project manager and editor Colleen Diamond for keeping me on track throughout this project — you've made this book a fantastic read! A hearty thanks to technical editor Bill Hughes for ensuring that the content in the book was technically sound. Also, thanks to Carole Jelen of Waterside Productions for bringing me yet another exciting project to share with the world. And finally, thanks to my wife, Debbie, and kids, Jeremy and Emily, for allowing me to take on yet another book.

Publisher's Acknowledgments

Executive Editor: Steve Hayes
Development Editor: Colleen Diamond
Copy Editor: Colleen Diamond
Technical Editor: Bill Hughes

Managing Editor: Ajith Kumar
Production Editor: Tamilmani Varadharaj
Cover Image: © Andriy Onufriyenko/Getty Images